MW01492051

Crude Capitalism

Crude Capitalism

Oil, Corporate Power, and the Making of the World Market

Adam Hanieh

VERSO
London • New York

First published by Verso 2024

1 3 5 7 9 10 8 6 4 2

Verso
UK: 6 Meard Street, London W1F 0EG
US: 388 Atlantic Avenue, Brooklyn, NY 11217
versobooks.com

Verso is the imprint of New Left Books

ISBN-13: 978-1-83976-342-7
ISBN-13: 978-1-83976-344-1 (UK EBK)
ISBN-13: 978-1-83976-345-8 (US EBK)

British Library Cataloguing in Publication Data
A catalogue record for this book is available from the British Library

Library of Congress Cataloging-in-Publication Data

Names: Hanieh, Adam, 1972- author.
Title: Crude capitalism : oil, corporate power, and the making of the world market / Adam Hanieh.
Description: London ; New York : Verso, 2024. | Includes bibliographical references and index.
Identifiers: LCCN 2024017590 (print) | LCCN 2024017591 (ebook) | ISBN 9781839763427 (hardback) | ISBN 9781839763458 (ebook)
Subjects: LCSH: Petroleum industry and trade—Influence. | Corporate power. | Capitalism. | Militarism.
Classification: LCC HD9560.5 .H36 2024 (print) | LCC HD9560.5 (ebook) | DDC 338.2/7282—dc23/eng/20240503
LC record available at https://lccn.loc.gov/2024017590
LC ebook record available at https://lccn.loc.gov/2024017591

Typeset in Minion by Hewer Text UK Ltd, Edinburgh
Printed and bound by CPI Group (UK) Ltd, Croydon CR0 4YY

Contents

Acknowledgements

This book has been a long time in the making, and would not have been possible without the support of many friends and family across the world. I am particularly grateful to students and colleagues at the universities of Exeter, Tsinghua, and SOAS, who have taught me so much over the past fifteen years. Since 2021 I have been fortunate to be based at the University of Exeter's Institute of Arab and Islamic Studies (IAIS). The collegiality, intellectual curiosity, and genuine interdisciplinarity of everyone at IAIS has sustained me throughout the past few years.

As this book's references attest, Verso has always been at the cutting-edge of publishing on energy and climate. At Verso, it has been a pleasure to work with Sebastian Budgen, who encouraged this project from the very beginning, and continued to give me much valuable advice and support. Ali Stewart, Natalie Hume, and Jeanne Tao were meticulous in their copy-editing and steering me through the production process. I am also very appreciative of grants from the Carnegie Corporation New York and the Independent Social Research Foundation, which helped support the research and writing of much of this book.

Books are never written by just a single author, and much of this one has been inspired through innumerable conversations with other scholars and activists over the years. I am especially thankful to Ahmad Shokr, Brenna Bhandar, Dale Tomich, and Gareth Dale, who generously gave their time to offer feedback on various chapters. Jeff Webber went through an entire draft with his typical thoroughness and eruditeness, making many valuable suggestions. I owe the largest debt to Rafeef, who has read every word of this book in its multiple iterations. She has not only helped shape its ideas, but also so much of the writing. Her love, brilliance, and *sumud* continue to be an anchor.

1

Approaching Oil

Nearly four decades ago, a large team of scientists from around the world launched a major global research programme called the International Geosphere-Biosphere Programme (IGBP). Their goal was to study the connection between human activities and changes to the earth's biological, chemical, and physical systems, and in 2004 they synthesised the results of their initial research phase in a 336-page report entitled *Global Change and the Earth System*. The report revealed that humanity was causing a series of unprecedented changes that were pushing 'the Earth System well outside of its normal operating range'.[1] Never before had the world's atmosphere, land, coastal zones, and oceans experienced change at the rate that was now occurring. This was 'a no-analogue situation' according to the IGBP authors, and raised the very real threat of catastrophic, non-linear, events that could destroy the natural systems on which the survival of humanity depends.[2]

Twenty years have elapsed since this report was issued, and the casual reader might be forgiven for dismissing it simply as an interesting historical artefact – one more example of an urgent warning ignored in a long road of climate inaction. But the IGBP synthesis made one distinctive and path-breaking observation that remains highly relevant

1 Will Steffen et al., *Global Change and the Earth System: A Planet under Pressure*, Berlin: Springer, 2004, 81.

2 Ibid., 81.

today: *something happened around the middle of the twentieth century.* The significance of this turning point is confirmed by the report in a series of iconic 'hockey-stick' graphs, which show environmental markers such as atmospheric concentration of carbon dioxide beginning gradually to increase from the 1750s, and then suddenly exploding around 1950.[3] As Ian Angus points out, the timing of this 'Great Acceleration' surprised the lead authors, who had expected to see changes to the earth's systems follow a steady, linear trend starting from the Industrial Revolution in the eighteenth century.[4] Instead, the IGBP report concluded:

> The second half of the twentieth century is unique in the entire history of human existence on Earth. Many human activities reached take-off points sometime in the twentieth century and have accelerated sharply towards the end of the century. The last 50 years have without doubt seen the most rapid transformation of the human relationship with the natural world in the history of humankind.[5]

Why was the mid-twentieth century *the* turning point in humanity's impact on the earth's systems? The simple – but incomplete – answer is *oil.* Oil first began to emerge as a significant energy source in the US during the early 1900s, although, at the time, coal remained the dominant fossil fuel. A major leap towards an oil-centred world occurred around the Second World War, when the shift from coal to oil was extended across Western Europe, and then later through newly industrialising countries in other parts of the world. The oil transition massively accelerated the world's consumption of fossil fuels and thus carbon emissions: nearly three-quarters of the human driven increase in the atmospheric concentration of CO_2 has happened since 1950, and about half since the 1980s.[6] Despite hopes of another great transition towards renewables, oil remains by far the world's most important

3 Ibid., 6.

4 Ian Angus, *Facing the Anthropocene: Fossil Capitalism and the Crisis of the Earth System*, New York: Monthly Review Press, 2016, 38.

5 Ibid., 38–9.

6 Will Steffen, Paul J. Crutzen, and John R. McNeill, 'The Anthropocene: Are Humans Now Overwhelming the Great Forces of Nature?', *AMBIO: A Journal of the Human Environment* 38, no. 8, 2011: 614–21, 617–18.

energy source today, making up around 40 per cent of all fossil fuels consumed in 2022 and one-third of the world's primary energy (renewables constituted slightly more than 14 per cent).[7] As the world's most traded product, oil's economic power also remains indisputable. Measured by revenue, four out of the six biggest companies in the world are oil companies, and in 2022, the Saudi Arabian oil giant Saudi Aramco made history by recording a profit of over $100 billion – the largest profit made by any company, in any industry, *ever*.[8]

Oil, in other words, remains at the core of our economy and our energy systems; without dislodging it from this position there is no possibility of ensuring a future for humanity. The focus of this book is the story of how we find ourselves in this predicament – with the hope that this might tell us something about what must be done to dismantle the fossil economy. But the approach taken here breaks with the way oil is usually written about. Too much of our everyday thinking about oil invests it with some kind of inherent magical power, capable of transforming and changing societies by its presence (or absence) – a kind of 'commodity determinism', in the words of Michael Watts.[9] This power is seen in the various labels often used to describe oil: a 'prize', 'curse', 'devil's excrement', and so forth.[10] Now, oil certainly does provide incredible wealth for some and has simultaneously been enormously destructive for others, but the problem with this way of thinking is that it ascribes a causal power to oil itself, which, at the end of the day, is simply a sticky black goo. The real secret to the oil commodity lies instead in the kind of society that we live in – the priorities, logics, and behaviours that derive from how society is currently organised.[11] These

7 Energy Institute, *Statistical Review of World Energy*, 2023, 9. The figure given here for renewables includes hydroelectricity.

8 'Companies Ranked by Revenue', companiesmarketcap.com.

9 Michael Watts, 'Resource Curse? Governmentality, Oil and Power in the Niger Delta, Nigeria', *Geopolitics* 9, no. 1, 2004: 50–80, 53.

10 The phrase 'devil's excrement' comes from the former Venezuelan oil minister, Juan Pablo Perez Alfonzo (see Chapter 6). For further discussion of the various ways that oil is spoken about and comes to stand for particular representations of society – its 'metonyms' – see 'Introduction', Hannah Appel, Arthur Mason, and Michael Watts (eds), *Subterranean Estates: Life Worlds of Oil and Gas*, Ithaca, NY: Cornell University Press, 2015.

11 Among others, this point is made cogently by Matthew Huber, *Lifeblood*, Minneapolis: University of Minnesota Press, 2013; and Andreas Malm, *Fossil Capital*, New York: Verso, 2016.

social relations are what give oil meaning; they are where oil's apparent 'power' comes from.

As the title of this book indicates, the 'kind of society that we live in' is referring here to capitalism. Capitalism's internal *raison d'être* is one of endless accumulation – a drive to continually accumulate money that overrides all other considerations. This social logic differs from all preceding human societies and has had a profound impact on energy use and energy systems. A starting assumption of this book is that, without foregrounding capitalism as a social system with its own distinct logics, we lack any explanatory reason for *why* and *how* oil emerged as the dominant fossil fuel through the twentieth century (and even more importantly, what must be done about it). The problem with most conventional writing about oil is that this historical uniqueness of capitalism as a social system is ignored – in fact, capitalism rarely makes an appearance.[12] The result is to naturalise the social system we currently live under. In turn, the emergence of an oil-centred world is treated as a self-evident outcome of oil's material qualities (such as its high energy density, transportability, and efficiency). Put differently, oil's power is assumed to derive from the natural properties of the commodity itself, separate from the social system that gives these properties meaning and significance.[13] The story of oil then falls back into descriptive narratives focused on the attempt to control this magical commodity: tales of swashbuckling early oil entrepreneurs, the intrigues of the major Western oil companies, or the geopolitical tussle to capture a supposedly scarce resource.

The past two decades have seen a large body of critical writing break with these conventional ways of telling oil's story. For example, Timothy Mitchell's work on the transition from coal describes oil's part in the emergence of modern democracy, and other important contributions also centre oil more

12 This is evident in the older classic histories of the oil industry – Daniel Yergin's *The Prize: The Epic Quest for Oil, Money and Power* (London: Simon & Schuster, 2009 [1991]), Anthony Sampson's *The Seven Sisters: The Great Oil Companies and the World They Shaped* (New York: Viking, 1975) – as well as more contemporary accounts of oil and our energy system. Take, for example, the prolific output of Vaclav Smil, a Canadian scientist who has authored more than 40 books on issues of energy and climate change. Smil's highly influential *Energy and Civilization: A History* (Cambridge, MA: MIT Press, 2017), is in many ways a remarkable book that provides a deep history of energy from early hunter-gatherer society to the contemporary moment. The book's five hundred pages, however, contain not a single mention of capitalism.

13 Huber, *Lifeblood*, 3.

fully in the making of contemporary capitalism, forms of political and economic power, and cultural life.[14] Scholars have retold the early history of oil from the perspective of anti-colonial protagonists in Latin America and the Middle East, situating these in the broader backdrop of the 'Third World' struggles of the post-war decades.[15] Other work has critically interrogated the claims of 'oil security' and supply scarcity that have long underpinned traditional accounts of US foreign policy around oil.[16] Outside of North America and Europe, there is a burgeoning literature looking at the much-neglected histories of workers in the oil industry, and the ways that oil has shaped distinct spaces of urban and rural life in non-Western settings.[17] Alongside this historical revisionism, a rich set of ecological accounts has sought to integrate oil more systematically into the rhythms of accumulation, profitability crises, and uneven global development – an analytical shift that bears directly on the challenges of climate change and any possibility of moving away from fossil fuels.[18]

---

14 Timothy Mitchell, *Carbon Democracy*, New York: Verso, 2011; Hannah Appel, *The Licit Life of Capitalism: US Oil in Equatorial Guinea*, Durham, NC: Duke University Press, 2019; Hannah Appel, Arthur Mason, and Michael Watts, *Subterranean Estates: Life Worlds of Oil and Gas*; Huber, *Lifeblood*; Stephanie LeMenager, *Living Oil: Petroleum Culture in the American Century*, New York: Oxford University Press, 2014; Carola Hein (ed.), *Oil Spaces: Exploring the Global Petroleumscape*, New York: Routledge, 2022.

15 Christopher Dietrich, *Oil Revolution*, Cambridge: Cambridge University Press, 2017; Giuliano Garavini, *The Rise and Fall of OPEC in the Twentieth Century*, London: Oxford University Press, 2019.

16 Mazen Labban, *Space, Oil and Capital*, New York: Routledge, 2008; Robert Vitalis, *Oilcraft: The Myths of Scarcity and Security That Haunt U.S. Energy Policy*, Redwood City, CA: Stanford University Press, 2020.

17 Touraj Atabaki, Elisabetta Bini, and Kaveh Ehsani (eds), *Working for Oil: Comparative Histories of Labor in the Global Oil Industry*, London: Palgrave Macmillan, 2018; Farah Al-Nakib, *Kuwait Transformed: A History of Oil and Urban Life*, Redwood City, CA: Stanford University Press, 2016; Nelida Fuccaro and Mandana Limbert (eds), *Life Worlds of Middle Eastern Oil: Histories and Ethnographies of Black Gold*, Edinburgh: Edinburgh University Press, 2023; Mattin Biglari, 'Refining Knowledge: Expertise, Labour and Everyday Life in the Iranian Oil Industry, c.1933–51', PhD diss., SOAS, University of London, 2020; Ed Kashi and Michael Watts (eds), *Curse of the Black Gold: 50 Years of Oil in the Niger Delta*, Brooklyn, NY: Powerhouse Books, 2010.

18 John Bellamy Foster, *The Ecological Revolution*, New York: Monthly Review Press, 2009; Jason Moore, *Capitalism in the Web of Life*, New York: Verso, 2015; Andreas Malm, *The Progress of This Storm*, New York: Verso, 2018, and *Fossil Capital*, New York: Verso, 2016; Geoff Mann and Joel Wainwright, *Climate Leviathan*, New York: Verso, 2018; Roberto J. Ortiz, 'Oil-Fueled Accumulation in Late Capitalism: Energy, Uneven Development, and Climate Crisis', *Critical Historical Studies*, Fall 2020, 205–40.

This literature has upended many of the traditional tropes that govern thinking about oil and refocused attention on the social processes in which oil is embedded and in turn helps to shape. Building upon these insights, this book aims to do three things. The first is to move beyond the emphasis in a lot of oil writing on the 'upstream' segment of the business – the exploration and extraction of subterranean crude reserves – to look instead at what oil *becomes* once it is pulled out of the ground. Oil is an extraordinary commodity that has little immediate use in its crude state, but which is destined to take on a diverse array of forms as it circulates through capitalist economies. These forms encompass much more than energy or transport fuels – and herein lies a key part to oil's secret. We will consider, for instance, oil's transformation into petrochemicals and plastics, a material substrate that now underlies all aspects of commodity production and consumption. We will also focus on the transformation of oil into oil *wealth*, which has played a foundational part in the making of global finance. By foregrounding the various forms that oil takes as it circulates, we gain a much fuller sense of how oil is given meaning under capitalism – and a better understanding of what it *does* for capitalism. Such an approach also reveals the crucial role of the industries, infrastructures, and workers that enable oil to move, change, and be consumed – ships and ports, refineries, chemical firms, banks, financial markets, and so on. Each of these sites plays no less a part in the story of oil than the struggle over prized reserves located deep underground.

Continually transformed, oil comes to saturate and shape all aspects of our social existence. Given this fact, a second major goal of this book is to ask how the shift to oil has also worked to produce and structure the world market across the twentieth century. Here, a key theme is the relationship between oil as the principal fossil fuel and the consolidation of US capitalism as the most dynamic pole of the global economy following the end of the Second World War. This relationship is a complex story that is not reducible to the direct control of physical crude oil reserves. Rather, the diverse ways that oil was embedded in capitalism also worked to reinforce and nurture US power. Understanding why this was the case necessarily involves looking closely at the development of the oil industry and capitalism in the United States and Western Europe. But it must also encompass major oil-producing regions outside these primary centres of the world market. Too much writing on oil reduces such non-Western producers to simply giant oil spigots – their societies remain as black boxes, destined only to enter history as an object of foreign domination. A key premise of this book is to insist that the social structures of major non-Western oil producers – especially the Gulf Arab states and Russia – are internal and active parts in the making of the contemporary world market (and often in surprising and unexpected ways). This is not about adding more national case studies to the history of oil, or a view that capitalism is everywhere the same, emanating out from the West to the peripheries. Rather, it is an approach that takes capitalism as global from its inception, formed through the interdependencies and 'reciprocal transformations' that take place across the world market.[19] And, as we shall see in later chapters, all of this bears significantly on the possibility of a further global transition – the decline of US hegemony and the rise of new centres of world power.

Finally, tracing how oil helps make the world market clearly requires an understanding of how it is controlled. To this end, a third major goal of this book is to provide a concrete mapping of the companies and other entities that control the circulation of oil today – where they came from, what they do, how they are organised, who owns them, and their connections to the state and other economic sectors. There is a long tradition in oil scholarship that has attempted to do this, mostly focused on the rise of the seven large Western firms that would dominate world oil for most of the twentieth century (the so-called Seven Sisters).[20] This book draws extensively on this older literature, but also emphasises that we must look beyond the very largest Western firms to really understand how the industry operates today. Most strikingly, a new axis of world oil is now emerging around giant non-Western firms in the Middle East and East Asia. This shift is closely related to the rise of China and wider Asia as core zones of global production and is dramatically changing the nature of corporate power in oil. It has, however, been largely ignored amid the Euro-American focus of much oil writing. A main take-away from this book is that these new oil powers need to be

19 Fernando Coronil, 'Beyond Occidentalism: Toward Nonimperial Geohistorical Categories', *Cultural Anthropology* 11, no. 1, 1996: 51–87, 78.

20 See John Blair, *The Control of Oil*, New York: Pantheon Books, 1976; Sampson, *The Seven Sisters*.

placed front and centre in the debate around the future of oil and the struggle against climate change.

Before laying out exactly how these various themes are explored in the chapters of this book, it is necessary to take a step back and consider some broader conceptual questions concerning energy, capitalism, and the historical transition to fossil fuels. What is so different about the dynamics of capitalism compared to other social systems? What do these specific logics of capitalism mean for the demand for energy, and the types of energy sources that are favoured under this social system? Why did the shift to fossil fuels (in the form of coal) begin to consolidate in Britain around the end of the eighteenth century, and what did this transition mean for capitalist development? What actually *is* an 'energy transition'? The answers to these questions are essential to explaining just why those hockey-stick graphs of the IGBP exploded in the middle of the twentieth century – and where they might be heading today.

Capitalism and Energy: Why Fossil Fuels?

Since the very earliest human societies emerged millennia ago, we have depended upon our interaction with nature to produce the means of our existence. This 'metabolic interaction' between nature and human beings takes place through socially organised and purposeful human labour, which transforms the material of the world around us into useful objects.[21] At the most abstract level, energy is what enables this labour to take place and what determines its relative strength.[22] For most of our existence, energy was delivered through human muscles powered by the food we eat: an energy source ultimately derived from solar radiation (either directly, through the photosynthesis of plants, or indirectly through other animals). Energy supplied by human muscles was later supplemented by domesticated animals, the burning of wood and other plant matter, and rudimentary machines that harnessed the kinetic

21 The concept of 'metabolic interaction' derives from Marx. For further discussion, see John Bellamy Foster, Brett Clark, and Richard York, *The Ecological Rift: Capitalism's War on the Earth*, New York: Monthly Review Press, 2010; Kohei Saito, *Marx in the Anthropocene*, Cambridge: Cambridge University Press, 2022.

22 H. T. Odum, *Environment, Power, and Society*, New York: Wiley-Interscience, 1971, 43.

energy of wind and water. This basic relationship between human beings and nature – an interaction mediated by labour and different kinds of energy sources – cannot be overcome, regardless of how society is organised.[23]

But the emergence of capitalism in the 1400s was to transform our relationship with nature in profound ways. Marx described capitalism as a system of 'generalised commodity production', meaning that most of the things we produce and consume are objects destined to be bought and sold on the market. Control over what, when, and how to produce these commodities is concentrated in the hands of a small number of capital owners, each acting in pursuit of their own private interests. Most of us are forced to sell our ability to work in return for a wage, which we then use to buy what we need from the market. This dependence on the market gives capitalist production a social logic that differs from all preceding societies. In pre-capitalist societies, production was primarily aimed at producing more things to satisfy the consumption of ruling classes, and was thus limited by the capacity of those classes to consume. But 'under capitalism, most production is for exchange: capital exploits labour and nature to produce goods that can be sold for more than the cost of production, in order to accumulate more capital, and the process repeats'.[24] What this means is that capitalism's underlying logic is one of 'endless accumulation' – a push to accumulate more capital (in the form of money) that overrides all other considerations.

This logic of endless accumulation is not the personal preference of individual owners of capital but is hard-wired into the system itself: capitalists *must* behave in this way if they are to survive as capitalists. The motor force of this compulsion is competition. Those capitalists with greater resources are able to engage in large-scale investments and out-perform smaller adversaries – they have better ability to produce cheaper commodities, invest in more efficient technologies, swamp markets, engage in price wars, and adopt a myriad of other strategies to beat their opponents. Under the whip of this market competition, capitalists are thus forced to maximise profit or face being swallowed by a more successful rival. One consequence of this is a tendency for increasing amounts of capital to be amassed in fewer and fewer hands – this

23 Saito, *Marx in the Anthropocene*, 19.

24 Angus, *Facing the Anthropocene*, 114.

'concentration and centralization of capital' is a feature of the oil industry that we shall see repeatedly illustrated throughout this book.

Capitalism's drive to perpetual growth means an ever-increasing output and variety of commodities – even to the point of producing more than the market can consume (hence the appearance, unique to capitalist societies, of 'crises of overproduction'). There is no societal control over this because decisions about production are made by atomised individuals competing against one another for market share. But, as John Bellamy Foster has pointed out, the level of this output is directly connected to the throughput of energy and other raw materials, and thus the spiral of capitalist production tends constantly to increase the demand for energy.[25] Even if energy use per unit of output decreases – say, through the use of more efficient machines – this typically translates into greater overall consumption of energy because it becomes even cheaper to produce more goods, a conundrum first described by the nineteenth-century economist William Stanley Jevons, in his study of English coal.[26] Capitalist accumulation thus tends towards demanding an ever-increasing throughput of energy, which is only interrupted at moments of severe economic crisis. As we shall see, this has important implications for how we think about the idea of an 'energy transition'.

A key factor driving the limitless expansion of commodity output is capitalism's propensity to displace, replace, and augment human labour by machinery and capital-intensive technologies. Machines can be operated continuously and do not agitate or go on strike. They enable overall output and labour productivity to grow exponentially, and thus serve increasingly to embed science and technology at the heart of capitalist production. According to Vaclav Smil's back-of-the-envelope calculations, the proportion of the world's 'work' carried out by inanimate

25 John Bellamy Foster, *The Vulnerable Planet: A Short Economic History of the Environment*, New York: Monthly Review Press, 1999, 123.

26 Jevons's book, *The Coal Question*, observed that the increased efficiency of steam engines tended to increase the quantity of coal consumed because greater efficiency made possible the production of even more goods (see Foster, Clark, and York, *The Ecological Rift*, ch. 7, for a discussion of this 'Jevons Paradox'). Likewise, Stephen Bunker argues that at a global level, consumption of energy and other raw materials tends to grow absolutely, even with increasing resource efficiency: Stephen G. Bunker, 'Raw Material and the Global Economy: Oversights and Distortions in Industrial Ecology', *Society and Natural Resources* 9, no. 4, 1996: 419–29.

machinery rose from 10 per cent in 1850 to 50 per cent by 1900, reaching 90 per cent by 1950 – with the share of human labour falling commensurably.[27] Of course, this does not mean that the importance of human labour has decreased in absolute terms; rather, mechanisation has inaugurated an age where the machine itself can leverage human labour into ever-accelerating growth and continual speed up.[28]

Machines are, by definition, energy convertors – they translate some kind of energy source into useful mechanical energy that can be utilised by humans. For this reason, there is a close connection between capitalism's tendency to mechanise – or, as Marx put it, to 'replace living labour with dead labour' – and the types and quantities of energy utilised by society. The greater the energy density of a fuel, the greater the power that can be delivered per unit of energy input (and thus the larger scale at which machinery can be deployed). Once machines start to drive machines – an important turning point in capitalist production that began with the hitching of the steam engine to the British factory system in the 1700s – human muscle is no longer able to supply the requisite amounts of energy.[29] Workers become increasingly divorced from direct control of the labour process, and subject to the heightened tempos and pace of the machine.[30] From that moment on, there is a need for large-scale energy production that can be carried reliably to points of production.[31] Energy density and the infrastructures of energy delivery – the ways in which energy is produced, stored, transported, and transmitted – are thus increasingly bound up with capitalism's ability to increase the scale of production.

Another fundamental dimension to the phenomenon of machines as energy convertors is found in capital's circulation. In seeking to maximise profit, capitalism pushes inexorably to expand the size of markets and to reduce the time it takes in circulating commodities through the necessary cycles of investment, production, and eventual sale to the

27 Smil, *Energy and Civilization*, 71.

28 Malm, *Fossil Capital*, 17.

29 Paul Burkett and John Bellamy Foster, 'Metabolism, Energy, and Entropy in Marx's Critique of Political Economy: Beyond the Podolinsky Myth', *Theory and Society* 35, 2006: 109–56, 131.

30 Matthew Huber, 'Energizing Historical Materialism: Fossil Fuels, Space and the Capitalist Mode of Production', *Geoforum* 40, 2008: 105–15, 109.

31 Burkett and Foster, 'Metabolism, Energy, and Entropy in Marx's Critique of Political Economy', 133.

consumer. The bigger the reach of the market, the more commodities that can be potentially sold. The quicker the 'turnover' of capital can take place, the greater is the number of cycles of profit that occur in any given period. Capitalism, in other words, tends to 'tear down every spatial barrier' and simultaneously 'annihilate this space with time, that is, to reduce to a minimum the time spent in motion from one place to another', as Marx famously observed.[32] This conquering of space and time is something that springs immanent from the nature of accumulation itself, manifested through the repeated revolutions in modes of transport (and the associated developments in logistics and communications). The characteristics of the energy sources underpinning the circulation of capital – especially their energy density and portability – thus play a major role in determining the limits to the acceleration and amplification of capital's reach.

Expand, accelerate, and revolutionise – these catchwords of a social system based on 'accumulation for accumulation's sake' sit at the core of the transition to fossil fuels that occurred across major industrialised economies during the nineteenth century. These fossil fuels (principally coal, oil, and natural gas) originate in the remains of organic matter that have been subject to high pressure and heat over lengthy periods deep beneath the earth's surface. The time taken for these environmental factors to work their transformative magic can range from a few thousand years (in the case of peat) to millions of years (in the case of coal).[33] Having lost most of their water and other impurities through the extreme conditions of their formation, fossil fuels have a much greater carbon content and thus higher energy density than other energy sources. And as discrete physical resources, they are also movable, a quality that differs from non-portable energy alternatives such as wind and water.

With their higher energy density, portability, and chemical flexibility, fossil fuels became the ideal energy substratum for powering ever-accelerating growth – satisfying both the quantitative and qualitative

32 Karl Marx, *Grundrisse*, Harmondsworth: Penguin Books, 1973, 579.

33 Peat is partially decomposed organic matter trapped in an anaerobic environment for thousands of years. It is not strictly a fossil fuel, although it is sometimes referred to as such because of its high carbon content and the fact that it can turn into coal under the right conditions. Peat played an important role as an energy source in the early emergence of capitalism in the Netherlands.

dimensions of energy use under capitalism.[34] Or, as Elmar Altvater notes, there is a 'congruence of [fossil energy's] physical properties with the socioeconomic and political logics of capitalist development'.[35] Fossil fuels enabled a constant increase in the scale of energy throughput, and were thus capable of meeting the insatiable requirements of the new machine age in ways that other energy sources could not. They could be transported to wherever there was a demand for their use; and once connected to an appropriate machine, they themselves could also power movement. Mobility of fuel supports mobility of capital, which in turn helps to liberate capital from the constraints of space and time. Displacement of human muscle power as the primary energy source also divorces the worker from control over production and independent means of survival, helping to generalise and extend a reliance on waged labour and subordination to the market.[36] Markets can grow, and capital can seek out labour where it is cheaper and better controlled. From this moment on, Andreas Malm observes, 'other sources of mechanical energy are pushed to the fringes . . . Capital expands in leaps and bounds, energised by fossil fuels.'[37]

Tethered in this way to capitalist accumulation, fossil fuels become a pivotal input into production and enable continuing capitalist growth.[38] Their relative importance only rises alongside mechanisation and the widening scale of production. This means that the costs

34 Fossil fuels of course were not unknown or unused prior to capitalism – coal has heated homes for millennia and was used in China during the Han Dynasty (206 BCE – 220 CE) for iron smelting. The combustibility of oil was known to the Ancient Romans, Greeks, and Persians. But because capitalism is the first social system in which the drive to accumulate, expand, and accelerate is the *sine qua non* of human activity, it has systematically revolutionised the types and quantities of energy consumed.

35 E. Altvater, 'The Social and Natural Environment of Fossil Capitalism', in L. Panitch and C. Leys (eds), *Socialist Register 2007, Coming to Terms with Nature*, London: Merlin, 2006, 37–60, 41.

36 Huber, 'Energizing Historical Materialism', 110. In this respect, Matt Huber notes that the energy shift from biological energy to fossil fuels needs to be seen as a critical dimension to how capitalist social relations were generalised through the late eighteenth and early nineteenth centuries.

37 Malm, *Fossil Capital*, 288.

38 Fossil fuels are, by definition, discrete resources restricted to limited areas of the earth's territory, and also require labour to be extracted and turned into a useful product (crude oil, for instance, must be refined). This gives them both a value and a price, and they thus tend to become commodities themselves (unlike the rivers or wind used in energy production).

(and means of pricing) of these fuels become increasingly bound up with the ebbs and flow of capitalist profitability.[39] Moments of high energy prices are typically associated with accumulation crises, as the costs of energy inputs push weaker firms to the wall. Alternatively, cheap energy emerges as a means to prevent and address downturns, a way of 'revving profits in periods of accumulation slumps' through reducing input costs and thereby increasing surpluses.[40] An easy way to cheapen energy is to avoid paying the full costs of its production – through, for example, utilising underpaid labour or dumping toxic waste products into the environment. For this reason, the places where energy is extracted and produced tend to become sites of deep social and ecological degradation.

All of this leads to an ever-widening chasm between the tempos of the earth's natural cycles and those of the market.[41] Capitalism's tendency to push beyond all limits means that the capacity of natural sinks – the atmosphere, forests, and oceans – to store and recycle the by-products of fossil fuel consumption (primarily carbon) becomes increasingly strained. At the same time, the cycles of nature and capital become increasingly interdependent. The huge quantities of carbon that were sequestered in fossil fuels across millions of years of formation are now released at a rate that overwhelms the earth's ability to dispose of this waste. It is this coupling of millennia-long processes with capital's voracious speed of energy consumption that lies at the root of today's climate crisis. Once again, this dysregulation of the earth's systems is an inevitable and predictable outcome of the logic of energy use under capitalist accumulation; it is not a product of errant polluters, too many people, or bad consumer choices. And, as we shall see in later chapters, it is one that was qualitatively transformed with the coming of the oil era.

39 This also means that the mechanisms through which fossil fuels are priced become increasingly important to overall profitability. Changes to pricing systems are a major gap in many discussions of oil, despite several crucial transformations that we shall look at in later chapters.

40 Ortiz, 'Oil-Fueled Accumulation in Late Capitalism', 209.

41 Clive Hamilton, 'Human Destiny in the Anthropocene', in Clive Hamilton, François Gemenne, and Christophe Bonneuil (eds), *The Anthropocene and the Global Environmental Crisis*, New York: Routledge, 2015, 32–43, 35.

King Coal: The First Fossil Fuel

> Our civilization . . . is founded on coal . . . The machines that keep us alive, and the machines that make the machines, are all directly or indirectly dependent upon coal.[42]

Throughout the first two centuries that followed capitalism's emergence in the 1400s, energy continued to be delivered overwhelmingly through traditional organic and animate means: wood, wind, water, and muscle. Across this period, the main machines used to produce mechanical energy were waterwheels and windmills, while domesticated animals helped human beings plough fields and provided land transport. Heat for houses and for cooking mostly came from burning wood and charcoal, so that the maintenance of larger human settlements depended upon their proximity to forests or access to regular supplies of wood. Charcoal was, likewise, the key fuel used in smelting iron and nonferrous ores, which meant that wood was also a prime factor in metallurgical development. Overseas trade, colonisation, and war-making relied upon the sail and human muscle, and journeys by sea were thus costly, lengthy, dangerous, and unpredictable.

Coal's ascendancy as the first of the major fossil fuels began in England in the sixteenth century. At that time, England was an aspiring European power whose subsequent rise would be propelled by a large overseas empire and the profits of transatlantic slavery that helped finance the country's industrial development.[43] Although coal had been used for millennia for heating and light, its availability had been limited to places where it could be easily found on the surface of the earth or dug out of shallow mines. However, from the early 1500s, shortages of wood in some areas – partly driven by the large volume of charcoal and timber needed for iron smelting and shipbuilding – spurred increases in the country's coal production. Most English coal fields were opened between 1540 and 1640, in mines excavated by human labour and using

42 George Orwell, *The Road to Wigan Pier*, Harmondsworth: Penguin Books, 1937, 18.

43 In the sixteenth century, what would later become Great Britain consisted of two states, the Kingdom of England (which incorporated Wales and controlled Ireland) and the Kingdom of Scotland. In 1707, the two kingdoms merged under the Act of Union to become the Kingdom of Great Britain.

waterwheels, windmills, and horses to help with water pumping and hoisting coal.[44] By the early 1600s, coal had become a common fuel used to heat houses, and had also found some uses as an energy source in industries such as brickmaking, soap and starch making, and extracting salt.[45]

However, coal's eventual dominance over charcoal, wind, and water hinged upon two technological innovations that took place in the 1700s. The first of these was the discovery that coke, a substance derived from coal, could be used as both an energy source and raw material in the smelting of iron. The use of coke instead of charcoal significantly cheapened the cost of making iron and enabled the construction of much bigger furnaces that produced iron of better quality. It also relieved pressure on Britain's wood resources, allowing iron smelting to be located away from forested areas. By 1750, coke-fired blast furnaces had become widespread in the British iron industry, enabling a rapid increase in the output of this crucial raw material. Dominance in iron production supported Britain's manufacturing pre-eminence, not least as the backbone of the shipbuilding and military industries that helped secure the country's lucrative overseas colonies. Quite remarkably, Britain was producing more than half of the world's iron by the mid-1800s.[46]

The second major technological innovation that drove increased demand for coal was the development of the Watt Steam Engine in the 1770s. This device was fired by coal and converted the back-and-forth motion of a piston into rotary motion – it was the first new 'prime mover' introduced since the adoption of the windmill 800 years earlier, allowing the chemical energy contained in coal to be transformed into useful work.[47] Between the 1780s and 1830s, steam engines gradually displaced the traditional waterwheels used in industries such as cotton spinning and weaving. This eventual supremacy of steam over waterwheels, however, was not an automatic process. As Andreas Malm's masterful history of this period shows, coal-fired steam engines were initially neither cheaper nor more reliable than water – rather, the critical advantage of coal was that it enabled the mill to become mobile,

44 Smil, *Energy and Civilization*, 230.

45 Ibid., 231.

46 Simon Pirani, *Burning Up: A Global History of Fossil Fuel Consumption*, London: Pluto Press, 2018, 22.

47 Smil, *Energy and Civilization*, 235.

freeing it from the waterways and rural areas to which it had previously been bound.[48] This new mobility gave factory owners greater control over and access to labour, allowing steam-powered factories to be located close to bigger cities and towns, where a large pool of unemployed workers helped push down wages. Once ensconced in the factory, the steam engine enabled individual tool-bearing machines to be driven by other machines, exponentially increasing labour productivity and output in major British industries such as weaving, spinning, transport, and milling.

These 'dark satanic mills' – forever immortalised in the poetry of William Blake and Marx's excoriating damnation of the factory system in *Capital* – were one of the first grim underbellies of a fossil fuel–fired capitalism. Another was the mining of coal itself, which depended heavily on the labour of small bodies capable of navigating the poorly ventilated and dangerous mines scattered across the British Isles. The coupling of coal to capitalism thus helps to explain the fact – and timing – of what E. P. Thompson would later describe as 'the drastic increase in the intensity of exploitation of child labour between 1780 and 1840'.[49] Such conditions confirm that every energy transition depends upon earlier forms of energy, and that the shiny worlds erected by fossil fuels have always worked to hide the kinds of labour that make them possible. As George Orwell would observe at the height of the coal era, 'in the metabolism of the Western world the coal miner is . . . a sort of grimy caryatid upon whose shoulders nearly everything that is not grimy is supported'.[50]

Coal's ability to make capital mobile stemmed from the fact that it was itself a portable commodity, unlike the wind and water that drove Britain's earlier industrial development. And, crucially, coal had a much greater energy density than alternative movable energy sources such as wood and animals: its energy per unit mass, for example, is about two to three times that of air-dried wood, the staple movable energy source for most of humanity's existence.[51] Closely connected to the high energy density of coal (and other fossil fuels) is its ability to deliver a greater

48 Malm, *Fossil Capital.*

49 E. P. Thompson, *The Making of the English Working Class*, London: Victor Gollancz, 1963, 331.

50 Orwell, *Wigan Pier*, 18.

51 Smil, *Energy and Civilization*, 12.

amount of energy from a specific area of the earth's surface – between 100–1,000 watts per square metre, compared to only 0.2 watts per square metre in the case of forests destined for charcoal production. The importance of this *power density* often goes unrecognised in discussion of fossil fuels, but it enabled a specific form of urbanism to emerge – high density and energy intensive towns and cities, filled with concentrated areas of residential and industrial facilities powered by fossil fuels.[52] The transition to coal, in other words, helps explain why Britain experienced rapid and large-scale urbanisation ahead of all other capitalist powers – by 1851, a majority of the country's population were living in urban centres.[53]

The new fossil fuel energy order did not simply transform Britain domestically; its effects were global and far-reaching. The development of locomotives and steamboats through the early decades of the 1800s – literal products of coal, iron, and steam – revolutionised global transport and must have played a visceral part in Marx's observation that space was now being 'annihilated by time'. And capital's newfound mobility was not simply restricted to accelerating the circulation of goods and people; it also vividly amplified the war-making capacities of the major world powers. A new phase of colonialism ensued that saw the forcible incorporation of previously unconquered – but non-fossil – territories across Africa, Asia, and the Middle East into an expanding world market.[54] With the eclipse of France in the early 1800s, this world system would become a mostly British-dominated affair by the middle of the century – an empire ruled on the back of

52 Smil, for instance, estimates that pre-industrial Beijing would have required a wooded area about a hundred times its size to supply the charcoal necessary for its energy consumption. By contrast, today's industrial cities can consume much higher levels of energy supplied by a 'coalfield or oil field whose size is no more than one-seventh and as little as 1/1000th of its built-up area' (Smil, *Energy and Civilization*, 352).

53 C. M. Law, 'The Growth of Urban Population in England and Wales, 1801–1911', *Transactions of the Institute of British Geographers* 41 (June 1967): 125–43, 125–6.

54 Bruce Podobnik, *Global Energy Shifts: Fostering Sustainability in a Turbulent Age*, Philadelphia: Temple University Press, 2006. A major turning point was marked by the so-called Opium Wars of the 1840s and 1850s, which saw China's much larger sail-based navy defeated by British coal-fired steamships. Pomeranz also links coal to Europe's ascendancy over China in the 1800s, describing Britain as a 'fortunate freak' due to its abundant and accessible coal supplies. K. Pomeranz, *The Great Divergence: China, Europe, and the Making of the Modern World Economy*, Princeton, NJ: Princeton University Press, 2000, 207.

sterling, guns, and the coal-fired machines that projected power both at home and abroad.[55]

Throughout all of this, it is essential to remember that coal did not *cause* these social and economic changes, and that Britain's stewardship of the first fossil fuel transition was not simply an accident of plentiful coal reserves. Rather, it was the multiple logics of the new capitalism that Britain embodied and led at the time – the drive to control and cheapen labour, automate and accelerate production, expand and increase output, widen the market – that invested coal with its meaning, power, and significance. The advances in output, productivity, and technology unleashed by the transition to coal worked synergistically, further reinforcing British economic and military dominance at the global level. In 1800, more than 80 per cent of the world's coal was produced by Britain, and all the way up to the 1870s the country was still responsible for half of global output.[56] But once this new energy order took hold, other participants in the capitalist world market were forced to follow suit. Sometime in the 1890s, coal surpassed wood and charcoal as the world's primary fuel. Between 1870 and 1900, global coal production increased more than threefold, with the United States and countries in Western Europe joining Britain as major producers.[57] From that moment on, capitalism had become irrevocably fossilised.

However, coal's supremacy was relatively short-lived – by the mid-twentieth century, global consumption of oil had surpassed that of coal, and oil became firmly established as the world's primary fossil fuel. The pace of this transition varied across the world, with the United States leading the way during the early 1900s, followed by Western Europe after the Second World War, then the rest of the world from the 1960s onwards. Of course, this transition to oil did not mean that coal consumption disappeared.[58] While coal's relative share of global fossil

55 In the context of the Middle East, On Barak has persuasively shown how new colonial dependencies also emerged with Britain's transition to coal. On Barak, *Powering Empire: How Coal Made the Middle East and Sparked Global Carbonization*, Oakland, CA: University of California Press, 2020.

56 Vaclav Smil, *Energy Transitions: History, Requirements, Prospects*, Westport, CT: Praeger, 2010, 31.

57 Pirani, *Burning Up*, 15.

58 It also did not mean that the entire world's population had access to commercial fossil fuels (either coal or oil). As recently as 2020, 10 per cent of the world's population had no access to electricity, and 30 per cent used biomass (wood, charcoal, animal dung) for cooking. Data from World Bank, 'World Development Indicators', databank.worldbank.org.

fuel consumption has shrunk over the past century, reaching about 33 per cent in 2022 (down from over 85 per cent in 1925) – overall consumption of coal has more than quadrupled since the beginning of the 'oil age' in around 1950.[59] The ever-growing demand for energy throughput under capitalism means that so-called energy transitions are best thought of as a process of *addition*, not displacement or replacement – a concept that, as we shall see, is critical to understanding the possibilities of alternative energy pathways under capitalism.[60]

What Comes Next?

Oil is a commodity with a curious character. On one hand, because of what it does for capital accumulation, it has become an indelible part of our social existence, embedded in the materiality of commodity production, our food systems, the kinds of urban spaces we live in, military power, and the global financial architecture that has emerged through the second half of the twentieth century. It is this *everywhereness* that makes the problem of oil so hard to unpack – and thus so difficult to challenge. But, at the same time, so much of what oil does for capitalism is invisible. We tend to think about it as simply a fuel or an energy source, and not in the myriad ways it underpins our social life today. Its very pervasiveness makes it difficult to see. One of the aims of this book is to shine a light on this everywhere-but-nowhere character of oil – to show the ways that oil holds up our contemporary world through remaining 'hidden in plain sight'.[61]

This book does not seek to provide a comprehensive history of oil across every place and time. Rather, by bringing out some of the lesser-known connections between the rise of oil and the making of our contemporary world, I hope to open up different ways of thinking about the problem of oil today. Our story begins in the late 1890s in the United States. This is the birthplace of a remarkable firm whose actions, structure, and ethos would do so much to shape the future of world oil across

59 Calculated by author Pirani, *Burning Up*, 64; Energy Institute, *Statistical Review of World Energy*, 9.

60 In this respect, On Barak argues that we should see oil's rise not so much as a transition, but as a process of carbon *intensification*. Barak, *Powering Empire*.

61 Fuccaro and Limbert, 'Introduction', *Life Worlds of Middle Eastern Oil.*

the next century: John D. Rockefeller's Standard Oil. Chapter 2 traces the origin of this company and the part it played in the nascent US oil industry. Across a period stretching between the 1870s and 1920s, we look at why the structure of the US oil industry became so important to the development of the world oil market, and how the unique nature of US property laws influenced the country's oil production. We discover how modern financial structures such as trusts originated in the oil industry, and why New Jersey – a US state with no crude oil reserves or production – came to play such a vital role in the development of world oil. We also explore how militarism and the global drive to war propelled oil to the centre of US state power, and also helped encourage the early international expansion of US oil firms, beginning in Latin America and the Caribbean.

One of the challenges in writing about oil is that so much of its history has been determined by secret gatherings of powerful people behind closed doors. The interwar years are a clear illustration of this, and, in Chapter 3, we look at a series of key agreements that set the stage for the governance of oil in the wake of the First World War. Within the conventional hagiography of this moment, a special place is often reserved for a mysterious meeting convened over whisky and a haunch of venison in the Scottish Highlands. As we shall see, however, a much more fundamental force was at play at this time: the steady emergence of an oil-fuelled global order that was becoming increasingly synonymous with a US-centred one. In this context, the discovery of oil reserves in the Middle East and elsewhere posed a substantial dilemma for the largest US oil companies: how to gain a foothold in those parts of the world where European colonial powers remained dominant? The resolution of this dilemma was a major milestone in the making of the US state as a global power. But, against a tendency to think about this moment as one of geopolitical competition over a supposedly limited resource – we show that the chief problem facing oil companies at this time was oil's abundance, not its scarcity. Moreover, within these global tussles, the internal structure of the US oil industry played a decisive role – and here we develop our first map of the US corporate oil landscape.

American oil supremacy was never a foregone conclusion. In Chapter 4, we look at the early oil industry in Baku, a global centre of oil production that rivalled the US through the early 1900s. Baku was later incorporated into the Soviet Union following the victory of the Bolshevik

Revolution in 1917, and Soviet oil policy during the early years of the revolution would have an extraordinary impact on the later evolution of world oil. The Soviet Union was the world's 'first OPEC', and it was the unintended effects of the Bolshevik Revolution that helped US oil firms expand their global reach ahead of their major British counterparts. At the same time, Soviet oil exports laid the ground for the emergence of key independent oil firms in Western Europe, undermining the apparent global dominance of the largest US and British firms. For the Soviet Union itself, these early years were just as much a revolution in oil as they were a moment of rapid social transformation; indeed, the sharp and remarkably frank debates that took place within the Bolshevik Party through the 1920s – around economic policy, foreign concessions, workers' rights, and especially the right to national self-determination – can only be fully understood in relation to oil.

Across the twentieth century, war and militarism have repeatedly served as the catalyst of oil's rise. The Second World War provides a vivid example, with the conflict driving a huge increase in the military and civilian use of petroleum. In the wake of the war, US dominance consolidated across most of Western Europe, in lockstep with a transition to oil as the primary fossil fuel. Accounts of this post-war moment typically emphasise the back-and-forth negotiations and shifting alliances between the US, Britain, and other major West European states in the context of the Soviet threat. In contrast, Chapter 5 centres the Middle East as the hidden crucible of Euro-American post-war relationships. We see how the changing structure of the oil industry in the Middle East was intimately connected to the rise of US power in Europe and explore the special place of the Middle East in Britain's attempt to resist imperial decline, especially in relation to sterling's role as a major global currency. We also discover how and why the US government makes a little-known change to its tax policy in the 1950s, which effectively diverts hundreds of millions of dollars in US tax revenues to major oil-producing states in Latin America and the Middle East.

With European states consumed by the oil-fuelled conflagration of the Second World War, a new surge in anti-colonial and national liberation struggles enveloped the colonised world during the two decades following the war. How did the shift to an oil-fuelled and US-centred world market shape this anti-colonial revolt? Chapter 6 explores this question, looking at the complex ways in which the control of oil – and the structure of corporate power in the oil industry – intersected with anti-colonialism. Approaching anti-colonialism through the global transition to oil complicates the easy binaries of *coloniser vs colonised* and reveals something new about the roots and contradictory character of Third Worldism. On the way, we look at the establishment of the Organization of the Petroleum Exporting Countries (OPEC) in 1960, and its fraught relationship to popular struggles in the Middle East and elsewhere. We also see the destabilising influence of an upstart Italian company, ENI: later a major force in the global oil industry, but whose leader was killed in murky circumstances that remain unclear to this day.

A decisive part in oil's emergence as the world's dominant fossil fuel was the so-called petrochemical revolution – a mid-twentieth century shift away from the use of naturally occurring substances towards plastics, artificial rubbers, synthetic fibres, and other materials that are ultimately derived from oil as the main raw input. Chapter 7 explores the causes and implications of this synthetic transformation. It is a strange tale that begins in the early twentieth century with the growth of the chemical industry in Germany and the US, subsequently moving through the rise of fascism and two world wars that pitted Germany's coal-based chemical giants against their weaker US counterparts. By the end of the Second World War, the US had emerged as the dominant global chemical power. Its dominance, however, relied on the use of oil as the main chemical feedstock, rather than coal. This petrochemical revolution enabled oil to entwine itself through all aspects of our lives and is one of the principal ways that oil has come to be located everywhere but nowhere. As such, the question of petrochemicals is a central part of the ecological crisis of the present – and forms a key thread within the story to come.

In the standard telling of oil through the 1970s, OPEC's Arab oil-producing states are often cast in the role of arch villain, with their 1973 oil embargo viewed as the prime reason behind two large spikes in the global oil price during that decade. Chapter 8 shows why this and other widely held beliefs about the 1970s oil shocks are false. Instead, we trace the roots of the price spikes to the deeper structural changes that occurred in the world oil industry during the 1960s. These changes involved a range of actors, including the Soviet Union, Libya, and newcomer European and American oil firms. We see why the distinctive structure of the oil industry in the US made the crisis immensely beneficial to the largest American firms. This reading of the 1970s highlights how changes in the oil market were fundamentally linked to a reworking of US power through this decade – a process that was also connected to the rise of a newly resurgent political Right, whose discourse of deregulation and market liberalisation would find a firm foothold globally during the 1980s.

The control of oil means the control of oil wealth, and this ties the major oil-producing states to the genesis of the modern financial system. In Chapter 9, we look at the foundational role played by the circulation of oil wealth from the Gulf Arab monarchies in the new financial system that emerged through the 1970s. These Gulf 'petrodollars' worked to cement the US dollar as the leading international reserve currency, strengthened the dominance of Anglo-American financial institutions, and underpinned the explosion of debt across most of the rest of the world. As such, the Gulf's oil surpluses helped renew and reshape US primacy in the 1970s, despite the extreme instability of the times. But this depended upon a deepening US relationship with the authoritarian monarchical states in the Gulf. US support would turn the Gulf into the centre of the world's arms trade. It would shore up states where up to 80 per cent of the population consists of rightless, poorly paid, and racialised non-citizens. All of this gives the Gulf a unique place in the structure of US power – and allows us to see the realities of militarism, imperial violence, and racial exclusion that continue to sit behind modern finance.

The 1970s crises were followed by the 'counter-shock' of the mid-1980s, a sharp fall in the price of oil that lasted until the late 1990s. This drop in oil prices was closely linked to a series of political and economic crises across the Soviet bloc, which culminated in the 1991 collapse of the Soviet Union. Chapter 10 returns again to Russia to look at how oil was linked to the demise of Soviet-style socialism. We explore the relationship between the oil industry and the emergence of a new class of billionaires in post-Soviet Russia, nurtured under the successive administrations of Boris Yeltsin and Vladimir Putin. Many of these wealthy Russians – including Roman Abramovich, Leonid Mikhelson, Mikhail Fridman, and Gennady Timchenko – would make headlines after 2022 for their support of Putin over the war in Ukraine. But against a widespread misconception that Russia's energy sector is now fully state-controlled and has little to do with the business activities of these individuals, we show why oil (and energy more broadly) needs to be seen as the continuing nexus that binds Putin's authoritarian rule to the wealth of Russia's billionaire business class.

While much has been written on the neoliberal economic turn of the 1980s and 1990s, a largely overlooked aspect is the deep connection between this policy shift and the structural transformation of the Western oil industry. Chapter 11 explores this connection, showing how the sale of state-owned oil firms revolutionised the nature and structure of financial markets and underwrote the initial ascendancy of neoliberalism in key Western states. In turn, we see how Western oil companies were themselves transformed through this period: slashing jobs to meet new shareholder imperatives, branding themselves as 'energy' firms rather than oil companies, and unleashing the largest wave of corporate mergers and acquisitions in history. This was a moment of growing public scrutiny of Western oil firms, partly due to greater awareness of climate change and a string of disastrous oil spills. But this did not mean that these firms became any less entangled in the physical production of oil. Instead, the dirty realities of the oil economy were increasingly concealed in offshore and remote locations. As part of this, we see how the continent of Africa emerges as a decisive site for Western oil extraction – producing some of the most destructive social and ecological outcomes recorded in the history of the industry.

Saudi Aramco's extraordinary 2022 profit results point to a major shift that has happened in the oil industry over the past two decades: the rise of huge national oil companies (NOCs) in non-Western countries that are now eclipsing the biggest Western oil companies in metrics such as oil production, reserves, market capitalisation, and export quantities. Chapter 12 examines this shift, contrasting the operations of both the largest Western firms and the NOCs. We map the various geographies of today's trade in crude oil and refined products, look at refining capacities in different regions of the world, and see how the make-up of the world's top fifteen refining companies has altered over the last two decades. The chapter explores the emergence of a new East–East hydrocarbon axis that links the oil industries of the Middle East and East Asia, and we trace the flows of capital and ownership ties that are now developing between these two regions. Much like the story of oil and US power in the twentieth century, this radical new geography of world oil bears directly on the rise of China as a potential competitor to US hegemony. It also has crucial implications for campaigns to halt the global fossil economy.

The final chapter draws together the multiple threads of this book to examine what they mean for dealing with the stark threat of catastrophic climate change. Oil firms are no longer simply the voices of climate change denialism but have, instead, transformed themselves into enthusiastic champions of the slogans of a supposed green transition, especially the concept of 'net zero'. We explore the dangers in accepting these slogans and the apparent greening of the oil industry at face value. Investigating the leading involvement of the oil industry (including the NOCs), in dubious climate techno-fixes such as carbon capture and storage, biofuels, electric vehicles, and hydrogen production, the chapter reveals how oil firms are not only endeavouring to hide their ongoing prioritisation of fossil fuels but are now attempting to seize leadership of the world's response to the climate emergency. The extreme peril of the current moment means that we can no longer ignore the logics of a social system that has brought us to this point: with oil so deeply interlaced with capitalism and the making of global power over the past century, any real hope of addressing the climate emergency must be coupled with a politics of deep-rooted system change.

2

Petro-Power: The Rise of the US Oil Industry

In 1859 when Colonel Drake drilled the first successful American oil well in the small town of Titusville, Pennsylvania, he could not possibly have anticipated what would follow.[1] Up until then, oil was typically collected from the surface of rivers or through natural rock seepage. Its primary use was in the manufacture of kerosene, which was a cheaper and more efficient fuel for lamps and lighting than alternatives made from coal or whale blubber. The kerosene business was highly profitable and would become even more so during the American Civil War (1861–65), when increased taxes on alcohol priced kerosene's other major competitor, camphene, out of the market. But, at this stage, there was little indication that oil would become anything other than a single-product industry focused on the manufacture of kerosene. In fact, as Drake sank his fateful well into the Pennsylvanian soil on 27 August 1859, the American energy system was still largely wood-based; it was not until 1885 that coal finally overtook wood to become the primary energy source in the US.[2]

1 Edwin Drake is often credited as being the first person in the world to drill an oil well, but this is incorrect: earlier wells had been drilled in Poland, Russia, and Canada. Brian Black's *Petrolia: The Landscape of America's First Oil Boom* (Baltimore, MD: Johns Hopkins University Press, 2000) presents a powerful account of Pennsylvania's early oil boom, with a particular focus on ecological consequences.

2 US Energy Information Administration, 'History of Energy Consumption in the United States, 1775–2009', *Today in Energy*, 9 February 2011, eia.gov.

Nonetheless, there was still plenty of money to be made in oil, and Drake's success meant that Pennsylvania soon attracted thousands of people from across the country hoping to make it rich (including the young actor John Wilkes Booth, who just a few years later would quit the oil business to find fame as Abraham Lincoln's assassin).[3] This was the world's first oil boom – dubbed the 'Great Oildorado' by journalists at the time – and it saw the population of Titusville explode from around 250 people to over 8,600 by 1870.[4] It was a boom that relied much upon absentee landlords and financial speculators from big cities such as New York, Cleveland, and Baltimore, who bought up land from existing residents and then divided it up for lease to the new arrivals.[5] All the hopeful prospector needed was a small plot on which to locate a mine and some kind of makeshift residence. It was here that the iconic imagery of the US oil landscape was born – rows of oil derricks lined up across heavily polluted and tightly packed parcels of land, each operated by small-scale producers eager to discover oil beneath their feet.[6]

Given their interest in what lay under the ground, these would-be oil barons may well have been familiar with the Latin phrase *cujus est solum, ejus est usque ad coelum et ad inferos*. Loosely translated, this legal maxim gives the owner (or leaseholder) of land, the right to possess what is above and below it – 'up to heaven and down to hell'. Dating back to Ancient Rome, the 'ad coelum' doctrine was codified in its modern form in 1766 by the English jurist William Blackstone. Following the invention of the hot-air balloon (and later mechanised flight), *ad coelum* became much more difficult to apply to ownership above the ground (as one disappointed Californian landowner was to discover in 1936 after he unsuccessfully sued an airline company for violating his private property rights).[7] But, in the US, unlike in many other countries, lawmakers did apply *ad coelum* to sub-soil mineral resources. If it lay

3 Booth set up the Dramatic Oil Company and began digging for Pennsylvanian oil in 1864. He was initially successful, but inadvertently shut down his mine after setting off an explosion in an attempt to increase production.

4 'The Oil Industry', United States Census Bureau History, August 2021, census.gov.

5 Black, *Petrolia*, 57.

6 Matthew Huber, *Lifeblood*, Minneapolis: University of Minnesota Press, 2013, 45.

7 Hinman v. Pacific Air Transport, United States Court of Appeals for the Ninth Circuit 84 F.2d 755, 1936.

under your soil, it was yours.[8]

However, unlike a solid mineral such as coal or gold, oil raised a legal conundrum. Who had the rights to a substance that might move around underground or be held in single basins split across numerous property titles on the surface? In 1889, amid the first oil boom, the Pennsylvanian Supreme Court considered this question and eventually concluded that subterranean oil and gas were similar to wild animals: 'They have the power and the tendency to escape without the volition of the owner.'[9] And like a hunted fox – the unfortunate subject of an earlier court deliberation – the 'fugitive and wandering existence' of oil meant that ownership went to whoever could capture it. Even if oil from underneath your land flowed into a well dug by someone far removed from your plot, it was now theirs.[10] With echoes of John Locke, what mattered most was whose labour brought oil to the surface – capture conferred possession.

The Pennsylvanian Supreme Court decision subsequently became known as the Rule of Capture, and it created a distinctive and long-lasting problem for the US oil industry. With each large oil discovery through the late nineteenth and early twentieth centuries – Pennsylvania, Ohio, California, Texas, and so forth – thousands of people flocked to the new fields in search of oil. The Rule of Capture gave these hopeful prospectors the right to all oil produced from their well, even if part of it might have come from an underground reservoir shared with adjoining lands. But, as Matt Huber observes, this meant that when oil was found, 'the only rational response . . . was to pump [it] as quickly as possible, in fear that if you held back your neighbor would suck the oil from underneath your property'.[11] Due to the highly fragmented nature of property ownership and the relatively large number of small-scale well owners, there was no way to restrict production at the aggregate

8 In Britain, for example, the Crown reserves the right to take control of underground deposits of valuable minerals, including coal, gold, and silver.

9 Ross Pfifer, 'The Rule of Capture in Pennsylvania Oil and Gas Law', Agricultural Law Resource and Reference Center, 2009.

10 The Rule of Capture is discussed in Daniel Yergin, *The Prize*, London: Simon & Schuster, 2009. For more analytical accounts, see Matthew Huber, 'Energizing Historical Materialism: Fossil Fuels, Space and the Capitalist Mode of Production', *Geoforum* 40, 2008: 105–15; and Huber, *Lifeblood*.

11 Huber, *Lifeblood*, 45.

level.[12] The problem confronting the early US oil industry was, in other words, *too much* oil, not too little.[13]

A chronic tendency towards overproduction was thus embedded at the heart of US oil. In effect, the industry was discovering that the extraction of crude was *uncontrollable*. Each new discovery of oil meant that there was plenty of it. And overall output was determined by the uncoordinated decisions of thousands of small-scale well owners, all hoping to maximise their share, and with little concern for the impact of their individual actions on the price of oil or the health of the oil field.[14] This structural tendency towards overproduction led to repeated cycles of oil booms and price busts during the early years of the industry, creating fantastic wealth for a few lucky well owners, while causing financial ruin for countless others. In these circumstances, it was difficult for any single firm to emerge that could directly control oil at the point of extraction.

Grasping the Eel

This problem of overproduction lay at the roots of a company that would forever transform US capitalism, Standard Oil. Standard was established in Ohio in 1870 by a small group of businessmen led by John D. Rockefeller and Henry Flagler. In the year Standard was founded, the Pennsylvanian oil industry was experiencing one of its first crises of overproduction, and as crude prices plummeted, Rockefeller and Flagler came to a crucial realisation. What mattered most in oil was not the control of extraction, but, rather, the fact that crude must be transformed into something else before it was useful (at that time, kerosene). For this transformation to happen, oil needed to circulate – it needed to be transported from oil fields to refineries, processed into kerosene, and

12 It should be emphasised this was true only for oil fields *on land*. Offshore fields developed under a different set of legal relations (see Chapter 8).

13 As Mazen Labban puts it, 'competition for oil is not to secure its continuous supply, but to secure that not so much of it is produced that may threaten the profitability of the industry'. Mazen Labban, *Space, Oil and Capital*, New York: Routledge, 2008, 7.

14 This situation also raised important questions around the conservation of oil fields. Unrestricted extraction of oil could deplete the gas pressure needed to force oil out of the ground, thereby reducing the extractable volume of oil from the field.

then marketed to the final customer. If Standard could control access to the infrastructure that made circulation possible – pipelines, storage facilities, railway lines, refineries, marketing, and so forth – then the wild animal spirits of oil might just be tamed.

In coming to this conclusion, Standard's founders foresaw something that would later become accepted wisdom in the oil industry: the infrastructures that took crude, transformed it into something useful, and then moved it to the consumer formed an integral part of the industry. As a leading US oil lobby group put it in 1936, these infrastructures were akin to 'the smoke stack of a factory . . . the pipe line, the tank ship, the railroad track car, the tank truck, the barge on ocean, lake, river or canal – all are closely articulated parts of the system. To amputate one would destroy the entire organism.'[15] A unique industry lexicon emerged to describe these interconnected segments of the oil 'organism': the upstream (crude extraction) and the downstream (whatever happened between the oil field and the customer). From this moment on, a tendency towards vertical integration – combining control of both upstream and downstream within a single company – would become the defining characteristic of the world's largest oil companies.

Standard was the first US oil company to become vertically integrated, employing techniques that were later mercilessly exposed by the so-called muckrakers – pioneers of investigative journalism led by the brilliant Ida Tarbell. Tarbell's classic history of Standard would be published in 1904, and in it she traced how Standard's power emerged through a careful strategy of infrastructural control. This included buying up pipelines that connected oil fields to railroads, colluding with the railroad industry to obtain favourable rates for transporting crude, and taking ownership of virtually all downstream refineries that converted crude oil into kerosene.[16] Through this control over the

15 American Petroleum Institute, *American Petroleum Industry: A Survey of the Present Position of the Petroleum Industry and Its Outlook toward the Future*, New York: American Petroleum Institute, 1936, 12.

16 Ida Tarbell's account explains Standard's market power through their predatory pricing policies, specifically the rebates gained from railroad companies that enabled Standard to transport oil at significantly cheaper rates than their competitors. Ida Tarbell, *The History of the Standard Oil Company*, New York: McClure, Phillips and Co, 1904. Later authors, however, have placed more emphasis on Standard's control over refineries and pipelines. For a discussion of these debates, see the '100 Years of *Standard Oil* Antitrust' symposium issue of the *Southern California Law Review* (85, no. 3, March 2012).

circulation and refining of oil, Standard forced the thousands of small well operators at the point of extraction to take the price for crude that the company demanded, while making ample profits on the final sale of kerosene to the customer. By the 1880s, Standard controlled virtually all refinery capacity and kerosene marketing in the US, and 35,000 out of the nation's 40,000 miles of pipeline were owned by the company.[17]

However, in the early stages of building this vertically integrated structure, the company faced a serious challenge. During the 1880s, American businesses were predominantly organised within individual states, and a wide variety of different legal systems, financial rules, and market conditions existed across the country. As Standard expanded beyond Pennsylvania, the company's empire grew to include dozens of affiliate firms operating in different states, meaning that a large number of shareholders, managers, and administrative staff were involved in the running of Standard's operations. Although majority control in each of these affiliate companies was held by John Rockefeller and just four other men, this inner core found it increasingly difficult to ensure effective planning and day-to-day management amid the various interests at play.[18] Vertical integration demanded a much tighter centralisation of control at the national scale, which would enable the inner core to coordinate and bridge the differences across individual states and affiliate companies. The challenge, as one of Rockefeller's close associates put it at the time, was how to bring about 'a more thorough unification of the [company's] interests'.[19]

The initial solution to this challenge was proposed by Standard's legal counsel, Samuel Dodd, in 1879. Dodd recommended that Standard establish a new corporate vehicle, the Standard Oil Trust, in which the top shareholders of the various companies that made up the Standard empire would deposit their stock. About forty shareholders were involved in this secret arrangement, and in return for depositing their

17 A. A. Fursenko, 'The Oil Industry', in Rondo Cameron and V. I. Bovykin (eds), *International Banking, 1870–1914*, Oxford: Oxford University Press, 1991, 443–67, 444.

18 The four were John D. Rockefeller's younger brother William Rockefeller, along with Henry Flagler, and Ohio businessmen Stephen Harkness and Oliver Payne. With John Rockefeller, these individuals owned around 57 per cent of the various Standard oil concerns. Ralph Hidy and Muriel Hidy, *Pioneering in Big Business, 1882–1911*, vol. 1, New York: Harper, 1955, 40.

19 Ibid.

stock, they would receive a trust certificate and guaranteed dividend payments. The trust itself would be governed by a board of nine trustees, including Rockefeller himself. The trustees would be given full management authority over all affiliated companies involved in production, pipelines, refining, and transport, thereby centralising power in their hands.[20] From the oil field to the customer, the trust structure would effectively unify control across the entire corporate structure.

In her withering critique of this structure, Ida Tarbell would later emphasise how it helped hide the company from public scrutiny and facilitated Standard's evasion of federal and state anti-competition laws. According to Tarbell, '[the trust] made no agreements, signed no contracts, kept no books. It had no legal existence. It was a force powerful as gravitation and as intangible. You could argue its existence from its effects, but you could never prove it. You could no more grasp it than you could an eel.'[21] This critique hits home and has proven enormously influential in later writing on Standard, but it can also distract from the key point: the trust was the corporate form that underpinned vertical integration – it was this organisational innovation that enabled Standard to become the first vertically integrated oil company in the world. With this concentration and centralisation of oil capital, Standard could emerge as the undisputed master of the entire American oil industry.

From Pennsylvania to New Jersey

Standard's trust structure was fully established by 1882, and quickly became a model for other large US industrial firms, including those involved in cotton, whisky, sugar, and lead. By 1890, just twenty-four trusts controlled all major sectors of US industry, although few matched Standard's extensive vertical integration and its far-reaching influence on the oil business.[22] However, even with its activities shielded behind this new corporate structure, Standard's control of US oil continued to attract significant criticism from journalists and a public that was

20 A list of the companies involved in the trust can be found in ibid., 47.

21 Tarbell, *The History of the Standard Oil Company*.

22 Joel Seligman, 'A Brief History of Delaware's General Corporation Law of 1899', *Delaware Journal of Corporate Law* 1, no. 2, 1976: 263.

decidedly distrustful of big business. With sentiment running high against Standard and other trusts across the country, numerous federal and state government investigations were launched into the company's structure and its impact on the oil industry. In 1890, this would culminate in the US Congress passing the Sherman Anti-Trust Act, a piece of legislation that made it illegal to 'restrain trade' through a trust or similar form of corporate combination.

Fully anticipating government action against the company, Standard's trustees began a series of intense deliberations in the wake of the Sherman Act's passage. By 1892, they had come to the realisation that little choice remained but to formally dissolve the trust. In its place, the trustees devised a plan that involved the consolidation of Standard's existing ninety-two affiliate firms into just twenty major companies. Some of these twenty companies bore the Standard name and that of the state in which they were registered, such as Standard Oil Company (New Jersey), and Standard Oil Co. (Ohio). Others, including the Buckeye Pipeline Company or the Atlantic Refining Company, showed no direct evidence of the Standard connection. Shares in these twenty companies were distributed on the basis of earlier holdings of trust certificates, which gave a tiny number of prominent owners – estimated by one study to be just seventeen stockholders from ten wealthy families – overall control within the reorganised structure.[23] These owners took most of the director positions in the twenty firms that now made up the Standard empire, with Rockefeller, Flagler, and other close colleagues from the early days remaining at the helm of this ownership clique.

Through most of the 1890s, this strategy of exerting control through majority share ownership served Standard's owners well. Rockefeller and others now described their vast national corporate network as 'Standard Oil Interests' rather than a trust. Despite an economic recession during this period, kerosene continued to be a very profitable business, and the company's production of the lighting fuel increased by more than half between 1890 and 1897. Additionally, other uses of oil were also gaining traction, especially the manufacture of fuel oil, which could be burnt in boilers to generate heat. Fuel oil was a viable alternative to coal in industries such as steel, bricks, and glass manufacturing, and it could also be used to power ships and locomotives. Standard's

23 Hidy and Hidy, *Pioneering in Big Business*, 227.

production of fuel oil increased more than sevenfold through the 1890s; and while kerosene continued to be the most important oil product by some margin, its contribution to Standard's overall revenues fell from about 70 per cent to 60 per cent between 1890 and 1897.[24]

Nonetheless, Standard's stark domination of the oil industry provoked several court cases and repeated accusations that it continued to operate as a trust in all but name. Fearful of these attacks, Standard's owners began discussing another major business reshuffle that could help them maintain their firm grip on the company and ensure its ongoing vertically integrated structure. This time, their focus was on the state of New Jersey, which had radically overhauled its corporate legal system in the late 1880s and early 1890s. The legislation that had been introduced in New Jersey was expressly designed to get around anti-trust measures and encourage companies such as Standard to relocate to the state (in fact, some legal theorists speculate that the lawyers of the largest trusts played a direct role in writing the new laws).[25] The state had become, as the *New York Times* later put it, a place where businesses could do 'just as business pleases'.[26]

For Standard, the most notable measure introduced in New Jersey was an 1889 statute that authorised and regulated the formation of companies whose sole purpose was to hold shares in other companies, including those outside the state. Such 'holding companies' were in effect legalised trusts: they could be used to control and coordinate the activities of a large number of separate companies within a single corporate structure. Other laws permitted companies registered in New Jersey to operate freely in other US states without authorisation from the New Jersey state legislature – a prerogative that might not appear extraordinary today, but which, at the time, was not possible anywhere else in the country.[27] The state also gave businesses the right to merge and consolidate as they wished, pay very little tax, and issue various kinds of stocks

24 Ibid., 289.

25 Charles M. Yablon, 'The Historical Race Competition for Corporate Charters and the Rise and Decline of New Jersey: 1880–1910', *Journal of Corporation Law* 32, no. 2, 2007: 324–80.

26 'How Delaware Became No. 1', *New York Times*, 9 May 1976: 112.

27 Sarath Sanga, 'The Origins of the Market for Corporate Law', 3 March 2020, ssrn.com: 2.

that could be used to limit the voting power of smaller shareholders.[28] By 1900, an estimated 95 per cent of large US businesses had flocked to New Jersey, and the state was earning so much from corporation filing fees and franchise taxes that it could abolish all property tax and yet still pay its entire state debt.[29]

In 1899, Standard's core ownership group decided to make use of New Jersey's liberal new corporate laws to reorganise all the company's affiliate firms under the umbrella of a single holding company, Standard Oil Co. New Jersey (SONJ). With this move, the twenty large Standard firms that had superseded the trust were now transformed into subsidiaries of SONJ. By absorbing these twenty companies and their affiliates, SONJ sat atop an empire consisting of about seventy firms in total, stretching across the US, Canada, Cuba, Puerto Rico, and several European countries. Under SONJ's vertically integrated structure, these firms were active in a diverse array of activities, including crude oil production, refining, pipelines, tanker ownership, and marketing. Coordinating all of this was a board of directors made up of thirteen individuals representing the interests of Standard's largest shareholders, first and foremost, the Rockefeller family.[30]

Standard's corporate structure would set the template for the global oil industry through to the present day. From this moment on, all leading oil companies would strive to become vertically integrated, creating intricate networks of subsidiaries engaged in extraction, transportation, refining, and marketing that were spread across the globe. By controlling the infrastructure that enabled each of these steps, the vertically integrated firm could block would-be competitors or demand prices that were much higher than internal costs. The integrated model allowed firms to adapt swiftly to changing supply and demand – emphasising either upstream or downstream activities depending on market conditions. This structure also enabled firms to hide and shift profit-making activities between different business segments, a useful tool for minimising tax and royalty payments. All of this would necessarily rely on constant innovations in financial and legal policies such as those

28 See Seligman, 'A Brief History', for a full discussion of the New Jersey laws.
29 Ibid., 267.
30 For these directors, see Hidy and Hidy, *Pioneering in Big Business*, 314.

pioneered by the state of New Jersey.[31] Already, from these early days, we can see the intimate connections that were beginning to develop between oil, finance, and political power.

The Break-Up of Standard

For Standard, the ability to operate as a vertically integrated firm was not simply important from a domestic perspective. About half of Standard's kerosene production was exported, and to control these markets, the company sought to buy up shipping lines, kerosene canneries, storage facilities, and other kinds of overseas infrastructure. Its major international competition came from Russia – where companies controlled by the Nobel and Rothschild families consciously emulated Rockefeller's strategy of pipeline and refinery control (see Chapter 4) – and the Dutch East Indies, where the Royal Dutch Petroleum Company (forerunner of today's Shell), produced and exported oil from Sumatra and Borneo. Fierce competition among these firms pushed Standard to build a network of international agents and allied merchants, who were subcontracted by Standard to manage the trade and distribution of kerosene in markets across the world.[32] The company also employed novel marketing techniques, such as giving away millions of free lamps to Chinese households in order to encourage the consumption of Standard's kerosene.[33] These early attempts at establishing a corporate

31 Other states replicated New Jersey's regulations, most notably Delaware, which became the destination of choice for firms following a reversal of New Jersey's policies after 1913. Standard Oil of New Jersey incorporated in Delaware in 1927, as did other leading oil companies. By the late 1930s, nine out of the top twenty oil firms in the US were Delaware-incorporated. R. C. Cook, United States Temporary National Economic Committee, *Control of the Petroleum Industry by Major Oil Companies*, Washington, DC: US Government Printing Office, 1941, 4.

32 See Sherman Cochran, *Encountering Chinese Networks: Western, Japanese, and Chinese Corporations in China 1880–1937*, Oakland, CA: University of California Press, 2020, 31–42, for a discussion of these corporate structures in China.

33 The slogan 'Oil for the lamps of China' became the title of a best-selling novel and movie, which critically portrayed the single-minded obsession of an oil company employee with corporate expansion in China against the backdrop of communist agitation. Standard held more than 70 per cent of the Chinese market until 1894, after which time exports from Russia and the Dutch East Indies began to encroach on its market share. Cochran, *Encountering Chinese Networks*, 29.

and logistical infrastructure outside the US were a vital precursor to the later dominance of international petroleum markets by Standard's descendant companies. By the early 1900s, Standard held a leading market share in kerosene across East Asia, Britain, Canada, Western Europe, and Latin America.[34]

Nonetheless, at the turn of the century, Standard's apparently unassailable position came under increasing challenge from other American firms that had begun to win a foothold in newly discovered US oil fields. Most significant here was the 1901 discovery of the huge Spindletop oil field in Texas, which was soon to account for half of US oil production and attracted tens of thousands of people from across the country hoping to make their fortunes.[35] Standard had been excluded from the field due to Texan anti-trust actions against the company. And, in its place, two new companies backed by large financial interests – Gulf Oil and Texaco – built a major presence in Spindletop, taking control over the transportation and refining of oil produced from the field.[36] Much like Standard itself, these new rivals were vertically integrated with involvement across all stages of the oil industry.

As these corporate rivals grew, a major shift was also beginning to take place in the US oil market: a move away from oil as a single-product industry centred on kerosene, towards one that involved multiple other kinds of refined products. From 1900, the rising commercial success of the internal combustion engine had increased demand for petrol and lubricating oils. Rudimentary automobiles had begun to make their appearance, and asphalt – another oil product – was being used to pave the roads on which these vehicles moved. The establishment of urban electricity networks and the growing adoption of electric street lighting from the early 1900s reduced the demand for kerosene.[37] But, at the same time, it increased the demand for fuel oil, which could be used as a combustion fuel in the steam engines that generated electricity.[38] By

34 Michael Tanzer and Stephen Zorn, *Energy Update: Oil in the Late Twentieth Century*, New York: Monthly Review Press, 1985, 27.

35 The population of the nearby town, Beaumont, tripled in just three months. Yergin, *The Prize*, 69. Chapter 4 of *The Prize* contains a colourful account of Spindletop.

36 One of Standard's global rivals, the London-based Shell Transport and Trading, also established an important position in Spindletop, marketing oil to the British Navy.

37 David Nye, *Electrifying America*, Cambridge, MA: MIT Press, 1990.

38 In 1909, kerosene's share of refined oil products in the US had fallen to 45 per cent, down from 62 per cent in 1904. By 1914, it would be 26.5 per cent. Nicoline

1909, kerosene no longer contributed the majority of the US oil industry's revenues – petrol, fuel oil, and other refined products were now more important.

With oil no longer a single-product industry, the activities of Standard's integrated rivals were substantially eroding the company's position in the US market. In refining, Standard's virtual monopoly had fallen to 65 per cent of US output in 1911, down from more than 90 per cent in 1880.[39] In upstream crude, Standard held only 14 per cent of US production. The final blow to the company came with a 1911 Supreme Court decision that found Standard guilty of violating the Sherman Anti-Trust Act, despite its attempts to reorganise itself in New Jersey, and ordering that it be broken up into thirty-four separate firms. Nonetheless, the formal end of the Standard empire did little to erode the wealth of the Rockefeller family. The assets of Standard were distributed back to their original shareholders, leaving dominant ownership across the now independent companies in the hands of John D. Rockefeller, who became the richest person in the world as a result of the decision.[40]

Out of the dozens of firms that came out of the dissolution of Standard, four quickly emerged as the most notable: SONJ (later Exxon); Standard Oil of New York (SOCONY, later Mobil); Standard Oil of California (SOCAL, later Chevron); and Standard Oil of Indiana (later merged

---

Kokxhoorn, *Oil and Politics: The Domestic Roots of US Expansion in the Middle East*, Frankfurt: Peter Lang, 1977, 2.

39 Bruce Everett, 'The Revenge of the Invisible Hand', *Foreign Policy*, 13 May 2011, foreignpolicy.com.

40 Yergin, *The Prize*, 113. Almost three decades later, a 1939 US government investigation would find that the Rockefellers remained in a controlling minority position in at least six of the major American oil companies, noting drily that: 'While all of these concerns are independent enterprises, with complete freedom to determine their own policies, it seems hardly likely, in view of the extent to which they are owned by the same people, that any one of them would pursue a course which was prejudicial to the interests of the others.' H. Dewey Anderson (Temporary National Economic Committee), *Investigation of Concentration of Economic Power: Final Report of the Executive Secretary*, Washington, DC: US Government Printing Office, 1941, 24. As the Federal Trade Commission commented more than a decade after the 1911 decision, there was 'an interlocking stock ownership in the different organizations [that emerged from the breakup of Standard Oil] which has perpetuated the very monopolistic control which the courts sought to terminate'. Cited in John Blair, *The Control of Oil*, New York: Pantheon Books, 1976, 127.

with BP). Each of these firms was highly integrated and inherited part of the logistical infrastructures of their parent company. They remained dominant within their individual geographic areas, operating in a domestic US market where thousands of smaller non-integrated firms were involved in crude extraction. Crucially, these four large firms were established as independent firms at a time when commercial use of the internal combustion engine was growing rapidly. They were thus strategically positioned – along with a handful of other major vertically integrated US firms (such as Gulf Oil and Texaco) – at the epicentre of the very birth of a new petroleum-fuelled world market.

US Oil and the First World War

The 1911 court action to dissolve Standard was not the cause of Standard's demise, but rather a reflection of changes that had *already happened* within the US oil industry. As the demand for oil expanded and the number of oil products diversified, it had become impossible for a single company to control the industry as the old Standard once had. The national market was now dominated by a handful of large integrated firms – some that came out of Standard – alongside a few newcomers that had got their start with oilfield discoveries in California, Texas, and Louisiana. Around this integrated core, a substantial ecosystem of smaller non-integrated companies existed (especially in the upstream crude segment). This integrated/non-integrated structure has remained the basic division within the domestic US oil market through to the present day. It will also take a central place in later chapters as we trace the development of the global industry over the rest of the twentieth century.

The outbreak of the First World War in 1914 vastly strengthened the power of these large integrated US firms. While coal remained the dominant commercial energy source during the war, the global conflict force-marched most of the world into adopting the deadly new technologies of petroleum-based warfare.[41] Particularly important here was

41 For accounts of oil and the First World War, see Timothy Winegard, *The First Oil World War*, Toronto: University of Toronto Press, 2016; Anand Toprani, *Oil and the Great Powers: Britain and Germany, 1914 to 1945*, Oxford: Oxford University Press, 2019.

the transformation of maritime fleets away from coal to oil-burning ships. Ships that ran on oil were much lighter, faster, and did not need space for bulky coal-storage areas; they could thus carry extra weapons and crew. Oil-powered ships could also be refuelled at sea, giving them greater operational flexibility. In Britain, naval planners, led by then head of the Admiralty, Winston Churchill, had taken the decision to transition the country's fleet to oil in 1911. By the end of the war, 40 per cent of the British fleet was oil-powered, and the navy's monthly consumption of fuel oil had more than doubled.[42] Similarly, the US government had also decided in 1906 to substitute oil for coal as the main fuel for its naval fleet.[43] To guarantee a stable supply of oil for these ships, US government planners noticeably accelerated the development of bunkers, port infrastructure, and transport capacity for refined oil products. Between 1913 and 1915, oil-storage capacity doubled in order to meet the projected US naval demand; by 1920, storage capacity would be more than three times pre-war levels.[44] The centrepiece of this policy was the establishment of massive overseas bases at Guantánamo Bay and Pearl Harbor, which together held more than one-third of the US Navy's fuel-storage capacity.[45]

But the impact of petroleum on war making extended far beyond its use as a naval fuel. In Britain, toluene, one of the by-products of oil refining, was used to manufacture TNT, an explosive that was in high demand due to the bloody trench warfare ravaging Europe.[46] Armies also became fully mechanised, reliant upon new petroleum-based forms of transport: in 1914 the British military had only 823 cars and fifteen motorcycles, but by the end of the war it had 23,000 cars, 63,000 trucks, and 34,000 motorcycles.[47] New technologies such as tanks, submarines, and the aeroplane were all introduced during this period – transforming war, in the words of one soldier, into something that was 'machine-like . . . an

42 P. Johnstone and C. McLeish, 'World Wars and the Age of Oil: Exploring Directionality in Deep Energy Transitions', *Energy Research and Social Science* 69, November 2020: 6; G. Gareth Jones, 'The British Government and the Oil Companies 1912–1924: The Search for an Oil Policy', *Historical Journal* 20, no. 3, 1977: 647–72, 655.

43 Stephen Powers, 'The Development of United States Naval Fuel-Oil Policy, 1866–1923', MA thesis, Houston, TX: Rice Institute, 1960.

44 Ibid., 35.

45 Ibid.

46 Jones, 'The British Government and the Oil Companies', 655.

47 Johnstone and McLeish, 'World Wars and the Age of Oil', 6.

industry of professionalized human slaughter'.[48] Off the battlefields, petroleum-fired machines made possible a huge increase in the output of military factories. Tractors and other kinds of mechanised machinery were also introduced into agriculture, thereby releasing the labour force essential to waging war. While it would take several more decades before petroleum-derived fertilisers, pesticides, and other chemicals bound global food production fully to the oil economy, the origins of this relationship can be dated to this moment.

All of this led Britain's Lord Curzon to quip famously that the Allied forces had 'floated to victory on a wave of oil'. But what Curzon declined to mention is that this oil was overwhelmingly *American*: remarkably, around 80 per cent of all the oil used by Allied forces during the First World War came from the US, with SONJ alone providing more than a quarter of this amount.[49] For the leading US oil companies, this huge increase in the global demand for petrol, fuel oil, lubricants, and other synthetic products, definitively pushed aside kerosene as the main oil product. It also tied the power of US oil firms to the deepening global war economy. From this point onwards, militarism would become a principal driver of oil consumption; indeed, today, the largest single institutional consumer of oil on the planet – and thus the largest institutional source of carbon emissions – is the US military.[50]

These close connections between the US state and the growth of the global oil economy were codified in a series of fateful steps that firmly placed the leading oil companies at the centre of government energy policy and planning. In 1917, just before the US joined the war, a government advisory board was formed that brought together the leaders of the six largest US oil companies. This National Petroleum War Service Committee (NPWSC) was headed by the chair of SONJ, Alfred Bedford,

48 Cited in Winegard, *The First Oil World War*, 5.

49 Ibid., 104.

50 O. Belcher et al., 'Hidden Carbon Costs of the "Everywhere War": Logistics, Geopolitical Ecology, and the Carbon Boot-Print of the US Military', *Transactions of the Institute of British Geographers* 45, no. 1, 2020: 65–80. Despite this connection with war-making, overseas military emissions have been deliberately excluded in global climate agreements: they were made exempt in the 1997 Kyoto Protocol after US lobbying, and military emission reporting is optional in the 2015 Paris Climate Agreement. See Patrick Bigger et al., *Less War, Less Warming: A Reparative Approach to US and UK Military Ecological Damages*, Common Wealth, 6 November 2023, available at common-wealth.org.

and was given a direct role in government decision-making, including the ability to set national oil production levels and refinery outputs. NPWSC facilitated an unprecedented level of direct intra-industry coordination among the largest firms; statistics on drilling operations, well numbers, production volumes, transport costs, and pricing calculations could be collected by these firms and shared with the US government for war-planning purposes. This was the first time in the history of the US oil industry – with the partial exception of the original Standard Oil's own internal book-keeping – that comprehensive data on crude production and refining was collected across the whole country.[51] In effect, the US government was endorsing intra-industry coordination among the largest firms around the key issues of supply, demand, and pricing. While many at the time believed that this was a clear violation of anti-trust regulations – occurring less than a decade after the 1911 decision to break up Standard – the government explicitly blocked the Federal Trade Commission from taking any action against the oil companies.[52]

Alongside this integration into political decision-making, a range of hugely consequential tax breaks and financial subsidies for US oil firms were also introduced at this time that went far beyond those provided to any other industry. The most astonishing of these was the 1918 'Oil Depletion Allowance', a deduction from taxable income that enabled oil producers to offset the depletion of their oil mine in a manner that resembled capital depreciation.[53] Over the next decade, the tax break would evolve into a 27.5 per cent annual deduction on the gross income from oil production – a figure that was arbitrarily chosen to make 'it

51 Joseph Pratt, 'Organizing Information about the Modern Oil Industry in the Formative Years of the American Petroleum Institute', *Business and Economic History* 9, 1980: 74–86. Due to the fragmented nature of private ownership in the oil industry it had initially been difficult to gather accurate statistics for oil production, consumption, and reserves, until the establishment of this government-sanctioned intra-industry coordination. In the US, there were at least eleven official investigations into the size of the nation's oil reserves between 1900 and 1925, most of which were subsequently proven to be wildly inaccurate.

52 Gerald Nash, *United States Oil Policy 1890–1964*, Pittsburgh: University of Pittsburgh Press, 1968, 32–7.

53 For a discussion of this law and its role in supporting the expansion of the oil industry, see P. Shulman, 'The Making of a Tax Break: The Oil Depletion Allowance, Scientific Taxation, and Natural Resources Policy in the Early Twentieth Century', *Journal of Policy History* 23, no. 3, 2011: 281–322.

appear as though it was scientifically arrived at' according to the Texan senator who supported the law in 1926.[54] The crucial detail of this tax regulation was that the total amount taken for depletion was unlimited over the life of the mine. As a result, the overall subsidy received by the oil company could end up being many times the original cost of investment – a fact that was later described by US Treasury Secretary Henry Morgenthau as 'perhaps the most glaring loophole in our present revenue law'.[55] Indeed, the tax advantages presented by this subsidy were so great that, by the 1950s, wealthy Hollywood stars such as Bob Hope, Frank Sinatra, Bing Crosby, and Jimmy Stewart decided to buy oil wells in order to shield their income from the tax office.[56]

This and other tax subsidies – including the deduction of 'intangible drilling expenses' – meant that the costs associated with the exploration and production of oil were effectively borne by the US state and taxpayer, not the oil companies themselves.[57] With oil's rising prominence to the world's energy matrix, the US state had become a guarantor for the accumulation of the largest oil firms that had emerged in the wake of the Standard break-up – underwriting high profit rates through increased state consumption of oil, building critical infrastructure, and providing substantial tax breaks and other cost subsidies. The growing interdependencies between government and the oil industry had been institutionalised in bodies such as NPWSC, which, in 1919, was renamed the American Petroleum Institute (API), and they continue to play a central role in US oil policymaking to this day. All of this was further reinforced by the 'revolving door' between oil company management and US politicians. These entanglements of American politics and the private

54 R. B. Woods, *LBJ: Architect of American Ambition*, Cambridge, MA: Harvard University Press, 2006, 230.

55 Gerhard Peters and John T. Woolley, 'Franklin D. Roosevelt, Message to Congress on Tax Evasion Prevention', American Presidency Project, UC Santa Barbara, presidency.ucsb.edu.

56 Shulman, 'The Making of a Tax Break'.

57 Intangible drilling expenses refer to items such as wages, fuel, machinery, and tools used in the drilling operation; and unlike any other industry, where these costs would be amortised over the life of the asset, oil companies could deduct them in the year that they occurred. 'The result of this extraordinarily rapid amortization is a huge first-year deduction which can be used to shelter an equivalent amount of taxable income from other sources' (Blair, *Control of Oil*, 192). Most of these subsidies, including the depletion allowance, remain in place today. They were later augmented by other tax advantages supporting the overseas operations of the oil industry (see Chapter 6).

business of oil would deepen and expand over subsequent decades, with profound implications for the future trajectories of world oil.[58]

The Interwar Years: Internationalisation of US Oil

Major wars are often followed by periods of rapid social change, and the end of the First World War was no exception. In the US, perhaps the most visible illustration of this was the extraordinary revolution in personal mobility that occurred through the 1920s. From just a few tens of thousands of cars manufactured in the US prior to the war, the number of vehicles produced in American factories would reach 6 million by 1918. Between 1918 and 1925, this figure more than tripled once again.[59] Looking back on this transformation in 1936, the American Petroleum Institute (API) would note that while 'George Washington could travel no faster than Julius Caesar, and Caesar no faster than Solomon', the US public had gone from '30 miles a day to 300 miles an hour . . . all within the last quarter of a century'.[60] This introduction of mass individualised transport was the beginning of a wholesale restructuring of US urban life: the dismantlement and mothballing of public transit systems; suburbanisation and the linking of cities through a spaghetti-like maze of tangled highways; and a revolution in corporate advertising that went hand in hand with the emergence of a road culture.[61] Among these social changes, large automobile manufacturers (such as General Motors and Ford) became a recognisable and powerful force in US politics, their interests closely aligned with those of the oil industry.

With the pervasive spread of automobiles came the emergence of a new social figure: the *driver*. It was no longer just industry and the

58 Other countries – notably Britain – experienced a similar entwining of politics and oil during the same period; see Jones, 'The British Government and the Oil Companies'. Importantly, Germany, which continued to lack access to oil in the wake of the war, instead sought to build a chemical industry that produced petroleum from coal. This had important implications for the later development of the oil industry in Europe (see Chapter 7).

59 American Petroleum Institute, *American Petroleum Industry*, 135.

60 Ibid.

61 See Huber, *Lifeblood*, 43. The automobile delivered 'individuated mobility', with the 'ecology of "buried sunshine" [i.e. petroleum]' powering a 'dispersed geography of atomized, auto-bound subjects'.

military that demanded ever-increasing quantities of petroleum: oil consumption was now propelled forward by the daily needs of the individual and the household. According to the API, the rise of the car had 'remodeled the face of this continent', with petrol firmly replacing kerosene as the industry's 'money commodity'.[62] The American driver's 'thirst for motor fuel' was insatiable – it knew 'no holidays, no Sundays, no relaxations' and demanded 'a revolution in nearly all processes and practices'.[63] All of this necessitated a major reworking of how crude moved from the oil well to the automobile tank: ever more complicated and expensive refineries, new marketing techniques, and a nationwide network of service stations – bound to one another, as always, through the infrastructures of pipelines, storage facilities, tankers, and road transport. By 1927, there were 143,000 US service stations, linked through more than 350,000 miles of highways made from that oft-forgotten oil product, asphalt.[64]

Western Europe also witnessed a significant increase in automobile use during the interwar years, albeit at levels lower than the US.[65] The emergence of this global market for automobiles meant that worldwide demand for oil rose considerably. By 1925, global consumption of oil and oil products had increased more than two and a half times compared to 1913. While coal easily continued to make up the largest share of the world's commercial energy mix (around 83 per cent), absolute levels of coal consumption were lower in 1925 than they had been in 1913. In contrast, oil's share of the world's commercial energy more than doubled over this same period, rising from 5.6 per cent to 13.2 per cent.[66] In the US, the growth in the oil economy was even more dramatic: by 1925, oil contributed more than one-fifth of the country's energy consumption.

In this context, the development of the domestic US oil industry was closely dependent upon what happened across the wider world market. While the US accounted for more than 70 per cent of world oil production in 1918 and was by far the largest source of consumer demand, the

62 American Petroleum Institute, *American Petroleum Industry*, 135, 129.

63 Ibid., 12–13.

64 Winegard, *The First Oil World War*, 108.

65 In 1927, there was one car for every 5.3 Americans, compared to just one for every forty-four people across Britain, France, and Germany. Ibid., 108.

66 Simon Pirani, *Burning Up: A Global History of Fossil Fuel Consumption*, London: Pluto Press, 2018, 19.

international position of the dominant US oil firms appeared much less assured at the end of the First World War.[67] Up until this moment, their international interests had largely focused on competing with European rivals over *export* markets for refined products made in the US from American crude – not the control of overseas sites of oil extraction. In Iran, the only oil-producing state in the Middle East at the time, oil production was fully controlled by the British-owned Anglo-Persian Oil Company (later BP). Further east, the British-Dutch firm, Royal Dutch Shell, held the main oil fields in the Dutch East Indies (Indonesia). In Romania and Poland, the two oil-rich countries of Europe, production was also dominated by Royal Dutch Shell, alongside other British and French investors.[68] And, in the Soviet Union, which was the third largest area of world oil production through the 1920s, the oil sector was controlled by the new Bolshevik government.

Breaking out of this geographical isolation was a major priority for the largest US oil firms through the interwar years. The reasons for this were closely connected to the persistent problems of overproduction in the US market. By the end of the First World War, it had become abundantly clear that measures to restrict production would be needed to stabilise prices in the domestic market. And while the exact content of these measures would not be fully agreed until the 1930s (see next chapter), various policies to control production for the US market were already under discussion between the oil industry, federal, and state governments by the 1920s. For the largest integrated US oil firms, these

67 B. McBeth, 'Venezuela's Nascent Oil Industry and the 1932 Tariff on Crude Oil Imports, 1927–1935', *Revista de Historia Económica/Journal of Iberian and Latin American Economic History* 27, no. 3, 2009: 427–62, 431.

68 Romanian oil accounted for 82 per cent of West European oil production in 1929; see *World Energy Supplies in Selected Years 1929–1950*, New York: UN, 1952, 50. The Romanian oil industry had been much more advanced than the US during the mid-nineteenth century – the country already possessed an oil refinery in 1856, three years before the first successful well was drilled in the US. Bucharest was also the first city in the world to use kerosene for street lighting, with 1,000 lamps illuminating the country's capital in 1857. Romania was the site of the 'Torch of Moreni', the largest oil fire in European history that began in 1929 and burned for over two years. Access to and control over the country's oil was an essential part to Nazi war efforts, particularly when Germany failed to gain control over the Baku oil fields during its invasion of the USSR in 1941. Following the Second World War, Romanian oil was nationalised and came under Soviet control. See Maurice Pearton, *Oil and the Romanian State*, Oxford: Clarendon Press, 1971, for an informative history of the country's oil industry.

discussions implied that the growing international demand for oil could no longer be reliably met from domestic US sources – instead, it would be more effective to supply their international markets from foreign reserves.[69] It was also clear that substantial foreign supplies existed outside the US, and these could be extracted at prices that were significantly cheaper than oil in the US (which, in turn, created further pressures around overproduction). In this context, control of foreign reserves became an imperative. As a director of SONJ would note in 1917: 'In protecting our foreign investments, we protect ourselves and our friends by controlling a greater percentage of the foreign business which comes directly into competition with US products. By owning it, we can influence its activity at times when production is too great or too small in America and maintain more regular conditions.'[70]

Latin America

The first target of US international oil expansion was Latin America, where US Secretary of State Robert Lansing proclaimed in 1918 'that no oil properties in the neighbourhood of the Panama Canal should be owned by other than Americans'.[71] One of the early successes of this policy was a 1.5-million-acre concession on the Colombia–Venezuela border, the Barco Concession, which was transferred to US ownership in 1918. As one of the first sites of oil exploration located *outside* US territory, Barco would become a potent symbol of American oil colonialism. The concession remained under the control of US firms until the 1960s – eventually becoming one of the most lucrative of all US business investments in Latin America (largely because the US oil companies running the concession deliberately understated production levels by at least half so as to avoid paying royalties).[72] Barco became a new frontier

69 This was a particularly pressing problem for SONJ, which was widely considered to be 'crude hungry' in the early 1920s: despite SONJ's dominant share of international markets for refined products, the firm was considerably short of adequate crude supplies to supply their refineries.

70 Cited in Kokxhoorn, *Oil and Politics*, 22–3.

71 Cited in Mira Wilkins, *The Maturing of Multinational Enterprise: American Business Abroad from 1914 to 1970*, Cambridge, MA: Harvard University Press, 1974, 27.

72 René de la Pedraja, *Energy Politics in Colombia*, London: Westview Press, 1989, 25, 73. The Barco Concession was held by Texaco and Mobil.

reimagined through notions of conquest and race – a place where, as one US government report later described, American oil companies 'literally had to carve their producing fields out of steaming jungles filled with wild animal life and infested with the most savage tribe of Indians extant in this hemisphere'.[73]

But, although Barco signalled a major step forward for US oil firms in Latin America, it was in Mexico and Venezuela that American oil expansionism really took hold in the decade after the First World War. Mexico ranked as the world's second largest oil producer until 1921, with oil concessions operated by firms such as SONJ, Shell, Gulf, Texaco, Sinclair, and Standard Oil of Indiana.[74] These companies supplied their international marketing channels with Mexican oil, and also viewed the country as a profitable market in its own right. However, their ongoing position in Mexico was by no means assured. The 1917 Mexican revolution had declared that the country's natural resources would be publicly owned, and although it was not until 1938 that Mexico became the second country outside the Soviet bloc to nationalise its oil industry, anger against the foreign ownership of oil ran high among oil workers and the country's militant labour and student movements.[75]

By the late 1920s, Mexican oil had begun to be eclipsed by a succession of oilfield discoveries in Venezuela, a country that was attractive to US oil firms for several reasons. Its plentiful oil supplies – concentrated around Lake Maracaibo – had an extraction cost significantly less than the US or other areas in Latin America. Its geographical proximity to the US meant that oil could be shipped to the Atlantic seaboard at cheaper rates than the interstate transport of domestic US oil by pipelines. Most importantly, unlike the nationalist threats against foreign oil ownership emanating from Mexican revolutionaries, the Venezuelan state served as a dependable ally to US and European oil firms. Although the country had a history of worker militancy, it had been ruled since 1908 by the

73 *American Petroleum Interests in Foreign Countries*: Hearings before a Special Committee, 1946, 227.

74 Jonathan Brown, 'Why Foreign Oil Companies Shifted Their Production from Mexico to Venezuela during the 1920s', *American Historical Review* 90, no. 2, 1985: 362–85.

75 Giuliano Garavini, *The Rise and Fall of OPEC in the Twentieth Century*, London: Oxford University Press, 2019, 41–2. The world's first non-Soviet oil nationalisation occurred in Bolivia in 1937.

autocratic general, Juan Vicente Gómez, who allowed oil companies to drill for oil without paying taxes or royalties.[76] Gómez would either sell concessions directly to oil firms, or pass them on to close allies who would then market them to foreign companies – helping him to cultivate a layer of support among Venezuelan elites that allowed his reign to last in one form or another until 1935.[77] Gómez's willingness to facilitate the activities of the oil industry in Venezuela helped make him the richest man in Latin America. By the time of his death, he oversaw a vast business empire that controlled the 'soap, paper, cotton, milk, butter, and matchmaking industries' in Venezuela, as well as major interests in foreign trade, ports, and shipping lines.[78]

Venezuela's place in world oil would transform the geography of the surrounding region. Soon after the discovery of oil, Gómez urged international oil firms to locate their refineries that processed Venezuelan oil in nearby Dutch-controlled Caribbean islands, rather than in Venezuela itself. He did so, according to the Venezuelan anthropologist, Fernando Coronil, 'to avoid creating large concentrations of workers [in Venezuela] with their attendant labour problems'.[79] Shell took up Gómez's suggestion in 1918, with the construction of its massive Isla refinery on the site of a former slave market in Curaçao. A second refinery, which eventually became the largest in the world, began operation in 1929 on the island of Aruba, under the ownership of SONJ.[80] These locations set a

76 Raúl Gallegos, *Crude Nation – How Oil Riches Ruined Venezuela*, Sterling, VA: Potomac Books, 2019, 58.

77 A detailed analysis of this concession system and its ultimate beneficiaries is available in B. McBeth, *Juan Vicente Gómez and the Oil Companies in Venezuela, 1908–1935*, Cambridge: Cambridge University Press, 1983, ch. 3.

78 Garavini, *The Rise and Fall of OPEC*, 20.

79 Fernando Coronil, *The Magical State*, Chicago: University of Chicago Press, 1997, 107. This connection between the potential threat of worker militancy and the spatial relocation of Venezuelan refining provides further confirmation of labour's active role in the restructuring of the global oil industry. For a rich discussion of why labour is so often occluded in the discussion of oil, see Touraj Atabaki, Elisabetta Bini, and Kaveh Ehsani (eds), *Working for Oil: Comparative Histories of Labor in the Global Oil Industry*, London: Palgrave Macmillan, 2018.

80 The Aruba refinery expanded significantly in the lead-up to the Second World War, after SONJ won a contract in 1938 to supply the British Air Force with high-octane fuel. SONJ was not permitted to provide this fuel from US territory because of American neutrality, but it could do so from Dutch-controlled Aruba.

later pattern of refinery expansion throughout the Caribbean.[81] Quite remarkably, the Dutch West Indies (which held no domestic oil resources itself) remained the world's largest centre of oil refining outside the US until the eve of the Second World War: in 1938, the two small islands of Curaçao and Aruba contributed more than a quarter of the world's total refining capacity outside the US and USSR.[82] As late as the 1980s, it was estimated that more than half of all refined petroleum products entering the US – including oil from Africa and the Middle East – had passed through Caribbean refineries.[83]

By the end of the 1920s, the large integrated US oil companies had built a complex network of pipelines, storage terminals, refineries, shipping tankers, and trucks that linked the oil wells of Venezuela's Lake Maracaibo to the US consumer via the islands of the Caribbean. In 1928, Venezuela would become the world's second-largest oil producer, responsible for around 8 per cent of global production.[84] At the time of Gómez's death in 1935, almost all this production was controlled by just three firms: SONJ, Gulf Oil, and Shell.[85] Venezuelan oil was immensely

81 The oil industry also expanded through British colonies in the Caribbean, especially in Trinidad and Tobago, where Shell and BP (then known as the Anglo-Persian Oil Company) controlled oil fields and refineries. Oil workers, including migrant workers from nearby Grenada, were at the core of a series of massive strikes that rocked the British Caribbean between 1934 and 1939. In Britain, C. L. R. James and George Padmore organised a solidarity movement; indeed, a convincing argument can be made that James's understanding of revolutionary movements and anti-colonial struggle, expressed in *The Black Jacobins* and *A History of Negro Revolt* for example, was heavily inspired by his close attention to this struggle. See C. J. Hogsbjerg, '"A Thorn in the Side of Great Britain": C. L. R. James and the Caribbean Labour Rebellions of the 1930s', *Small Axe: A Caribbean Journal of Criticism* 15, no. 2 (35), 2011: 24–42.

82 Vernon Mulchansingh, 'The Location of Oil Refining in Latin America and the Caribbean', *Revista Geográfica* 75, December 1971: 85–126, 94.

83 Bonham Richardson, *The Caribbean in the Wider World, 1492–1992*, Cambridge: Cambridge University Press, 1992, 116.

84 McBeth, 'Venezuela's Nascent Oil Industry', 430.

85 Through a complex series of mergers and acquisitions in the 1920s and early 1930s, SONJ took over the interests of Standard Oil of Indiana (and those of other smaller American producers) in Venezuela. SONJ relied heavily on Venezuelan oil as the lynchpin of its international trade. Prior to the First World War, the company had held no production sites outside the US; by 1927, more than a third of its total global crude production (including from the US and Canada) came from Latin America (mostly Venezuela). This was crucial for the company's dominant position in the world trade of refined products (controlling nearly a quarter of all refined products consumed outside the US, compared to 16 per cent for Shell). Kokxhoorn, *Oil and Politics*, 22–3.

profitable for these firms – it was much cheaper to extract, refine, and transport than crude in the US, and authoritarian rule made it even cheaper. Nonetheless, for the US oil market as a whole, Latin America created a dilemma: the continent's oil might have been cheap, but there was, once again, too much of it. The extra volumes of oil now flowing into the US only amplified the problems of overproduction that had plagued the industry since the first Pennsylvanian oil boom. This challenge of *too much* oil would remain at the heart of the problems confronting the world oil industry over the next two decades.

3

The Middle East and the Seven Sisters

Across the Atlantic, vertical integration was also quickly becoming an important feature of the burgeoning European oil industry. The best illustration of this was Royal Dutch Shell, a company formed in 1907 by the merger of the Netherlands-based Royal Dutch Petroleum Company and the British-owned Shell Transport and Trading Company. The Dutch concern held extensive production interests in oil fields across the Dutch East Indies but lacked the means to transport that oil efficiently to Europe. Shell had made its start in shipping shells from the Far East to Britain during the 1850s, capitalising on the craze for shell boxes that swept Britain at that time.[1] By the early 1900s, the British firm controlled an extensive shipping network, including the rights to transport oil through the Suez Canal. The 1907 union was thus a true child of Dutch and British colonialism, bringing the upstream and downstream together in the first of Europe's large integrated oil companies. Shell would soon rival Standard in size and international reach.[2]

The second of Europe's major oil companies emerged through the active assistance of the British state. In 1914, following lengthy and acrimonious parliamentary debate, the British government made the

1 Stephen Howarth, *A Century in Oil: The Shell Transport and Trading Company, 1897–1997*, London: Weidenfeld & Nicolson, 1997.

2 Subsequent references to Shell refer to the merged Royal Dutch Shell, rather than the Shell Transport and Trading Company.

momentous decision to take a 51 per cent controlling stake in the Anglo-Persian Oil Company (APOC), a firm that had been founded in 1909.[3] APOC held exclusive rights to most of the oil fields in Iran, a country that was then under British influence.[4] The government's objective in taking over APOC was to establish a dependable and secure source of oil, which was essential to the planned transition of the British Navy into an oil-based fleet. Other suppliers, such as Shell, could not be relied on as their oil reserves were located in territories outside British imperial control, leaving them vulnerable at times of war.[5] Alongside these strategic considerations of the British state, APOC's private owners also actively lobbied for government investment.[6] At the time, APOC lacked a robust shipping network to transport oil products from its refinery in Iran to Europe or anywhere else (in fact, the company had been forced to sign an agreement with Shell in 1912 to help ship and market its oil). A relationship with the British state provided APOC access to a large government-owned tanker fleet, as well as a guaranteed market for its oil products (especially fuel oil). British government support thus helped push APOC into the front ranks of Europe's large vertically integrated firms, second only to Royal Dutch Shell. Decades later, the company would be renamed British Petroleum – known today as BP.

The First World War erupted just a few months after the British government's decision to invest in APOC. The war greatly accelerated the shift in global economic power away from Western Europe towards the US, due in part to a massive boom in the export of US goods to the Allied powers – including oil, weapons, and other industrial and agricultural products. While the conflict devastated countries across Europe, the US experienced its longest continuous economic expansion since

3 APOC was established as a subsidiary of the Burmah Oil Company, the first wholly British-owned oil firm. Burmah Oil Company operated oil fields in Burma at the time, and held an effective monopoly on the oil industry in India up until the 1950s. For a history, including the establishment of APOC, see T. A. B. Corley, *A History of the Burmah Oil Company*, vol. 1, *1886–1924*, London: William Heinemann, 1983.

4 Although it was known as Persia until 1935, for clarity the term *Iran* will be used throughout.

5 Most of Shell's reserves were located in Russia, the Dutch East Indies, and Romania. Winegard, *The First Oil World War*, 61.

6 G. Gareth Jones, 'The British Government and the Oil Companies 1912–1924: The Search for an Oil Policy', *Historical Journal* 20, no. 3, 1977.

the Civil War, a forty-four-month stretch lasting from December 1914 to August 1918.[7] Importantly, the US also benefited from its role as creditor to European states seeking to finance their military expenditures. Total Allied debts reached $19.4 billion between 1914 and 1918, equivalent to the entire stock of British foreign assets just before the war, and about half of these loans came from the US.[8] The US was the only country involved in the war that did not need to take out foreign loans, and as it became banker to the world, Wall Street emerged as a major financial centre, rivalling the City of London in its global influence. By war's end, US capitalism had clearly overtaken the heavily indebted and conflict-ravaged countries of Europe. As one prominent scholar of American history concluded, 'in an economic sense, the United States was the sole victor of World War I'.[9]

Nonetheless, despite its obvious economic ascendancy, the expansion of US capitalism faced a major *political* obstacle in the wake of the First World War. The roots of the war lay in the struggle of the older European powers to re-divide the world, and large parts of Africa, the Middle East, and Asia remained under various kinds of European colonial rule. For centuries, European global dominance had rested upon the systematic extraction of resources from these areas. And, to maintain this dominance, states such as Britain and France kept tight rein on economic structures in their colonies – including the development of monetary systems tied to sterling or the franc, the control of banking and industrial policy, and restrictions on the entry of other foreign competitors. These spaces of economic exclusion thus effectively blocked the expansion of US capital from much of the world and ensured that colonial wealth continued to flow predominantly into the older imperial centres.

The oil industry served as the immediate and direct arena for tensions between a rising US power and the enduring realities of European colonialism. With the US positioned as the world's largest producer and

7 Benjamin O. Fordham, 'Revisionism Reconsidered: Exports and American Intervention in World War I', *International Organization* 61, no. 2, Spring 2007: 277–310, 286.

8 Youssef Cassis, *Capitals of Capital: A History of International Finance Centres, 1780–2005*, Cambridge: Cambridge University Press, 2006, 147.

9 Frank Costigliola, 'Anglo-American Financial Rivalry in the 1920s', *Journal of Economic History* 4, 1977: 911–34, 914. The outcome included a $4.7 billion war debt owed by Britain to the US.

consumer of oil, the emergence of oil as a *globally* significant energy source acted in mutual effect with the concurrent rise of American capitalism, simultaneously bolstering the international power of the largest US oil firms. Yet, in the post-war redivision of the world, most oil reserves beyond the US and Latin America had fallen under the effective control of European powers. In these territories, it was Shell and APOC who stood poised to become the main beneficiaries of the expected oil bonanza. The ensuing tussle around access to these global reserves was the main issue confronting the world oil industry through the 1920s. This was far more than simply a contest over the corporate control of oil – it was a struggle that would determine the nature of European power and the place of American capitalism in the world market for decades to come.

Opening the Door in the Middle East

The historian James Gelvin has pointed out that, while the First World War is commonly seen as a conflict fought entirely in Europe, in truth, it was a war that extended far beyond European borders. Many of these non-European battlefields were located in the Middle East, where a deep-seated political crisis erupted as the region was drawn into the conflict. Across the territories of the centuries-old Ottoman Empire, which stretched from modern-day Turkey through Syria, Palestine, Iraq, and beyond, nearly 25 per cent of the population perished – more than twice the death rates of France and Germany.[10] Iran experienced similarly high casualty levels, even though the country was formally neutral during the war. At the end of hostilities, the Ottoman Empire was broken apart by the victorious European powers, with new borders imposed that demarcated various spheres of European influence and control. This was the birth of the region's contemporary state system, and as Gelvin observes, it made the First World War 'the single most important *political* event in the history of the modern Middle East'.[11]

10 James Gelvin, *The Modern Middle East: A History*, Oxford: Oxford University Press, 2011, 180.

11 Ibid., 182.

Control over oil reserves was a principal factor in this post-war territorial carve-up of the Middle East. While the region was not yet a major oil producer, it was keenly recognised that substantial reserves existed across Iran and the former Ottoman territories. Britain, in particular, placed utmost strategic priority on gaining dominance over these areas. The goal of British oil policy, according to Winston Churchill, was to become 'the owners, or at any rate the controllers at the source, of at least a proportion of the supply of natural oil which we require . . . and to draw our oil supply, so far as possible, from sources under British control or British influence'.[12] The Sykes–Picot Agreement, a secret pact drawn up between Britain and France in 1916, had allocated to Britain most of what became Jordan, Palestine, and Iraq.[13] In addition, Britain was the dominant colonial power in Iran, Egypt, Kuwait, and the smaller Gulf sheikhdoms situated along the Arabian Peninsula. Political and economic control over these countries gave Britain privileged access to the most promising areas of oil exploration. It also meant that Britain would govern many of the prospective transhipment routes and ports that were necessary for moving oil out of the Middle East (including the Haifa Port in Palestine, and the Suez Canal in Egypt).

The obvious focus of British oil interests in the Middle East was APOC's presence in Iran: by 1923, Iran accounted for 29 per cent of British global oil imports, compared to only 4 per cent in 1920.[14] But it was in neighbouring Iraq where the most significant struggles around the control of the region's oil unfolded through the 1920s. Prior to the war, the Ottoman government had promised concessionary rights for Iraqi oil to a European consortium, the Turkish Petroleum Company

12 Cited in United States Senate, Special Committee Investigating Petroleum Resources, *American Petroleum Interests in Foreign Countries*, 78th Congress, 1946, 298.

13 Palestine was initially given over to an international administration, but later came under British control. Formerly, Britain and France were given 'mandate power' over these areas in the Middle East, meaning they were supposed to guide the territories towards self-government and eventual independence. In reality, however, this meant they had control over all elements of decision-making, including economic and financial questions. The Sykes–Picot Agreement also committed the British and French governments to supporting their respective nationals in any negotiations around oil in Romania and Russia. The agreement would only be publicly revealed following the 1917 Bolshevik Revolution in Russia, when a copy was found in one of the czar's safes.

14 Nicoline Kokxhoorn, *Oil and Politics: The Domestic Roots of US Expansion in the Middle East*, Frankfurt: Peter Lang, 1977, 27.

(TPC), whose leading shareholders included APOC, Shell, the German-based Deutsche Bank, and Calouste Gulbenkian, an Armenian entrepreneur. War had disrupted TPC's exploration plans, however, and with the end of the conflict, an intense discussion flared around what to do with the German share of TPC. Eventually, an international conference held in San Remo in 1920 decided to hand over Deutsche Bank's holdings (25 per cent of TPC) to a French firm, the Compagnie française des pétroles (forerunner of today's French oil giant, TotalEnergies). This so-called San Remo Oil Agreement also committed France to allowing any future oil produced in Iraq to be transported through French-controlled territories (Syria and Lebanon) to ports on the Mediterranean.

The largest US oil companies understood well the enormous potential of Iraq's oil, especially those fields located around the city of Mosul, whose inclusion within British-controlled Iraq was then under challenge from Turkey. But the problem faced by these American firms was that they were effectively barred from access to the country's oil riches: TPC had exclusive rights to all Iraqi oil, and there were no US shareholders in the company. Additionally, Britain, the dominant political force in Iraq, was intent on blocking the entry of US firms into the Middle East.[15] In response to this exclusion, the US government strongly attacked the San Remo Agreement, and instead called for an open-door policy that would allow firms of any nationality to hold concession rights to oil in the region. In making this argument, the US government reasoned that it had played a major role in the Allied victory in the First World War and was thus deserving of equal rights to resources in areas such as Iraq. Indeed, as the US ambassador in Britain put it, the US had only agreed to 'the acquisition of certain enemy territory by the victorious powers' on the understanding that it too would be allowed to benefit.[16] The world was changing. Colonialism had to be made to work for *all* aspiring powers, not simply the old European colonisers.

15 Further afield, non-British firms were also officially barred from petroleum exploration in British-controlled India and Nigeria.

16 Letter from US Ambassador to Great Britain John Davis, to British Foreign Secretary George Curzon, 12 May 1920, cited in Annie Tracy Samuel, 'The Open Door and U.S. Policy in Iraq between the World Wars', *Diplomatic History* 38, no. 5, November 2014: 926–52, 931.

The US wielded several powerful weapons in its efforts to 'open the door' to oil in the Middle East. For one, US oil exports met around 60 per cent of the total foreign demand for oil in 1921, making Britain and other European countries vulnerable to any fluctuations in American supplies.[17] In Britain alone, a subsidiary of SONJ controlled over half of the oil market, and British military planners held long-standing concerns over their ability to secure adequate amounts of oil if the US remained neutral during any future global conflict (indeed, this was another reason why Shell and SONJ had decided to locate their refineries for Venezuelan oil in the Dutch West Indies, rather than in the US).[18] It is not publicly known whether the threat of withholding oil exports was ever used to pressure Britain to open up access to Middle East oil, but the possibility was at least discussed by SONJ, according to a later US government investigation into the American oil industry.[19]

The sheer size of the US domestic oil market was another strong lever used in attempts to open the region to American firms. In February 1920, just a few short weeks before the San Remo Agreement was concluded, US President Woodrow Wilson signed into law the Mineral Leasing Act of 1920.[20] The Act was introduced to regulate access to minerals on land owned by the US Federal Government, and to ensure that private companies who mined the land paid royalties to the government. But the first paragraph of the Act contained another decisive provision: no foreign company would be allowed to gain mineral rights on US public land if their government denied the same rights to US citizens in other areas of the world. It was a move that placed immense pressure on the British, French, and Dutch governments: any European oil company that aspired to be truly global could not afford to be shut out of the US market.[21] Shell, in particular, was especially worried about the implications of the new law: in 1920, about 15 per cent of the

17 Federal Trade Commission (FTC), *Foreign Ownership in the Petroleum Industry*, Washington, DC: US Government Printing Office, 1923, 53.

18 G. Gareth Jones, 'The British Government and the Oil Companies'.

19 FTC, *Foreign Ownership in the Petroleum Industry*, 53.

20 The text of this act, *Mineral Leasing Act of 1920 as Amended*, is downloadable from the Bureau of Land Management, blm.gov, 1.

21 Giuliano Garavini, *The Rise and Fall of OPEC in the Twentieth Century*, London: Oxford University Press, 2019, 28. The FTC's *Foreign Ownership in the Petroleum Industry* contains a detailed discussion of European restrictions on American oil production across various parts of the colonised world.

company's crude production came from the US, and soon after the law was passed, an American subsidiary of Shell was denied an exploration permit in Utah until it was able to 'satisfy the [US government] that the Governments of Great Britain and the Netherlands do not discriminate against Americans'.[22]

Ultimately, the dominant weight of the US in global oil markets stymied European plans to exclude American companies from the Middle East. Following some difficult discussions between 1920 and 1922 – which were closely connected to ongoing diplomatic considerations around Turkey's claim over Mosul – US firms, led by SONJ and SONY, were finally invited to negotiate for a share of TPC.[23] In 1928, following six years of debate, a comprehensive agreement was reached with all shareholders of TPC.[24] Under the terms of this agreement, 95 per cent of the shares in TPC were equally apportioned between APOC, Royal Dutch Shell, the French-owned CFP, and a consortium of US oil

22 FTC, *Foreign Ownership in the Petroleum Industry*, 14.

23 In 1922–23, Britain needed American diplomatic support in negotiations around the future borders of Mosul. Eventually the League of Nations decided in Britain's favour.

24 These negotiations threatened to violate the US State Department's open-door policy, as TPC's rights over Iraqi oil would potentially block the entry of other competitors. The American oil companies' position on this was based on earlier negotiations between the US Department of the Interior and the Osage Nation in Oklahoma; see FTC, *International Petroleum Cartel*, Washington, DC: US Government Printing Office, 1952, ch. 4. Oil had been discovered on Osage land in 1897, and until 1916 the lease for the land was monopolised by a single firm, the Indian Territory Illuminating Oil Company (which eventually became a subsidiary of the Cities Service Oil Company, owner of the original lease for the Barco Concession in Colombia). In 1916, leases for the Osage land were opened up for competitive bidding through a public auction process, with members of the Osage tribe assigned an annual royalty payment from the oil production. The American oil companies initially proposed a similar system for Iraq, with part of the country's oil fields run by TPC, and another part opened up to bidding from other companies who would be required to pay royalties. We can only speculate whether the American oil companies who proposed this arrangement consciously thought of Iraqis as they did Native American populations, but these companies would undoubtedly have been aware of the various laws that governed the relationship between the US state and the Osage Nation. These defined full-blooded tribal members as 'incompetent', 'wasteful', and 'extravagant', and mandated the assignment of white 'guardians' to control their financial affairs. In the 1920s this led to the Osage Reign of Terror, when dozens (perhaps hundreds) of tribal members were murdered, and the rights to their land and oil wealth inherited by their white guardians; see Matthew L. Fletcher, *Failed Protectors: The Indian Trust and Killers of the Flower Moon*, 117 Mich. L. Rev.1253, 2019.

companies called the Near East Development Corporation. Each of these four parties received 23.75 per cent of TPC, with the remaining 5 per cent held by Calouste Gulbenkian (subsequently known as 'Mr Five Percent'). In 1929, TPC was renamed the Iraq Petroleum Company (IPC).

The formation of IPC was a crucial milestone. Through it, SONJ and SONY – the initial majority shareholders in the Near East Development Corporation – gained their first permanent foothold in the Middle East.[25] Iraq's prospective oil reserves were believed to be enormous, and IPC had managed to capture an extraordinarily favourable concession from the Iraqi government: rights to all oil over the entire territory of the country *for the next seventy-five years* (except for a small area near the town of Basra in the south), as well as exclusive marketing rights for petroleum inside Iraq.[26] This concession was won through negotiations with the government of the Iraqi monarch, King Faisal I – a man who held no previous connections to Iraq, but who had been installed by Britain as ruler in 1921 following the bloody suppression by the British Air Force of a mass, nationwide revolt.[27] IPC's control over Iraq's oil thus fully rested on the support of British colonialism – including, of course, Britain's effective monopoly over the means of violence. It was, in other words, through *partnering* with Britain as the colonial power in

25 SONJ and SONY each held a 25 per cent share in NEDC, with Gulf Oil, Atlantic Refining, and the Pan-American Petroleum and Transport Company holding the rest. Between 1928 and 1934, a series of mergers and share sales saw ownership of NEDC reduced to two companies: SONJ and Socony-Vacuum (a merger of SONY and the Vacuum Oil Co.).

26 These negotiations were concluded with TPC in 1925 (before the formation of IPC). The initial agreement also provided for a small area of Iraq to be opened up to subleases for other companies not involved in TPC, helping to satisfy the US government calls for an open door. In reality, however, TPC would have retained control over the bidding process and could thus reject any rival bids; Gulbenkian later called the idea that other nations would be given the rights to explore for Iraqi oil 'eyewash'. Cited in G. S. Gibb and E. H. Knowlton, *The Resurgent Years: The History of the Standard Oil Company (New Jersey), 1911–1927*, vol. 3, New York: Harper & Brothers, 1956, 297.

27 The 1920 revolt saw Britain employ a new strategy of 'air control' that involved the indiscriminate aerial bombing of hundreds of Iraqi villages and towns. Up to ten thousand Iraqis were killed during the revolt, which remains an important reference point for Iraqi nationalism and political identity today. See Toby Dodge, *Inventing Iraq: The Failure of Nation Building and a History Denied*, New York: Columbia University Press, 2003; and Priya Satia, 'The Defense of Inhumanity: Air Control and the British Idea of Arabia', *American Historical Review* 111, no. 1, February 2006: 16–51.

Iraq that US firms were able to enter Middle Eastern oil production for the first time.[28]

The IPC agreement signalled a growing convergence between British and US interests at the global level. For Britain, this alliance helped guarantee the stable supply of oil – whether from the US in times of peace, or the Middle East in times of war. Additionally, IPC's distinct corporate structure contributed greatly to Britain's strategy of repositioning the City of London as a global hub for financial and legal services at a time of reduced international influence. While ownership of IPC was internationalised, the company was headquartered in London, and its chairperson was required to be British. The US and French partners were also considered to be domiciled in London for legal purposes, and thus subject to English law and English courts in the case of any dispute.[29] British banks serviced the company, especially the Eastern Bank (today part of Standard Chartered), which had branches in Iraq but was headquartered in London.[30] All of this firmly established the City of London as the key intermediary between flows of oil wealth from the Middle East and the rest of the world – a role that would later become an essential part of Britain's place in an increasingly US-centred world.

Iraq, however, gained no such advantages from the establishment of IPC. Early on in the negotiations around the structure of the company, the US firms had insisted that IPC be incorporated as a non-profit, whose main activity was the distribution of crude oil to the company shareholders.[31] Instead of taking a monetary dividend, the owners of IPC received a pro rata share of the oil produced in Iraq, valued at a price that was set at a minimal level to cover production, transportation, and operating costs.[32] Ostensibly this structure was chosen because it meant that the US and French participants could avoid paying double

28 This argument is persuasively made in the case of Iraqi oil by William Stivers, *Supremacy and Oil: Iraq, Turkey, and the Anglo-American World Order, 1918–1930*, London: Cornell University Press, 1982, 118–30.

29 William Stivers, 'International Politics and Iraqi Oil, 1918–1928: A Study in Anglo-American Diplomacy', *Business History Review* 55, no. 4, Winter 1981: 517–40, 521.

30 Geoffrey Jones, *Banking and Oil: The History of the British Bank of the Middle East*, vol. 2, Cambridge: Cambridge University Press, 1987, 21.

31 For a discussion of these negotiations, see Gibb and Knowlton, *The Resurgent Years*, ch. 11.

32 FTC, *International Petroleum Cartel*, 61.

taxation (they were essentially being paid in oil at cost price rather than in money). In reality, however, this structure gave APOC, Shell, CFP, and the US partners the ability to hide the actual value of the oil extracted by IPC (and hence the royalties due to the Iraqi government, which were based on this value). The 'price' of IPC's crude was effectively an arbitrary transfer price set internally by the companies themselves, bearing little resemblance to the actual market price of crude. IPC's component companies then made their real profits on the downstream refining, transport, and marketing of oil products, and information on this was buried in confidential company reports.[33] IPC's directors had learned well the lesson first taught by John D. Rockefeller's Standard Oil: vertical integration, hidden behind creative corporate structures, was the key to power in the global oil industry.

Closing the Door

Importantly, however, the real significance of IPC lay not so much in what it meant for the *increased* production of oil, but rather the power it gave its member firms to *restrict* production. By placing decisions around oil production in a collectively managed consortium, IPC enabled these firms to control the amounts of oil being produced – a task that would have been much more difficult to achieve if each company were competing individually over market share. The challenge of restricting the quantity of oil entering the world market was posed particularly sharply during the late 1920s and early 1930s, given the impact of the 1929 Great Depression on global demand and the large supplies of Venezuelan oil that had also become available around that time. US producers were especially vulnerable to the oversupply of oil following the discovery of a huge field in East Texas in 1930 – a field that quickly became the largest oil-producing reservoir in the US.

33 Moreover, the Iraqi government could not determine royalties on the basis of IPC profits because the company operated as a non-profit firm. This arrangement was only detrimental to Gulbenkian, who did not own an oil company and thus had no interest in being paid in crude oil. Gulbenkian refused to accept this point and blocked negotiations for six years; in the end, he agreed to it on the proviso that the French CFP buy back his 5 per cent of IPC's crude at market price (CFP were short of crude oil at that time and looking for extra sources).

This collective and coordinated approach to restricting the production of oil in the Middle East was operationalised through another agreement struck between the IPC partners in 1928. Known as the Red Line Agreement (RLA), this arrangement specified a large area comprising most of the former Ottoman Empire, including the oil-rich Arabian Peninsula (excluding the emirate of Kuwait).[34] Within this area, the component companies of IPC agreed not to seek individual oil concessions except in the name of IPC itself. The main effect of this was to restrict inter-firm competition over concessions outside Iraq: the companies that made up IPC (the largest oil firms in the world) were prevented from bidding separately or acting in joint ventures with independent firms that were not part of the consortium.[35] With competition over the region's oil limited in this manner, the RLA helped IPC win control through the 1930s over oil concessions in Syria, Jordan, Abu Dhabi, Qatar, Oman, and Yemen, in addition to their holdings in Iraq. Only in Saudi Arabia and Bahrain were the rights to explore and produce oil won by two non-IPC firms, Standard Oil of California (SOCAL, now Chevron), and Texaco.[36]

A confidential French government memorandum noted in 1929 that the signing of the RLA 'marked the beginning of a long-term plan for

34 According to the mythology that has developed around the agreement, none of the participants in the negotiations knew the borders of the Ottoman Empire except for Gulbenkian, who drew a line on a map of the proposed territory in thick red pencil, stating: 'That was the Ottoman Empire which I knew in 1914, and I ought to know. I was born in it, lived in it, served it.' The story was fabricated by Gulbenkian for his autobiography; in reality, extensive negotiations took place between the oil companies and their respective governments over where the border should be delineated. See William Stivers, 'A Note on the Red Line Agreement', *Diplomatic History* 7, no. 1, Winter 1983: 23–34.

35 This restriction on bidding also prevented local rulers from playing off one company against the other, and thus gave IPC increased weight over Middle East governments.

36 SOCAL first discovered oil in Bahrain in 1932, and the following year was awarded a concession to explore for oil in Saudi Arabia. SOCAL's overseas marketing facilities were weak, and in order to strengthen its ability to sell its Middle East oil it formed a joint venture with Texaco in 1936. The new company, Caltex, played a crucial role in developing the Bahraini and Saudi concessions. At the time, however, the implications of this expansion in Gulf oil production, driven particularly by Saudi Arabia's massive fields, were not immediately obvious – either to IPC or the new American entrants. It was only in the years following the Second World War that their profound impact on the world oil order would become apparent.

the world control and distribution of oil in the Near East'.[37] Across the large stretches of territory that it controlled, IPC deliberately sought to limit the overall production of crude according to the downstream needs of the partner companies. In Iraq, for example, IPC dragged its feet on exploration and production, restricting production to only 0.5 per cent of the country's total area, despite the fact it controlled most of the country's oil fields.[38] In neighbouring Syria, the company deliberately drilled shallow wells in areas where it was confident that no oil would be found, to create a pretence that it was complying with the terms of the concession agreements.[39] Alongside these mechanisms, IPC stalled the development of oilfield infrastructure, delayed the building of oil pipelines, and bought up concessions in order to take potential oil supplies off the market. Actions such as these were to continue through the 1950s and 1960s, much to the chagrin of local governments eager to maximise oil production (and thus royalties). Indeed, Iraq's eventual confiscation and nationalisation of IPC oil fields in the early 1970s came directly on the back of these kinds of deliberate attempts to restrict the country's oil production, not as a consequence of any kind of unbridled extraction by Western oil firms.[40]

While the RLA sought to carefully control the production of oil in the Middle East, a parallel agreement was also being developed at the global scale. In August 1928, shortly after the signing of the RLA, the leaders of APOC, SONJ, Gulf Oil, and Shell met secretly in a remote Scottish Highlands castle, Achnacarry, to hammer out details for managing oil production across the world oil market (outside the US).[41] To avoid the appearance of collusion, the secret seventeen-page agreement concluded

37 Cited in FTC, *International Petroleum Cartel*, 112.

38 John Blair, *The Control of Oil*, New York: Pantheon Books, 1976, 81.

39 Ibid., 82.

40 Ibid., 90.

41 The story of the Achnacarry meeting has been recounted many times, including in Daniel Yergin, *The Prize*, London: Simon & Schuster, 2009; and Anthony Sampson, *The Seven Sisters: The Great Oil Companies and the World They Shaped*, New York: Viking, 1975. But it is undoubtedly told with most gusto by the former Scottish Tory MEP, Struan Stevenson, who confidently asserts that the men meeting at the castle crowned their eventual agreement with a glass of 1904 Stronachie Malt Scotch Whisky Special Reserve and a sumptuous meal of smoked salmon, roast grouse, and haunch of venison (for which he provides the recipe). According to Stevenson, this was one of 'ten meals that changed the world'. Struan Stevenson and Tony Singh, *The Course of History: Ten Meals That Changed the World*, Edinburgh: Birlinn, 2017.

between the company heads was never signed and its existence was only publicly revealed in 1952.[42] Entitled 'Pool Association', this document has become better known as the 'As Is' or Achnacarry Agreement. Its key feature was the apportionment of the world's oil production outside the US between the leading oil companies based on their respective market shares in 1928 (hence As Is). In its preamble, the agreement noted that 'excessive competition [in the oil industry] has resulted in the tremendous overproduction of today, when over the world the shut-in production amounts to approximately 60 percent of the production actually going into consumption'. The problem lay in the fact that each of the large companies 'has tried to take care of its own overproduction and tried to increase its sales at the expense of someone else. The effect has been destructive rather constructive competition.'[43]

In this global imitation of the RLA, the oil executives meeting at Achnacarry sought to restrict their production within their respective shares, and only increase the supply of world oil if global demand increased. Oil infrastructure (such as refineries, storage, and pipelines) would not be built except in case of increased demand, and existing facilities would be shared at minimal cost between the partners to the agreement in order to discourage duplication. Oil would be supplied from the nearest geographical area, and the companies were prohibited from using surpluses in one area to destabilise prices in another. They also agreed to establish a jointly owned pool of tanker vessels to carry oil and enable the exchange of any excesses necessary to maintain their respective shares.[44]

In addition, the agreement concluded at Achnacarry included an innovative pricing system, which guaranteed considerable profits for the largest oil producers. At the time, new oil discoveries in the Middle East, Venezuela, Romania, and the Dutch-controlled East Indies could be extracted at a price significantly cheaper than those in the US. Achnacarry set all world oil at the price of a barrel at the Gulf of Mexico, plus the freight cost of shipping oil from Houston, Texas to the destination where it was sold. This 'Gulf-plus' system meant that cheaper oil produced outside the US was sold at the price of the higher-cost US oil.

42 Sampson, *The Seven Sisters*, 91.
43 Cited in FTC, *International Petroleum Cartel*, 200.
44 Ibid.

It also meant that oil shipped to relatively near destinations (for example, oil from APOC's facilities in Iran transported to Italy) would be charged *as if* it had been shipped from the more distant Gulf of Mexico. The substantial profits made on these artificially high prices were pocketed by the large oil firms. Furthermore, the companies agreed on the reciprocal exchange of oil between themselves to ensure that markets were supplied from the closest production area. This 'phantom freight' – as the savings made in transport costs through this exchange were called – was shared between the oil firms at the expense of buyers.[45]

Two decades later, as part of an investigation into the cartel-like behaviour of American oil firms, the US government would describe Achnacarry as 'a constitution, or charter, which, in broad terms, sets out general principles, objectives, and procedures for market stabilization'.[46] This 'constitution' was operationalised through regional arrangements such as the RLA, and soon came to be accepted by all large players in world oil markets, including the other major internationalised US firms outside IPC – Gulf Oil, SOCAL, and Texaco.[47] By calibrating world supply and coordinating extraction and refining levels, the largest oil companies sought to shield themselves from the destructive consequences of overproduction. The ingenious Gulf-plus pricing system guaranteed super-profits on oil produced outside the US, while ensuring the ongoing profitability of the domestic American industry, the largest market in the world at the time. The extremely high costs involved in the exploration, production, transport, and retailing of oil acted as major barriers to would-be competitors; by agreeing to share these infrastructure facilities among themselves, the largest oil firms were able substantially to reduce their own costs and deepen their vertical integration and market control.[48] And of course, these firms ultimately controlled extraction at source of all the world's crude outside the US – the minimal amounts paid to governments headed by individuals such as Gómez and Faisal I merely serving to disguise the organised plunder made possible by colonial rule.

45 See Sampson, *The Seven Sisters*.

46 FTC, *International Petroleum Cartel*, 210.

47 Sampson, *The Seven Sisters*, 92.

48 Edith Penrose, *The Large International Firm in Developing Countries: The International Petroleum Industry*, Cambridge, MA: MIT Press, 1968.

The US Domestic Oil Market to the Second World War

Taken as a whole, these global initiatives helped buttress and protect the market dominance of a handful of powerful, internationalised oil firms, led by those based in the US. Yet, while international expansion was a major strategic priority of the largest US firms through the 1920s and 1930s – ensuring super-profits on low-cost oil and enabling growing international demand to be met through non-US production – the US domestic market remained by far the largest and most important in the world. Backed by the rapid growth in automobile use and the needs of an oil-fuelled military, US oil consumption reached 173 million tonnes of coal equivalent in 1929, compared to just 30 million tonnes in Western Europe.[49] A decade later this imbalance would have narrowed slightly, but US oil consumption continued to remain at more than five times that of Europe until the eve of the Second World War.[50] Outside North America and Europe, the rest of the world's oil consumption was comparatively insignificant at this time.

Given the overwhelming preponderance of the US market, the international power of the largest US oil companies depended firmly on their domestic strength. Here, a clear pattern of ownership and control had become evident through the 1920s, which was later laid out in some detail by the US economist John Blair, in his classic work *The Control of Oil*. According to Blair's analysis – one supported by numerous other studies of this period, including US government investigations – the major division in the US oil industry was between twenty large vertically integrated firms that controlled all stages of the oil commodity circuit in the US, and thousands of smaller non-integrated firms and producers, who were involved in one or more oil-related activity (most commonly at the extraction stage). In addition to this split between integrated and non-integrated firms, Blair identified a further division within the top twenty itself: a core group of eight dominant firms who, alongside their domestic activities, were also leading international expansion. Four of these top eight firms came out of the break-up of Standard Oil, and the other four had emerged as major players in US oil at the time of the Spindletop Field discovery.

49 UN, *World Energy Supplies, 1929–1950*, 60–2.

50 Ibid., figures for 1937.

Table 3.1 shows the top eight and top twenty integrated firms as they appeared in 1938. Over the next few decades there would be numerous mergers, acquisitions, and name changes among these firms – but the basic three-part division (what Blair called a 'trichotomy') would persist through to the 1970s. The reality of this corporate structure is demonstrated in Table 3.2, which confirms the pronounced control that these large vertically integrated firms had obtained over the US oil industry on the eve of the Second World War. In 1938, the top twenty firms controlled more than 70 per cent of all major sectors of the domestic US oil industry, aside from crude production and domestic wells. Among the top twenty, the top eight integrated firms listed in Table 3.1 were clearly dominant – holding more than half of the assets in each branch, again with the exceptions of wells and crude production.

Table 3.1. US Oil Industry, Vertically Integrated Firms (as of 1938)

Top eight firms	**Other top twenty**
SONJ	Empire Gas and Fuel
SOCONY-Vacuum Oil Co.	Phillips Petroleum Co.
Standard Oil (Indiana)	Tide Water Associated Oil Co.
Standard Oil Co. of California	Atlantic Refining Co.
Texas Corporation	Pure Oil Company
Gulf Oil Corporation	Union Oil Co.
Sinclair Oil Corporation	Sun Oil Co.
Shell Union Oil Corporation	Continental Oil Co.
	The Ohio Oil Co.
	Standard Oil Co. (Ohio)
	Mid-Continent Oil Petroleum Co.
	Skelly Oil Co.

Table 3.2. Concentration of Control Over the US Oil Industry by Largest Firms (1938)

Branch of industry	**Top eight firms**	**Top twenty firms**	**Non-integrated firms**
Total investment	50%	67%	33%
Domestic producing wells	13%	24%	76%
Production of crude	32%	53%	47%
Crude mileage of pipelines	55%	72%	28%
Tanker tonnage	52%	87%	13%
Production of gasoline	59%	84%	16%
Refining capacity	53%	76%	24%
Domestic sales of gasoline	54%	80%	20%

Source: Calculated by author from data in Annex Tables, Cook, 1941, 57–94.

Despite the clear dominance of the top twenty firms across the oil circuit, non-integrated firms continued to play an important role in the US oil industry. It is evident from Table 3.2 that control of the upstream sector in the US was more diffuse than downstream activities, with non-integrated firms holding a significant position in the ownership of wells and production of crude oil. This arrangement served the integrated firms very well. The cost and risks of exploring for oil were high, and in times of overproduction, the downward pressures on the bottom line of oil producers were sizeable. By controlling downstream activities such as pipelines, tanker tonnage, refining, and marketing, the integrated firms could purchase any extra crude oil they required from the smaller producers while shifting the risks of production and exploration onto these firms. In doing so, the top twenty firms' control over the entire oil circuit – the very fact of *being* integrated – allowed them to ensure a consistent supply of crude oil that could fluctuate depending on market conditions.[51] The significant costs of this flexibility were mainly borne by the smaller producers. Moreover, the large, fixed capital expenses associated with vertical integration – most of which were funded internally by the oil companies themselves – acted as a considerable barrier to new entrants.[52]

Dividing the World Oil Market

US domestic oil policy in the 1920s ultimately sought to preserve this division between integrated and non-integrated firms, allowing the latter to exist as a necessary (and flexible) appendage to the former. By the early 1930s, however, this structure was imperilled by the renewed threat of overproduction – the Great Depression had caused a big drop in demand for oil, yet supply was continuing to increase, particularly

51 In the retail sector, non-integrated firms also played a useful role by purchasing refined products from integrated producers who had manufactured more than their own marketing needs.

52 The TNEC reported that between 1930 and 1938, 95 per cent of expenditures for plant and equipment were met by internal sources for eleven of the largest oil companies. Temporary National Economic Committee, *Concentration of Economic Power*, Washington, DC: US Government Printing Office, 1941, 229.

after the discovery of another massive oil field in East Texas in 1930.[53] Adding to this glut were growing levels of oil imports, particularly from Venezuela, which had become the second-largest oil producer in the world following a 600 per cent increase in oil production between 1925 and 1930.[54] Total oil imports to the US were estimated at around 10 per cent of daily domestic demand in 1930 (most of which came from Venezuela).[55] In the face of this inexorable oversupply, crude oil prices fell by almost half between the end of the 1920s and early 1930s.[56]

This was the context, of course, that framed international discussions around the Red Line and Achnacarry agreements. At the level of the US domestic market, however, a complex set of debates took place throughout the interwar years aimed at tackling the twin challenges of overproduction and excess imports. These debates involved federal and state legislatures, as well as lobby groups representing the oil industry itself. The stance of the large integrated firms was presented by the American Petroleum Institute (API), which – while purportedly representing the industry as a whole – was led, funded, and staffed by the top twenty leading integrated firms.[57] Alongside the API, other smaller organisations sought to represent the sometimes divergent interests of non-integrated producers. The proposals made by these various lobby groups necessarily navigated the distinct geography of US politics – the prerogatives of individual states (particularly oil-rich states such as Texas) often stymied or held back the formulation of national policy.

Given this institutional milieu, both integrated and non-integrated firms viewed the issue of domestic overproduction as a major problem that was deeply destabilising to the industry as a whole. Integrated firms sought to resolve this through federal legislation around *conservation*, attempting to manage the amount of oil that could be produced in line

53 Discoveries earlier in the decade, including large fields in Arkansas and California, had increased the supply of crude oil by 134 per cent between 1920 and 1923. B. McBeth, 'Venezuela's Nascent Oil Industry and the 1932 Tariff on Crude Oil Imports, 1927–1935', *Revista de Historia Económica/Journal of Iberian and Latin American Economic History* 27, no. 3, 2009: 427–62, 436.

54 Ibid., 432.

55 Kokxhoorn, *Oil and Politics*, 39.

56 McBeth, 'Venezuela's Nascent Oil Industry', 428.

57 In 1937, 85 per cent of the members of API policymaking boards and committees were employees of the large integrated firms. Kokxhoorn, *Oil and Politics*, 68.

with demand predictions. In contrast, the smaller non-integrated firms – typically operating at the state level and opposing federal controls over the industry – advocated state *prorationing* legislation: control of production based upon estimated demand in the state, which was then allocated to individual fields depending on oilwell capacity and expected life of the field. Prorationing orders were first passed in Oklahoma in 1928, and then later in Texas in 1930 (where martial law was declared in order to enforce restrictions on production). While integrated firms had generally preferred a federal rather than state-level solution, they soon came round to support state prorationing legislation. Indeed, prorationing held considerable benefits for the large integrated firms – because of their integrated structure they could compensate for limits in one state with more production in another, and they were able to evade rationing limits by selling oil across state borders.[58]

Non-integrated firms (and those integrated firms in the top twenty that were primarily domestic oriented) were also concerned with the impact of foreign oil imports on supply. Of particular significance were Venezuelan imports, which in 1929–1930 represented around 70 per cent of crude oil and refined products entering the US.[59] More than 90 per cent of Venezuelan oil was produced at the time by three of the large integrated companies shown in Table 3.1: Shell, Standard Oil (Indiana), and Gulf Oil.[60] These firms exported to US markets through two routes: either in the form of crude oil supplied directly from Venezuela, or indirectly, by first sending Venezuelan crude to their large refinery complexes in the Dutch West Indies, and then exporting the refined products to the US. Venezuelan oil was much cheaper than that produced in the US, and this was particularly important for US states on the East Coast, such as Maine and Maryland, which met just under a quarter of their annual consumption through oil imported from Venezuela and the Dutch West Indies.[61]

Given the significant impact of these imports on oil supplies, domestic

58 Ibid., 69.

59 McBeth, 'Venezuela's Nascent Oil Industry', 432.

60 In the mid-1930s, SONJ took over Standard Oil (Indiana)'s share of Venezuelan oil.

61 McBeth, 'Venezuela's Nascent Oil Industry', 446. McBeth estimates that Venezuelan oil was US$0.45 cheaper than a barrel of US domestic oil (taking into account transport costs, different oil grades, and refinery output), 442.

oil companies and major US oil-producing states began lobbying in 1929 for a tariff on oil imports. A protracted and fraught set of negotiations took place involving different industry and political interests, with legislation eventually passing in 1932 that established a USD$0.21 tax on crude oil imports and larger amounts on refined products such as petrol and motor oils. Crucially, however, this tax excluded so-called *bonded* oil – which was imported into the US, refined, and then exported somewhere else. Partly due to this exclusion, the large internationally oriented integrated firms (the top eight firms listed in Table 3.1) supported the initiative.[62] Following the introduction of the import tax, these firms redirected their foreign production towards Western Europe rather than US markets (with Europe supplied either directly from Venezuela or through bonded oil refined in the US). As a result, Venezuela's share of the world oil market increased substantially over the next decade, with the country becoming the largest supplier to Western Europe by the mid-1930s.[63]

Thus, at the cusp of the Second World War, the US oil industry had been stabilised through a set of policies that divided the world market into two distinct spheres. On the one hand, a large US domestic market dominated by just twenty integrated firms that existed in a synergetic relationship with thousands of smaller independent producers and retailers. On the other, a world market where the core group of the US top twenty firms collaborated with the biggest European firms to carve up the international trade in oil, ensuring access to cheap reserves and minimising overproduction. Straddling this bifurcated world market were a handful of large companies that were later to become known as the Seven Sisters: Standard Oil Company of New Jersey (now part of ExxonMobil); Standard Oil Company of New York (now part of ExxonMobil); Gulf Oil (now part of Chevron); Texaco (now part of Chevron); Standard Oil Company of California (now part of Chevron); Royal Dutch Shell; and the Anglo-Iranian Oil Company (renamed from APOC in 1935, now BP).

62 The import tax also helped support the US-based refinery operations of the largest firms, by protecting them from cheaper Venezuelan products. For a discussion of the different forces involved in the debate around oil imports and the respective positions of integrated and non-integrated firms, see Kokxhoorn, *Oil and Politics*, 166–71.

63 At the beginning of the Second World War, nearly half of Britain's oil market was being supplied from Venezuela. McBeth, 'Venezuela's Nascent Oil Industry', 453–4.

4

A Russian Interlude: From Baku to the Bolsheviks

> It is quite as hazardous to estimate the underground oil reserves of a given patch of oleous territory as it is to guess the quantity of gin a child in swaddling clothes will swallow by the time it is grey and rheumatic . . . Yet everyone who dabbles in this dangerous realm of judging the volume of the dark green-brown rivers which flow unseen hundreds of feet below the earth's surface invariably gives Russia a place quite near the top of the list of countries.[1]

Writing on the eve of the Second World War, the historian Glyn Roberts once observed that a 'history of the world from 1898 to 1938' could well be written 'in form of a history of Baku'.[2] Located on the coast of the Caspian Sea in modern-day Azerbaijan, Baku had been known since antiquity for its 'eternal fires' – undying flames fed by the steady seep of petroleum gases through the region's sandy topsoil. Innumerable cults and religious beliefs found inspiration in these flames, including the followers of Zoroastrianism, which would become the state religion of Persia for more than a millennium. Yet, from the mid-nineteenth century onwards, a 'new breed of fire-worshippers' had begun to make

1 Louis Fischer, *Oil Imperialism: The International Struggle for Petroleum*, London: Routledge, 2018 (1927), 10.

2 Glyn Roberts, *The Most Powerful Man in the World: The Life of Sir Henri Deterding*, New York: Covici-Friede, 1938, 41.

Baku their home.[3] These were the oil barons – mostly Europeans, Russians, and Armenians – whose sole devotion was to the black gold that nourished Baku's holy fires. In a few short decades, Baku would become the largest city in the Caucasus – 'one of the first successful oil-producing regions outside of North America and the first major oil industry in or around the Middle East'.[4] By 1901, Baku and its immediate environs were supplying more than half of the world's crude.

Much like Titusville, Pennsylvania, Baku's rapid growth in population transformed it into one of the first examples of an *oil town* – a metropolitan landscape where urban planning and design were consciously rooted in the needs of the oil industry. Most of the oil refineries and workers' accommodation were located just outside the city in a notorious soot-covered area known as Black Town. Developed in 1876 in a grid layout that fused the infrastructures of oil – pipelines, storage containers, railway tracks, and so forth – with the living quarters of workers, Black Town was the first instance of planned zoning in Russia.[5] Crammed into Black Town's densely packed workers' housing were Russians, Azerbaijani, Armenians, Azeri and other migrants, a cosmopolitan melange that gave Baku's working classes a much more multi-ethnic character than other parts of the Czarist Empire.[6] The tough, dangerous lives of these workers sat in stark contrast to the inhabitants of the spacious tree-lined boulevards and palatial mansions that earned Baku-proper the title 'Paris of the East'.

But Baku was not just known for its distinctive urban layout. As the centre of the Russian oil industry, the grimy quarters of Black Town also formed the base of a militant workers' movement, led by the rival Bolshevik and Menshevik factions of the Russian Social-Democratic Labour Party (RSDLP). It was here that a young Georgian, nicknamed Koba, made his home in the RSDLP underground between 1907 and 1909. Twenty years later, Koba, then known as Joseph Stalin, would recall that those 'three years of revolutionary work among the workers

3 Michael Johnson, 'From the Big Bang to Baku: A Primer on the Beginnings of the Petroleum End Times', *Southwest Review* 95, no. 3, 2010: 426–43, 435.

4 Jonathan H. Sicotte, 'Baku: Violence, Identity, and Oil, 1905–1927', PhD diss., Georgetown University, Washington, DC, 2017, 52.

5 Eve Blau, *Baku: Oil and Urbanism*, Zurich: Park Books, 2017.

6 Sara Brinegar, 'The Oil Deal: Nariman Narimanov and the Sovietization of Azerbaijan', *Slavic Review* 76, no. 2, 2017: 372–94, 373.

of the oil industry tempered me as a practical fighter and as one of the local practical leaders'.[7] While Leon Trotsky had a much more measured assessment of Stalin's record in Baku, he would also highlight the centrality of Baku and Black Town to the formation of the Russian revolutionary tradition, noting that a general strike in the oil industry during the spring of 1904 had 'unleashed an avalanche of strikes and demonstrations throughout the South of Russia' that could be seen as 'the beginning of the [1905] Revolution'.[8]

The ultimate success of this revolutionary movement would still be some years away, but the agitation and propaganda of the RSDLP factions and other militant groups nonetheless provoked deep anxiety among the leading oil magnates of Baku. By the turn of the nineteenth century, the pre-eminent force in Baku's oil industry was the Petroleum Production Company Nobel Brothers (known as Branobel), which was founded and led by the Swedish industrialists, Robert and Ludvig Nobel (older brothers of Alfred, the inventor of dynamite and creator of the Nobel Prize). By pursuing an aggressive strategy aimed at controlling refineries and transport infrastructure, Branobel prefigured many of the features of the largest vertically integrated oil firms.[9] Alongside ownership of oil fields and refineries in Baku, the Nobel brothers built Russia's first oil pipeline in 1878, and, in the same year, contracted a Swedish shipbuilder to construct the world's first steam-powered oil tanker, appropriately named *Zoraster* after the spiritual founder of the fire-worshipping Zoroastrian faith. With control of this infrastructure, Branobel was the major competitor with Standard Oil for the global

7 Cited in Ronald Grigor Suny, 'A Journeyman for the Revolution: Stalin and the Labour Movement in Baku, June 1907–May 1908', *Soviet Studies* 23, no. 3, January 1972: 373–94, 373.

8 In his unfinished biography of Stalin, cut short by his assassination at the hands of one of Stalin's agents, Trotsky noted that the documentary evidence pointed much more towards Stalin's secondary role as a 'committee man', concerned with narrow underground organisational tasks, and far removed from the leadership of trade union activities or worker struggles. See Trotsky, 'Stalin – An Appraisal of the Man and his Influence', 1940, marxists.org.

9 Branobel was incorporated as a stockholding company in 1879 and listed on the Berlin Stock Exchange. It adopted an innovative corporate form structured around individual accounting segments that ran as autonomous profit-maximising units; this structure prefigured the corporate form that was later generalised throughout the oil and petrochemical industries (see Chapters 7 and 11).

kerosene market.[10] By 1899, this strategy of vertical integration had won Branobel control of around 18 per cent of total Russian oil production, 8.6 per cent of world production, more than a quarter of Russian kerosene exports, and half of the domestic kerosene market.[11]

Alongside the Nobels, British investors had also begun to take a keen interest in Russian oil in the early 1900s. Many of the leading Russian oil firms were British-funded or were domiciled in London, and there had been a large inflow of British capital into Baku following the damage to oil fields that occurred during the 1905 Revolution. British influence increased substantially in 1912, following the acquisition by Royal Dutch Shell of the Russian oil assets of the French Rothschild family. Shell also monopolised Russian oil exports to Asia, thanks to the firm's control of shipping routes through the Suez Canal. These British commercial interests supported the broader goals of the British Empire: American oil firms had failed to win any presence in Russian crude production, and Britain saw Baku as the key link in a future chain of British-controlled oil fields, military bases, and shipping routes, which could block the global ambitions of an upstart US state.[12] Spanning Europe, Central Asia, and the Middle East, this would be Britain's 'own great oil empire, competing with Standard everywhere', where oil was wielded to subdue 'the insolent United States . . . by their own weapon'.[13]

10 Branobel's global rivalry with Standard in the 1880s became known as the Kerosene Wars. At its general shareholders meeting in 1883, Branobel noted the significance of Russian oil to this conflict: 'Having on its side the undoubted advantage of the Baku oil sources over American ones . . . The company's goal was first to displace American kerosene from Russia, and then begin to export kerosene to other countries . . . American kerosene has now been completely displaced from Russian markets, and in the past year the company had already begun to export its products to Austria and Germany.' Cited in Vagit Alekperov, *Oil of Russia: Past, Present and Future*, Minneapolis: East View Press, 2010, 129.

11 By the early 1900s, Russia accounted for just under a third of all world kerosene exports, second behind the US and far in advance of the other major exporters: the Netherlands (8.4 per cent); Romania (2.7 per cent); and Galicia (2.3 per cent) (Alekperov, *Oil of Russia*, 131). These exports were significantly aided upon the completion of a pipeline connecting Baku and the port terminal of Batumi (on the Black Sea in Georgia) in 1906, which made the transportation of Baku's oil to markets in Western Europe, the Mediterranean, and Asia much more efficient.

12 Britain also viewed control over Baku as a means to thwart Germany's attempt to expand from Berlin to Baghdad, and from there to India.

13 Roberts, *The Most Powerful Man*, 60.

The Russian Revolution

British success in this strategy would have taken the subsequent history of world oil down a very different path. However, in October 1917, British designs on Baku and the wider Caucasus faced a new obstacle following the outbreak of a revolution across Russia that overthrew the old Czarist order and transferred power to a Bolshevik-led government. For Vladimir Lenin and the other Bolshevik leaders, the future of Baku was inseparable from the survival of the revolution itself: more than 80 per cent of Russia's oil came from Baku, and this oil was not only critical to meeting internal energy needs but also to earning hard currency.[14] Confronted with these realities – and a little over six months into a civil war that would last until 1922 – the new Soviet government issued a decree on 28 June 1918 that expropriated all foreign oil assets without compensation. The move had a dramatic effect on the Russian oil industry: at the time, foreign investment in Russian oil was greater than in any other industrial sector, and more than half of the capital invested in Russian oil was held abroad.[15] Facing this Soviet decree, Emanuel Nobel – who had inherited control of Branobel from his father Ludvig – is said to have described nationalisation as 'a beautiful word for a very ugly thing'.[16]

Nonetheless, one problem remained for the Bolshevik leaders: Baku *was not Russian*. As the capital of Azerbaijan, the city was solidly part of what Lenin had described prior to the revolution as the Czarist 'prison house of nations'. Its multi-ethnic workforce included a large Muslim population that was suspicious of Bolshevik rule and desirous of independence, and it was neighboured by two other non-Russian republics, Georgia and Armenia, where Menshevik parties were strong and willing to ally with external powers against the Bolsheviks. A key site of the civil war battles, control over Baku alternated for two years between Ottoman Turkish, British, and Bolshevik-aligned forces. Throughout this period, Baku and its oil provided much of the subtext for debates within the

14 Philip S. Gillette, 'American Capital in the Contest for Soviet Oil, 1920–23', *Soviet Studies* 24, no. 4, April 1973: 477–90, 478.

15 Hans Heymann Jr, 'Oil in Soviet-Western Relations in the Interwar Years', *American Slavic and East European Review* 7, no. 4, December 1948: 303–16, 303.

16 Brita Åsbrink, 'Nationalisation Is a Beautiful Word for a Very Ugly Thing', 15 August 2011, branobelhistory.com/society.

Bolshevik Party around the right to national self-determination for republics such as Azerbaijan.[17] Eventually, on 28 April 1920, the Bolsheviks managed to bring Azerbaijan (and shortly after, Armenia and Georgia) under their control. Baku became allied with the new Soviet government as the capital of the Azerbaijan Soviet Socialist Republic.

Bolshevik victory in the Caucasus finally appeared to make a reality of the 1918 oil nationalisation decree. At that stage, however, many foreign oil companies continued to believe that the Soviet government still faced imminent collapse due to the ongoing civil war. One of these firms was the US major SONJ, which saw this is as an opportune moment to gain the first American foothold in the prized region. In July 1920, the company bought half of the Nobel brothers' assets in Russia, located primarily in Baku and Grozny, in the hope of a Bolshevik defeat and an eventual reversal of the nationalisation decree.[18] One estimate gives the value of Nobel's Russian oil assets bought by SONJ at a staggering tenth of all US property claims against the Bolsheviks.[19] Alongside SONJ, Sir Henri Deterding of Royal Dutch Shell had also bet on Soviet defeat, buying up land owned by expropriated Russian oil tycoons in Baku, and fully expecting that as the largest 'owner' of oil assets in the Caucasus, he

---

17 On one side of these debates, Lenin consistently advocated for supporting the right of independence in the nations across the Caucasus, while encouraging their eventual federation as equal republics with Russia. On the other side, Stalin's 'Great Russian Chauvinism' – heavily criticised by Lenin – subordinated the national question (and Baku's oil) to decisions made in Moscow. With Lenin's death in January 1924, Stalin's position came to dominate an increasingly bureaucratised Soviet Union (formed at the end of 1922). The reality of these unresolved national tensions would have long-term consequences for the later development of the Russian oil industry. Sara Brinegar presents a fascinating account of the role of oil and Lenin's negotiations with the Azerbaijani Muslim communist Nariman Narimanov, arguing that 'the need to secure and hold energy resources – and the infrastructures that support them – was critical to the formation of the Soviet Union' and that these issues need to be better integrated into our understanding of the formation of the Soviet state; see Brinegar, 'The Oil Deal', 394. It cannot be coincidental that the Communist International's Congress of the Toiling People of the East was convened in Baku in 1920.

18 Prior to the 1917 Revolution, the Nobel assets in Russia constituted a third of Russian production, 40 per cent of Russian refining, and 60 per cent of Russian distribution (Gillette, 'American Capital in the Contest for Soviet Oil', 480).

19 Marshall I. Goldman, *Petrostate: Putin, Power, and the New Russia*, New York: Oxford University Press, 2008, 25.

would gain a decisive advantage over his American rivals.[20] The main battle lines for the next decade had been drawn: on one side were warring US and British oil companies hoping to regain access to Russian oil and thereby strengthening their position on the world scale; on the other side was the Soviet Union.

SONJ *vs* Shell and the First Concessions

By 1920, civil war and foreign invasion had reduced the main oil-producing areas in Russia to around a third of their pre-war production levels.[21] Faced with the desperate need to increase production both for domestic energy and to earn hard currency through exports, the Bolshevik leadership prioritised the expansion of the industry in Baku and the surrounding region. Key prerequisites to this were more capital investments and improved technology and technical capacity – all of which were in short supply because of the civil war. It was in this context that Lenin and other Bolshevik leaders began to explore the idea of offering oil concessions to foreign oil companies in return for tax payments, profit sharing, and technology transfer. Alongside their crucial economic dimension, Lenin viewed concessions as a means of aggravating rivalries between different imperialist powers, and potentially encouraging some Western states to recognise the Soviet government. 'Concessions', as Lenin put it in a 1920 speech defending the new policy before a group of workers in Moscow, 'do not mean peace; they too are a kind of warfare, only in another form, one that is to our advantage . . . here we do not destroy our productive forces, but develop them.'[22] After months of vigorous debate, the Bolshevik Party voted to support the strategy of concessions, and negotiations began with a range of different Western oil interests.[23]

20 Roberts, *The Most Powerful Man*, 183.

21 Gillette, 'American Capital in the Contest for Soviet Oil', 479.

22 V. I. Lenin, speech delivered at a meeting of cells' secretaries of the Moscow organisation of the RCP(B), November 1920, marxists.org.

23 Many Bolshevik leaders opposed the idea of concessions, seeing in them a return to the domination of foreign capital in the oil industry. This was part of a wider discussion around what became known as the New Economic Policy, a move towards limited opening of market-based activities in order to encourage economic activity following the damage of civil war. The NEP was eventually adopted by a majority of delegates at the Tenth Party Congress of the All-Russian Communist Party in March 1921.

For the Western oil majors, these negotiations created a significant predicament: all wanted access to Russian oil (and to deny access to their rivals); but, at the same time, an agreement with the Bolsheviks that gave de facto recognition to nationalisation would legitimise the earlier expropriation of oil assets and undermine the property claims of companies such as SONJ and Shell. Faced with this dilemma, various firms including APOC, Shell, SONJ, and Sinclair Oil entered separate discussions with the Soviet government between 1920 and 1922. These negotiations were overseen by Lenin personally, although conducted through the Russian ambassador in London, Leonid Krasin. The Bolshevik side placed strict restrictions on the terms that were offered to Western firms, including a refusal of any compensation for nationalised assets. Largely as a result of this refusal, no agreement was reached between the Western firms and the Bolshevik government.

These inter-imperial and inter-firm rivalries over Russian oil came to a head at the Genoa Economic and Financial Conference, a major international meeting convened between the leading European powers in Genoa, Italy, in mid-1922. The conference aimed at resolving the relationship of Europe to both Germany and Soviet Russia in the aftermath of the First World War. While the question of Russian oil was not openly on the conference agenda, it was well understood that the discussions were, in fact, a backdrop to a deeper conflict over this oil. As Louis Fischer would note in his 1927 book, *Oil Imperialism*, the conference 'was to be the field on which the battle for Russian oil would be fought . . . [with] oil kings, great and small . . . flock[ing] to the Italian city'.[24] Most directly, this was a battle between US and British oil – and, unsurprisingly, the two key protagonists were SONJ and Royal Dutch Shell.

The US government did not directly participate in the conference but was present as an observer. For its part, a major concern was that all deals with the Bolsheviks should remain off-limits without recognition of SONJ's newly acquired assets in Russia. On the British side, Royal Dutch Shell had been secretly negotiating with Krasin on terms for a large oil concession from the Bolsheviks. When rumour of a successful deal – denied by all sides – was leaked, the conference proceedings exploded. Fearing the dominance of British oil interests if Shell won access to Russian oil, the US observer declared his government's

24 Fischer, *Oil Imperialism*.

opposition to any settlement that did not take 'into account the principle of the open door for all and recognized equal rights for all'.[25] This position was also supported by the French and Belgian delegations, who were against any deals with the Bolsheviks that might give tacit or *de jure* endorsement of nationalisation. The conference disbanded without agreement, leading one French newspaper to attribute the collapse 'entirely to the fight between Royal Dutch and Standard Oil [New Jersey]. The conference participants are not interested in the question of rebuilding Europe; they need only Caucasian oil.'[26]

In September 1922, shortly after the failed Genoa conference, sixteen of the world's largest oil companies, including Royal Dutch Shell and SONJ, agreed to join in a boycott of Russian oil. Nonetheless, despite this attempt at presenting a united front against Soviet oil, Lenin and the Bolshevik government were correct in predicting that inter-firm and inter-state competition would trump any coordinated effort to isolate the Soviet Union. While none of the major Western firms signed operating concessions in the Soviet Union at this time, smaller oil companies were happy to fill the breach. Most important here was the International Barnsdall Corporation (IBC), a US firm run by Henry Mason Day, which signed a fifteen-year concession with the Russian government in September 1922 to develop oil fields in Baku. Day was careful to give assurances to the US government that he would not work on assets that had been nationalised by the Bolsheviks, although, as Steve LeVine points out, he was plainly doing just that.[27] By bringing in advanced drilling equipment then currently unavailable in Russia, as well as electrical pumping machinery and technical expertise, IBC increased drilling in Baku by a factor of ten and halved costs of oil production. Baku's oil production was restored to the levels that existed prior to the civil war. In return, IBC received a 15 per cent royalty on crude produced from existing wells and 20 per cent on successful new wells. Alongside the agreement in Baku, IBC also won concessions to export oil, coal, timber, and tobacco in Georgia.[28] Although IBC's contract in Baku was terminated

25 Cited in Heymann, 'Oil in Soviet-Western Relations', 306.

26 Cited in Alekperov, *Oil of Russia*, 729.

27 Steve LeVine, *The Oil and the Glory: The Pursuit of Empire and Fortune on the Caspian Sea*, New York: Random House, 2007, 110.

28 Ibid., 111. The US firm Sinclair Oil (see Table 3.1), was negotiating concessions with the Soviet government at the same time as IBC. One outline of the negotiations

early, the introduction of advanced drilling technology and the opening-up of new wells transformed levels of oil production in the region.[29]

With this rehabilitation of oil fields and transfer of new technology, the Bolshevik government had managed to address the crucial obstacles facing oil production at the end of the civil war. They had done so without relinquishing any direct control over Russian oil assets, relying instead on service and royalty contracts (as in the case of Day's IBC). Much of the increased oil production enabled by these agreements went to exports: between 1922 and 1932, the volume of Soviet oil exports increased more than a hundredfold.[30] According to official Soviet statistics, oil made up more than a third of the value of all Soviet industrial exports by 1927–28 – it thus became an essential vehicle for earning hard currency and financing other imports.[31] Numerous European countries came to depend heavily on these exports. By 1927, around half of Italy's oil came from the Soviet Union – proportions were also high in France (18 per cent), Germany and Belgium (17 per cent), and Spain (15 per cent).[32] The largest market for Soviet oil through the 1920s was Britain, where a company known as Russian Oil Products (ROP) was formed in 1924.[33] By the end of the decade, ROP would hold a 10 per cent share of the British petroleum market, with distribution organised through an extensive network of trucks, tankers, and railways.[34]

---

states that Sinclair would have been given twenty-five-year rights to the richest parts of the Grozny oil field in return for a $250 million loan (Gillette, 'American Capital in the Contest for Soviet Oil', 488). Sinclair, however, was unable to attract other investors and the deal fell apart.

29 A few years after the IBC concession, the Soviet government also gave a concession to a Japanese company, the North Sakhalin Oil Company (NSOC), for oil production on Russia's Sakhalin Island, located off the Pacific coast of Siberia. NSOC was established in 1927 and its main shareholders were Japan's leading industrial conglomerates: Mitsui; Mitsubishi; and Sumitomo.

30 Jonathan Sicotte, 'Baku and Its Oil Industry through War and Revolution: 1914–1920', *The Extractive Industries and Society* 5, no. 3, 2018: 384–92, 387.

31 Soviet Union Information Bureau, 'Foreign Trade', 1928, marxists.org.

32 Soviet Union Information Bureau, 'Industry', 1928, marxists.org.

33 ROP was a subsidiary of the state-owned Soviet export monopoly, the Naptha Syndicate, which controlled all Soviet oil sales abroad.

34 Alekperov, *Oil of Russia*. According to Marshall Goldman, ROP was forbidden from importing oil directly from the Soviet Union because of Western property claims in Baku. Instead, it supplied itself through Soviet oil imported by Finland, and then exported to the UK. Finland, in other words, became a significant oil exporter despite the fact it had no domestic oil resources; see Goldman, *Petrostate*, 45.

Reconsidering World Oil and the Early Soviet Union

The repercussions of the 1917 Bolshevik Revolution highlight the deep interplay between political dynamics inside Russia and the development of the global oil industry. By blocking the leading Western powers, especially the British Empire, from territorial control in the Caucasus, the revolution separated Western oil firms from what was then the world's most important oil-producing area outside the US (the Middle East was not yet a significant producer). This was followed by the Bolsheviks' 1918 nationalisation decree, which went far beyond anything that OPEC would ever do in the 1960s and 1970s (and was carried out in much more difficult conditions). Today, it is often forgotten that 1917–20 was the first time in history that Western oil companies faced full and direct expropriation. Bolshevik Russia was, in effect, the world's first iteration of OPEC, and the subsequent history of the global oil industry would have followed a very different path if Branobel, Royal Dutch Shell, and other European industrialists had continued to dominate Baku's oil.

But beyond the seizure of oil fields in Baku, the Bolshevik Revolution also had far-reaching effects on oil export markets, especially in Europe. In major European states such as Germany, Italy, Spain, France, and Portugal, Soviet oil imports were organised through European companies that lay outside the big British and US majors. These European companies held monopoly concessions on the import of Soviet oil, and also ran petroleum retail and distribution networks within their respective countries. In some cases, these were state-owned firms controlled by fascist and authoritarian governments (in Italy and Spain, for example).[35] In other cases, large private business and banking interests

35 In Italy, the firm AGIP was established by Mussolini in 1926, and would become ENI in the 1950s (see Chapter 6). AGIP held a monopoly on Soviet oil imports into Italy through the 1920s, and although state-owned, its management was dominated by leading Italian industrialists, such as Giovanni Agnelli (founder of FIAT) and Piero Pirelli (owner of Pirelli tyre company). See Daniele Pozzi, 'Capabilities, Entrepreneurship, and Political Direction in the Italian National Oil Company AGIP/ENI (1926–1971)', in Franco Amatori, Robert Millward, and Pier Angelo Toninelli (eds), *Reappraising State-Owned Enterprise: A Comparison of the UK and Italy*, Abingdon, UK: Routledge, 2011. In Spain, the state-owned Campsa was formed in 1927 under the dictatorship of Primo de Rivera. Campsa was established through the nationalisation of the three main oil companies in Spain: the subsidiaries of Shell and Standard, and the Spanish-owned Porto Pi that held the monopoly on Russian oil (Gabriel Tortella, 'Oil Policies in 20th

managed the import of Soviet oil (as in France and Germany).[36] Operating through these new supply chains, Soviet oil exports thus served to open up space for an embryonic European oil industry independent of the US and Britain. Today, many of Europe's most prominent energy companies – ENI, Repsol, TotalEnergies, Wintershall DEA – find their early roots in this Soviet trade. An analogous process also occurred in Japan, where production from Russian-controlled Sakhalin Island was supplying around 13 per cent of oil by 1929, squeezing the Western oil majors' presence in the country.[37] Sakhalin's oil was particularly important for the Japanese military and was thus linked to the rise of Japanese imperialism through the 1930s.

From 1923 onwards, Soviet oil also helped strengthen the international reach of large American oil firms that had previously found it difficult to compete in markets outside the US. Key examples of this were Standard Oil New York (SONY) and Vacuum Oil Company, two of the top eight American firms (see Table 3.1) that would later merge to become Mobil (now part of ExxonMobil). In the early 1920s, these firms lacked access to oil reserves outside the US and Latin America, and were thus at a disadvantage to Royal Dutch Shell and APOC who could supply international markets more cheaply through their substantial oil fields in Romania and the Middle East.[38] To remedy this situation, the two US firms began negotiations in 1923 to buy oil

---

Century Spain', in Alain Beltran's *A Comparative History of National Oil Companies*, Lausanne: PD Lang, 2010, 143–62). It was privatised in 1992 and is today part of the Spanish oil giant, Repsol.

36 In France, the French subsidiary of Belgium's Petrofina held the monopoly on Soviet oil. Although Petrofina was a Belgian company, its major shareholders were French banking and financial interests; see Chapter 4 of Gregory P. Nowell, *Mercantile States and the World Oil Cartel, 1900–1939*, Ithaca, NY: Cornell University Press, 2019. In 1999, Petrofina merged with France's Total. In Germany, Soviet oil imports were managed through DEA Deutsche Erdoel, which was controlled by German banking interests. This company now exists as part of Wintershall DEA, one of the largest oil and gas companies in Europe (currently owned by the German chemical giant BASF and the Russian billionaire Mikhail Fridman; see Chapter 10).

37 Alekperov, *Oil of Russia*.

38 A 1928 statement by SONY notes: 'As the Royal Dutch had large production in Rumania [*sic*] . . . it was in a position to be fairly independent of supplies of Russian oil, whereas, unless Standard Oil of New York was assured of products on a favourable basis in its south eastern European markets and Asia Minor, it would be involved with substantial losses.' 'Standard Oil Defends Deal with Soviets', *New York Herald Tribune*, 16 January 1928.

directly from Soviet Russia, which they could then use to compete in markets across Europe, Asia, and the Middle East. By 1926, SONY and Vacuum had agreed a five-year contract to purchase 10 million dollars' worth of oil annually from the Soviet Union. SONY also signed a concession to build a refinery on the Black Sea coast, to produce kerosene from Russian oil for export to India, Indonesia, and other Asian countries.[39] These deals transformed SONY and Vacuum into truly *global* companies, able to compete as equals with SONJ, Royal Dutch Shell, and APOC. And, as such, the Bolshevik revolution helped recalibrate the balance of power *among* the emerging Seven Sisters cartel, shifting the control of world oil away from Britain towards the US during these critical interwar years.

The SONY/Vacuum deals with the Soviet Union were angrily opposed by the chairman of Shell, Henri Deterding, who declared in response that Russian oil 'was stolen property, its owners never having been compensated for it' (despite having earlier permitted a Shell subsidiary to purchase Soviet kerosene for sale in India).[40] Nonetheless, with the potential for Russian oil to flow now into new markets through the export channels of these US oil firms, the ability of the Western majors to *restrict* the volume of global oil supplies became much more difficult, and the perennial curse of oversupply re-emerged. Competition between Shell and the US firms first erupted in a major price war in India in 1928, which then quickly spread to Egypt and other regions. This was the fundamental trigger for the secret negotiations between the major oil companies in Achnacarry in 1928, which attempted to contain and manage the global flow of oil surpluses. Once again, the unintended consequences of revolution in Russia were evident; the attempted cartelisation of world oil by the leading US and British firms was as much a product of the Bolshevik nationalisation of oil as it was a result of the oil riches in the Americas and the Middle East.

39 Alekperov, *Oil of Russia*, 219.

40 'Standard Oil Defends Deal', *New York Herald Tribune*. Deterding was concerned not only about the competition that SONY and Vacuum presented in markets such as India and Egypt, but also the encroachment of Russian oil into his home market in the UK (where Russian petroleum had reached 10 per cent of the market share by the late 1920s). Heymann, 'Oil in Soviet-Western Relations', 307.

5

Post-war Transitions I: Europe's Shift to Oil

> This is a war of engines and octanes. I drink to the American auto industry and the American oil industry.
>
> Joseph Stalin, toasting Winston Churchill at the British prime minister's birthday drinks, 1943.[1]

Even more than the conflict of 1914–18, oil stood at the centre of the Second World War. The air, naval, and motorised vehicles that so greatly amplified the destructive power of war depended on ever-increasing supplies of petroleum, and securing those supplies became a major preoccupation of all the leading protagonists. Germany's lack of domestic oil reserves animated Hitler's war preparations through the 1930s, driving Nazi attempts to produce liquid fuels from coal and the subsequent development of the chemical industry (see Chapter 7). The strategic importance of oil was also clearly understood by US planners, who massively ramped up the supply of oil to Allied forces throughout the conflict. Indeed, the eventual Allied victory in the war is sometimes credited – with only a hint of exaggeration – to the two enormous Inch pipelines built between 1942 and 1943, connecting the oil fields of Texas to refineries on the New Jersey seaboard and providing 500,000 barrels

1 Cited in Timothy Winegard, *The First Oil World War*, Toronto: University of Toronto Press, 2016, 14.

of petroleum each day for Allied forces in Western Europe.[2] Oil's military importance would only continue to grow with the end of the war, with the US military eventually becoming the largest single consumer of oil in the world.[3]

After the war, as military and civilian life came fully under the sway of petroleum, oil finally overtook coal to become the world's principal fossil fuel. This fossil fuel transition occurred first in the US, where the consumption of oil surpassed coal in 1950, followed by Western Europe and Japan in the 1960s. Across the OECD, oil made up less than 28 per cent of total fossil fuel consumption in 1950; by the end of the 1960s, it held a majority share.[4] This did not mean that coal was no longer consumed, or even that there was an overall decline in its use. Rather, across this period, 'oil-fueled accumulation . . . was superimposed on coal-based accumulation'.[5] Overall, this addition of oil to the world's energy matrix set off a huge surge in the global consumption of fossil fuels, which *doubled* in just fifteen years between 1950 and 1965.[6] The 'Great Acceleration' in carbon emissions noted decades later by the scientists of the International Geosphere-Biosphere Programme had begun.

The massive growth in oil consumption across the two decades following the Second World War was driven by oil's utilisation in three primary ways: (1) a significant expansion in oil's use as a fuel for electricity production, industry, and in heating; (2) a considerable rise in the consumption of petroleum-based liquid transport fuels; and (3) the development of petrochemicals and other synthetic products, ultimately

2 The Big Inch (24 inches in diameter) was designed to transport oil, and the Little Inch (20 inches in diameter) for transporting oil products such as kerosene. They were the largest and longest pipelines ever constructed (US pipelines were generally 8 inches or smaller in diameter at the time). Keith Martin, 'The Big Inch: Fueling America's WWII War Effort', National Institute of Standards and Technology, 26 March 2018, nist.gov. The Inch pipelines and the wider infrastructure of oil were celebrated by leading Hollywood film companies of the time, including in the appropriately titled short *Oil Is Blood* (RKO-Pathé, 1943).

3 Neta Crawford, 'Pentagon Fuel Use, Climate Change, and the Costs of War', Costs of War Project, 13 November 2019.

4 Simon Pirani, *Burning Up: A Global History of Fossil Fuel Consumption*, London: Pluto Press, 2018, 64.

5 Roberto J. Ortiz, 'Oil-Fueled Accumulation in Late Capitalism: Energy, Uneven Development, and Climate Crisis', *Critical Historical Studies*, Fall 2020, 205–40, 236.

6 Pirani, *Burning Up*, 64.

derived from oil as a basic feedstock. These three uses were distinct but closely interlinked; more demand for oil in one area tended to increase the need for oil in another. The dynamic of the oil transition was thus acutely self-reinforcing and incessantly revolutionising – creating new products, needs, and desires that further served to push forward the thirst for oil. As energy source, liquid fuel, or raw material, various forms of oil now underlay all moments of commodity production and circulation – capitalism's endless spiral of accumulation was now conclusively oil-based.

The consumption of oil as an *energy source for electricity generation, industry, and heating* is sometimes downplayed because, at a global level, and especially in the US, other energy sources such as coal and hydropower remained predominant. The problem with this perspective is that it ignores the decisive role of oil in energy production across specific regions and countries that lacked alternative energy sources, including numerous countries in Western Europe and Asia. In the electricity sector, for example, oil-fired plants came to supply a majority of all power in Denmark, Italy, Portugal, Japan, Greece, Ireland, and Belgium during the post-war period. Across the wider OECD, the use of oil in electricity generation grew from negligible levels in the early 1950s to contributing more than a quarter of all electricity by the early 1970s.[7] Likewise, oil's share of energy consumption in West European industry and manufacturing rose from around 10 per cent in 1950 to 50 per cent in 1970.[8] Oil also displaced wood and coal as a major residential heating fuel across the OECD during the 1950s and 1960s; by the early 1970s, more than a third of all houses in the US, France, Denmark, Germany, Canada, Japan, Sweden, and Norway relied on oil for heating purposes.[9]

---

7 Craig S. Bamberger, 'Oil in Power Generation', Paris: OECD/IEA, 1997, 26. After the oil price spikes of the 1970s, natural gas took on an increasingly important role in electricity production (see Chapter 9).

8 John A. Hassan and Alan Duncan, 'The Role of Energy Supplies during Western Europe's Golden Age, 1950–1972', *Journal of European Economic History* 18, 1989: 479–508.

9 Lee Schipper and Andrea N. Ketoff, 'Residential Energy Use in the OECD', *Energy Journal* 6, no. 4, 1985: 65–85, 71. Japan figures from A. Doernberg, *Energy Use in Japan and the United States*, Washington, DC: US Department of Energy, Office for the Assistant Administrator for Planning Analysis and Evaluation, 1977, 44. Heating oil was cheaper than coal and considered cleaner because it did not release black smoke and soot (although it did release other invisible particles that were also dangerous). In

Overall, between 1940 and 1970, oil's share of total primary energy supply in the OECD rose from around 20 per cent to 50 per cent, while that of coal dropped from 62 per cent to 23 per cent.[10]

Across all these major countries, oil allowed the provision of cheap energy and mass electrification – and this played a key part in restoring capitalist profitability after the lengthy economic slump of the pre-war period.[11] Prices of oil and oil products were lower than coal prices – for reasons that will be explored below – and oil had much less volume, was easier to handle, and possessed a greater energy density.[12] This meant that the storage, labour, and transportation costs for a given quantity of energy were much cheaper than coal, lowering the energy costs for industry even as other production costs rose (such as wages, buildings, and machinery).[13] Oil's role in enabling mass electrification likewise had a powerful impact on capitalist profitability and the dynamics of consumption. As households gained access to electricity, a range of new markets opened up for consumer goods such as dishwashers, televisions, washing machines, refrigerators, vacuum cleaners, and electric cookers.[14] In industry and manufacturing, the introduction of electrical machinery helped drive the growing automation of post-war European

London, the 1952 Great Smog killed 5,000 people in a few days, prompting moves for clean-air laws that favoured oil for heating purposes.

10 Odinn Melsted and Irene Pallua, 'The Historical Transition from Coal to Hydrocarbons: Previous Explanations and the Need for an Integrative Perspective', *Canadian Journal of History* 53, no. 3, 2018: 396–422, 396.

11 Ortiz, 'Oil-Fueled Accumulation', 209.

12 Oil is also easier to control during industrial processes, and this enabled considerable reductions in manufacturing time (and thus lower costs).

13 One study documents a 44.5 per cent fall in the cost of petroleum relative to wages in France, and a 25.6 per cent fall in West Germany for the same ratio over the 1956–72 period. The cost of petroleum relative to buildings and machineries fell by an even greater amount over the same period: 77.4 per cent in the case of France, and 41.2 per cent in the case of West Germany. Hassan and Duncan, 'The Role of Energy Supplies', 494.

14 In *Burning Up*, Pirani notes that in 1957 only 2 per cent of Italian households and 12 per cent of West German households had a refrigerator. By 1974, this had risen to 94 per cent in Italy and 93 per cent in West Germany. This 'industrialisation of the home' carried significant implications for patterns of social reproduction, and also led to an explosion in new service industries and related activities (such as advertising) Jean-Claude Debeir, *In the Servitude of Power: Energy and Civilization through the Ages*, London: Bloomsbury, 1991, 136.

factories.[15] The turn to oil as an energy source also carried significant implications for class politics: as Timothy Mitchell points out, oil was largely imported from overseas, its use thus helped weaken the power of those militant miners who had traditionally taken a leading role in labour struggles across Europe.[16]

The second dimension to the post-war fossil fuel transition was petroleum's function *as a liquid transport fuel*. After the Second World War, petroleum definitively displaced coal across all modes of transport, fully revolutionising the movement of people and commodities. In the maritime sector, 'steam ships had almost completely disappeared from the world's seas' by the mid-1960s, replaced by vessels running on oil-fired engines.[17] Likewise, steam-powered locomotives 'became practically extinct' during the middle of the twentieth century, as diesel engines displaced coal for railway transport, and rail networks expanded across continental Europe, the United States, and Asia.[18] Of course, the biggest changes took place in road and air transport, where petroleum products did not actually displace coal but rather made possible new forms of commercial transportation that would have been impossible without liquid fuels. World automobile production quadrupled between 1938 and 1960, as the car became a widespread form of personal transport and mass automobile markets emerged in Western Europe under US-backed reconstruction plans.[19] Between 1960 and 1970, production levels doubled again in Western Europe, and a large car market emerged in Japan. Commercial transcontinental flights using new jet-plane technology also began in 1952, benefiting from a 1944 international treaty that exempted aviation fuel from taxation (a huge subsidy for carbon emissions that continues to this day).[20] These petroleum-based mass-transport systems – particularly the booming automobile sector – were among the most profitable areas of capitalist production in the post-war years. They would also bring profound changes to consumption norms across Western Europe and North America, reshaping cultural

15 Ernest Mandel, *Late Capitalism*, London: Verso, 1972.

16 Mitchell, *Carbon Democracy*, 19–27.

17 Melsted and Pallua, 'The Historical Transition', 410.

18 Ibid., 408.

19 D. Jones and J. Womack, 'Developing Countries and the Future of the Automobile Industry', *World Development* 13, no. 3, 1985: 393–407, 394.

20 Pirani, *Burning Up*, 23.

practices, individual subjectivities, and the set of social aspirations associated with the 'good life' and the 'American dream'.[21]

Liquid fuels were cheap, portable, and more energy dense than coal. This meant that commodities could be moved around much faster and at lower cost, and prices of shipping, rail, and road transport fell.[22] In this manner, petroleum helped underpin the radical reorganisation of global production and consumption that took place in the 1950s and 1960s. With far-flung international markets now linked through air travel, the new oil-based global transport infrastructures were particularly propitious for US firms seeking to establish subsidiaries and production facilities outside their home market: in Western Europe alone, a nearly fourfold increase in the number of US manufacturing subsidiaries occurred between 1950 and 1965.[23] A new term – *multinational corporation* – was coined to describe this territorial expansion of the world market, which ultimately embodied capitalism's ceaseless push to overcome barriers to its circulation, and a shortening of the cycles of production and consumption. Marx's prescient image of the 'annihilation of space by time' would be manifest through oil's emergence as the primary transport fuel.

The third fundamental dimension to oil's post-war rise – one that we look at in more detail in Chapter 7 – was the birth of a world composed of *petrochemical* products, i.e. plastics and other synthetic materials made from petroleum. From the 1950s onwards, a wide array of naturally derived substances – wood, glass, paper, natural rubber, natural fertilisers, soaps, cotton, wool, and metals – were systematically displaced by plastics, synthetic fibres, detergents, and other petroleum-based chemicals. The proliferation of these entirely novel and artificial commodities was marked by the change from coal to oil as the main chemical precursor in their manufacture (and the associated

21 Matthew Huber, *Lifeblood*, Minneapolis: University of Minnesota Press, 2013.

22 In the UK, the switch from steam to diesel railways was largely responsible for a fivefold reduction in the net energy requirements for the sector between 1960 and 1972; Hassan and Duncan, 'The Role of Energy Supplies', 498.

23 Burton I. Kaufman, 'Multinational Corporations, 1955–1990', *Encyclopedia of American Foreign Policy*, 2002, americanforeignrelations.com. Particularly important here was Britain, which became the second largest destination for US overseas investment (after Canada) in the decades following the war. Geoffrey Jones and Frances Bostock, 'U.S. Multinationals in British Manufacturing before 1962', *Business History Review* 70, no. 2, Summer 1996: 207–56.

destruction of Germany's coal-based chemical industry in the aftermath of the Second World War). This petrochemical revolution enabled the synthetisation of what had previously been encountered and appropriated only within the domain of nature; the very substance of life was transformed, alchemy-like, into various derivatives of petroleum. Here is oil, not as energy source or transport fuel, but as feedstock – the raw material of commodity production itself.

It is difficult to overstate the significance of the petrochemical revolution. Through it, oil enabled an exceptional increase in both the variety and quantity of goods produced across the world market. The production of food, for example, was transformed through the application of chemical fertilisers, pesticides, defoliants, and herbicides – new synthetic products all ultimately derived from oil. Along with the introduction of agricultural machinery such as tractors that ran on petroleum, this so-called Green Revolution 'turn[ed] oil and natural gas into food . . . farming was no longer farming. It was petro-farming'.[24] Elsewhere, the pervasive spread of plastics and other synthetic materials produced from petroleum rapidly colonised all aspects of everyday life, driving the emergence of new spheres of household and industrial consumption. Moreover, this petrochemical revolution became a crucial factor in expelling living labour from the production of commodities – the automated fabrication of cheap, machine-reproducible plastics transformed whole branches of industries. Mechanisation and automation were indissolubly linked to oil's new role as petrochemical feedstock.

Woven into capitalism in these three diverse but connected ways – energy, transport, and petrochemicals – the post-war consolidation of oil as the primary fossil fuel drove forward a two-decade economic boom that was the fastest period of growth in history.[25] The years before the war had been marked by a lengthy period of world economic stagnation, declining profit rates, and the overaccumulation of capital; few profitable outlets for investment existed, intensifying the struggle to control markets and resources. Oil made possible new goods and commodity markets, accelerated the speed of production and

24 Jason Moore, *Capitalism in the Web of Life*, New York: Anchor, 2015, 251–2.

25 UN DESA, *World Economic and Social Survey 2017*, New York: UN, 2017, 26, un.org. Of course, another key factor in enabling this economic upturn was the destruction caused by the war itself.

consumption, and expanded the sphere of circulation. It helped cheapen costs of manufacturing, restructure labour processes, and became the foremost input into most of the essential consumption goods that regulated the value of labour power.[26] In all these ways, the oil transition contributed decisively to the long wave of capitalist expansion that began around 1950 and lasted until the late 1960s, a period many economists came to describe (albeit in somewhat Eurocentric terms) as the 'Golden Age of Capitalism'.

Alongside this economic boom, oil's insertion at the core of capitalist production was also coactive with US political and economic dominance. As the world's first real 'oil power', the largest US oil firms dominated the new oil markets through their command over crude production and their ability to deliver the downstream oil products essential to the emergent transport and petrochemical industries. The expansion of foreign markets for other commodities closely connected to oil – such as automobiles, chemicals, heavy machinery, mass consumer goods, and agro-industrial food – also primarily benefited the largest US industrial firms, which leveraged their long-established leadership in their domestic market to gain a major position across Western Europe and elsewhere.[27] With the US holding a 60 per cent share of world manufacturing output and just over a quarter of global GDP, American exports increased more than 450 per cent in the decade following the war.[28] By 1956, forty-two of the top fifty industrial corporations in the world were American.[29] This overwhelming US corporate dominance was likewise supported by a new global financial architecture centred on the US dollar, a restructuring of global finance that would later be deeply interlaced with oil and the flows of so-called petrodollars into the world market (see Chapter 9). Oil, in short, served to bolster all aspects of US power.

26 Ortiz, 'Oil-Fueled Accumulation', 207.

27 From 1959 to 1964, US companies set up international subsidiaries at the rate of more than 300 per annum, more than ten times the period immediately before the Second World War. More than a third of these subsidiaries were established in Western Europe. N. Grimwade, *International Trade: New Patterns of Trade, Production, and Investment*, New York: Routledge, 2000, 119.

28 UN DESA, *World Economic and Social Survey 2017*, 38.

29 Satoshi Ikeda, 'World Production', in Terence Hopkins and Immanuel Wallerstein, *The Age of Transition: Trajectory of the World-System, 1945–2025*, London: Zed Books, 1996, 74.

US Oil and Europe's Fossil Fuel Transition

What did this new petroleum-based political and economic order mean for the control of world oil? In the years immediately following the war, the dominance of the large American and European integrated oil firms appeared unassailable. By 1949, around two-thirds of the world's known crude reserves, and more than half of the world's crude production, refining, and cracking capacity (used in the manufacture of petrochemicals), were controlled by the seven companies that we encountered in Chapter 3. Outside of the US and USSR, these Seven Sisters held more than 82 per cent of all known crude reserves, 86 per cent of crude production, 77 per cent of refining capacity, and 85 per cent of cracking plants.[30] As ever, the power of these seven firms rested on their fully integrated nature, and the immediate post-war years saw an even greater concentration in their command over key oil infrastructures. Between them, it was estimated that the Seven Sisters owned at least half the world's tanker fleet in 1949, and around two-thirds of privately controlled tankers.[31] Similarly, outside the US and USSR, *all* the world's pipelines were owned and operated by one or more of the Seven Sisters at the end of the war.[32] Coupled with their dominance over the production and refining of oil, the Seven Sisters' control over these crucial circulatory infrastructures gave them power over the marketing and retailing of oil across the world. Indeed, assessing these ownership structures in 1952, the US government concluded that 'there are no other companies operating in international markets capable of supplying petroleum products', and the 'power of these [seven] major companies is so substantial as to be virtually unchallengeable'.[33]

Notwithstanding the overwhelming collective power of the Seven Sisters, the largest US firms continued to be dominant within this structure. As Tables 5.1 and 5.2 indicate, the American Sisters held a much greater share of the all-important US oil market than did British Petroleum or Royal Dutch Shell. The sheer size of the US market – and

30 See Tables 5.1 and 5.2.

31 FTC, *International Petroleum Cartel*, Washington, DC: US Government Printing Office, 1952, 27.

32 Ibid., 28.

33 Ibid., 29.

the physical and financial resources that were made available to the largest American firms as a result – translated into international strength: by the end of the war, the American Sisters controlled significantly more crude reserves, oil production, and cracking capacity *outside the US* than did their European rivals.[34] At the same time, the fully internationalised operations of the American Sisters helped to consolidate their domestic power (especially as the US was to become a net oil importer following the war). In this manner, the two sides of the bifurcated world oil market continued to exist in mutual interplay; the structure of the US oil industry served to condition – and was itself conditioned by – the control of world oil outside the US.

Part of the reason for the international strength of US firms was the significant increase in the domestic demand for oil and oil products that occurred in the lead-up to and during the war itself. Between 1939 and 1941 – before the US entered the war – American oil consumption rose by around a fifth.[35] Much of this extra demand for oil came from the US military, and this continued to expand throughout the war; indeed, the US military's consumption of oil grew from 1 per cent of total refined oil in 1939 to more than 33 per cent in 1945, while the total production of refined products increased by 44 per cent over the same period.[36] As a result of this demand growth, any concerns around domestic oil overproduction quickly evaporated. At the same time, the US government reinforced the power of the leading US oil firms in other ways, including investment in critical oil infrastructure – such as the aforementioned Inch pipelines – and offering major strategic support to the development of petrochemicals, which were to become decisive to the war effort itself (see Chapter 7). As with the formation of the NPSC during the First World War, the US government also tightened its connection to the largest oil companies, establishing new institutional linkages between the state and the oil industry, which effectively gave the latter direct control over devising and implementing policy around oil.[37]

34 Refining capacity was about equal (see Table 5.2).

35 Kokxhoorn, *Oil and Politics*, 77.

36 Ibid., 81.

37 In 1941 US President Roosevelt appointed a petroleum coordinator for national defense, Harold Ickes, who tapped the vice-president of SOCAL, Ralph Davies, to act as his deputy. All pending anti-trust actions against the oil industry were halted, and a new committee – the Petroleum Industry War Council – was established, composed of seventy-two leaders of the major US oil firms, which devised oil policy during the US war effort.

Table 5.1. The Seven Sisters: Global Oil Reserves and Production, 1949

	Reserves (billions of barrels)			**Production (thousands of barrels daily)**				
	US	Outside US	Total	US	Latin America and Caribbean	Middle East	Other Eastern Hemisphere	Total
British Petroleum	0	13.9	13.9	0	0	704.7	1	705.7
Royal Dutch Shell	0.8	4.5	5.3	211	458.9	51	136.2	857.1
American Sisters	8.6	22.9	31.5	1,376.3	990	664.5	68	3,098.8
Industry total	28	50	78	5040	1799	1435	257	8531
Seven Sisters' share of industry total (per cent)	33.6	82.1	65.0	31.5	80.5	99.0	79.8	54.6

Table 5.2. The Seven Sisters: Global Refining and Cracking Capacity, 1949

	Refining capacity (thousands of barrels daily)			**Cracking capacity (thousands of barrels daily)**		
	US	Outside US	Total	US	Outside US	Total
British Petroleum	0	707.9	707.9	0	137.5	137.5
Royal Dutch Shell	367	891.9	1,258.9	248.3	270.3	518.6
American Sisters	2,631	1,507.4	4,138.4	1,624	499.6	2,123.6
Industry Total	6,750	4,010	10,760	3,980	1,065	5,045
Seven Sisters' Share of Industry Total (per cent)	44.4	77.4	56.7	47.0	85.2	55.1

Source: Adapted by author from Tables 8, 9, 10, 11, United States Federal Trade Commission, United States Congress, Senate Select Committee on Small Business, Subcommittee on Monopoly, *The International Petroleum Cartel* (reprint), staff report, Washington, DC: US Government Printing Office, 1975, 23–6. Figures exclude USSR and Eastern Europe.

Beyond the increase in the domestic demand for oil, however, the key factor behind the clear dominance of the largest US firms in world oil was the post-war expansion of oil-centred economies in Western Europe. Prior to the war, more than 90 per cent of Western Europe's energy requirements had depended on coal.[38] With the Allied victory, US administrators consciously sought to shift European countries away from this reliance on coal towards the use of oil. A major focus of these efforts was Germany, which due to a lack of domestic oil supplies had built its war economy around technologies that used coal to produce synthetic fuels and other chemicals. At the conclusion of the war, the Potsdam Conference of July 1945 banned Germany from utilising coal as a feedstock in this manner – a move that forced the expansion of oil refining in order to satisfy the country's need for liquid fuels.[39] In 1951 this order was rescinded, but by that stage all four German coal-to-fuel plants in Western-controlled zones had either been deactivated or converted to processing oil.[40]

Alongside these kinds of explicit restrictions on coal-to-fuel technologies, US-backed reconstruction efforts also worked to reinforce the transition to oil in Western Europe. Between 1948 and 1952, around US$13 billion was directed towards European reconstruction as part of the Marshall Plan, equivalent to the transfer of one per cent of US GNP each year.[41] This reconstruction significantly strengthened US dominance, with Marshall Aid funds providing purchasing power for European countries to buy US goods and services.[42] More than a

---

38 David Painter, 'Oil and the Marshall Plan', *Business History Review* 58, no. 3, Autumn 1984: 359–83, 361.

39 A. Stranges, 'Germany's Synthetic Fuel Industry, 1927–1945', in J. E. Lesch (ed.), *The German Chemical Industry in the Twentieth Century, Chemists and Chemistry*, vol. 18, Dordrecht: Springer, 2000, 213.

40 A similar shift occurred in Japan under post-war US military occupation. Japan was heavily reliant on imported energy – indeed, the lure of coal in Manchuria and oil in South-East Asia was a major factor in the rise of Japanese imperialism during the 1930s and 1940s. After the war, the share of oil in Japanese energy consumption grew from less than a tenth in 1950 to more than three-fifths by the 1970s. American companies were supplying more than 60 per cent of Japanese oil by the mid-1960s. Michael Tanzer and Stephen Zorn, *Energy Update: Oil in the Late Twentieth Century*, New York: Monthly Review Press, 1985, 72.

41 UN DESA, *World Economic and Social Survey 2017*, 39.

42 Of course, American post-war dominance in Europe was by no means a foregone conclusion. The mood across Europe coming out of the war was decidedly

tenth of this Marshall Aid was spent on oil, a greater proportion than that spent on any other single commodity.[43] Large amounts of Marshall Plan funding also went to oil-related industries such as automobiles, other kinds of petroleum-based transport, and petrochemicals. And importantly, because Marshall Aid was provided in US dollars, it enabled US oil companies to sell oil to European countries despite the chronic shortage of US dollars at the time. US companies became the leading suppliers of oil to Europe, with more than 70 per cent of oil shipments financed by the US coming from just three US companies (SONJ, Mobil, and Caltex).[44] The beneficial effects of this on the US oil industry were well recognised by American planners, including Walter Levy, the head of the Marshall Plan oil division and a former economist for Mobil, who would later remark that without the Marshall Plan, 'the American oil industry in Europe would have been shot to pieces'.[45]

In short, US post-war reconstruction plans drove Europe's oil transition. The success of this project, however, depended fundamentally on a simultaneous realignment in the geography of global oil production. Due to tight supply at the time, increased American oil exports to Europe would have impacted US domestic prices, and for this reason, the Marshall Plan explicitly stipulated that Europe's oil should come from outside the US.[46] In this context, the Middle East was to emerge

---

anti-capitalist, particularly given the leading role of Communist Parties and other left-wing organisations in the resistance to fascism across countries such as France, Spain, Yugoslavia, Italy, and Greece. Nonetheless, through the 1950s, any potential challenge to American dominance was largely neutralised through a combination of repression and the relative dynamism of US capitalism, of which the Marshall Plan was an important dimension.

43 Painter, 'Oil and the Marshall Plan', 362. Despite the weight accorded to oil in Marshall Plan funding, a leading historian of this period has noted that 'most studies of the Marshall Plan ignore oil . . . This neglect is striking because oil played a key role in the origins, operations, and impact of the Marshall Plan.' David S. Painter, 'The Marshall Plan and Oil', *Cold War History* 9, no. 2, 2009: 159–75, 160.

44 Painter, 'The Marshall Plan and Oil', 165. Mobil was formed through a merger of SOCONY and Vacuum Oil Company in 1955; Caltex was a joint venture of SOCAL and Texaco (now part of Chevron).

45 Cited in Edward Shaffer, *The United States and the Control of World Oil*, New York: St Martin's Press, 1983, 94.

46 Painter, 'The Marshall Plan and Oil', 165. Supplying Europe with oil from Latin America was also difficult because much of this was directed to American oil consumption.

over the next decade as the principal source of crude oil supplies to Europe (and later, the rest of the world). The region had plentiful supplies, which, by the mid-1950s, would amount to nearly 40 per cent of the world's proven reserves.[47] Middle East oil also sat in closer proximity to many European countries, and its costs of production were much less than anywhere else in the world.[48] Seemingly unlimited quantities of low-cost Middle East oil could thus be supplied to Europe at prices lower than coal, while ensuring that domestic US oil markets remained insulated from the effects of increased European demand.[49] The recentring of Europe's oil consumption around the Middle East was a remarkably rapid process: between 1947 and 1960, the share of Europe's oil originating from the region essentially doubled, rising from 43 per cent to 85 per cent.[50]

Sterling Oil and British Imperial Decline

The Middle East's centrality to Western Europe's post-war oil transition gave the region an increasingly pivotal place in US power – a fact explicitly recognised at the time by leading post-war American strategists, including Walter Levy. This was also signalled in the growing proportion of Middle East oil held by US firms. The jewel in the American

47 Figures for 1957. Kokxhoorn, *Oil and Politics*, 123. In 1949, the US had held more than a third of the world's crude reserves (Table 5.1).

48 One estimate for 1950 put the cost of production at $0.18/barrel in the Middle East compared to $1.18/barrel in the US. Zuhayr Mikdashi, *A Financial Analysis of Middle Eastern Oil Concessions*, New York: Praeger, 1966, 168. Producers in the Middle East were making around $1.96 profit on a barrel compared to $1.37 in the US (Kokxhoorn, *Oil and Politics*, 139).

49 Debeir, *In the Servitude of Power*, 136. For graphs of the relative costs of coal and refined products such as heating oil and heavy fuel oil, see Melsted and Pallua, 'The Historical Transition'. Another important factor in lowering the cost of petroleum was the increasing size of tankers: in 1960, tankers were being built between three to ten times larger than those of the mid-1950s, significantly reducing the cost of transporting oil; see Pirani, *Burning Up*, 81. The increased size of tankers was partly made possible by oil's energy density (relative to coal) – another illustration of how oil's effects were expressed synergistically across the commodity circuit. For a discussion of oil, shipping, and tankers, see Laleh Khalili, *Sinews of War and Trade*, London: Verso, 2020.

50 Kokxhoorn, *Oil and Politics*, 127.

presence in Middle East oil was Saudi Arabia's Aramco, which had come under the control of four leading US firms in 1947 and eventually became the largest oil producer in the world.[51] Alongside Aramco, US oil firms also managed to break the British oil monopoly in Iran, with a group of US firms taking a 40 per cent share of British Petroleum's Iranian oil interests in 1954 (see Chapter 6). In 1940, US companies had held only 10 per cent of Middle East oil; by the early 1950s, this proportion had become a majority share. This was part of a wider global shift that reflected the diminishing capacities of European colonial powers. In the years immediately following the war, US oil companies entered India, Indonesia, Mozambique, Angola, and Ethiopia for the first time ever.[52]

For Britain, the implications of this went far beyond oil's status as the world's most important energy source and raw material. Control over oil was hugely significant to the strength of the British currency.[53] Although the British Empire was much weakened following the war, sterling continued to account for a large share of world trade and international reserves across an assortment of British colonies, protectorates, and allied settler-colonies.[54] Within this international system, sterling functioned as a kind of quasi-international currency, operating as means of payment and wealth accumulation. Positioned at the centre of this imperial structure, the flow of both goods and currency within the sterling area supported Britain despite a substantial deficit *vis-à-vis* the rest of the world. In this manner, Britain sought to negotiate a place in the new world hierarchies of post-war capitalism by displacing the costs of decline onto subordinate states through the mechanism of sterling.[55]

51 In 1947 Aramco was rearranged to give SONJ and Socony-Vacuum a 40 per cent share, while the original shareholders SOCAL and Texaco retained 30 per cent each. In taking a share of Aramco, SONJ and Socony-Vacuum broke with the Redline Agreement, which they chose not to renew in 1946. For a discussion of these negotiations and the entry of SONJ and Socony-Vacuum into Saudi Arabia, see John Blair, *The Control of Oil*, New York: Pantheon Books, 1976, 35–40.

52 Tanzer and Zorn, *Energy Update*, 51–2.

53 Stephen Galpern, *Money, Oil, and Empire in the Middle East: Sterling and Post-War Imperialism, 1944–1971*, Cambridge: Cambridge University Press, 2009.

54 Catherine Schenk, *Britain and the Sterling Area: From Devaluation to Convertibility in the 1950s*, London: Routledge, 1994.

55 Ibid.

Stephen Galpern's pioneering work demonstrates how Britain's Middle East oil interests formed the centrepiece of this sterling strategy. Control over oil in Iran, Kuwait, Iraq, and elsewhere gave Britain the ability to denominate oil exports in sterling rather than dollars. British-owned firms such as British Petroleum (then known as Anglo-Iranian) sold their oil to Britain in sterling, rather than dollars, and thus enabled Britain to conserve precious dollars 'on a commodity that represented the greatest drain on the country's dollar supply'.[56] These firms were also domiciled in Britain, which meant that the sterling payments they received for oil stayed within the sterling bloc. Furthermore, the oil sold by these firms to countries outside the sterling bloc was paid for in dollars, so these firms also became a lucrative source of dollar flows into the sterling area.[57] This goal of maintaining sterling oil against dollar oil formed a key strategic priority in Britain's attempt to hold its position in the world order.

Closely related to sterling oil was the issue of what happened to the wealth that ruling monarchies in the region earned from royalty payments received from British oil companies.[58] Once again, this was a critical element of Britain's Middle East policy, with Britain going to extraordinary lengths to ensure that Middle East rulers were serviced by British banks, held their reserves in sterling, and deposited their earnings in London, rather than dollar-based jurisdictions. This link between oil, financial markets, and Britain's colonial domination of the Middle East was all the more important given the success of independence movements in South and South-East Asia. With independence, and as part of the broader shift towards the US dollar as the dominant international currency, numerous countries began to reduce their sterling reserves and replace these with dollars.[59] To a significant degree, Middle

56 Galpern, *Money, Oil and Empire*, 38. Oil represented nearly half of the sterling area's dollar outlays in the years following the Second World War. Matthew Shutzer, 'Oil, Money and Decolonization in South Asia', *Past and Present* 258, no. 1, February 2023: 212–45, 223.

57 Galpern, *Money, Oil and Empire*, 16.

58 Geoffrey Jones, *Banking and Oil: The History of the British Bank of the Middle East*, vol. 2, Cambridge: Cambridge University Press, 1987.

59 In India, Britain saw 'the problem of decolonization not as a loss of manufacturing or trading wealth, but as the prospective further weakening of Britain's capacity to control the value of sterling'. Shutzer, 'Oil, Money and Decolonization', 220. Shutzer shows that India's attempt to nationalise oil in the 1950s was centrally motivated by a

East oil producers formed the final backstop for sterling on the world market – a position that had much to do with Britain's unswerving support for the autocratic monarchs who ruled the Gulf.[60]

As we shall see in Chapter 9, it was not until the 1970s that all Middle East states in the Gulf region finally established their independence from British colonial rule. By the time this happened, the US had emerged as the dominant foreign power in the Middle East, oil was denominated in dollars, and the direct British presence in the region had been much diminished. But Britain's decades-long control over oil in the Middle East – from the early operations of APOC in Iran, the formation of the Iraq Petroleum Company in the 1920s, through to the continued weight of Shell and British Petroleum in the 1950s and 1960s – gave British capitalism a unique advantage in navigating its own imperial decline *vis-à-vis* the rising US. Much more than any other European state, Britain could position itself as an important, albeit subordinate, partner to US power. The control over oil – both the physical crude *and* the oil wealth that emanated from the Middle East – was fundamental in enabling Britain to establish this special place for itself in a US-centred world order.

Oil and the Anti-colonial Moment

Prior to the oil transition, a country's consumption of energy typically depended on coal and other resources that were present within its own borders.[61] Oil changed this situation. Unlike coal, which was bulky and much more difficult to transport over long distances, oil was the first energy commodity to be *internationalised*: produced, transported, and refined for global consumption. As early as 1949, around 30 per cent of all oil produced was traded across borders (compared to less than 8 per cent

desire to confront the power of sterling (and the dollar) over the Indian economy, not simply the control of material resources.

60 Schenk, *Britain and the Sterling Area*, 48. In the two decades after the war, South Asia's share of overseas sterling balance dropped from around 60 per cent to around 5 per cent. Over the same period, the Middle East share increased from a negligible amount to reach 20 per cent by 1958. Ibid., 25–6. The other major prop to sterling at this time was gold exported from apartheid South Africa.

61 Tanzer and Zorn, *Energy Update*, 16.

of coal), and oil represented nearly 70 per cent of all internationally traded energy (today, around 60 per cent of oil production is internationally traded, compared to around 15 per cent of coal).[62] This international character of world oil meant that, as it became increasingly intertwined with European post-war capitalism, control over its extraction and circulation – including, of course, its price – became ever more inseparable from the trajectories of European development. Long-standing logics of colonial domination were thus indelibly etched into the very heart of Europe's transition to oil – a fact frequently downplayed in standard histories of the energy transition.[63]

At the time, however, the well-established patterns of control in the world oil industry were themselves increasingly threatened by nationalist and radical anti-colonial movements in the colonised world. Many of these movements had a history stretching back beyond the twentieth century, but the devastation suffered by the major European powers during the Second World War had given new impetus to the anti-colonial struggle. The presence and prestige of the Soviet Union as a rival to Europe and the US had also broadened the space available to them (although not without presenting its own dangers). Despite the fact that these movements expressed a range of often counterposed and contradictory social interests within the colonised world, the question of oil – the control over its extraction and price, and the distribution of oil rents – loomed large in their political imaginary.[64] This was expressed most sharply in Latin America and the Middle East, where anti-colonial and anti-imperialist movements increasingly raised demands for the nationalisation of oil or the renegotiation of oil concessions on improved terms.

A major complaint shared by both governments and popular movements in oil-producing states concerned the system of oil pricing that was then prevalent. This system was based on the so-called *posted price* – a public price that was set by the Seven Sisters, and which was used to

62 Figures for 1949. 'World Energy Supplies in Selected Years, 1929–1950, *Statistical Papers*, Series J, no.1, unstats.un.org, 11, 35.

63 See, for example, Vaclav Smil, *Energy Transitions*, Westport, CT: Praeger, 2010, which contains no mention of colonialism.

64 Two books stand out for their attempt to recentre the anti-colonial movement within the story of oil: Giuliano Garavini, *The Rise and Fall of OPEC in the Twentieth Century*, London: Oxford University Press, 2019; and Christopher Dietrich, *Oil Revolution*, Cambridge: Cambridge University Press, 2017.

calculate the tax due to host governments. Posted prices in no way represented the actual market value of crude. Rather, because the vast majority of oil produced outside the US circulated *within* the integrated channels of the Seven Sisters (from one of their oil-producing companies to a downstream subsidiary also owned by them, for example), the posted price was in effect the *cost* at which these intra-company transfers were valued.[65] The Seven Sisters were simultaneously the 'seller/producers as well as the buyers/refiners of the oil', and a lower price for crude simply shifted profits towards the downstream segments of the same company.[66] Crucial to this system was the fact that posted prices determined the amount of revenue payable to host governments – any reduction in the posted price thus also lowered the overall tax obligations of the largest oil firms. Taken together, these features of the posted-price system allowed the Seven Sisters to keep the cost of crude relatively low through the post-war boom, undercutting the price of coal in Western Europe and thereby facilitating the transition to oil. Buttressed by the extraordinary advance in consumption volumes that accompanied Europe's oil transition (growing at around 10 per cent each year), the Seven Sisters' control over pricing guaranteed them continuously high profits in both the upstream and downstream segments of the industry. Indeed, one calculation for the four largest oil firms operating in the Middle East shows them earning net profits at more than 50 per cent of net assets through most of the 1950s, a rate of profit far in excess of other industries at the time.[67]

Fully cognisant of these booming profit rates, governments in Latin America and the Middle East began to assert pressure on the major oil

65 During US government hearings convened in 1969, it was estimated by one oil industry consultant that 80–90 per cent of oil produced in the Eastern Hemisphere moved within the integrated channels of the largest oil majors. United States Senate, *Governmental Intervention in the Market Mechanism: The Petroleum Industry: Hearings before the Subcommittee on Antitrust and Monopoly of the Committee on the Judiciary*, 91st Congress, First Session, S. Res. 40, 1969, Parts 1–4, 47.

66 Edith Penrose, *The Large International Firm in Developing Countries: The International Petroleum Industry*, Cambridge, MA: MIT Press, 1968, 160. This crucial point highlights why it is so important to foreground the integrated nature of the largest oil firms. As Penrose noted in her testimony before the US Senate in 1969: 'Neither the history of the international [oil] industry or its present troubles can be understood except with reference to the economic significance of vertical integration, for this provides the essential key'. Penrose in United States Senate, *Governmental Intervention in the Market Mechanism*.

67 Blair, *Control of Oil*, 50.

companies to renegotiate oil concession terms. The initial push for these improved terms came from Venezuela, where a series of popular uprisings and military coups through the 1940s had culminated in the formulation of a new fifty–fifty profit-sharing model in 1948. As the name suggests, the model utilised a combination of royalties and taxes to guarantee the Venezuelan state half of the net income of any oil concession operated by the international majors. This arrangement was largely the brainchild of Juan Pablo Pérez Alfonzo, minister of development in the government of Venezuela's first freely elected president, Rómulo Gallegos.[68] Although it did not challenge the posted-price system, the fifty–fifty model nonetheless promised to increase the amount of oil rent captured by the Venezuelan state. In addition to taking an equal share of oil income, Pérez Alfonzo also sought to expand Venezuela's involvement in downstream petroleum activities, through the construction of state-owned refineries. His subsequent efforts were to have a major impact on the trajectory of the world oil industry, including the formation of OPEC (see Chapter 6).

It should be emphasised that the leading oil concessionaries in Venezuela (principally SONJ and Shell) were not opposed to the fifty–fifty model and were actually closely involved in the negotiations with the Venezuelan state around its implementation (along with the US State Department).[69] The reasons for this willingness to renegotiate stemmed partly from political pragmatism: the oil majors and the US government were much more concerned with the potential threat of complete nationalisation of oil, a move that had taken place in nearby Mexico in 1938, and which Venezuelan unions and leftist organisations were calling for through strikes and street protests. But perhaps even more significant was a highly advantageous tax law that the US government had also introduced, which allowed for any taxes that were paid overseas by oil companies to be used as a credit towards taxes owed in the US.[70] Because

68 An earlier hydrocarbon law had been passed in 1943 that contained the seeds of the fifty–fifty agreement, but it took Pérez Alfonzo's intervention in 1948 to pass an amendment guaranteeing Venezuela receipt of half the net oil revenues by using additional taxes if royalty payments were not sufficient. For a thorough discussion of Pérez Alfonzo and the fifty–fifty model, see Garavini, *The Rise and Fall of OPEC*, 2019.

69 Ibid., 54–62.

70 This foreign tax credit had been on the books since 1918 but was not used by oil companies until the fifty–fifty model came into effect.

the fifty–fifty model was largely implemented through taxation (and at a tax rate lower than the US), the overall impact on oil company revenue was neutral – money was simply being paid to the Venezuelan government rather than the US Treasury.

Venezuela's success in adopting the fifty–fifty model had a powerful impact on other major oil producing states, notably Saudi Arabia, which was rapidly emerging as the most important oil producer following the 1948 discovery of the world's largest oil field at Ghawar, in the eastern part of the country. In 1950, a delegation from Venezuela visited countries in the Middle East – including Kuwait, Egypt, Iran, and Syria – in order to sound out a common approach towards the world oil market and the Seven Sisters.[71] Although Saudi Arabia did not meet with the Venezuelan delegation during their visit to the region, the ruling Saudi monarch, Ibn Saud, was keen to replicate the fifty–fifty arrangement for the Aramco concession. At the time, Ibn Saud was receiving a 12 per cent royalty from Aramco, while its US owners were earning profit rates in excess of 50 per cent on their total initial investment in Saudi oil.[72] The initial discussions with Aramco's owners, however, did not yield any agreement on changing the royalty rates. While Saudi-based Aramco officials and the US State Department were sympathetic to Ibn Saud's demand – recognising that any refusal could potentially destabilise his position as a key American ally in the region – the consortium partners back in the US were strongly reluctant to see such extraordinary profit rates disappear.

The ultimate solution to this dilemma provides a text-book illustration of US state support to the international expansion of the largest US integrated oil firms. Following consultations with the oil companies, the US State Department, and the Treasury, the National Security Council secretly ruled in 1950 that the increase to a fifty–fifty share for the Aramco concession would be made up through a new payment by the US oil companies to Saudi Arabia, which would be classified as foreign

71 Garavini notes that while the trip sometimes seemed a 'comedy of errors' due to the very different cultural and political backgrounds of the participants, it nonetheless represented the first attempt at direct conversation between oil-producing nations in the South without the mediation or involvement of the oil majors; Garavini, *The Rise and Fall of OPEC*, 65. The implications of this point were not lost on American or British officials in the Middle East – and with hindsight, these meetings can be seen as a precursor of what would later be institutionalised in OPEC.

72 Blair, *Control of Oil*, 197.

tax rather than a royalty (even though Saudi Arabia did not have any form of corporate or income tax at the time).[73] As a foreign tax payment, this amount could then be used to offset other taxes owed by the Aramco concessionaires to the US government. In effect, the US was agreeing to transfer money it would have received as tax from the oil companies directly to the Saudi monarchy. This arrangement – later described by John Blair as 'an act of pure genius' – was not revealed publicly until 1955, and became a prominent topic of investigation during a 1974 US Senate hearing into the overseas activities of American oil companies.[74] As a direct subsidy by the US government (and US taxpayers) of the business expenses of the largest US oil firms, it was estimated that the tax arrangement effectively transferred $50 million from the US Treasury to Saudi Arabia in its first year of operation.[75] By 1955, this figure had risen to $192 million, and Aramco was paying zero tax in the United States.[76] A similar arrangement was later applied to US oil companies operating in Kuwait, Iran, and other oil-rich states.

The tax benefits offered by the US government helped increase the flow of oil rents to producer countries (at no expense to the oil firms themselves) and had a considerable effect on the political economy of these states.[77] These financial arrangements, however, also had major ramifications for the US oil industry itself. With preferential tax credits available only to those companies operating overseas – along with ownership of the cheapest oil on the planet and access to the booming petroleum markets of Western Europe – the gap between the largest internationally oriented US oil firms and their domestic rivals widened even further. The handful of large integrated oil firms that had managed

73 The role of the National Security Council in this secret tax ruling was revealed by Ambassador George McGhee who was assistant secretary of state for Middle Eastern affairs between 1951 and 1953, in testimony before the US Senate in 1974. United States Senate, Subcommittee on Multinational Corporations, *Multinational Corporations and United States Foreign Policy*, Part 4: Committee on Foreign Relations, 1974, 13.

74 Blair, *Control of Oil*, 198, and fn. 32, 414. See also United States Senate, *Multinational Corporations*, 90.

75 Blair, *Control of Oil*, 198.

76 Ibid., 202.

77 Adam Hanieh, *Money, Markets, and Monarchies: The Gulf Cooperation Council and the Political Economy of the Contemporary Middle East*, Cambridge: Cambridge University Press, 2018.

to internationalise were earning some of the highest profit rates of any industrial sector in the US. Indeed, by 1960, the profits of the six largest US oil firms (all internationally active) represented around a seventh of *all* profits earned by the entire Fortune 500.[78] Through the second half of the 1960s, the net income of the largest internationally active US majors doubled, while that of their domestically oriented rival majors remained virtually unchanged.[79]

Looking Forward

Across the tumultuous two decades following the Second World War, oil had systematically displaced coal as the world's key fossil fuel. Oil's rise was transformative to capitalism: the restoration of the post-war rate of profit, the internationalisation of capital, the qualitative growth in new consumption markets and commodities, the acceleration in the circulation of goods and services – all these vital changes to post-war economies were closely attached to oil's ascension as the primary fossil fuel. To be clear, oil was not the *reason* for these changes – ultimately, they were an expression of capitalism's deeper logics – but oil's new place within commodity production helped make them possible. Closely bound up with these changes was a simultaneous shift in global political and economic power, with the US definitively dislodging European dominance across the world market. The US pushed forward the post-war diffusion of an oil-centred mode of production – beginning first in Europe, and then elsewhere – using copious reconstruction funds, political and military power, and the continued international expansion of US multinational firms. As the foremost strength in world oil at the time, the rise of the US was mutually linked to oil's newfound centrality to capitalist production.

Integral to this fossil fuel transition was the further concentration of corporate ownership and control within the world oil industry itself. US oil firms remained the most important force, and saw their power deepened by the transition away from coal and the generalisation of oil-centred economies throughout Western Europe and beyond. The control

78 According to the 1960 Fortune 500 list, available at money.cnn.com.

79 United States Senate, *Multinational Corporations*, 105.

of US domestic oil markets by the largest integrated American firms supported their international growth; global ascendance would have been impossible without dominance of the largest oil market in the world. Alongside the US oil giants, the European firms Royal Dutch Shell and British Petroleum also held a substantial share of the world oil market, rounding out the Seven Sisters sorority. As always, what ultimately gave these seven oil companies their overwhelming power was not the ownership of crude oil concessions per se, but their ability to move oil from the field to the consumer via the integrated control over transport, storage, processing, and marketing.

Underlining all of this was the providence of post-war colonialism in the Middle East. Europe's fossil fuel transition fully depended on the Seven Sisters' command over Middle East oil production, which enabled a stable and cheap flow of oil from the region to West European states. The expansion of European capitalism through the 1950s and 1960s was thus inextricably bound to the ongoing realities of colonial rule in the Middle East and, even more so, to the deepening alliances between the US and ruling monarchies in countries such as Saudi Arabia and Iran. Accordingly, from this moment onwards, the struggles for national sovereignty and popular antipathy against European and American influence in the Middle East would be central to shaping how oil was controlled, priced, and consumed at the global scale.

6

Post-war Transitions II: Anti-colonial Revolt and OPEC

Given the generous tax benefits and promise of cheaper oil, many US oil firms sought to expand overseas in the period immediately following the Second World War. Nearly two hundred US companies were exploring for oil across ninety-one different countries by the end of the 1950s, a figure that had jumped from only twenty-eight firms and seventy-eight countries in 1946.[1] These overseas oil interests sat at the forefront of the wider post-war international growth of US capitalism – quite remarkably, more than a third of all foreign investments made by US private firms between 1946 and 1959 came from the oil sector.[2] As a result of these international activities, the total volume of proven reserves held by US oil companies increased more than sevenfold over the 1950s. Naturally, a major focus of this expansion was the Middle East, where around four-fifths of the price of a barrel of crude was simply pure profit.[3]

1 George Stocking, *Middle East Oil: A Study in Political and Economic Controversy*, Nashville, TN: Vanderbilt University Press, 1970, 404.

2 Nicoline Kokxhoorn, *Oil and Politics: The Domestic Roots of US Expansion in the Middle East*, Frankfurt: Peter Lang, 1977, 132.

3 United Nations Economic Commission for Europe (UNECE), 'The Price of Oil in Western Europe', 1955, 16. Mikdashi estimates that in 1955, the rate of return on equity for Gulf Oil was only 6.3 per cent in the US compared to 82.7 per cent in the Eastern Hemisphere, most of which was produced in the Middle East. See Zuhayr Mikdashi, *A Financial Analysis of Middle Eastern Oil Concessions*, New York: Praeger, 1966, 212–13.

In addition to the lure of such lucrative profit rates, large integrated US firms that were not part of the Seven Sisters (that is, those included in the other top twenty companies discussed in Chapter 3) also sought access to Middle East oil for their domestic crude needs. At the time, prorationing restrictions on production in the US served to limit the availability of domestic oil. Production in the Middle East could thus provide large independent integrated firms with access to a ready supply of oil for their own downstream activities, thereby lessening any need to purchase crude from competitors. In this manner, competitive pressures in the US domestic market helped drive the international expansion of a second tier of large integrated American firms; at the same time, access to oil in the Middle East further consolidated their vertical integration. With the growing amounts of oil being imported into the US through the integrated channels of American firms operating abroad, the US became a net oil importer between 1946 and 1959.[4]

One initial outcome of this overseas expansion was the creation of the American Independent Oil Company (AMINOIL), a consortium formed by a group of domestic-focused integrated firms in 1947. Registered in Delaware, AMINOIL was established to purchase an oil concession in the 'neutral zone' south of Kuwait – an area that had been formed in the 1920s to allow nomadic Bedouin to move freely between Saudi Arabia and Kuwait despite the presence of national borders.[5] In 1948, the Kuwaiti emir awarded AMINOIL a sixty-year concession in the neutral zone, charging them $7.5 million in cash, a minimum royalty of $625,000 per annum, 15 per cent of profits, and a million-dollar yacht.[6] In the same year, Saudi Arabia granted rights in the neutral zone to another US firm, the Pacific Western Oil Company (Getty Oil), which was controlled by the billionaire industrialist Jean Paul Getty. These were the first concessions offered by either the Kuwaiti or Saudi governments to firms outside the Seven

4 In 1959, the US government introduced the Mandatory Oil Import Quota Program, which restricted the amount of crude oil and refined products that could be imported into the US.

5 By the early 1920s, Delaware had eclipsed New Jersey as the destination of choice for firms wishing to register in a tax- and regulation-light US state. Just before the Second World War, nine out of the top twenty US oil firms were Delaware incorporated.

6 Yergin, *The Prize*, 438. Aminoil was bought by the tobacco firm R.J. Reynolds in 1970 for the price of $40 million. In 1984, it was sold again to Phillips Petroleum for $1.7 billion.

Sisters. Throughout the 1950s, independent US oil firms also successfully obtained concessions in Dhofar (a province in the south of Oman), Libya, and Iran, and were exploring for oil in Jordan, Syria, Lebanon, and Tunisia.

Beyond the second-tier US integrated firms, other companies also began to enter Middle East oil markets from the 1950s. The most significant of these was the Italian state-owned company Ente Nazionale Idrocarburi (National Hydrocarbon Agency, ENI), which was established in 1950 through the merger of Italian companies involved in exploration, refining, transport, and marketing of oil and gas. ENI was headed by Enrico Mattei, an influential figure in Italian politics who styled himself as a supporter of anti-colonial struggles in the Middle East and was the first to coin the term 'Seven Sisters' to describe the oligopoly controlling world oil.[7] Under Mattei's tutelage, ENI doggedly sought to undermine the dominance of the Anglo-American oil majors in the Middle East by offering more advantageous concessionary agreements to oil-producing countries.[8] Instead of the fifty–fifty arrangement that had become standard by the late 1950s, ENI proposed a 75:25 profit split and promised to engage producer countries as partners in oil exploration and production. ENI also delivered training to engineers, geologists, and other specialists from the Middle East, and set up a graduate training school in Italy to develop a cadre of professionals for the Middle East oil industry. Agreements based on the so-called 75:25 'Mattei Formula' were successfully negotiated with countries across the region, including Iran (1955), Egypt (1955), Libya (1957), Morocco (1958), Algeria (1958), Sudan (1959), Tunisia (1961), and Nigeria (1962).[9]

7 Mattei also headed a second Italian state-owned firm, Azienda Generale Italiana Petroli (General Italian Oil Company, AGIP), which was established by the Fascist regime in 1926 with the goal of exploring for oil and gas overseas. AGIP owned the majority share of two Romanian oil companies and had also unsuccessfully sought oil in Italian colonies such Libya, Eritrea, Ethiopia, and Somalia. It was later absorbed into ENI.

8 Inside Italy, the company established a monopoly for oil exploration in the Po Valley and also rolled out a national network of well-equipped service stations that gained a majority share of the retail market for petroleum. Claudio Fogu, *The Fishing Net and the Spider Web: Mediterranean Imaginaries and the Making of Italians*, London: Palgrave Macmillan, 2020, 252.

9 Ibid., 251.

Mattei's opposition to the largest international majors had the support of Italy's Christian Democracy party, which sought to project Italy as a 'bridge between Europe and the Arab world . . . [and] a mediator between Arab nationalist leaders and the Atlantic Alliance'.[10] As such, ENI led Italy's attempt to consolidate its own regional footprint in the Middle East during the decades following the war; indeed, ENI's influential position in formulating Italian foreign policy was reflected in frequent references to the company as 'a state within the state'. The company spared no effort in projecting itself as a central actor in the remaking of the wider Mediterranean region, and produced a set of captivating neorealist films that depicted ENI's oil infrastructure as the backbone to a new community of Mediterranean-basin peoples and governments.[11] The famed Italian director Bernardo Bertolucci even made a film for ENI about the journey of oil from Iran, via Italy, to Germany.[12]

Under Mattei's leadership, ENI garnered numerous enemies both within and outside Italy. In 1962, he was killed when his private plane crashed as it approached an airport in Milan. The crash is widely believed to have been caused by a bomb, with responsibility variously attributed to the CIA, the Mafia, or far-right French paramilitaries opposed to his support of Algerian independence.[13] Following Mattei's death, ENI adopted a less confrontational position towards the Seven Sisters, pulling back from direct extraction in the Middle East and signing deals to import oil produced by US firms such as SONJ and Gulf Oil instead.[14]

10 Elisabetta Bini, 'A Transatlantic Shock: Italy's Energy Policies between the Mediterranean and the EEC, 1967–1974', *Historical Social Research* 39, no. 4 (150), 2014: 145–64, 147.

11 Some of these films can be viewed online at ENI's historical archive, archiviostorico.eni.com.

12 James Marriott and Mika Minio-Paluello, *The Oil Road: Journeys from the Caspian Sea to the City of London*, London: Verso, 2012, 313, fn. 7.

13 Mattei's death was followed by the kidnapping and murder of investigative journalist Mauro de Mauro while he was working on Francesco Rosi's award-winning film, *Il caso Mattei* (The Mattei Affair, 1972). During later court hearings into Mauro's death, the last of which was held in 2015, high-level Mafia informants declared that Mauro had been killed because he was about to reveal the Sicilian Mafia's responsibility for Mattei's assassination. The Mafia informants also linked Mattei's death to US oil interests because of the damage he had done to the position of American oil companies in the Middle East.

14 Bini, 'A Transatlantic Shock', 150.

Nonetheless, ENI continued to build its infrastructure and global hydrocarbon assets through the 1970s and 1980s, later becoming one of the largest energy companies in the world (see Chapter 11).[15]

The international expansion of oil firms such as AMINOIL, Getty Oil, ENI, and others that were outside the Seven Sisters club had a major impact on the structure of oil markets in the Middle East.[16] The attempt by these companies to develop their international crude asset base at a time of oil's increasing centrality to the world market overlapped with the emergence of powerful anti-colonial and left-wing movements across the key producing regions of the Middle East and Latin America. Nationalist leaders sought – and were pushed by movements from below – to increase their share of oil wealth, particularly as the end of formal colonial rule brought with it the need to fund and develop more sophisticated state structures (including military and security forces). For newcomer oil companies, especially the US firms, the necessity of having an international presence was in many ways determined by domestic considerations, and this made them willing to offer much more competitive terms than those available from the Seven Sisters. The 1950s and 1960s were thus a meeting of these two mutually reinforcing trends: the definitive, albeit gradual and limited, erosion of the Seven Sisters' control of upstream oil resources, and the increased share of the oil wealth that accrued to producer governments.

15 The company continues to hold a dominant market share in the retailing and distribution of oil products in Italy and is also active in the retail petroleum markets of other European countries such as Austria, Switzerland, and Germany. Through the 1970s and 1980s, ENI played a pioneering role in building and operating the energy infrastructure that now links Africa to Europe, notably the 2,475 km Trans-Mediterranean Pipeline that runs from Algeria through Tunisia to Italy. In 2000, this pipeline was renamed the Enrico Mattei Pipeline.

16 Another significant entrant into Middle East oil markets at this time was Japan's Arabia Oil Co., which signed a deal with Saudi Arabia for exclusive rights in the offshore area of the neutral zone between Saudi Arabia and Kuwait in 1957. As part of this deal, the Japanese company agreed to pay 56 per cent of net profits and also to give Saudi Arabia part ownership of the company following the discovery of oil. A similar agreement was reached with Kuwait. Over 80 per cent of Japan's oil was to come from the Middle East through the 1960s and 1970s, and thus was an essential factor in the country's rapid industrialisation over this period, particularly in relation to electricity. Oil's share in electricity generation rose from around 35 per cent in 1965, to more than 70 per cent by the early 1970s. See Loftur Thorarinsson, 'A Review of the Evolution of the Japanese Oil Industry, Oil Policy and Its Relationship with the Middle East', Oxford Institute of Energy Studies, Working Paper 76, 2018, 8.

A Splutter of Musketry Too Far

In the Middle East, this growing nexus between oil and anti-colonialism was best illustrated in the case of Iran. As we saw earlier, Iran had been a major target of British oil interests stretching right back to the formation of the Anglo-Persian Oil Company (APOC) in the early twentieth century. In 1933, APOC had been granted a concession that gave it exclusive rights to all of Iran's oil for the next sixty years. Renamed the Anglo-Iranian Oil Company (AIOC) in 1935, the firm's Abadan oil refinery grew to be the largest in the world. AIOC's control of Iranian oil was immensely profitable to the British state, earning hundreds of millions of pounds in taxes and a hefty dividend payment from the government's majority ownership of the company. Up to 85 per cent of the British Navy's fuel was supplied by AIOC, and the firm was a major prop to the continued strength of British sterling.[17] As the British Foreign Office put it in a letter to the US State Department in the early 1950s, Iran's oil was '*the* major asset which we hold in the field of raw materials [globally]. Control of that asset is of supreme importance . . . [and] the loss of this, our only major raw material, would have cumulative and well-nigh incalculable repercussions.'[18]

The terms of the 1933 concession had clearly indicated Iran's vassal status: while the British government was taxing AIOC at a 30 per cent rate, the Iranian government received royalties of just 15–20 per cent.[19] In response to Iranian anger at these inequities, secret discussions were opened in 1949 with AIOC to renegotiate the terms of the concession. As part of these negotiations, AIOC offered to raise the royalty rate, as well as increase the share of profits from 17 per cent to 24 per cent. Iran, however, sought a fifty–fifty profit share in line with Venezuela and Saudi Arabia, as well as other changes to the concession, including a reduction in the length of the contract, payment of royalties in a currency other than sterling, an end to the British Navy's access to subsidised oil, and the right to purchase oil at the cost of local production, rather than

17 Ervand Abrahamian, 'The 1953 Coup in Iran', *Science and Society* 65, no. 2, Summer 2001: 182–215, 185.

18 Ibid., 189.

19 Ian Speller, 'A Splutter of Musketry? The British Military Response to the Anglo-Iranian Oil Dispute, 1951', *Contemporary British History* 17, no. 1, 2003: 39–66, 40.

being forced to pay market prices for their own national resource (perhaps the most egregious legacy of British colonialism).[20] These demands were flatly rejected by AIOC and British government officials, with the British minister of fuel and power noting that, while Iran was 'morally entitled to a royalty', to claim 'that they are entitled to 50 per cent, or . . . even more of the profits of enterprises to which they have made no contribution whatever, is bunk, and ought to be shown to be bunk'.[21]

Amid these fraught negotiations, political movements across Iran were demanding that the government nationalise AIOC's assets. During a period wracked by large street mobilisations and labour strikes in Abadan and elsewhere, the Iranian prime minister was assassinated in February 1951. He was replaced by Mohammad Mossadegh, a nationalist leader who strongly supported the popular calls for AIOC's nationalisation. On 2 May 1951, Mossadegh brought the Nationalisation Law into effect, cancelling the 1933 concession and taking AIOC's assets under the control of the Iranian state. The immediate reaction in Britain was one of shock, with British officials viewing the nationalisation as 'the insolent defiance of decency, legality and reason by a group of wild men in Iran who proposed to despoil Britain's government', according to the memoirs of Dean Acheson, then US Secretary of State.[22] But behind the predictable racialised tropes of British imperial rule lay a much deeper problem: Iran's actions were not so much driven by a dispute over royalties and profit share; at a more fundamental level they posed the question of who would actually *control* Iranian oil.[23] By nationalising AIOC, Mossadegh was making a broader assertion of Iran's national sovereignty – specifically, the country's right to determine how much oil should be produced, when and to whom it would be exported, and, potentially, at what price and currency it might be sold. For the largest Anglo-American oil companies, this scenario threatened to upset the careful arrangements they had put in place over the past half century with respect to the supply, price, and distribution of world oil. Moreover,

20 Abrahamian, 'The Coup in Iran', 186.

21 Mark Curtis, *Ambiguities of Power: British Foreign Policy since 1945*, London: Zed Books, 1995, 88.

22 Dean Acheson, *Present at the Creation*, New York: Signet, 1969, 507.

23 Abrahamian, 'The Coup in Iran'.

the Iranian move raised the real possibility of inspiring other oil-producing countries to take a similar step.[24]

Initially, direct military intervention to seize Iran's oil facilities was on the table and supported by both the British foreign secretary and defence minister in Clement Atlee's Labour government of the time.[25] After some debate, Britain opted not to invade, leading Winston Churchill to remonstrate later that 'a splutter of musketry would have ended the matter'.[26] Instead, British personnel were evacuated from Abadan and Iran's sterling assets in London were frozen. Aided by their control over shipping and transport infrastructure, the international oil majors led a boycott of Iranian oil that was widely observed and caused Iranian oil exports to fall from $400 million in 1950 to less than $2 million in 1953: without this infrastructure, Iran simply could not transport oil.[27] US oil firms were also given anti-trust exemption to coordinate oil supplies around the world, and production levels increased significantly in Saudi Arabia, Kuwait, and Iraq to cover any shortfall from the loss of Iranian oil. As these measures took hold, British and American officials were putting in place a plan to remove Mossadegh by military coup – and, in August 1953, Mossadegh was ousted. This was the first time the US government had deposed a foreign ruler during peacetime, and the CIA's leading role in this coup marked an important precursor for later US interventions such as the 1954 coup in Guatemala and the overthrow of Chile's Salvador Allende in 1973.[28]

Ultimately, the first attempt to nationalise oil resources in the Middle East had failed. As a result of the coup, Iran's Pahlavi monarchy, headed by Mohammed Reza Shah, returned to power in Iran and remained a

24 Homa Katouzian, *Musaddiq and the Struggle for Power in Iran*, London: I. B. Tauris & Co., 2009 (1990, 1999), 145. The Iranian nationalisation had reverberations even in countries that were not significant oil producers. In India, for example, Mossadegh's actions were openly supported by Indian politicians who saw them as inspiration for the nationalisation of British oil interests in the country. See Matthew Shutzer, 'Oil, Money and Decolonization in South Asia', *Past and Present* 258, no. 1, February 2023: 212–45, 220.

25 Curtis, *Ambiguities of Power*, 90.

26 Speller, 'A Splutter of Musketry'.

27 John Blair, *The Control of Oil*, New York: Pantheon Books, 1976, 79.

28 Tim Weiner, *Legacy of Ashes: The History of the CIA*, New York: Doubleday, 2007.

loyal US ally until the 1979 Iranian revolution.[29] Nonetheless, despite the apparent failure of nationalisation – and the bloody repression of the shah's dictatorship for the next twenty-six years – Iran's attempt to wrest control of its oil from Britain would irrevocably change the world oil market. From that moment on, AIOC (renamed British Petroleum in 1954) would lose its monopoly on oil in Iran. With American insistence, and the waiving of US anti-trust laws, Iranian oil was opened up to a new international consortium between the Seven Sisters, the Compagnie française des pétroles (CFP), and a group of smaller US oil majors.[30] The consortium would establish two operating companies registered and headquartered in Iran, with two Iranian directors on their boards. Iran's share of oil profits also increased, rising to the fifty–fifty share that was quickly becoming the norm across the world. The period of the agreement was reduced to twenty-five years, much shorter than the original sixty-year concession outlined in the 1933 agreement.[31]

In 1957, just four years after the overthrow of Mossadegh, Mattei's ENI also won the right to explore and develop oil in Iran. Crucially, this agreement provided for profit-sharing on the basis of the Mattei Formula – a 75:25 split – with the further kicker that Iran would only need to contribute half of the expenses if oil was actually discovered, otherwise ENI would bear the full costs of exploration. The agreement caused considerable consternation in Washington and London, with one secret US intelligence memo noting that the deal 'represents a significant and radical change from the pattern now prevalent throughout the Middle East in which profits are split 50-50'. It also noted that the result would almost certainly lead to 'demands in the Middle East that current arrangements be revised. Should the Italian concession prove to be

29 For a recent nuanced account of the connections between Pahlavi authoritarianism, oil, and US Cold War policy, see Gregory Brew, *Petroleum and Progress in Iran: Oil, Development, and the Cold War*, Cambridge: Cambridge University Press, 2022.

30 This arrangement was agreed in a memorandum signed on 9 April 1954, which established a consortium made up of British Petroleum (40 per cent), Royal Dutch Shell (14 per cent), SONJ, Socony, Socal, Texas and Gulf (8 per cent each), and CFP (6 per cent). This was modified a year later with each of the US companies giving up 1 per cent of their holding so that 5 per cent could be distributed to a consortium of a further nine independent American companies.

31 The agreement provided for the possibility of three five-year extensions, but these were conditional on a reduction in the area covered by the oil concession.

successful, these pressures will become increasingly difficult to resist. And the opening of this bargaining may well further contribute to the instability of the Western position in the area.'[32] One year later, the first US company broached the fifty–fifty line, when Pan American Petroleum (a subsidiary of Standard Oil Indiana) agreed a 75:25 deal in Iran in the same area as ENI's concession.[33]

The experience of Mossadegh and the 1953 coup highlighted the seismic shift that had taken place in the politics of the post-war world order. The leading role of the US in both planning the response to Mossadegh and steering the coup and its aftermath indicated that the apotheosis of British rule in the Middle East had passed. While British officials and MI6 played a major part in the coup, this was ultimately a US-led operation. Britain was unable to employ direct military force, despite the wishes of leading politicians and military personnel.[34] US leadership was also symbolised in the new arrangements for the exploitation of Iranian oil – the British monopoly was broken, and American firms controlled 40 per cent of the consortium that would run the country's oil industry. Perhaps even more significantly, the US would take the leading political role in Iran, building a tight partnership with the shah for the next two decades as a lynchpin of US foreign policy in the Gulf and wider Middle East. Underpinning this was US support to the shah's violent autocratic rule – including the 1957 establishment of the hated secret police, the SAVAK, the banning of political parties, and the widespread arrest and torture of opposition activists. And as we shall see in Chapter 9, a core element to how this relationship with the shah evolved – notably the recycling of oil revenues through arms sales and Iranian investments in US financial markets – would come to underly US relationships with other rulers of oil-rich states in the Middle East.

---

32 Memorandum from the Secretary of State's Special Assistant for Intelligence (Cumming) to the Under Secretary of State (Herter), 20 August 1957, history.state.gov/historicaldocuments/frus1955-57v12/d403.

33 Jane Perry Clark Carey and Andrew Galbraith Carey, 'Oil and Economic Development in Iran', *Political Science Quarterly* 75, no. 1, 1960: 66–86, 71.

34 Speller, 'A Splutter of Musketry'.

The Rise of OPEC

Iran's first foray into oil nationalisation was inseparable from a wider transnational climate of anti-colonial struggle and thought. Through his short reign, Mossadegh himself travelled and spoke before the International Court of Justice (ICJ) and the UN Security Council, framing the domestic jurisdiction over oil as a basic principle of national sovereignty.[35] As Christopher Dietrich points out in his illuminating study of anti-colonial elites and the oil industry, Mossadegh understood that self-determination ultimately required economic independence.[36] This sentiment was reflected in debates across a range of international institutions, including at the UN General Assembly, where a December 1952 resolution explicitly linked sovereignty to the right of countries to use and exploit their own national wealth.[37] These debates were not simply about the politics of the present but confronted a much longer history of colonial wealth extraction. Through the 1950s, notions such as 'unequal exchange' and various theorisations of the relationship between poorer and richer countries were beginning to take shape. In 1955, partly reflecting the agitation of newly independent states, the Third Committee of the UN General Assembly adopted a resolution stating that 'all peoples have the right to self-determination' and 'to freely dispose of their natural wealth and resources' – the only opposition to the resolution came from the three countries where the Seven Sisters were headquartered: the United States, Britain, and the Netherlands.[38]

This global anti-colonial context helps us understand how the control of oil was a question of transnational significance – not simply an internal issue for the major oil producing states. In the Middle East, a key illustration of these transnational anti-colonial synergies were the events that transpired in Egypt through the 1950s. In 1952, while Mossadegh was defending oil nationalisation in Iran, a popular Egyptian military officer, Gamal Abdel Nasser, led a coup that overthrew the country's

35 Christopher Dietrich, *Oil Revolution*, Cambridge: Cambridge University Press, 2017, 34.

36 Ibid., 35.

37 Ibid., 36.

38 Cyrus Bina, *A Prelude to the Foundation of Political Economy: Oil, War, and Global Polity*, London: Palgrave Macmillan, 2005, 106.

British-backed monarch, King Farouk. Nasser immediately set out a programme of social transformation that weakened the position of Egypt's tiny land-owning elite and improved living standards for the country's poorer classes.[39] The British military presence in Egypt ended in 1956, and Egypt's newfound sovereignty was crowned with the nationalisation of the British- and French-controlled Suez Canal that same year, a move that met with wide popular acclaim in other Arab states.[40] Nasser's rhetoric and actions resonated deeply across the region, inspiring other anti-colonial and nationalist movements, including in Sudan, Yemen, and nearby Algeria, where, in 1954, a bloody war for national liberation was launched against the French occupation of the country.[41] A major factor behind Nasser's regional appeal was his view of oil as 'an inalienable Arab right' that could be used to unify the Arab world against imperialism.[42] The slogan 'Arab Oil for the Arabs' soon gained widespread popularity, as did Nasser's strident condemnation of Saudi Arabia and other oil monarchies.[43]

These challenges to the old colonial order further consolidated a shift away from British and French dominance, and towards a much more active role for the US in the Middle East. On 5 January 1957, then US president Dwight Eisenhower elaborated the so-called Eisenhower Doctrine as part of his 'Special Message to the Congress on the Situation

39 Despite these measures, Nasser's relationship to the Left in Egypt was complicated and often fraught, involving repression and the stifling of independent social mobilisation. For a discussion of Nasserism and its relationship to nationalism and class formation in Egypt, see Adam Hanieh, 'Class, Nation, and Socialism', *International Politics Reviews* 9, 2021: 50–60.

40 The Anglo-Egyptian Treaty to end the British military occupation of the Suez Canal zone was concluded in 1954, but it took another two years for British troops to withdraw. It was around this time that Enrico Mattei developed his 75:25 formula, meeting with Nasser and launching joint projects with Egypt, including a pipeline linking the Suez Canal to Cairo.

41 The Algerian independence struggle was to profoundly shape the character of anti-colonial thought over subsequent decades. Although French rule did not end in Algeria until 1962, the Algerian revolt was a significant factor in pushing France to grant formal independence to Morocco and Tunisia in 1956.

42 Nelida Fuccaro, 'Oilmen, Petroleum Arabism and OPEC: New Political and Public Cultures of Oil in the Arab World, 1959–1964', in Dag Harald Claes and Giuliano Garavini (eds), *Handbook of OPEC and the Global Energy Order*, New York: Routledge, 2020, 15–30, 16.

43 Ibid. Nonetheless, Fuccaro points out that Nasser's call to use oil as an anti-imperialist weapon was mostly rhetorical, and lacked any concrete policies.

in the Middle East'.[44] Decrying the threat of 'international communism', Eisenhower guaranteed US readiness 'to employ the armed forces of the United States to assist to defend the territorial integrity and the political independence of any nation in the area'. Although Eisenhower's speech was framed by the supposed Soviet threat, much of what he said addressed events in Egypt, particularly the 1956 nationalisation of the Suez Canal. Eisenhower noted that the canal 'enables the nations of Asia and Europe to carry on the commerce that is essential if these countries are to maintain well-rounded and prosperous economies', and that the Middle East was a 'gateway between Eurasia and Africa . . . [with] about two-thirds of the presently known oil deposits of the world . . . The nations of Europe are peculiarly dependent upon this supply, and this dependency relates to transportation as well as to production.'

Eisenhower's doctrine was first put to the test in Jordan, where a pro-Nasser government, led by Suleiman al-Nabulsi, had come to power in 1956 and sought to curb the powers of the British-backed monarch, King Hussein. Building upon the anti-British sentiments that were running high following the nationalisation of the Suez Canal, Nabulsi cancelled a treaty between Jordan and Britain and called for closer relations with China, the Soviet Union, and Egypt. In response, King Hussein dismissed the Nabulsi government, banned all political parties, and placed Jordan under martial law. After Hussein expressed tacit support for the Eisenhower Doctrine, the US responded with financial and political aid, effectively supplanting Britain as the major Western ally of Jordan.[45] As this crisis unfolded, the US also moved to support pro-Western forces in Syria through backing conservative politicians and encouraging Turkish and Iraqi plots against the country. Here the attempts failed, serving only to generate further support for communist and Arab nationalist forces. In 1958, Egypt and Syria formed the United Arab Republic (UAR), a short-lived attempt by Nasser to form a union based on Arab nationalism, which was embraced by Syrian elites in an attempt to undercut the strength of the communist movement in Syria. Responding to the formation of the UAR, Jordan and Iraq formed the

44 Dwight Eisenhower, 'Special Message to the Congress on the Situation in the Middle East', 5 January 1957. Gerhard Peters and John T. Woolley, The American Presidency Project, presidency.ucsb.edu.

45 Lawrence Tal, 'Britain and the Jordan Crisis of 1958', *Middle Eastern Studies* 31, no.1, January 1995.

Arab Union, a federation of the two monarchies that was set up as a pro-Western counterpoint to Arab nationalism. As these Western allies struggled, British troops were despatched to Jordan to support King Hussein (with the help of Israel and the US), while US Marines landed in Lebanon to bolster the pro-Western government of President Camille Chamoun.

The oil-rich states of the Gulf were not immune from this political awakening. In Saudi Arabia, the racially segregated work camps of Aramco were hit by a huge wave of labour strikes through the 1950s.[46] In 1956, the Saudi monarch, King Saud, was met with large demonstrations during a visit to the Aramco headquarters in Dhahran, with protestors chanting slogans in support of Nasser and demanding an end to the influence of the US-controlled Aramco, the legalisation of trade unions, and the creation of a constitutional monarchy.[47] In Bahrain in 1954, the Gulf's first organised political movement was formed: among other activities, the Higher Executive Committee (HEC) protested in support of Egypt's nationalisation of the Suez Canal and called for the expulsion of the British political resident, Charles Belgrave, from the country.[48] The same year, a large militant trade union, the General Trade Union (GTU), was also established in Bahrain, working closely with communist activists from Iraq and Iran who had sought refuge in the country.[49] With British support, the ruling Al Khalifa monarchy crushed both the HEC and GTU in 1956, exiling many of their leaders to the British-controlled island of Saint Helena in the South Atlantic.[50] Pro-Nasser, nationalist, and communist movements were also visibly active in other states across the Arabian Peninsula.

46 Robert Vitalis, *America's Kingdom: Mythmaking on the Saudi Oil Frontier*, Stanford, CA: Stanford University Press, 2007, 177–84.

47 Giuliano Garavini, *The Rise and Fall of OPEC in the Twentieth Century*, London: Oxford University Press, 2019, 93.

48 The political resident was a British official who effectively held power in Bahrain. Belgrave was the 'head of the police, the supervisor of all government departments, [and sat] on higher and lower courts and municipal councils'. Omar Hesham AlShehabi, 'Divide and Rule in Bahrain and the Elusive Pursuit for a United Front: The Experience of the Constitutive Committee and the 1972 Uprising', *Historical Materialism* 21, no. 1 (2013): 94–127.

49 'Abd al-Hadi Khalaf, 'Labor Movements in Bahrain', *Middle East Report* 132, May/June 1985, merip.org.

50 Simon Smith, *Britain's Revival and Fall in the Gulf: Kuwait, Bahrain, Qatar, and the Trucial States, 1950–71*, London: Routledge, 2004, 22.

Of all the major oil-producing states, it was the 14 July 1958 revolution in Iraq that best captured the centrality of oil to the nationalist movements shaking the region at this moment.[51] Here, Iraqi military officers headed by Abd al-Karim Qasim and Abdul Salam Arif led an uprising that overthrew the pro-British monarch, King Faisal II, and his prime minister, Nuri al-Said. A range of different nationalist and left-wing currents were active in the tumult. These included the Communist Party of Iraq, one of the largest CPs in the Middle East, which commanded a significant mass base among the country's ethnically diverse working classes and peasantry. Another important political actor was the Iraqi section of the Ba'th Party, an organisation founded in Syria in 1947, whose strategy focused on winning over members of the armed forces.[52] In the end, Qasim emerged as the leader of the post-monarchical regime – a development that alarmed US officials because of his apparent closeness to the communist movement at the time.[53] With calls to nationalise the Iraq Petroleum Company (IPC) at fever pitch, the US government debated different means of overthrowing Qasim. These even included a plot to send a poisoned monogrammed handkerchief to one of Qasim's leading allies – the unlucky recipient of the bizarre scheme has never been publicly revealed, although scholars have speculated as to his identity.[54]

Against this febrile backdrop of nationalist revolt, the Middle East formed one link in a wider chain of radical struggles that stretched from Latin America, across Africa, through to Asia. The leaders of these struggles actively sought ways to foster deeper collaboration and transnational solidarity, and one chief step in this regard was the 1955 Bandung Conference, a gathering held in Indonesia that brought together twenty-nine newly independent countries in order to explore

51 For an illuminating account of Iraqi politics and the struggle to nationalise IPC across the decades following the Second World War, see Brandon Wolfe-Hunnicutt, *The Paranoid Style in American Diplomacy*, Oakland, CA: Stanford University Press, 2021.

52 A classic account of Iraq's political movements and the rise (and fall) of Qasim can be found in Hana Batatu, *The Old Social Classes and the Revolutionary Movements of Iraq: A Study of Iraq's Old Landed and Commercial Classes and of Its Communists, Ba'thists, and Free Officers*, Princeton, NJ: Princeton University Press, 1978.

53 Much like Nasser in Egypt, Qasim alternated between a strategy of accommodation and repression against the communist movement.

54 For a discussion of this plot and its place in American attempts to undermine Qasim, see Wolfe-Hunnicutt, *Paranoid Style*, ch. 2.

ways of strengthening ties outside the dominant Cold War powers. A principal instigator of Bandung was Ahmad Sukarno, who had become Indonesia's first president following the country's successful independence struggle against Dutch colonialism. Indonesia – like many of the Middle East states in attendance at Bandung – was oil-rich, and the dominance of the Seven Sisters emerged as a significant topic of discussion at the meeting.[55] Alongside calls for economic and cultural cooperation, world peace, and the respect of national sovereignty, the meeting's final communiqué urged 'exchange of information on matters relating to oil, such as remittance of profits and taxation, [that] might eventually lead to the formulation of common policies'.[56]

Building on these discussions at Bandung, oil experts from the Middle East and Latin America began to meet through the latter half of the 1950s in order to explore ways to establish a united front against the largest Western firms. The driving force in these discussions comprised two individuals who identified closely with the rising tide of nationalist sentiment at the time: Juan Pérez Alfonzo of Venezuela; and Abdullah Tariki of Saudi Arabia (known as the Red Sheikh among the international oil companies).[57] Tariki was then serving as director general of petroleum and mineral resources in the Saudi government, and was closely associated with a pro-Nasserist current within the Saudi ruling family, known as the Free Princes Movement.[58] He was also the central figure among a transnational network of Arab oil technocrats who embraced varying shades of Arab nationalism, and saw the control of oil as a means of political, cultural, and economic renaissance for the region.[59] By 1959, discussions between Pérez Alfonzo and Tariki culminated in a series of secret meetings held in the Cairo suburb of Maadi, along with other representatives from Kuwait, Iran,

55 The Middle East countries that attended Bandung were Egypt, Turkey, Yemen, Lebanon, Jordan, Syria, Iraq, Iran, Saudi Arabia, and Libya.

56 'Final communiqué of the Asian-African conference of Bandung', 24 April 1955, available at cvce.eu.

57 For an account of the oil companies' view of Tariki, see Vitalis, *America's Kingdom*, 208–10.

58 On this movement in the Saudi ruling family, see Madawi al-Rashid, *A History of Saudi Arabia*, Cambridge: Cambridge University Press, 2002, 108–20.

59 Fuccaro, 'Oilmen, Petroleum Arabism and OPEC', 17–18.

Syria, and Egypt.[60] The agreement that came of out these clandestine meetings, the so-called Maadi Pact, proposed the establishment of a joint committee that would monitor petroleum matters in the interests of oil-producing states. The participants agreed to seek an increase in the government profit share to 60:40, establish national oil companies that could develop the necessary expertise in upstream and downstream activities, and push to locate refinery operations locally rather than in North America or Europe.

Although the Maadi Pact was not made public until 1961, the key issues it tackled would not have surprised anyone familiar with the world oil industry at the time. In addition to the question of profit shares and the development of downstream expertise, the most pressing concern for oil-producing states was the system of posted prices described in the previous chapter. With excess international supplies of oil available on the world market during the late 1950s – due partly to the introduction of mandatory quotas on oil imports into the US in 1959, as well as the fact that more independent oil firms were now active in overseas production – the actual delivery price for oil was less than its posted price.[61] Responding to this attack on their bottom line, the largest international oil firms sought to reduce their tax obligations to producer governments by unilaterally lowering posted prices in 1959 and again in early 1960 – a move that naturally caused considerable anger among oil-producing states.[62]

Attempting to find some way to take control over oil pricing, Pérez Alfonzo and Tariki continued discussions after their initial agreement in Cairo. After preparatory meetings in Venezuela, they successfully brought representatives from Iraq, Iran, Saudi Arabia, Kuwait, and Venezuela to a conference in Baghdad in September 1960, at which the five countries announced the formation of the Organization of the Petroleum Exporting Countries (OPEC). As Garavini points out, this

60 The discussion here can only provide a telegraphic overview of the background and negotiations that led to the formation of OPEC. An excellent recent account can be found in Garavini, *The Rise and Fall of OPEC*.

61 Kokxhoorn, *Oil and Politics*, 182

62 In August 1960, for example, Exxon unilaterally reduced the posted price by just over 7 per cent, causing tax receipts of oil-producing states in the Middle East to fall significantly.

was the first global initiative led by governments from the so-called Third World, and predated the founding of the Non-Aligned Movement by a year.[63] At that time, the five countries constituting OPEC produced around 37 per cent of world crude and a majority of all oil outside of the US.[64] Over the following decade, the organisation's membership would continue to expand, incorporating Qatar (1961), Indonesia (1962), Libya (1962), Abu Dhabi (1967, replaced by the UAE in 1974), Algeria (1969), and Nigeria (1971). Today, most major oil producers – excepting the US, Canada, and Russia – are members.[65]

The Counter-revolutionary Turn

The establishment of OPEC in 1960 was followed by a series of counter-revolutionary events that profoundly shaped the character of the new organisation. In Saudi Arabia, the Free Princes Movement was quashed following the coming to power of a new Saudi king, Faisal, in 1964. Faisal's ascension was fully backed by the US and the major American oil companies, who saw in him an effective counterforce to the radicalising impulses of figures such as Abdullah Tariki. For his part, Tariki was exiled in 1962, forced to live out his life in Beirut and later Cairo, where he edited a magazine that railed against OPEC's timidity and called for oil nationalisation and the redistribution of oil wealth across the region.[66] Meanwhile, in Iraq, Abd al-Karim Qasim was ousted by a US-supported coup in February 1963, bringing the Ba'th Party to power amid a bloody massacre of thousands of

63 Garavini, *The Rise and Fall of OPEC*, 8.

64 Iran, Iraq, Kuwait, Saudi Arabia, and Venezuela produced 7.89 million barrels of oil per day in 1960, compared to US production of 7.04 million barrels per day. The world total in that year was 20.99 million barrels per day.

65 As of early 2024, OPEC had twelve member countries: five from the Middle East, six from Africa, and one from Latin America. These countries account for around 80 per cent of the world's proven oil reserves.

66 Fuccaro points out that, until recently, the legacy of Tariki has been largely erased in accounts of Arab nationalism and the popular imagining of this period: 'Oilmen, Petroleum Arabism and OPEC', 26. Juan Pablo Pérez Alfonzo had been oil minister in Venezuela, but a few years before his death in 1979 he was calling oil the 'devil's excrement' because of its associations with governmental waste, corruption, and authoritarianism.

communist and left-wing militants.[67] The killings were made possible in part because US intelligence agents had supplied the Ba'th with the details of Communist Party members in advance of the coup. As Brandon Wolfe-Hunnicutt observes, this moment was foundational to a new American counter-insurgency strategy, in which local US-backed forces were deployed to assassinate left-wing opponents. Henceforth, American military planners would systematically apply the same policy across the world – perhaps most horrifically illustrated in the killings of over a million Indonesians in a US-backed military coup against Ahmad Sukarno in 1965.[68]

Another crucial moment in the counter-revolutionary wave across the Middle East came with the 1967 Arab–Israeli War, which saw the Israeli military destroy the Egyptian and Syrian air forces and occupy the (Egyptian) Sinai Peninsula, (Syrian) Golan Heights, and Palestinian territories in the West Bank and Gaza Strip. Israel's victory dealt a decisive blow to the project of Arab unity and resistance that had crystallised most sharply under Nasser. In Egypt, the military defeat brought severe economic consequences: the Suez Canal remained shut for several years, the US halted deliveries of food aid to the country, and Israel's occupation of the Sinai Peninsula cut off access to oil reserves in the area.[69] As a result, Egypt's ability to acquire hard currency was heavily restricted at a time of growing military expenditures. Israel's victory was symbolically reinforced by Nasser's death in 1970 and the coming to power of Anwar Sadat, who subsequently moved to reverse many of Nasser's more radical policies. While nationalist and anti-colonial struggles continued to rock the Middle East after the war – notably in North and South Yemen, Libya, and the Dhofar province of Oman – a political vision that looked to a regionwide transformation became much more distant. Israel's defeat of the Arab states in 1967 also encouraged the United States to cement itself as the country's primary patron; from this

67 In November 1963, another coup occurred, bringing a group of pro-Nasserist officers to government. A further coup took place in 1968, returning the Iraqi branch of the Ba'th Party to power (including the country's future president, Saddam Hussein).

68 This US counter-insurgency strategy has been described by scholars as 'the Jakarta Method' because of the events in Indonesia.

69 See Aaron Jakes and Ahmad Shokr, 'Capitalism in Egypt, Not Egyptian Capitalism', in Joel Beinin, Bassam Haddad, and Sherene Seikaly (eds), *A Critical Political Economy of the Middle East and North Africa*, Stanford, CA: Stanford University Press, 2020, 123–42; 137–8.

point forward, billions of dollars' worth of US military hardware and financial support would flow to Israel as a fundamental leg of US power in the Middle East.

All of this illustrates the complex, contradictory significance of oil's place in the wider anti-colonial moment. The leading figures associated with OPEC's establishment, especially Pérez Alfonzo and Tariki, were deeply influenced and embedded in the radical anti-colonial movements of the period and held firmly to a vision of oil wealth as a tool to reverse the centuries of colonial predation. Their vision was by no means one of national autarchy. The anti-colonial spirit of the time was a transnational phenomenon that inevitably raised questions around the cross-border distribution of oil wealth, especially in regions such as the Middle East where colonial powers had played a major role in drawing national borders in the first place. The perception of oil as a source of wealth that everyone should benefit from – including the poor *outside* oil-rich states – was a palpable part of the political moment, and these wider regional antagonisms played into the negotiations between national elites and the international oil companies. Placing oil in the anti-colonial moment helps make sense of the racialised epithets that were later thrown at OPEC as a supposed cartel holding the world hostage during the oil crises of the 1970s. As we shall see in later chapters, OPEC was never a cartel – in reality, it was formed in opposition to the cartel-like behaviour of the Seven Sisters.

Yet it would be a mistake to present OPEC as some kind of leading vanguard of Third Worldism. To a large degree, OPEC was made possible through struggles that came from below – the strikes, protests, radical movements, and revolutions in (and in near proximity to) the main oil-producing states. The demands articulated by these movements were often directed *against* the rulers of countries where oil was found, notably the monarchies of Saudi Arabia, Iran, and the Gulf sheikhdoms. As the radical edge of the 1950s was blunted and these oil-rich states fell firmly within the orbit of American power, the potential for OPEC to become something other than an instrument for the enrichment of ruling elites disappeared. Instead, oil wealth helped create new social forces whose interests stood decidedly against the vast majority of those living in regions such as the Middle East. In this sense, OPEC's establishment highlights the problem with collapsing the so-called Third World into a simple opposition between colonised and colonising countries. Without careful attention to the internal social and economic differences within oil-producing areas – both nationally and regionally – it is impossible to understand the varied impacts of oil wealth. We shall return to these dynamics of nationalism and oil in Chapters 8 and 9 – but before doing so, it is necessary to look in greater depth at that other crucial component to oil's post-war place in capitalism: the petrochemical industry.

7

Petrochemicals and the Emergence of a Synthetic World

> I just want to say one word to you. Just one word . . . Plastics.
>
> Mr McGuire offering career advice to Benjamin in the *The Graduate* (1967)

There was little indication in the early 1900s of the sweeping transformations that would be ushered in by the petrochemical revolution just fifty years later. At the turn of the century, the chemical industry was largely focused on dyestuffs, utilising coal as the main precursor for chemical production. Globally, the industry was dominated by Germany's 'Big Three' chemical companies – BASF, Bayer, and Hoechst – which, in 1916, established the IG Farben (IGF) cartel in order to coordinate research and divide up European and international markets.[1] At that time, Germany's chemical industry supplied around 90 per cent of the world's synthetic dyes and was vastly superior to that of the US or any other European country. The US dye industry consisted of only seven firms in 1913, employing a mere 528 people with a product value of $2.4 million; by comparison, the German industry was worth $65 million and employed 16,000 people. German dominance was maintained through an aggressive policy of overseas patent protection: one 1912 survey estimated that 70 per

1 Peter Hayes, *Industry and Ideology: I.G. Farben in the Nazi Era*, New York: Cambridge University Press, 1987.

cent of all US patents granted on synthetic organic chemicals were German-owned.[2]

Much like the oil sector, the First World War gave a powerful impetus to the growth of the chemical industry across Europe and the US. In Germany, IGF played a central role in war efforts, pioneering the development of poison gas weapons using by-products from dye manufacturing, as well as synthetic nitrates that could replace saltpetre in the production of explosives and fertilisers.[3] All of this was extremely profitable for IGF, and despite Germany's defeat and the crushing terms dictated by the Treaty of Versailles, IGF's component companies remained intact and continued to be recognised as world leaders in chemical research and production after the war. In 1925, the cartel was formally reorganised as a single entity, becoming the largest corporation in Europe and the most important chemical company in the world.[4]

Across the Atlantic, leading US chemical companies also profited handsomely from the war.[5] In addition to increased demand for basic chemicals, a pivotal moment for the US chemical industry came with the passage of the Trading with the Enemy Act (TWEA) in October 1917 and the establishment of a new government position called the alien property custodian (APC). Through this office, the US state seized German-owned patents and German-owned businesses – specifically targeting the chemical industry. Initially, this property seizure was viewed as a temporary act – after all, 'the United States is not a pirate nation', opined a 1917 *New York Times* editorial.[6] However, less than a

2 Kathryn Steen, *The American Synthetic Organic Chemicals Industry: War and Politics, 1910–1930*, Chapel Hill: University of North Carolina Press, 2014, 17, 64, 55.

3 Synthetic nitrates allowed Germany to manufacture explosives despite the British blockade of Chile, then the world's major exporter of saltpetre.

4 Joseph Borkin, *The Crime and Punishment of I. G. Farben*, New York: Free Press, 1978, 37. The author of this fascinating book served on the team that prosecuted IGF for war crimes at the conclusion of the Second World War.

5 It has been estimated that DuPont earned $89 million through its wartime expansion, a windfall of retained earnings that enabled the company to expand research and production significantly after the war; see Keith Chapman, *The International Petrochemical Industry*, Oxford: Basil Blackwell, 1991, 65. Likewise, around 90 per cent of Dow Chemical's production was devoted to materials such as explosives and mustard gas during the war; see Jason Szilagyi, 'American Chemical Companies in the First World War', Proceedings of Armistice and Aftermath: A Michigan Tech Symposium on WW1, 2018, 9.

6 Benjamin Coates, 'The Secret Life of Statutes: A Century of the Trading with the Enemy Act', *Modern American History* 1, 2018: 151–72, 158.

year later, German industrial firms were to be denounced by the APC A. Mitchell Palmer as 'spy centres' and 'a knife at the throat of America'.[7] At the end of the war, the APC held an estimated $700 million worth of seized German assets in 30,000 trust accounts.[8]

For the nascent US chemical industry, the TWEA turned out to be an immensely fortunate turn of events. Just one week before armistice was declared on the Western Front, the act was amended to allow the permanent confiscation of chemical patents; thousands of these patents were then sold at a pittance of their reputed value to the newly established Chemical Foundation, a non-profit organisation that was headed by the APC himself. From there, the Chemical Foundation issued non-exclusive licences to US-owned chemical firms. This mechanism for appropriating German technical knowledge was developed in conjunction with leading American companies, including DuPont, the largest chemical firm in the US at the time, which drew up a precise list of patents that should be targeted for seizure.[9] The APC explicitly identified the TWEA and the Chemical Foundation as a means of Americanising the chemical industry, and in later Congress debates, one representative would describe the Act as 'the only safeguard . . . to the existence of the new chemical industry in this country'.[10] In this manner, the law constituted a massive lever of capital accumulation for America's burgeoning chemical industry.[11]

The establishment of the Chemical Foundation as a means of transferring patents within the US industry was formally designed to prevent the monopolisation of scientific techniques by a handful of firms. However, a small number of companies emerged as leaders through the 1920s, most notably DuPont; Union Carbide & Carbon Corporation; Dow Chemicals; and Monsanto. These firms benefited greatly from the transfer of German patents, applying new techniques to expand their output and range of basic chemicals. Of particular importance to these firms was the expanding automobile industry, which provided a steady source of demand for new chemical products at a scale that made

7 Ibid.

8 Steen, *The American Synthetic Organic Chemicals Industry*, 23.

9 Ibid., 299.

10 Coates, 'The Secret Life', 159.

11 The TWEA became a permanent mechanism of US foreign policy, including the later use of international sanctions. For a discussion, see ibid.

production profitable. US chemical companies grew in lockstep with the major car manufacturers, supplying fuel additives such as the anti-knocking agent tetraethyl lead, synthetic rubber for tyres, and the first synthetic plastic, Bakelite, for components such as spark plugs, batteries, steering wheels, and instrument panels. Indeed, the close association between the chemical and automotive industries was expressed in joint ownership structures – DuPont, for example, owned up to 38 per cent of General Motors in the interwar years, and when Pierre du Pont passed the presidency of the company to his brother in 1919, he went on to become chairman of General Motors.[12]

From Coal to Oil: The Petrochemical Revolution

The 1920s and 1930s were vital decades in basic chemical research, focused particularly on polymers, large molecules made up of repeated chains of smaller molecular units, called monomers. The German scientist Hermann Staudinger first discovered this basic structure of polymers in 1920.[13] His ideas were initially met with scepticism but soon found practical application in the development of new synthetic compounds. Through the interwar years numerous polymers were discovered (mostly accidentally) in the labs of the largest chemical companies, including plasticised polyvinyl chloride (PVC) (1926), neoprene synthetic rubber (1930), polyethylene (1933), nylon (1935), and Teflon (1938).[14] However, with the exception of nylon – developed by DuPont scientists over an eleven-year period – these polymers generally lacked significant commercial application. Most importantly, coal remained the key feedstock utilised in their production and in the wider chemical industry.

The Second World War, however, drove three major changes to chemical production: first, an immense increase in the diversity, output, and commercialisation of polymers; second, the emergence of the US as

12 Steen, *The American Synthetic Organic Chemicals Industry*, 443.

13 Staudinger was later employed as a consultant by IGF during the interwar years; see Chapman, *International Petrochemical Industry*, 45. He was nonetheless sympathetic to pacifist ideas, and his first wife Dorothea was an active socialist.

14 The leading developers of these polymers were IGF, DuPont, the British firm ICI, and Dow.

the dominant global chemical power (along with the decline of the German chemical industry); and, third, most significant for the major oil firms, a shift towards the use of oil rather than coal as the basic feedstock for polymer production. These three changes were closely related, implicitly pitting the German and US chemical industries against one another through the mediation of war and a different choice of fossil fuel substrate. In both Germany and the US, there was an intimate connection between the development of industrial chemical techniques, the rapid growth of the leading chemical firms, and the initiative and material support of the state.

In the years preceding the war, IGF continued to be the clear leader in the world chemical industry despite the increased prominence of US firms such as DuPont and Dow Chemicals. IGF was central to Nazi war preparations, with the company's efforts focused particularly on the use of coal to produce synthetic fuels and artificial rubber. Hitler had identified these materials as essential to the success of Germany's future expansion. Lacking the direct colonies of other European powers and facing the surety of naval blockade on rubber supplies from Malaysia, Nazi planners placed enormous priority on the development of synthetic alternatives that could ensure German self-sufficiency. By 1937, IGF had become 'completely Nazified . . . almost all of the members of the I.G. managing board who did not already belong now joined [the Nazis] . . . all Jewish officials of I.G. were removed, including a third of the supervisory board'. The company was essentially transformed into the industrial arm of Germany's military – producing almost all the country's synthetic gasoline (derived from coal), as well as 'synthetic rubber, poison gases, magnesium, lubricating oil, explosives, methanol, sera, plasticizers, dyestuffs, nickel, and thousands of other items necessary for the German war machine'.[15]

15 Borkin, *Crime and Punishment*, 58, 60. This relationship with the Nazi war machine was highly profitable for IGF: with each successful German conquest, it took over factories and looted assets of rival European firms – a stepwise expansion encompassing Austria, Czechoslovakia, Poland, Norway, and France. IGF also benefited enormously from the seizure of Jewish property and the use of forced labour in Hitler's concentration camps – indeed, the firm built a huge industrial complex in Auschwitz for the production of synthetic rubber and oil that was run by an 'almost limitless reservoir of death camp labor . . . [and] used as much electricity as did the entire city of Berlin' (ibid., 7). The company's profits between 1941 and 1943 were nearly five times those of 1935, and huge amounts were invested in the expansion of new plants such as those at

Prior to its entrance into the war in December 1941, the US similarly sought to develop synthetic polymers as potential replacements for metals, natural rubber, wood, and cotton.[16] Due to the looming shortage of basic raw commodities, these new materials would find widespread use in aircraft, submarines, tanks, tents, parachutes, and other essential military items – one US army order even mandated that the rubber combs carried by soldiers be replaced by a plastic version.[17] Over the course of the war, production of vinyl resins (such as PVC) increased nearly fiftyfold; acrylic polymers (such as 'Plexiglas') increased by a factor of ten, and overall production of plastics nearly quadrupled.[18] Even the development of radar technology and the atomic bomb was dependent on two newly invented polymers, polyethylene and Teflon. The First World War is sometimes described as the 'Chemists' War' due to the innovations it drove in the development of poison gas and other weapons – but given the supreme importance of new synthetic materials to war efforts in the Second World War, it would be little exaggeration to term this later conflict the 'Polymers War'.

As with Germany, US production of these new polymers initially utilised pre-war technologies based on the conversion of coal and other organic materials. Over the course of the war, however, a radical transformation occurred in manufacturing techniques. Driven by escalating military demands, production shifted decisively towards the use of oil as the primary feedstock for synthetic manufacture. This transition was enabled by innovations in petroleum cracking, a

---

Auschwitz. For documentation and further discussion, see Wollheim Memorial, 'I. G. Farben at the End of the Second World War', wollheim-memorial.de. Esther Leslie presents a detailed account of Farben's link to the Nazis as part of her investigation of Western aesthetics and the rise of the chemical industry in *Synthetic Worlds: Nature, Art and the Chemical Industry*, London: Reaktion Books, 2005.

16 With the entry of the US to the war in December 1941, the old Trading with the Enemy Act was once again employed to confiscate German patents, which were made available to any member of the general public willing to pay $15; see Arnold Krammer, 'Technology Transfer as War Booty: The U.S. Technical Oil Mission to Europe, 1945', *Technology and Culture* 22, no. 1, January 1981: 68–103, 75.

17 Susan Freinkel, 'A Brief History of Plastic's Conquest of the World', *Scientific American*, 29 May 2011, scientificamerican.com.

18 John Kenly Smith, 'The American Chemical Industry since the Petrochemical Revolution', in Louis Galambos, Takashi Hikino, and Vera Zamagni (eds), *The Global Chemical Industry in the Age of the Petrochemical Revolution*, Cambridge: Cambridge University Press, 2007, 175.

technique that oil companies had been experimenting with through the 1920s and 1930s as part of efforts to increase the quantities of gasoline produced in their refineries.[19] In addition to improving gasoline output, cracking also generated significant quantities of other highly reactive hydrocarbons – known as olefins and aromatics – which could be utilised as building blocks for synthetic polymers. In the minds of US government planners, this new petrochemical industry was fundamental to the supply of essential military materials, including various plastics, aviation fuels, and chemicals such as toluene (used in the manufacture of explosives).[20] By shifting to petroleum as a basic feedstock, the abundance of US oil would enable these materials to be produced cheaply and at scale.[21]

Considerable levels of US government funding were thus directed into petrochemical research and refinery construction during the war, and manufacturing volumes for basic petrochemicals grew at an unprecedented pace. Between 1940 and 1946, the production of ethyl benzene (used in synthetic rubber) rose from 500 to 135,000 tons, ethylene dichloride (for PVC) from 9,000 to 27,000 tons, ethyl chloride (anti-knocking gasoline additive) from 3,000 to 28,500 tons, and ethylene oxide (an antifreeze and fumigation agent) from 41,500 to 78,000 tons.[22] These products were not only utilised by the US military but were essential to supporting other Allied powers. Notably, SONJ's Baton Rouge refinery played a vital role in producing petrochemical feedstocks and was the largest source of aviation fuel for the Allies during the war.[23]

19 Prior to the Second World War, this largely involved the use of very high temperatures and pressures to achieve greater control over the yield of refinery products, a technique known as thermal cracking. In the early years of the war, however, this was replaced by catalytic cracking – the use of a catalyst to achieve the same results but in easier operating conditions. This change in technique both cheapened the cost of production and enabled a substantial increase in refinery volumes.

20 Toluene production had traditionally derived from coal; by 1944, however, 81 per cent of US toluene was made from petroleum. See Chapman, *International Petrochemical Industry*, 74.

21 Kenneth Geiser, *Materials Matter: Toward a Sustainable Materials Policy*, Cambridge, MA: MIT Press, 2001, 43.

22 Peter Spitz, *Primed for Success: The Story of Scientific Design Company*, New York: Springer, 2019, 40.

23 More than half of total capital expenditure on Baton Rouge came from the US government; see Chapman, *The International Petrochemical Industry*, 74. In 2010, ExxonMobil used this support to sue the US government for reimbursement on

Baton Rouge was said to 'have saved England in the Battle of Britain' – it also inaugurated the 136 km strip of toxic land later known as Cancer Alley; populated mostly by African American residents, around a quarter of US petrochemical production is now located there.[24]

Arguably the most important petroleum-based industry that emerged in the US during the war was that of synthetic rubber. Before 1939, 90 per cent of the world's natural rubber originated from just three countries – Ceylon (Sri Lanka), India, and Malaysia – but with Japan's conquest of Asia, US access to these supplies disappeared.[25] The US government took various initiatives to conserve rubber – including mandating the first ever national speed limit in May 1942 – but these measures could not satisfy the tremendous demand for rubber coming from all branches of the military.[26] Indeed, just six months after the US entered the war in December 1941, Ferdinand Eberstadt, then chair of the Army and Navy Munitions Board and destined to be an instrumental figure in the creation of the National Security Council, claimed that the US would 'have no alternative but to call the whole thing off' – meaning the war – unless synthetic rubber could be produced in large enough quantities.[27] Driven by these fears, the US government embarked on a massive programme to build synthetic rubber plants that could produce rubber derived from petroleum.[28] These plants would be government-owned, but operated by private firms on a 'cost plus

---

environmental damages it had been required to pay at this refinery. In 2020, the US government lost the case and was ordered to pay $20.3 million and partially foot the bill for future clean-up costs.

24 Spitz, *Primed for Success*, 32. Cancer Alley stetches from Baton Rouge to New Orleans. The area became the centre of the US petrochemical industry because racial segregation enabled firms to locate heavily polluting refineries there without political opposition. See Richard Misrach and Kate Orff, *Petrochemical America*, New York: Aperture Books, 2014.

25 Paul Samuelson, 'The US Government Synthetic Rubber Program 1941–1955, An Examination in Search of Lessons for Current Energy Technology Commercialization Projects', Working Paper MIT-EL 76-027WP, November 1976, 4.

26 The so-called Victory Speed Limit lasted from May 1942 until the end of the war in August 1945.

27 Cited in William M. Tuttle Jr, 'The Birth of an Industry: The Synthetic Rubber "Mess" in World War II', *Technology and Culture* 22, no. 1, January 1981: 35–67, 38.

28 Initially, there was an inter-industry dispute over whether synthetic rubber should be produced from alcohol (derived from grain) or from petroleum. In the end, oil companies won out; for an account of these disputes, see Tuttle, 'Birth of an Industry'; and Chapman, *The International Petrochemical Industry*, 69–72.

management fee' basis. By the end of the war, over 2 million tons of synthetic rubber had been produced by more than fifty plants.[29] This huge expansion permanently altered the nature of American rubber production: in 1941, just under 99 per cent of all US domestic rubber consumption was natural; by 1945, this figure had fallen to 15 per cent.[30] Perhaps most remarkably, the US – which up to 1939 was the world's largest importer of rubber – emerged from the war as its largest exporter.

With the end of the war, the US government sought to divest ownership of this immense network of rubber plants to the private sector. Plans were initially delayed by the beginning of the Korean War in 1950, but just ten days after the end of that conflict the US Congress passed the Rubber Producing Facilities Disposal Act of 1953. Much like the seizure of German patents in the wake of the First World War, this act represented another major transfer of wealth to the US chemical industry, with plants worth a total of $700 million sold for a mere $260 million. During Congressional hearings in 1954, one opponent protested that the sale should properly be 'labelled a giveaway', and accurately predicted that it 'would bring about complete domination of the industry by a few mammoth corporations'.[31] Indeed, the ultimate beneficiaries of the sale were a handful of oil, rubber, and chemical firms, including SONJ, Shell, Goodyear, Firestone, and Dow Chemicals. By 1958, just six firms controlled 79 per cent of all US plant capacity for the main type of synthetic rubber production.[32]

The story of rubber illustrates the extraordinary impact that the petrochemical revolution would have on American capitalism and the US oil industry. At the beginning of the war, a commercial petrochemical industry did not exist in the US. By 1950, half of the US output of organic chemicals would be made from petrochemicals; and by the end of the 1950s, this figure would reach just under 90 per cent.[33] This transformation of synthetic production was not simply a result of

29 Kenly Smith, 'American Chemical Industry', 175.

30 Tuttle, 'Birth of an Industry', 65.

31 James Patton, President of the National Farmers Union, in United States Senate, *Rubber Facilities Disposal: Hearings before a Subcommittee of the Committee on Banking and Currency*, 84th Congress, First Session, on S. 691, 4a.

32 Stanley E. Boyle, 'Government Promotion of Monopoly Power: An Examination of the Sale of the Synthetic Rubber Industry', *Journal of Industrial Economics* 9, no. 2, April 1961: 151–69, 158.

33 Kenly Smith, 'American Chemical Industry', 178.

technological innovation or the contingent choices of US war planners. Crucially, the petrochemical revolution embodied the fundamental energy shift that we have traced over preceding chapters: the rise of oil as the fulcrum of fossil capital. The expansion of the oil industry massively increased the availability of basic feedstocks for chemical production; this considerably cheapened the cost of material manufacture because the inevitable by-products of fuel production were now transformed into a profitable input for petrochemicals. What was essentially waste had suddenly become an indispensable raw material. In short, at the heart of the petrochemical revolution was a radical change to the nature of production itself: *the materiality of commodity production had become a derivative – or a by-product – of the production of energy*.

Moreover, and no less significantly, all of this occurred under the virtual domination of the US oil industry. As we have seen, at the time of the petrochemical revolution, the US was the world's largest producer of crude oil, and also held over 70 per cent of global refining capacity (compared to only 7 per cent in Western Europe).[34] In the decade that followed the Second World War, almost all the world's production capacity for ethylene – the fundamental building block of petrochemical production, now frequently described as the 'world's most important chemical' – was located in the US.[35] This gave US oil companies, especially the five American Sisters, substantial control over all basic petrochemical production.[36] There was thus a mutually reinforcing relationship between the rise of a US-centred world market, the shift to an oil-based global energy regime, and the revolution in commodity production inaugurated by petrochemicals.

34 Chapman, *International Petrochemical Industry*, 60.

35 In 1950, more than 98 per cent of the world's ethylene capacity was based in the US; see ibid., 17.

36 As we saw in Table 5.2, about 80 per cent of the world's cracking capacity was located in the US in 1949, and about 40 per cent of the US total was controlled by the five American Sisters.

Europe Follows

In late 1944, with Allied leaders looking in growing anticipation to the end of the war, the issue of Germany's long-standing and powerful chemical industry loomed large in the various scenarios of post-war planners.[37] Much of the physical infrastructure of German industry lay in rubble or was in territory that had fallen into the hands of the Soviet Union. There was, however, considerable scientific expertise and decades of chemical experimentation scattered throughout research facilities and laboratories across Germany. Cognisant of this potential treasure trove of knowledge, US oil company executives began lobbying US officials in August 1944 for a plan to seize this research in the event of Germany's defeat. Competing interests in the US government initially failed to agree on how to approach this issue, but by the end of the year an audacious scheme had cohered.

Two-dozen leading US oil company managers and scientists were temporarily drafted as colonels of the US Army, provided with uniforms, and secretly ushered into German territory to visit industrial facilities and collect documents from IGF and other German firms.[38] Between February and August 1945, these teams gathered material that ran to over 300,000 pages; their visits continued after the war, and by 1948, a dedicated office set up by President Truman would report that 'more than five million microfilmed pages of technical documents, all in German, containing drawings, flow sheets, reports of chemical experiments and meetings of German technical societies' were still being processed. One later historian would describe these events as akin to 'technology transfer' through 'war booty', commenting that 'never in the history of the modern world has a sophisticated industrial nation had at its complete disposal the industrial secrets of another nation'.[39]

With the conclusion of the war, the inextricable connections between German fascism and the German chemical industry were formally recognised at the Nuremberg war crime trials. Twenty-four leading

37 For a detailed account of the development of the West German chemical industry after the Second World War and its transition to oil, see Raymond G. Stokes, *Opting for Oil: The Political Economy of Technological Change in the West German Industry, 1945–1961*, Cambridge: Cambridge University Press, 1994.

38 Ibid., 41–7.

39 Krammer, 'Technology Transfer', 97.

executives of IGF were indicted and tried at Nuremberg, with thirteen eventually found guilty of war crimes including slavery, mass murder, and plunder.[40] In a pattern replicated throughout post-war German big business, however, those convicted received extremely short prison sentences and early pardons, and were quickly reintegrated into the top echelons of West German industry. IGF was broken up into its original constituent parts: Bayer, Hoechst, and BASF. Heading each of these companies into the 1950s and 1960s were those same IGF managers of the Nazi era, including those who had served time for war crimes.[41] Beyond the reconstitution of the Big Three under the authority of former war criminals, other leading IGF directors were released early from prison and went on to prosperous careers with the US government and American chemical firms.[42]

Alongside the diffusion of German scientific knowledge, post-war planners also sought systematically to change Germany's chemical industries away from the use of coal-based technologies towards oil.[43] As we saw in Chapter 5, the Potsdam Conference of 16 July 1945 went so far as to ban Germany from utilising coal as a feedstock for fuel production – thereby shifting the country's manufacture of liquid fuels

40 Borkin, *Crime and Punishment*, 121. Another of the post-war revelations was IGF's deep ties to SONJ, which involved the exchange of patents, technical assistance, and secret agreements to divide global markets between the two companies. These ties continued throughout the war itself and meant that IGF 'received money for every litre of aeroplane fuel produced in the US and delivered to Britain'; see Leslie, *Synthetic Worlds*, 213. The head of Texaco, Torkild Rieber, was also an ardent fascist sympathiser who provided cheap oil to Franco during the Spanish Civil War and to the Nazis in the Second World War; see Adam Hochschild, 'The Untold Story of the Texaco Oil Tycoon Who Loved Fascism', *Nation*, 21 March 2016.

41 IGF board member Friedrich Jähne, who had been convicted of war crimes at Nuremberg, was hired as the chairman of the Hoechst supervisory board in 1955. Fritz Ter Meer, also convicted of war crimes at Nuremberg, became chair of the board of directors for Bayer in 1956. IGF board member Carl Wurster, former Wehrwirtschaftsführer (military economy leader) and 1943 recipient of a Knight's Cross for War Service, became chief executive of BASF in 1952 (he had been acquitted of war crimes at Nuremberg).

42 One of these was Otto Ambros, who was found guilty of crimes against humanity (the use of slave labour) at Auschwitz and is credited with the invention of Sarin gas. Granted clemency by the US government in 1951, he became an advisor to the US Army Chemical Corps and various leading US chemical firms, including Dow Chemicals. 'Ambros, Otto / W.R. Grace and Company', Ronald Reagan Presidential Library and Museum, October 2020, reaganlibrary.gov.

43 See Stokes, *Opting for Oil*.

to oil instead.[44] As oil became more available and necessary infrastructure such as pipelines were built, BASF, Hoechst, and Bayer entered the petrochemical industry through partnerships with British and US oil firms. By 1961, oil and gas had overtaken coal as the primary feedstock for the German chemical industry – and by 1963, 63 per cent of all German chemical production was derived from petroleum.[45]

A similar transition away from coal occurred in other West European states. Despite some initial opposition by US oil companies who feared losing their dominant position in world oil markets, funding from the Marshall Plan supported a large expansion of European refining capacity in the immediate post-war years.[46] European refinery capacity increased fivefold between 1948 and 1955, and by 1960 Europe's share of global refining capacity stood at 16 per cent (up from 7 per cent in 1940).[47] The increase in the output of refined oil derivatives enabled a decisive shift towards petroleum-based production of chemicals. This was most evident in the UK, where more investment went into petrochemicals than any other branch of British industry between 1948 and 1958.[48] By 1962, around two-thirds of all British chemical production would be petroleum-based. In that same year, petrochemicals averaged 58 per cent of chemical production across Western Europe as a whole – a figure that had increased from negligible levels in just over a decade.[49]

This expansion of the European petrochemical industry occurred under the auspices of the Seven Sisters – especially SONJ, Texaco, British Petroleum, and Shell – sometimes acting in joint ventures with other large West European chemical firms such as BASF, Bayer, and the

44 A. Stranges, 'Germany's Synthetic Fuel Industry, 1927–1945', in J. E. Lesch (ed.), *The German Chemical Industry in the Twentieth Century*, vol. 18, *Chemists and Chemistry*, Dordrecht: Springer, 2000, 213.

45 Ulrich Wengenroth, 'The German Chemical Industry after World War II', in Galambos, Hikino, and Zamagni, *Global Chemical Industry*, 149.

46 David S. Painter, 'Oil and the Marshall Plan', *Business History Review* 58, no. 3, Autumn 1984: 359–83.

47 Chapman, *International Petrochemical Industry*, 83.

48 Wyn Grant, 'The United Kingdom', in Galambos, Hikino, and Zamagni, *Global Chemical Industry*, 299.

49 Chapman, *International Petrochemical Industry*, 82. The frontrunner in this transition was the UK. British scientists had participated in the secret teams that visited IGF plants between 1944 and 1945, and the UK was the first West European country to utilise petroleum feedstocks for chemical production.

UK-based Imperial Chemicals Industries.[50] For the integrated oil firms, the petrochemical industry was the next logical downstream step, enabling them to profit from the by-products generated during the refining of fuel oils for industry and electricity plants.[51] In this manner, the expansion of oil as a post-war energy source in Europe was co-active with the rise of a European petrochemical industry dominated by the Seven Sisters.[52] The crude oil that fed this nascent petrochemical production came largely from oil fields controlled by the Seven Sisters in the Middle East, and thus a direct thread connected the emergence of a synthetic world with the patterns of colonial domination that we have traced in earlier chapters. As an integral part of Europe's broader transition to oil in the post-war period, the petrochemical revolution was now as much a Middle Eastern story as it was a European one.

Chemical Century

The post-war petrochemical revolution inaugurated an unprecedented transformation in patterns of industrial production and consumption. The synthetic materials derived from petroleum became ubiquitous and created new industries – such as plastics and packaging – and it reshaped social, cultural, and aesthetic practices.[53] Business historians have subsequently described this period as the 'chemicalisation' of industry, with virtually all forms of commodity production linked to petrochemicals in some manner. In the US, the chemical industry moved to the centre of economic development through the 1950s and 1960s,

50 For a survey of different European countries, see Galambos, Hikino, and Zamagni, *Global Chemical Industry*. For a detailed analysis of the relationship between West German chemical firms and the large integrated oil companies, especially British Petroleum and Shell, see Stokes, *Opting for Oil*, 131–75.

51 The main by-product was naphtha, a hydrocarbon fraction that is produced alongside the manufacture of fuel oil and is an essential raw material in the production of plastics. With the expansion of fuel oil manufacture, oil companies found a use for their surpluses of naphtha.

52 It also strengthened their control of a network of shipping terminals, pipelines, refineries, and petrochemical plants, mostly concentrated in Northern Europe, particularly the UK, the Netherlands, and West Germany.

53 For analysis of the relationship between the chemical industry and artistic forms from the era of coal through to the post-war petrochemical revolution, see Leslie, *Synthetic Worlds*.

experiencing growth rates double that of GDP and profit rates at least 25 per cent higher than those found in other manufacturing industries.[54] With the chemical business unmatched 'by any other in growth, earnings, and potential', normally circumspect pundits of the post-war era foresaw a future in which 'most industries will be absorbed into the chemical industry'.[55] This was the beginning – proclaimed a *Fortune* magazine headline in 1950 – of the 'Chemical Century'.

One notable consequence of this petrochemical revolution was its impact on science. With chemical research located ever more at the heart of commodity production, the chemicalisation of industry was associated with a parallel phenomenon, more broadly described by Harry Braverman as the 'transformation of science itself into capital'.[56] In the US, this was expressed through the growing collaboration between the chemical industry and university chemistry departments, as well as the increasing prominence of chemical engineering as a distinct branch of academic research.[57] Chemical engineering itself became organised largely around the notion of unit operations, a kind of theoretical Taylorism that approached chemistry through a small number of generic processes (including separation, crystallisation, distillation) easily transferable across the development of new synthetic products. Large firms became major donors to chemistry departments, often mandating the prioritisation of research connected to product development. At the same time, chemical engineers gained increasing prominence as managers and executives of chemical firms, coming to identify 'the scientific transformation of America and the corporate transformation of America [as] one and the same'.[58]

With science increasingly an appurtenance to business calculus, the internal organisation of firms in the chemical industry was also transformed. Historians of the chemical industry frequently point out that the major challenge presented by petrochemicals for business was not the act of discovering new chemical products – this was relatively

54 Kenly Smith, 'American Chemical Industry', 169.

55 'The Chemical Century', *Fortune Magazine*, March 1950: 116–21, 70.

56 Harry Braverman, *Labor and Monopoly Capital*, New York: Monthly Review Press, 1974, 167.

57 Spitz, *Primed for Success*, 20–1.

58 David F. Noble, *America by Design: Science, Technology, and the Rise of Corporate Capitalism*, New York: Alfred A. Knopf, 1977, 19.

straightforward given the basic structure of polymers – rather, the main issue was inventing a *use* for them. As a result, chemical firms increasingly prioritised activities such as marketing and product commercialisation. In turn, companies began to structure themselves around individual product lines rather than generic activities. Associated with this internal reorganisation were innovations in accounting – DuPont, for example, pioneered the introduction of return on investment (ROI) as an accounting measure, a means to capture the costs of invention, marketing, and revenue for discrete products.[59] And because this enabled individual units to be easily valued and then offered for sale by their parent companies, this form of organisation propelled repeated waves of consolidation in the chemical industry. Consequently, the industry became dominated by a small number of the largest oil firms and a few specialised chemical companies such as DuPont.[60]

At the same time, a handful of basic petrochemical products (such as ethylene, propylene, benzene, and toluene) formed the core inputs for more complex derivative chemicals. The production of these essential precursors was increasingly associated with huge increases in the size of petrochemical plants as producers sought to achieve economies of scale. One industry expert described this as the proliferation 'of massive, integrated industrial complexes' where basic petrochemical production was connected to the manufacture of more complex derivative products through a spaghetti-like maze of pipes, tubes, and specialised storage hubs.[61] Between 1950 and 1970, the size of such plants in the US increased by a factor of ten and could take up to forty-two months to construct, with some components so large that they required on-site manufacture.[62] These massive upfront costs typically exceeded the

59 Alfred D. Chandler Jr, 'The Competitive Performance of U.S. Industrial Enterprises Since the Second World War', *Business History Review* 68, Spring 1994: 1–72, 11–12.

60 By the 1960s, it was estimated that just fifteen companies controlled most US petrochemical production; see Geiser, *Materials Matter*, 49. This concentration and centralisation of capital is a long-standing feature of the chemical industry. Indeed, the 1925 formation of IGF occurred because the German chemical giant BASF could not afford the commercialisation of a newly discovered means of producing synthetic fuels on its own; see Borkin, *Crime and Punishment*, 39.

61 M. F. Cantley, 'The Scale of Ethylene Plants: Backgrounds and Issues', IIASA Working Paper. IIASA, Laxenburg, Austria, WP-79-043, 1979, 17.

62 Ibid., 12.

capacity of individual firms, and thus further drove significant industry consolidation through mergers, exclusive partnership agreements, and joint ventures.[63]

While the basic costs of materials, fuel, and machinery in the petrochemical industry were high, the proportion of labour costs was extremely low – indeed, considerably less than other industrial sectors. In this respect, petrochemicals were one of the first branches of industry to exhibit what Ernest Mandel described as the 'third technological revolution': almost full automation, where plants were designed around 'automated flow systems', integrated networks of machinery, containers and pipes that ran continuously with only a few workers monitoring the process.[64] Indeed, the cost of labour for the petrochemical industry in the early 1970s was calculated at much less than 1 per cent of total production expenses.[65] And, as the size of petrochemical complexes increased, the need for extra labour was estimated by industry analysts as 'not significantly different from zero': that is, for a certain size of plant, it was theoretically possible to increase plant output to '*any level* by merely increasing other inputs while holding labor at a fixed level'.[66] For these reasons, petrochemicals have consistently had higher levels of productivity than any other branch of industry.

But the degree to which petrochemicals drove the 'replacement of living labour by dead labour' extends far beyond petrochemical plants themselves. At a more elemental level, petrochemicals marked a *qualitative shift in the nature of commodity production*: the substitution of naturally occurring, labour-intensive goods – often sourced from far-flung colonial territories – with synthetic materials that had an average

63 Another structural change associated with this process was the emergence of specialised chemical engineering firms that developed petrochemical processes and innovations in plant designs and would then license these technologies to manufacturers (rather than proprietary engineering knowledge remaining exclusively in the hands of individual firms). This innovation helped encourage the post-war diffusion of petrochemical plants through Europe and Japan. The leading example was the Scientific Design Company, which, after a series of acquisitions, is today owned by a joint venture between Saudi Arabia's SABIC (see Chapter 12) and the Swiss multinational, Clariant; for a history of the company, see Spitz, *Primed for Success*. Many of the world's largest engineering firms (such as KBR) have their origins in these activities.

64 Ernest Mandel, *Late Capitalism*, London: Verso, 1972, 184–223.

65 Charles Levinson, *Capital, Inflation and the Multi-nationals*, London: Allen & Unwin, 1971, 228–9.

66 Cantley, 'Scale of Ethylene', 27.

necessary labour content approaching zero. This was not simply an increase in the quantity or scale of production. Rather, the functional attributes of natural materials such as wood, cotton, or rubber would now be served by petroleum-derived chemicals.[67] By de-coupling commodity production from nature, there was a radical reduction in the time taken to produce commodities, and an end to any limits on the quantity and diversity of goods produced. This qualitative transformation in the substance of commodity production came with far-reaching ecological implications. As synthetic materials began to accumulate in ever-increasing quantities throughout the environment, their disruptive toxic effects soon became apparent – yet another manifestation of the Great Acceleration enabled by the transition to oil.

Moreover, the development of these synthetic materials had a major impact on other industrial sectors. By the early 1950s, a new generation of materials known as thermoplastics had become widespread. These plastic polymers become malleable when heated and hard when cooled, as opposed to thermosetting plastics that permanently keep their initial shape. With the development of injection-moulding machines through the 1950s and 1960s, thermoplastics enabled the automated fabrication of cheaply reproducible components that transformed whole branches of industrial production, including the manufacture of heavy machinery, automobiles, medicine, construction, consumer goods, packaging, and so forth.[68] Akin to modern-day alchemy, a bag of small pill-like thermoplastic pellets could be transformed into any simple commodity with the appropriate mould. And, once a mould was in place, there was little extra cost to manufacturing each additional item; this not only further accelerated the expulsion of labour from an even wider sphere of commodity production, it also encouraged enormous increases in commodity output.[69]

---

67 One of the first people to highlight this qualitative transformation in the nature of post-war commodity production – and its enormous ecological implications – was the American scientist Barry Commoner in his pioneering works *The Closing Circle* (New York: Knopf, 1971) and *Poverty of Power: Energy and the Economic Crisis* (London: Jonathan Cape, 1976). For recent insightful accounts of plastics, petrochemicals, and the ecological crisis, see Alice Mah, *Plastic Unlimited: How Corporations Are Fuelling the Ecological Crisis and What We Can Do about It*, Cambridge: Polity Books, 2022; and the work of Rebecca Altman, available at rebecca-altman.com.

68 Geiser, *Materials Matter*, 70.

69 As Barry Commoner pointed out in *The Closing Circle*, 'If you asked a craftsman to make you a special pair of candlesticks he would be delighted; if you asked for two

In this manner, the petrochemical revolution was inseparable from the chronic levels of commodity overproduction that came to mark the post-war era. As huge quantities of new and easily reproducible synthetic goods displaced natural materials during the first decades after the Second World War, producers were faced with the obstacles of limited market size and the restricted needs of the post-war consumer. Ever-accelerating quantities of waste, inbuilt obsolescence, and a culture of disposability became the hallmarks of capitalist production – a situation presciently described by Vance Packard in his 1960 classic, *The Waste Makers*. As he noted, the solution to this dilemma lay with another relatively new industry, advertising, which aimed at inculcating the mass consumer 'with plausible excuses for buying more of each product than might in earlier years have seemed rational or prudent'.[70] But all branding needs skin, and here advertisers turned to petrochemicals for inspiration. The pervasive supply of cheap and malleable petrochemicals enabled a huge expansion in packaging and labelling, which soon began to adorn all consumer goods. Packaging quickly became the largest end-use for plastics, and now makes up more than a third of the current global demand for plastics.[71]

We shall return in later chapters to the subsequent evolution of the petrochemical industry, especially the rise of large petrochemical producers located in the Gulf States and East Asia. At this stage, it is simply important to stress once more the centrality of petrochemicals to both the history and the future of oil. Petrochemicals are a key means through which oil was embedded across all parts of our daily lives. These synthetic materials drove the post-war revolutions in productivity, labour-saving technologies, and mass consumption. The unbridled output of new commodities was only made possible through this synthetic shift.[72] Birthed in war and militarism, they helped constitute

million pairs he would be appalled. Yet if you asked a plastics molder for one pair of candlesticks he would be appalled, but delighted if you asked for two million pairs.' Today, around 90 per cent of plastics are thermoplastics; see Geiser, *Materials Matter*, 70.

70 Vance Packard, *The Waste Makers*, New York: David McKay, 1960.

71 International Energy Agency (IEA), *The Future of Petrochemicals: Towards More Sustainable Plastics and Fertilisers*, IEA, 2018, 19; Alice Mah, 'Future-Proofing Capitalism: The Paradox of the Circular Economy for Plastics', *Global Environmental Politics* 21, no. 2, 2021: 121–42.

72 One clear example of this is 'fast fashion,' the move by major fashion retail chains to launch up to a hundred micro-seasons of clothing per year, rather than the few

a US-centred world order. Today, it is almost impossible to identify an area of life that has not been radically transformed by the presence of petrochemicals. Whether as feedstocks for manufacture and agriculture; the primary ingredients of construction materials, cleaning products, and clothing; or the packaging that makes transport, storage, and retail possible – our social being is bound to a seemingly unlimited supply of cheap and disposable petrochemicals. Synthetic materials derived from petroleum have come to define the essential condition of life itself – yet simultaneously, their ubiquity has made them almost invisible to our everyday consciousness. They have become normalised as *natural* parts of our daily existence. This paradox must be fully confronted if we are to move beyond oil.

seasons that formerly characterised the industry. This shift was only made possible by the massive expansion of polyester production, which untethered the industry from supplies of wool and cotton (and created disastrous ecological consequences due to the mountains of clothing waste now generated). The annual production of polyester and other synthetic fibres now consumes more oil than Spain.

8

A Moment of Rupture: Myths and Consequences of the First Oil Shock

On 17 September 1973, the US magazine *Newsweek* hit the streets with a cover that for many would come to symbolise the crisis-ridden decade of the 1970s – an angry-looking Arab man adorned in the Gulf's traditional head-dress, who cradled in his arm a petrol station pump much as he might a rifle. Under the tagline of 'Arab oil squeeze', the imagery resonated with the mood of the times: the world was being held to ransom by a band of unreasonable Arab oil barons, whose newfound control over crude was driving up prices, creating shortages of petrol and other fuels, and triggering spiralling inflation and economic stagnation. Within the popular imagining of this crisis, OPEC's actions were akin to weaponising oil against the West, leaving the traditional oil majors helpless and with few viable responses to the sharp price spikes that were looming.[1] Shortly after the issue of *Newsweek* appeared, oil prices quadrupled in what became known as the first oil shock (1973–4). They would subsequently double again during a second shock at the end of the decade (1979–80). Oil was now discussed in terms of 'scarcity' and 'national security' – with voices from across the political spectrum urging for

1 This perception of the oil companies as weak and isolated was found across the political spectrum. For documentation, see Francesco Petrini, 'Counter-Shocked? The Oil Majors and the Price Slump of the 1980s', in D. Basosi, G. Garavini, and M. Trentin (eds), *Counter-Shock: The Oil Counter-Revolution of the 1980s*, International Library of Twentieth Century History, London: I. B.Tauris, 2016, 76–96.

a turn to Western energy autarchy and a break with the dangerous addiction to Middle East crude.

This OPEC-as-villain interpretation of the 1970s continues to be widely held in both popular culture and much academic writing. But, echoing the *Newsweek* cover photograph – which was really a Madison Ave model dressed up in Gulf attire – it is a superficial blend of misperceptions and myths. Notions of oil scarcity, or the belief that petrol prices spiked because of an OPEC embargo, are incorrect, reflecting a tendency to conflate events with the perceived intent of various actors. Many of these mistaken ideas arise from a poor grasp of how oil circulates – especially the significance of downstream activities and the integrated corporate form – which obscures not only the mechanisms, but also the ultimate beneficiaries of price increases. There is also a habit of viewing the oil shocks in aggregate terms, without disentangling their varied impacts across different geographies, social classes, and the oil industry itself. All of this makes it difficult to understand the true significance of the multiple crises of the 1970s.

So how might we understand both the causes and consequences of the 1970s oil shocks? To answer this question, we must shift our attention away from a singular focus on OPEC to examine the changes that were taking place across other segments of the world oil market during this period. Most important here is the US, where the thoroughly hierarchical oil industry – divided between the top twenty integrated firms and many smaller, non-integrated companies – underwent a deep structural transformation in the years immediately preceding the momentous shifts in the upstream control of Middle East oil. The changes to the American oil market were closely connected to the main OPEC states, not least through the vertically integrated corporate structures that continued to move most oil around the world. At the same time, a new surge in Soviet oil exports also occurred through this period, with significant implications for the balance of power in the world industry. Tracing the interdependencies between these different geographies of world oil can reveal much about what happened to pricing, corporate structures, and the characteristics of oil production through the 1970s. In essential ways, they also prefigure contemporary patterns in the control and ownership of oil.

US Oil before the Shock

An important dimension of the post-war global oil transition that we encountered in Chapter 6 was the growing international activity of oil firms that were not part of the Seven Sisters club. The major driving force behind this international expansion was the second tier of top twenty US firms listed in Chapter 3 – companies such as Occidental, Phillips, and Getty Oil.[2] While not as powerful as the Seven Sisters, these so-called 'independents' were still large and integrated, combining both upstream and downstream activities (including refining and marketing) within the same corporate structures. As global oil consumption exploded in the two decades following the war – doubling between 1950 and 1960, and then doubling again by 1970 – these independent firms sought overseas crude as a means of breaking into the new markets that had emerged in Western Europe, Japan, and elsewhere.[3] As we have seen, a chief consequence of this increasingly diverse industry landscape was the undermining of the highly advantageous concessionary terms that the Seven Sisters had held in areas such as the Middle East. Coupled with the global wave of anti-colonial revolt, all of this played an essential part in the eventual establishment of OPEC in 1960.

But this international expansion of the second-tier independents also carried key implications for the structure of the *domestic* US oil industry. Most importantly, in an environment of booming world consumption and generous tax subsidies, those US oil companies that had managed to make the leap beyond US borders found themselves accumulating enormous cash reserves through the 1950s and 1960s. These reserves far exceeded those of any other industrial sector, and by 1968, it was estimated that the top twenty oil firms in the US were sitting on a pile of surplus cash worth around $9.6 billion – an amount 'equal to the assets of more than 60 percent of the total number of all [US] manufacturing

2 The other major newcomer companies were of course ENI and Japan Oil, but most of the oil firms that were exploring overseas in the 1960s were from the US. Nicoline Kokxhoorn, *Oil and Politics: The Domestic Roots of US Expansion in the Middle East*, Frankfurt: Peter Lang, 1977, 175.

3 The consumption of oil and oil products tripled in Western Europe between 1960 and 1970, and grew more than fivefold in Japan during the same period; see ibid., 181.

corporations'.[4] While some of these cash reserves were used to fund internal operating costs, the bulk went to financing other investments – frequently the purchase of other oil companies.[5] As a result, the US oil industry experienced an unparalleled wave of corporate consolidation throughout the 1960s.

These events are documented in a remarkable set of US Senate hearings that took place between 1964 and 1970, and which ran to over 4,500 pages when published in its final version. The hearings focused on the concentration of corporate power across all branches of US industry, including oil. A prominent figure in the proceedings was John Blair, then chief economist of the Senate Subcommittee on Antitrust and Monopoly, who would go on to write a pathbreaking account of the oil industry, *The Control of Oil*.[6] According to Blair's testimony before the hearings, oil companies spent more than $3.9 billion on mergers and acquisitions (M&A) in the US between 1955 and 1966 – more than any other industry and equivalent to 15 per cent of all manufacturing M&A over this period.[7] As such, the oil sector sat at the leading edge of a profound concentration in corporate control and ownership that occurred during this time: more than a third of *all* acquisitions between 1948 and 1968 were made by just twenty-five companies – and eight of these were petroleum firms, a greater proportion than any other sector.[8]

There were four main types of M&A that took place in the US oil industry through the 1960s. The first of these involved the merger of

4 United States Senate, *Economic Concentration: Hearings before the United States Senate Committee on Antitrust and Monopoly*, 88th Congress, second session, 89th Congress, 90th Congress, 91st Congress, Washington, DC: US Government Printing Office, pt 8-8A, 4873, catalog.hathitrust.org/Record/100666195.

5 At this stage, the phenomenon of debt-based financing was not a prominent means of corporate acquisition. It would become so with the rise of financialisation in the 1980s (see Chapter 9).

6 *The Control of Oil* was published in 1974 shortly after Blair's death. Much of this book was based on the FTC's Staff Report on the International Petroleum Cartel, published in 1952, of which Blair was the director and main author. This FTC report was censored by President Truman prior to its publication, at the urging of the Department of State and the CIA. Darius W. Gaskins, John R. Haring Jr, and William A. Vogely, 'Review: The Control of Oil by John Blair', *Land Economics* 54, no. 4, 1978: 531–7, 531.

7 United States Senate, *Economic Concentration*, 4902.

8 Ibid., 4558–9.

firms from within the second tier of top twenty petroleum companies.[9] By joining together, these firms could better fund their international expansion as well as complement their activities across different regional markets in the US (for example, a California-focused firm could acquire interests in Ohio). They could also grow their capacities in sectors where they had been relatively weak (such as refining activity, or marketing). These kinds of mergers constituted around a third of all acquisitions in the US oil industry between 1961 and 1968 and meant that the second tier of integrated US oil firms grew substantially in asset size but simultaneously shrank in number.[10] Because so much of this M&A activity involved deals between firms located in different regional US markets, the concentration and centralisation of ownership bolstered the nationally organised character of the US oil industry, while also squeezing smaller firms whose activities were limited to individual states. In subsequent decades, most of the companies created through this wave of mergers were themselves swallowed up by the largest integrated firms from among the top eight.

The second kind of M&A activity involved investment in downstream activities, especially the distribution and marketing of refined oil products such as petrol. Distribution and retailing of oil products made up around a quarter of all M&A purchases by the twenty largest petroleum companies between 1956 and 1968, with just under 23,000 independent service stations in the US taken over by them during this period.[11] Ownership of these retail outlets enabled the biggest oil companies to improve the balance between crude output and marketing, thereby reducing the amount of excess crude requiring disposal in the open market. The increased control of the largest firms over downstream sales also reduced the number and market strength of smaller retailers, including their ability to offer lower prices for oil products. These smaller retailers (known as private branders) had played an essential role in the suburbanisation of the US by setting up service stations on the major highways and selling petrol cheaper than the big oil majors – they even

9 These included the mergers of Union Oil with Pure Oil in 1965; Phillips with Tidewater in 1966; Sun Oil with Sunray in 1968; Atlantic Refining with Richfield Refining in 1966, and with Sinclair Oil in 1969.

10 United States Senate, *Economic Concentration*, 285.

11 Through the 1960s, Continental, Marathon, Shell, Occidental, and Ashland all made purchases of these types. Ibid., 301.

introduced the now ubiquitous practice of self-service as a means of reducing their operating costs. As we shall see below, the collapse of these private branders through the late 1960s was to have wide-ranging ramifications for how the oil shocks of the 1970s were experienced in the US.

Third, the largest oil firms also made a significant turn towards the chemical industry at this time. The production and distribution of chemicals – including fertilisers, plastics, and raw materials – made up more than a fifth of all domestic M&A purchases by the twenty largest US petroleum firms between 1956 and 1968.[12] Through the early 1960s, American oil firms spent as much on petrochemical plants as they did on oil refineries, taking control of the majority of domestic capacity for some of the most important chemical products, including synthetic rubber, ethylene, propylene, and acetone.[13] By 1968, thirteen of the fifty largest firms selling chemicals in the US were fully owned by petroleum companies.[14] As we saw in the previous chapter, these interlocking ownership structures across the US oil and chemical industries developed just as petrochemicals were becoming critical to industrial production in other parts of the world, especially Western Europe. They thus worked to solidify the global dominance of the US petrochemical industry through the 1960s and 1970s.

Finally, the fourth kind of M&A during this period saw the expansion of oil firms into a diverse range of non-oil activities. This included other forms of primary-energy production (such as coal and nuclear energy), as well as companies that lay outside the energy sector, including truck manufacturing, ship building, aircraft engines, concrete and cement production, road and highway construction, military equipment, heating and air-conditioning equipment, and real estate.[15] These non-oil investments comprised over a quarter of all M&A purchases made by the largest US oil firms between 1961 and 1968.[16] They indicate

12 Ibid., 4784.

13 John Blair, *The Control of Oil*, New York: Pantheon Books, 1976, 134; United States Senate, *Economic Concentration*, 304.

14 United States Senate, *Economic Concentration*, 307.

15 Coal investments represented around 8 per cent of all M&A purchases made by the largest petroleum companies between 1961 and 1968. In 1966, the largest US coal company, the Consolidated Coal Company, was bought by one of the top eight oil firms, Continental Oil. Ibid., 285–6.

16 Ibid., 285.

how US petroleum firms were beginning to evolve into larger industrial conglomerates that, while continuing to be centred on oil and energy, increasingly encompassed other economic sectors beyond oil. As we shall see in later chapters, this shift continues to mark the structural evolution of the largest US oil firms.

As the largest US oil companies made these various investments through the 1960s, a further important development was occurring within the oil industry: the emergence of American offshore exploration, especially in the Gulf of Mexico. Although drilling experiments along the coastal and wetland areas of Louisiana had begun in the 1930s, it took until the 1950s for improvements in drilling and exploration technology to enable extraction from deeper, open-water areas.[17] The huge expense of offshore extraction meant that its financial viability depended on relatively high oil prices, and this was much aided by Eisenhower's 1959 decision to restrict US oil imports and thus keep domestic oil prices higher than those outside the US.[18] The US government also offered sizeable tax incentives and subsidies for technological research and equipment to oil companies involved in offshore exploration during this period.[19] As a result, offshore production supplied an increasingly larger share of US oil through the 1950s and 1960s.

The biggest oil companies were the foremost beneficiaries of this expansion in offshore oil, in part due to a crucial difference that existed between the governance of property rights in onshore and offshore areas. Unlike the parcellised private property rights over numerous small plots that typified many onshore US oil fields (see Chapter 2), in 1953 the federal government had taken sovereign jurisdiction over 'submerged lands' more than three miles from the US coast, introducing

17 Tyler Priest, 'Extraction Not Creation: The History of Offshore Petroleum in the Gulf of Mexico', *Enterprise and Society* 8, no. 2, 2007: 227–67.

18 As noted in Chapter 6, this programme had been established to keep domestic US oil prices higher in the face of cheaper oil available elsewhere in the world (especially the Middle East); it had also been tacitly supported by the Seven Sisters, which hoped to discourage potential newcomers from entering overseas markets (because they would no longer be able to supply their own domestic US operations with foreign-produced oil). Through the 1960s, however, both the established majors and newcomer firms came out in opposition to these import quotas due to the increased competition and low prices that were now rocking the industry outside the US.

19 Priest, 'Extraction Not Creation', 240. As Priest points out, the absence of worker and environmental regulations also provided a significant boost to offshore oil.

a government-managed system for bidding on offshore exploration leases. Known as 'bonus bidding', this system awarded leases to companies that offered the highest upfront cash bid per acre.[20] The deep pockets of the largest firms enabled them to offer huge sums, and effectively excluded smaller companies from participating in offshore extraction. Thus, the offshore industry became dominated by a tiny number of the largest firms, almost exclusively from the top twenty, often bidding jointly for leases. This was to set the stage for later patterns of global oil production (and environmental destruction), with deep-water (and recently *ultradeep*) extraction supplying much of the crude base of today's corporate oil giants (see Chapter 11).

Taken as a whole, these changes within the US oil industry signalled the acute concentration of ownership that occurred across the sector through the 1950s and 1960s. The power of the largest integrated US firms (both the top eight and the broader top twenty) grew extensively – and was extended backwards and forwards across the oil value chain (and into other energy and non-oil industries). The domination of the US oil market by these large firms – including the sale of oil products such as petrol – was increasingly elaborated at the national scale, rather than in the discrete regional markets that had hitherto marked the structure of US oil. Alongside this process of industry consolidation, the position of smaller non-integrated oil firms and retailers weakened considerably, and entry barriers were raised for any potential competitors (especially in offshore exploration). The conditions that had initially allowed smaller non-integrated firms to emerge and prosper in the US – the relative imbalances of oil supplies between the different segments of the largest integrated firms (see Chapter 2) – were largely shut down. Ultimately, what this restructuring of the US oil industry enabled was a recalibration of where and how accumulation took place across the oil industry; as such, the largest American firms were able to insulate themselves from the seismic changes that were about to unfold in the international market.

20 Alternative proposals that would have awarded leases based on the long-term royalty rates offered by the companies were rejected. For a discussion, see Blair, *Control of Oil*, 140.

Back in the USSR

Nonetheless, despite their strengthened domestic position, the largest US firms did face several challenges at the international level. One of these was the resumption of Soviet oil exports, which, after a two-decade lull, had started to increase again following oil discoveries in the Volga-Ural region in the mid-1950s, and then the opening up of drilling and exploration across West Siberia through the 1960s.[21] As the location of the so-called 'supergiant' Samotlor oil field – the largest in Russia, and sixth largest in the world – West Siberia enabled a doubling of Soviet oil production between 1960 and 1970, catapulting the Soviet Union into the position of the world's top producer, ahead of the US and Saudi Arabia. Importantly, West Siberia also possessed vast natural gas reserves, which meant that gas could be used for domestic energy needs (especially in industry), while oil could be exported.[22] A complex pipeline network – soon to become the longest in the world – carried this oil and gas to refineries and energy-intensive industries in the Urals, from where petroleum products could then be transported to domestic consumers or exported to Europe and further afield. Overall, Soviet oil exports increased from just 3.7 million tons in 1955 to 85.8 million tons by 1968 because of West Siberian production.[23]

---

21 These geographical shifts illustrate an important characteristic of Russia's oil industry: as older oil fields were depleted or became less prolific, the industry moved to new regions that enabled the country to maintain (and increase) overall production levels. The first of these shifts took place with the move of oil production from Baku to the Volga-Urals in the 1940s and 1950s; the second occurred in the 1960s with the opening up of West Siberia. See Mazen Labban, *Space, Oil and Capital*, New York: Routledge, 2008, 100–2.

22 Oil, in the pithy phrasing of Gustafson, 'pays the bills abroad, while gas subsidizes the economy at home'. Thane Gustafson, *Wheel of Fortune: The Battle of Oil and Power in Russia*, Cambridge, MA: Belknap Press, 2012, 3. It should be noted that the transition to oil and gas for domestic use occurred later in the Soviet Union than most West European countries. Up to 1959, nearly two-thirds of all consumption of energy in the Soviet Union was based on coal and biomass. S. A. Ermolaev, 'Soviet Oil and Gas Dependence: Lessons for Contemporary Russia', *Problems of Economic Transition* 61, nos 10–12, 2019: 800–16, 802. While oil and gas had become the dominant primary fuels by the 1970s, the use of private cars, a key driver of the hydrocarbon economy, was still largely the preserve of a small section of the elite until the 1991 collapse of the Soviet Union; see Simon Pirani, *Burning Up: A Global History of Fossil Fuel Consumption*, London: Pluto Press, 2018, 93.

23 Jeronim Petrovic, *Cold War Energy: A Transnational History of Soviet Oil and Gas*, London: Palgrave Macmillan, 2017, 11.

This staggering increase in Soviet oil exports meant that more and more oil was entering the world market outside the integrated channels of the Seven Sisters. And, because this Soviet oil was frequently bartered or sold at a discount, it provided an attractive alternative to the oil controlled by the Western majors. This had vital political implications for the Soviet Union. On one side, Russian oil helped bind allied countries to the Soviet bloc: in Europe, for example, five Comecon trading partners – Bulgaria, Poland, East Germany, Hungary, and Czechoslovakia – relied on the Soviet Union for around 90 per cent of their oil needs.[24] Subsidised and bartered Russian oil also went to Cuba, and many former European colonies in Africa and Asia. Alongside this oil trade with its allies, around half of Soviet oil exports were flowing to Western Europe by the 1960s – weakening US-led attempts to force an isolation of the USSR by the West.[25]

By the early 1960s, Western intelligence circles had begun to speak of the 'Soviet oil offensive', which, according to one US senator, represented 'a grave threat to the free world' and was 'designed to undermine the commercial activities of the free enterprise system . . . the economic independence of Western Europe and the future of private enterprise in the underdeveloped countries'.[26] While comments such as these were certainly charged with Cold War zealotry, they underlined the deeply unsettling effects of Soviet oil exports on the entire edifice of a US-centred post-war order. For one, Soviet expertise broke the monopoly that Western companies held on knowledge about the oil industry. This included the technical skills required to build refineries or explore for oil (as happened in India, Ethiopia, Turkey, and Pakistan). It also gave newly independent countries a better understanding of the industry's arcane pricing mechanisms and the implications of vertical integration. In the context of the Bandung moment and the anti-colonial struggles discussed in Chapter 6, Soviet assistance helped create the space (and

24 This oil flowed through the Druzhba (Friendship) pipeline, which ran via the Soviet republics of the Ukraine and Belorussia into the Eastern bloc countries. Druzhba was completed in 1964 (despite NATO attempts to prevent supplies of large-diameter pipes reaching the Soviet Union) and remains the longest oil pipeline in the world. The only East European country with significant oil supplies was Romania.

25 Petrovic, *Cold War Energy*, 11.

26 United States Senate, *Defense Production Act, 1962: Hearings before the Committee on Banking and Currency*, 87th Congress, Second Session, 1962, 68.

technical capacity) for countries to pursue alternative development strategies, including the nationalisation of oil industry infrastructure. In Ceylon (Sri Lanka), for example, oil marketing was taken over by the state in 1962 (after Western oil majors refused to use cheaper Soviet oil instead of oil from their own subsidiaries). In Cuba, the Western oil majors were expelled in 1960, and nationalised oil refineries could be run with Soviet support.

All this had a major impact on the structure and balance of power within the world oil industry. The increased capacity of oil-consuming states to manage the import and refining of oil by themselves (or with Soviet support) meant an expansion in the number of independent buyers of oil on the world market (whether governments or independent refiners). No longer would the buying and selling of world oil take place almost exclusively within the internal subsidiaries of the largest Western firms. This made it much more difficult for the Seven Sisters to manage the flow of global surpluses and control the price at which oil was sold.[27] It also diminished their power over oil-*producing* states. From the 1960s onwards, it would be difficult to imagine Western majors waging an effective boycott of an oil-producing country, such as had occurred following the 1951 nationalisation of oil in Iran (see Chapter 6).

By eroding the Seven Sisters' power over where oil was produced, refined, and sold – and how it was priced – Soviet oil exports were directly consequential to the rise of oil nationalism, the establishment of OPEC, and the upsurge of national liberation movements that reached their peak across much of the so-called Third World in the 1960s and 1970s. For the Soviet Union itself, the hard-currency income earned through oil came to underwrite the country's development trajectories – not least in enabling the ruling bureaucracy to mollify internal tensions and address domestic shortages through imports of grain, technology, and consumer goods. Living standards could improve despite the stifling political climate and state repression of social movements – or the flagrant inefficiencies of bureaucratic central planning. In this manner,

27 It will be recalled that, at this time (the early 1960s), the price of oil was determined at two 'basing points' in the Persian Gulf and the Gulf of Mexico. The price in any given market was equal to the posted price (set by the majors) at that base plus the transport cost from the base to the consumption market, regardless from where that oil *actually* came from.

the future of Soviet-style socialism was increasingly tied to the volume of oil produced from the frosty marshlands of West Siberia. But there was an important corollary to this: oil also became the fundamental route through which the country was integrated into the wider world market, and oil thus emerged as a key transmission belt of global crises. As we shall see in Chapter 10, this was to have fateful consequences following the deep global economic downturn of the 1980s.

Libya and the 'Leapfrogging Effect'

The tremendous impact of Soviet oil exports on the world market illustrates once again why major international oil companies were so preoccupied with the problems of an oversupply of crude through much of the twentieth century. Attempts to restrict and limit the circulation of oil surpluses had driven the formation of the Iraq Petroleum Company, the Red Line Agreement, and subsequent secret arrangements designed to keep oil off the world market. These arrangements had brought limited, albeit temporary, success in restricting supplies. But through the 1960s – as the number of buyers and sellers outside the Seven Sisters multiplied – the interests of the main producer states (outside the US) stood opposed to any restriction of oil production. For the Soviet Union, oil exports were a lifeline in a hostile global political and economic environment. OPEC producers also sought to maximise the quantity of oil extracted and exported, because royalty payments were based on the volume of oil produced. In this context, it was becoming increasingly difficult for the Western majors to manage the problem of global crude surpluses.

However, soon after the establishment of OPEC in 1960, a new factor was to emerge within this tussle over global production levels: the entry of Libyan oil onto the world market. Oil exploration had begun in Libya in the early 1950s and significant reserves were discovered in 1959. Not only was Libyan oil plentiful and easy to extract, but it was also much closer to European markets than oil from the Gulf, and its extremely low sulphur content – a so-called 'sweet oil' – made it cleaner and cheaper to refine. Through the 1960s, the country's oil production grew faster than anywhere else in the world, and in 1968 Libya overtook Kuwait to become the fourth-largest OPEC producer, just behind Venezuela, Iran, and Saudi Arabia. By this stage, almost a third of Europe's oil was being supplied from Libya.[28] But within the leading group of OPEC producers, the structure of the Libyan oil industry was distinctive: many more of the country's concessions were in the hands of the large US independents (such as Occidental, Continental Oil, and Marathon), rather than the Seven Sisters. Indeed, by 1970 more than half of Libya's oil production was produced by independents, compared to an average of 15 per cent across OPEC as a whole.[29]

For the Seven Sisters, Libya's strong connection to independent producers created a major dilemma. Because these independent firms lacked established markets, they were willing to sell their Libyan oil at a lower price than that offered by the Seven Sisters (a similar strategy, in many respects, to that of the Soviet Union).[30] Faced with the problem of oversupply and the pressure that falling market prices placed on profit rates, the Seven Sisters could not unilaterally reduce the posted price, because this would jeopardise the already shaky relationship between the oil companies and the main producer governments.[31] At the same time, if the Seven Sisters cut back on their production elsewhere in the Middle East to make way for Libyan production, countries such as Saudi Arabia and Iran would protest the impact of this on oil exports (and thus government revenue). But, if the international majors chose not to produce in Libya, then the share of production held by independents would continue to increase, and these newcomers would have little incentive to stop selling oil at rock-bottom prices.[32]

The situation was finally brought to a head in 1969 with the overthrow of Libya's ruling monarch, King Idris. He was ousted in a coup

28 Andrew Scott Cooper, *The Oil Kings: How the U.S., Iran, and Saudi Arabia Changed the Balance of Power in the Middle East*, New York: Simon & Schuster, 2011, 109.

29 Blair, *Control of Oil*, 211.

30 According to figures cited by Blair, the delivery price of Middle East oil purchased by countries such as Japan, Argentina, and Uruguay had fallen around 10 to 15 per cent between 1965 and 1967.

31 As discussed in previous chapters, the posted price determined the tax revenues received by the producer states.

32 Another little-noticed consequence of this global expansion of independent firms was their role in spurring the development of National Oil Companies (NOCs), with whom they typically entered into joint ventures for the exploration and production of domestic resources. The growing technical capacity acquired by NOCs through these joint ventures was a crucial step towards the eventual full nationalisation of crude oil in the main oil-rich states (see Chapter 12).

led by the Libyan colonel Muammar Gaddafi, who – echoing the nationalist mood traced in Chapter 6 – immediately moved to impose a forty-cent increase in the price of oil for the companies operating in Libya. This demand was initially refused by the independent firms, but after being threatened with the confiscation of their concessions they had little choice but to give in to the price increase. For both the Seven Sisters and the independent firms, Libya's willingness to confront the foreign concessionaires raised the dangerous logic of what one oil firm lawyer described as a 'leapfrogging' effect: any improvement in concession terms won by the Libyan government would be generalised to oil producers in the Gulf, but this would then be followed by further demands in Libya, which would then be echoed in the Gulf, and so on, ad infinitum.[33] Much like Venezuela's fifty–fifty model in the early 1950s, the real threat posed by Libya's pushback against the international oil majors lay in its potential cross-border reverberations – not in its immediate ramifications for any individual national oil producer.

Conscious of this threat, the leading oil companies attempted to insist on collective negotiations that would be binding across all major producing countries. This, however, was refused. Instead, negotiations between twenty-two international oil companies and six Gulf producers took place in Tehran in February 1971, followed by a separate round of negotiations with the Libyan government in Tripoli in April the same year. The conclusion to these negotiations confirmed the oil companies' fear of escalating demands, with producer governments achieving an increase in tax rates to 60 per cent and successfully imposing a higher posted price on the Western oil majors. Closely connected to these negotiations was an even greater challenge: the nationalisation of Western oil assets. In February 1971, Algeria would nationalise 51 per cent of the French oil and gas concessions in the country, and in July, Venezuela passed a law mandating the eventual nationalisation of all concessions by 1983. In September, an OPEC resolution passed in Beirut committed countries to taking joint ownership of oil concessions operating within their borders. And on 5 December 1971, Libya nationalised British Petroleum's oil concessions in the country (representing more than a quarter of all its reserves), followed soon after by further

33 Blair, *Control of Oil*, 223.

nationalisation of the concessions held by Shell, Socal, Texaco, and some of the independents.

The First Oil Shock

As this momentum for oil nationalisation gathered pace, the pre-eminent position of the US within the wider global political economy was also under considerable strain. By the end of the 1960s, many of the factors underpinning the post-war economic boom had begun to weaken. Two decades of fast-growing production levels had led to the re-emergence of overaccumulation at the global scale – particularly following the expansion of global manufacturing output by European and Japanese firms able to benefit from low wages, long working hours, and the introduction of new technological techniques.[34] The high profit rates in the US and Western Europe that had been sustained through rising productivity and cheap energy were under pressure from labour and political movements seeking wage increases and better working conditions. Amid the upsurge of social revolt in the 1960s – closely connected to the Vietnam War and the national independence struggles across the colonial world – US global supremacy no longer appeared so assured.

One critical manifestation of the challenges facing American dominance was the role of the US dollar within the global financial system. Since the establishment of the Bretton Woods monetary system in 1944, global finance had been structured around the pegging of other international currencies to the dollar, which was then convertible to gold at a price of $US35/ounce (hence its description as the dollar-gold standard). With the dollar serving as the central currency for international transactions, the US supplied dollars to the rest of the world, and other currencies were adjusted in value through an exchange-rate system overseen by the International Monetary Fund (IMF). This gave the US an 'exorbitant privilege' in the words of French Minister of Economy and Finance Valéry Giscard d'Estaing, because it could create dollars for a few cents while other countries were forced to exchange real goods

34 Robert Brenner, *The Boom and the Bubble: The US in the World Economy*, London: Verso, 2000.

and services for the US currency.[35] By the early 1970s, however, the large quantities of US dollars held by private and central banks outside the US made it increasingly difficult for the US to maintain a fixed value of its currency in terms of gold. Through 1970, several European countries had demanded redemption of their US dollar holdings for gold – and with vastly more US dollars in circulation outside the US than could be covered by US gold reserves, US President Richard Nixon took the dramatic decision on 15 August 1971 to suspend (with certain exceptions) the convertibility of the dollar into gold.

For the major oil-exporting countries, Nixon's decision had immediate and severe ramifications. With the US dollar no longer pegged at a fixed value to gold, its value dropped significantly in 1971 and 1972.[36] Crucially, however, most oil sales were priced in dollars, which meant that the reserve holdings of oil producers depreciated in step with the weakening of the US dollar. At the same time, import costs were also growing for OPEC states because a large proportion of goods they consumed came from countries whose currencies were now more expensive in relation to the dollar (such as Germany, France, and Japan).[37] In the face of these deteriorating financial conditions, OPEC negotiated several increases in the posted price in the first half of 1973. At the same time, the leading oil-producing states continued to take greater control over the production of crude itself – whether through outright nationalisation of foreign concessions (Algeria, Iran, Iraq, and Libya), or through participation agreements, which gave producer governments a share of the oil produced, which was then sold back to

35 Barry Eichengreen, *Exorbitant Privilege: The Rise and Fall of the Dollar*, Oxford: Oxford University Press, 2011.

36 Immediately after the Nixon Shock, the US began negotiations with ten major allies to set a new level for international exchange rates. In December 1971, the so-called Smithsonian Agreement was reached, which effectively devalued the US dollar by 7.9 per cent in relation to gold, and appreciated the yen (16.9 per cent), Deutsche mark (13.6 per cent), French franc (8.6 per cent), British sterling (8.6 per cent), and Italian lira (7.5 per cent). This agreement lasted around fifteen months, when speculative pressure led the OECD and Japan to agree to a system of floating exchange rates in March 1973.

37 According to the OPEC Secretary General Adnan Pachachi, 60 per cent of OPEC imports came from countries whose currencies were appreciating relative to the dollar, and in 1971 this increased OPEC's import bill by $570 million, or around 10 per cent (cited in Giuliano Garavini, *The Rise and Fall of OPEC in the Twentieth Century*, London: Oxford University Press, 2019, 200).

the oil majors at a discount rate (Saudi Arabia and the smaller Gulf producers).

The steps taken by OPEC throughout 1972 and the first half of 1973 ultimately served to challenge a long-standing assumption that had underpinned international oil pricing since the early years of the twentieth century: the prerogative of the largest oil majors to control the price of oil at the point of extraction. And, on 16 October 1973, this system came to an irrevocable end. On that day, following a week of failed negotiations with the oil companies, five Arab members of OPEC along with Iran declared that they would now take the decision of oil pricing into their own hands. The posted price was immediately raised by 70 per cent, increasing from \$3 to \$5.11 – the largest jump in history. Over the next few days, six of the Arab members of OPEC (Saudi Arabia, Kuwait, Abu Dhabi, Qatar, Libya, and Algeria) announced oil production cuts and an embargo on oil exports to the US and the Netherlands for as long as Israel's occupation of Arab lands continued.[38] On 1 January 1974, a further OPEC meeting in Tehran again raised the posted price to \$11.65. Over a four-year period, the posted price had increased sixfold. The first oil shock of the 1970s was at the door.

Myths and Consequences

At this stage, it is important to clarify a range of misperceptions about the first oil shock, beginning with the oil price spike itself. As Timothy Mitchell carefully details in *Carbon Democracy*, the price rises that began in 1971 and culminated on the 16 October 1973 concerned the posted price, not the market or arms-length price at which crude oil (let alone oil products, such as petrol) were necessarily sold.[39] As such, the rise in the posted price had little to do with prices in the way we usually think of them – in reality, this was a *tax reference price*, which was administratively set in order to determine the amount of tax that oil concession holders (primarily the Seven Sisters) were required to pay to producer governments. Despite the vital role of Soviet oil exports, it was

38 Kuwait and the UAE announced an embargo on oil exports to the US on 18 October. This was at first rejected by Saudi Arabia, but the country joined on 19 October.

39 Timothy Mitchell, *Carbon Democracy*, New York: Verso, 2011, 181–8.

the large Western oil companies who continued to control most of the worldwide *refining* of oil – and thus the actual market price of oil products.[40] Given this position, they did exactly what would be expected of them: pass the increase in their tax rate through to consumers. Indeed, during the peak of the price explosion between July 1973 and January 1974, the cost of petrol in the US more than doubled, light fuel oil tripled, and residual oil (used in power plants and industry) nearly quadrupled.[41] Moreover, because the increase in the posted price was, in reality, an increase in *tax* payments, it meant that the largest American oil companies were also able to make use of the foreign tax credit scheme described in Chapter 3 – that is, they could book the increased amount paid to foreign governments against other taxes on overseas revenue owed to the US government. In this manner, the rise in the posted price simply represented a re-routing of tax payments away from the US government into the treasuries of OPEC.

It should also be remembered that, at this time, the concessions between the largest oil companies and many of the core OPEC producers (notably Saudi Arabia and the smaller Gulf states) were arranged through participation agreements.[42] According to these agreements, both the producing government and the foreign concession holders were entitled to a specific share of the crude produced in a particular country. From the perspective of the foreign oil company, the cost of producing a barrel of oil in the Middle East was still very cheap – around eighteen cents – and higher world prices meant they could either sell

40 In 1973, it was estimated that more than 90 per cent of world oil sales (outside the US and Soviet Union) were made by Western international majors. Brian Levy, 'World Oil Marketing in Transition', *International Organization* 36, no. 1, 1982, 113–33, 121. In fact, these companies sold very little OPEC crude oil on the world market, most of it went into their own integrated subsidiaries, where it was refined and sold to consumers. It took until the late 1970s before a significant proportion of world oil was bought and sold outside the integrated channels of the majors (see discussion next chapter).

41 Blair, *Control of Oil*, 270.

42 Participation agreements were largely the initiative of Ahmad Zaki Yamani, the Saudi oil minister appointed following the ouster of Abdullah Tariki. Yamani argued that these participation agreements 'would be indissoluble, like a Catholic marriage' and would 'save [the international oil majors] from nationalization'. Yamani's main aim was to convince the international majors that what mattered 'was not so much who owned the oil, as who was able to buy it'. Anthony Sampson, *The Seven Sisters: The Great Oil Companies and the World They Shaped*, New York: Viking, 1975, 278–9.

their share of oil on the market at considerable margin or alternatively utilise it within their own integrated downstream subsidiaries (enjoying a significantly lower cost than oil obtained through the world market). Naturally, these advantages were not available to other firms who lacked foreign concessions. Moreover, as part of the participation agreement, foreign oil companies were entitled to buy back the host government's share of oil production at a discount price. This oil was solely earmarked for the concession holders and gave them a further advantage over those who had to purchase their oil on the open market. Indeed, it was estimated by Saudi oil minister Ahmed Yamani that this discount had earned oil companies an extra forty to fifty cents per barrel during the first half of 1973 – a remarkable profit rate that Yamani felt should be split equitably with the Saudi government.[43] All told, the profit per barrel for foreign oil companies operating in the Middle East *tripled* during 1973 as a result of OPEC's actions.[44]

Closely related to these misperceptions around oil pricing is the notion that prices spiked *because* of a worldwide oil scarcity caused by the Arab embargo. Once again, this story is largely a myth, supported by an erroneous understanding of who did what, and when. To begin with, we must be clear that this was never an embargo that involved *all* of OPEC – it was, rather, a limited set of actions taken by just some of the Arab members of OPEC. The five-month embargo was primarily directed at the US and the Netherlands, and later extended to Portugal, Rhodesia, and South Africa. This limited international scope meant that oil shipments could be diverted from one place to another by the oil majors to make up for any potential shortages.[45] Many of the largest oil-producing countries did not participate in the embargo – such as Iraq, Iran, Venezuela, Nigeria, and Indonesia – and the US possessed its own considerable domestic reserves. As a result, global oil production could

43 'Subjects for Discussion at Sept 15 OPEC Meeting', 13 August 1973, Public Library of US Diplomacy, wikileaks.org. From the perspective of the Western majors, the one drawback to these participation agreements was that payments made to foreign governments for oil became straightforward purchases and the foreign tax credit was thus no longer available to help subsidise their overseas activities. This problem was accentuated through the 1970s as increasing quantities of upstream oil were fully nationalised by producer governments.

44 Kokxhoorn, *Oil and Politics*, 219.

45 In the case of the Netherlands, for example, Shell and BP rescheduled oil from Nigeria and Iran that would have previously gone to the UK.

be increased relatively easily to compensate for any shortfalls in crude. Moreover, because the global shipment and transport of oil remained in the hands of the largest oil companies, it was very difficult to exercise control over the ultimate destination of tankers once they had left Arab ports – even supposedly hard-line OPEC states such as Libya and Algeria reportedly showed little concern over where their oil was ultimately being shipped.[46] All in all, there was never any real shortage of oil as a result of the embargo. Indeed, to a significant degree, the embargo can be read as little more than a performative act, ultimately aimed at convincing Arab audiences that an anti-colonial front was possible between the oil-rich monarchies and the more radical nationalist movements of the region.[47]

Nonetheless, while the Arab embargo did little to impact global supplies of crude oil between October 1973 and March 1974, there were sizeable shortages in some oil products *before* the embargo itself – and, indeed, prior to the 1973 price rise. In the US, these shortages were largely driven by a series of reductions in refining capacity by the largest integrated firms between 1970 and 1972. The reason for these cutbacks was thoroughly documented in an investigation by the US Federal Trade Commission (FTC) in 1973. According to the FTC, there was no

---

46 Duco Hellema, Cees Wiebes, and Toby Witte, *The Netherlands and the Oil Crisis: Business as Usual*, Amsterdam: Amsterdam University Press, 2004, 65. Indeed, as early as January 1974, Saudi oil minister Ahmed Yamani admitted that the boycott against the United States and the Netherlands was ineffective. The US never experienced crude oil shortages through this period, and Rotterdam (the key port for oil shipments into the Netherlands) was receiving 96 per cent of pre-crisis shipments of oil products by January 1974. Bo Heinebäck, *Oil and Security*, Stockholm: Almqvist & Wiksell, 1974, 151.

47 While the Arab embargo turned out to be largely ineffectual shadow-play, it might have had a very different effect if it had involved a broad united OPEC front. The Netherlands, which relied upon the Middle East for around two-thirds of its crude, was particularly exposed. Dutch officials were genuinely concerned and undertook a range of measures to combat the threat, including petrol rationing, car-free Sundays, and a redirection of oil imports from other oil producers. Moreover, as one of Europe's key export terminals, the Dutch port of Rotterdam held major strategic significance for the rest of the continent – around a quarter of Europe's imports of Arab oil arrived there. Hellema, Wiebes, and Witte, *The Netherlands*, 99–100. All of this meant that a genuine cut to oil supplies to the Netherlands could have had highly disruptive effects on Western Europe as a whole. Much of the literature on this moment tends to focus on the US, ignoring the experience of the Netherlands and Western Europe.

shortage of oil or oil products for the largest integrated firms – what was in short supply were the surpluses that these firms had previously sold to smaller retailers (the private branders mentioned above). By cutting back on refinery output, the largest firms were able to deny smaller retailers access to enough refined products (such as petrol), thereby pushing them out of business.[48] The result was a further narrowing of control in the retail and marketing segment of the US oil industry. In 1972, private branders had made up 28 per cent of the US market; by May 1974 this proportion had fallen to 18 per cent.[49] A similar squeeze affected smaller refining companies that were denied crude supplies from the largest integrated firms and thus forced to cut back on their capacity.[50]

Alongside the evisceration of their smaller competitors, high oil prices had another extremely significant consequence for the largest integrated firms: the sudden profitability of more expensive exploration and drilling projects, especially in offshore areas. Faced with the looming threat of losing direct access to upstream reserves in the Middle East, the Western majors expanded their non-OPEC supplies through the early 1970s, focusing in particular on Alaska, the North Sea (between the UK and Western Europe), and the Gulf of Mexico. Some of these projects – such as British Petroleum's Trans-Alaska Pipeline (TAP) and Phillips Petroleum's production from fields in the North Sea – had been planned prior to the 1973 crisis, but only became feasible following the huge spike in crude prices of that year. Deploying the language of 'energy independence', the US and British governments rapidly cleared regulatory barriers to these projects. In the US, President Richard Nixon announced in September 1973 that the TAP would be a priority of his administration, and by the end of the year Congress had passed legislation authorising the pipeline, despite strong objections from environmental and indigenous groups who had been protesting the project for

48 United States Senate, *Preliminary Federal Trade Commission Staff Report on Its Investigation of the Petroleum Industry*, 93rd Congress, First Session, Washington, DC: U.S. Government Printing Office, 1973.

49 Kokxhoorn, *Oil and Politics*, 235.

50 Likewise in Western Europe, a diversion of oil from Rotterdam towards the US during 1972 and 1973 – prior to the October 1973 price rise or the Arab embargo – led to a temporary shortage of oil and a rise in product prices, which put many smaller, independent European firms out of business.

years.[51] Coupled with state-supported investment into drilling technology, the offshore industry experienced a massive boost that would permanently stamp the character of the Western oil industry (see Chapter 12). In this respect, as Tyler Priest observes, the 1973 crisis was a transformative moment that pushed forward the territorial and technological frontiers of the oil industry in ways that could not have been foreseen.[52] The legacies of this moment are inscribed in the most dangerous and destructive edges of oil today – illustrated perhaps most calamitously in the 2010 BP Deepwater Horizon spill in the Gulf of Mexico, widely regarded as the one of the worst environmental disasters in history.

In all these diverse ways, the 1973 crisis provided a powerful boost to the profitability and market strength of the largest integrated oil majors. But these outcomes were not fated; they were driven forward by the lobbying activities of the majors themselves. In the US, the American Petroleum Institute (API) embarked on a campaign that framed the crisis as a problem of too much government regulation, which kept prices artificially low and discouraged drilling and the establishment of new refineries. In this context, the OPEC bogey – and the related notion of oil scarcity – provided a convenient scapegoat for skyrocketing prices and partial shortages, as well as confirmation of what might happen if the industry continued to be shackled by government bureaucrats. This message was at one with the early advocates of deregulation, monetarism, and fiscal austerity – including Milton Friedman, the young Alan Greenspan, and the future Enron CEO Kenneth Lay (then chief assistant to the Federal Energy Commission) – who all cut their teeth on arguments around US oil in the early 1970s. For these pro-market ideologues, the roots of the energy crisis were simple: government overregulation, too much bureaucracy, and the stifling of market competition.[53] The reform of the oil industry, in this sense, stood as synecdoche for what would later be described as the

51 Tyler Priest, 'Shifting Sands: 1973 Oil Shock and Expansion of Non-OPEC Supply', in Elisabetta Bini, Giuliano Garavini, and Federico Romero (eds), *Oil Shock*, London: I. B Tauris & Co., 2016, 117–41.

52 Ibid., 134.

53 A detailed account of the evolution of these arguments and the effect of the oil shock on American politics can be found in Meg Jacobs, *Panic at the Pump: The Energy Crisis and the Transformation of American Politics in the 1970s*, New York: Hill and Wang, 2016.

'neoliberal revolution'. William E. Simon, Nixon's Secretary of the Treasury (later reappointed by Gerald Ford), put it succinctly: 'We must lift the deadening hand of government from the many areas of our economy such as energy where overzealous government regulations are now cramping our growth and hopes for the future.'[54] The solution proposed by the oil companies and their ideological interlocutors was straightforward: American energy independence from the Middle East, to be achieved by the relaxation of environmental and clean air laws, the opening up of TAP, support for more offshore drilling, an end to import restrictions, and allowing US oil prices to rise in line with the rest of the world. These demands were implemented in their essential outline by the Nixon and Ford administrations between 1972 and 1977.

54 Cited in ibid., 177.

9

US Power, Oil, and Global Finance

The 1970s was bookended by two major oil price shocks: the 1973–74 crisis, and then a second major price spike in 1979–80, following the Islamic Revolution in Iran. As we have seen, no matter how painful these two shocks may have been for the average Western consumer, they did little to damage the interests of the largest oil firms operating in North American and European markets. Nonetheless, OPEC's actions did constitute a much more serious challenge to their international upstream position, as an ever-growing share of oil reserves and world crude production came under the direct control of producer governments. In 1970, the Seven Sisters or other Western oil companies held more than 90 per cent of international oil reserves outside the US and Soviet Union; by the end of the decade, this share would fall to less than a third (see Table 9.1). Even in Saudi Arabia, which had become the world's largest oil exporter in the early 1970s, the government would take a 60 per cent stake in Aramco in 1974 and had fully nationalised the company by 1980. For the first time ever, Western firms were no longer the dominant producers of crude at the global level.

Coupled with price rises, this upstream nationalisation drove a remarkable increase in the collective income of the leading OPEC states. Between 1965 and 1986, Middle East OPEC members alone would make around $1.7 trillion from the sale of oil, with Saudi Arabia earning over 40 per cent of this total (see Figure 9.1). These enormous pools of money – which soon became known as 'petrodollars' – signalled a unique shift in the global distribution of wealth. A tiny group of former colonies and states that were previously marginal to the world system suddenly controlled large amounts of capital, mostly earned through payments that came *from* the core capitalist countries. Such a transfer of wealth was historically unprecedented. Many oil-producing countries, particularly those in the Middle East Gulf, had domestic economies that were too small to absorb the large revenues derived from oil sales, so these states were poised to become major *exporters* of capital – a transformation that would reconfigure patterns of ownership and the control of assets throughout the world.

Table 9.1: Ownership of crude oil and oil sales outside the US and USSR 1950–79

Crude holdings	**1950**	**1957**	**1966**	**1970**	**1979**
Seven Sisters	98.2	89.0	78.2	68.9	23.9
Other international companies	1.8	11.0	21.8	22.7	7.4
Producing countries	-	-	-	8.4	68.7
Oil sales	**1950**	**1957**	**1966**	**1973**	**1979**
International oil companies – integrated channels	92.8	82.4	80.0	69.6	46.6
Third party sales	7.2	17.6	20	22.5	11.2
Direct marketing by producing governments	negligible	negligible	negligible	7.9	42.2

Source: Adapted by author from Brian Levy, 'World Oil Marketing in Transition', *International Organization* 36, no. 1, 1982, 117, 121.

Figure 9.1: Middle East OPEC revenues (1965–85), Billions of US dollars

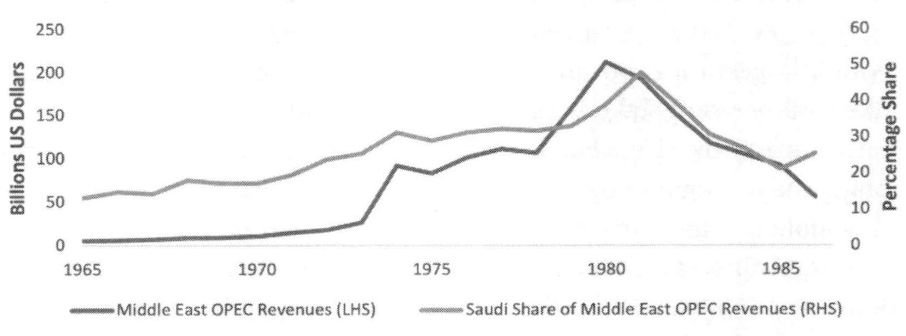

Source: Organization of the Petroleum Exporting Countries, Annual Statistical Bulletin, 2022, interactive version.

Yet, as these new geographies of accumulation were beginning to take shape, a range of other political and financial stresses was also apparent. Skyrocketing oil prices meant large fiscal deficits for most oil-importing countries, and these deficits presented a major threat to the development strategies of newly independent countries across Africa, Asia, and the Middle East. In the industrialised West, many states reeled from stagflation – the combination of high inflation rates and stagnant growth. New geopolitical fissures were also opening up alongside these financial strains. Throughout this period, the influence of the Soviet Union was growing rapidly across much of the former colonised world, linked in no small part to the oil boom occasioned by West Siberia's enormous energy reserves. While the US state and its largest corporations maintained their global strength, competing blocs were consolidating around powerful multinational firms based in Western Europe and Japan. The 1971 collapse of the dollar-gold standard also raised questions around continued US financial hegemony: the US dollar had been integral to buttressing American predominance through the post-war boom, but there was no guarantee that such a role could be maintained under the new system of floating international exchange rates. All of this posed serious questions around the continued viability of US dominance.

Against this backdrop, decisions about petrodollar *recycling* – where to invest OPEC's surpluses, who would control them, and in what currencies they would be held – drove a complex rerouting of capital flows through the 1970s. A new global financial system materialised, structured at the apex around the transatlantic connectivity of financial markets in the US and those in Western Europe. Dominated by Anglo-American financial institutions, this new architecture of global finance would help re-embed the primacy of the American state and the US dollar at a time of major political and economic uncertainty. It would also enable the appearance of new modes of wealth extraction and dependency across much of the globe, expressed most particularly through the chains of debt that emerged following the oil shocks. Rooting oil in these wider transformations of global finance and US power not only clarifies the real legacies of the 1970s and the so-called OPEC revolution – but also helps to illuminate oil's place in the contemporary world.

US Power in the Middle East

Much conventional economics literature approaches the 1970s as a moment in which the world faced a straightforward technical challenge: how to address global financial imbalances by matching surpluses in one part of the world with deficits in another. The problem with this perspective is that it abstracts economic decisions from the realities of social power, masking the continued influence of Western states across major oil-producing areas. It was certainly true that formal colonial rule had disintegrated amid post-war anti-colonial struggles, and that the direct ownership of upstream crude by Western firms was no longer possible in most circumstances. But oil-producing countries, especially in the Middle East, were now ruled by regimes that were seen as corrupt, self-serving, and autocratic by anti-imperialist, nationalist, and left-wing movements across their wider regional neighbourhoods. In this situation, Western states sought to cultivate new alliances with the national elites that had taken control of upstream oil. By selectively extending support to these regimes – integrating them into a subordinate position within the dominant power bloc – direct colonial rule was replaced by indirect forms of influence and control. Petrodollar flows emerged as a key mechanism through which this unequal but mutually beneficial arrangement was consolidated.

Most important here were the realities of American power in the Middle East. By the time of the first oil shock, the US had become the major foreign force in the region, a position that gave it significant influence over the main oil-exporting states in the Gulf. At the centre of the US presence in the region were alliances with ruling families in Saudi Arabia and pre-1979 Iran – the Al Saud and Pahlavi dynasties. These two autocratic monarchies were the undisputed leaders of OPEC, yet they were deeply disliked throughout the wider region and lived in perpetual fear of domestic revolt. As the influence of British colonialism waned, US support helped assure the survival of these monarchies while simultaneously binding them to US regional and global pre-eminence (or so it appeared in the case of Iran until the 1979 revolution). Alongside Saudi Arabia and Iran, the other oil-producing Gulf sheikhdoms were also essential US allies in the region. These states had all gained their independence by 1971, and while maintaining a strong link with Britain, they soon became a mainstay of US policy. Outside the Gulf, the other central pillar to US power in the region was Israel, which had proven its usefulness as a major force against Arab nationalism during the 1967 war with Egypt, Syria, and Jordan.

Following the first oil shock, the circulation of petrodollars became fundamental to the maintenance and reproduction of these relationships between the US and the Gulf monarchies. On one side, the US government consciously sought to attract petrodollar investments, and to encourage the purchase of American-made goods and services through a range of joint economic, technological, and commercial initiatives; in this manner, the revenues earned by the Gulf's oil sales flowed back into US businesses and the wider US economy, providing a vital source of global demand in a sluggish economic environment.[1] At the same time, with many of their investments held in dollar-denominated assets based in the US, the Gulf monarchies gained a stake in the stability and continued growth of the US economy. Most importantly, these economic linkages came with formal political ties and US support for the Gulf's ruling monarchies. This implicit guarantee of regime survival was essential in a regional climate of nationalist and radical-left agitation that viewed the Gulf monarchies as primary agents of Western influence in the Middle East.

At the heart of these 'petrodollar interdependencies' was the sale of US weapons and military hardware.[2] The country's military exports to Saudi Arabia increased more than tenfold between 1972 and 1978, to comprise more than 80 per cent of all arms bought by the Kingdom over that period.[3] Even more significant were US exports to the shah of Iran, which totalled \$8.3 billion between 1973 and 1978, just before the overthrow of the Pahlavi monarchy.[4] In 1974 alone, Iran agreed to purchase more US arms than did the rest of the world combined in any other previous year.[5] For the ruling monarchies in Iran and Saudi Arabia – and the narrow layer of elites that supported them domestically

1 For discussion of these initiatives, see David M. Wight, *Oil Money: Middle East Petrodollars and the Transformation of US Empire, 1967–1988*, Ithaca, NY: Cornell University Press, 2020, esp. ch. 3.

2 Ibid.

3 Stockholm International Peace Research Institute (SIPRI), Military Expenditure Database, sipri.org.

4 Leslie M. Pryor, 'Arms and the Shah', *Foreign Policy* 31, Summer 1978: 56–71, 57.

5 US Government General Accounting Office, 'Issues Related to U.S. Military Sales and Assistance to Iran', Department of Defense, Report to Congress, 1974, 38.

– these military sales confirmed unequivocal US support. They also offered lucrative profits for those close to the regime (and within the ruling family) through kickbacks and commissions for the arrangement of arms sales. On the US side, the export of weapons routed a considerable proportion of the Gulf's petrodollar surpluses into the pockets of the leading echelons of the country's war industry. This 'weapondollar–petrodollar' coalition remains an integral part of the economics of oil today.[6]

Military exports also had a direct (and often overlooked) consequence for trajectories of state formation in the Gulf itself. The sale of military hardware necessarily brought with it an ongoing US military presence to provide technical oversight, training, equipment repairs and upgrades, and to ensure the interoperability of domestic weapons systems within the wider security umbrella that the US maintained across the Gulf region. As a result, military transfers were not a simple one-off transaction: they served to embed US officials and advisors at the heart of the Gulf's state apparatus. Decisions around defence and security matters – a principal concern of the Gulf's paranoid rulers – were inseparable from this US presence, and served to fuse the highest ranks of the Gulf's military with the US state.[7] And in this manner, the sale of weapons allowed a concurrent shift in US geopolitical strategy amid the crisis of the Vietnam War – countries such as Iran and Saudi Arabia were repositioned as proxies for US regional interests, avoiding the scrutiny of the American public while hiding US military engagement behind the scrim of arms-length military transfers.[8]

These state-to-state connections helped carve out other routes for petrodollar recycling, notably the purchase of US government debt. Of key importance here was Saudi Arabia – now acknowledged as the world's leading oil producer and the largest holder of petrodollar surpluses within OPEC. Following a visit by US President Richard

6 Jonathan Nitzan and Shimshon Bichler, 'The Weapondollar-Petrodollar Coalition', in *The Global Political Economy of Israel*, London: Pluto Press, 2002.

7 The British also continued to maintain a strong connection with militaries in the Gulf, especially in the smaller Gulf sheikhdoms that had received their independence following British withdrawal from the region in 1971. This was particularly the case in Bahrain, the UAE, and Oman.

8 This strategy was codified in 1969 as the so-called Nixon Doctrine. For a discussion, see Andrew Scott Cooper, *The Oil Kings: How the US, Iran and Saudi Arabia Changed the Balance of Power in the Middle East*, London: Simon & Schuster, 2011.

Nixon to the country in 1974 (the first ever presidential visit to the Kingdom) and further delegations led by US Secretary of the Treasury William E. Simon, the US negotiated a secret arrangement that would see Saudi Arabia deposit billions of dollars in US Treasury bonds outside the normal auction for such securities.[9] By the end of 1977, Saudi Arabia would hold a fifth of all Treasury notes and bonds owned by central banks outside the US.[10] This remarkable level of Saudi bond purchases not only provided the US government with access to a 'huge pool of foreign capital', it also became vital to supporting the global dominance of the US dollar.[11] As Spiro points out: 'Having agreed to invest so much in dollars, the Saudis now shared a stake in maintaining the dollar as an international reserve currency . . . dollars constituted 90 percent of Saudi government revenues in 1979, and . . . Saudi investments were, roughly at the same time, 83 percent dollar denominated.'[12]

In this manner, Saudi financial surpluses played a central part in fortifying US dollar hegemony following the end of dollar–gold convertibility in 1971. At the same time, the status of the US dollar as the main international reserve currency was also directly connected to the denomination of oil itself in dollars. In the early 1970s, the dollar-denominated oil that we know today was not a foregone conclusion – about a fifth of international oil transactions were conducted in British sterling (see Chapter 5), and several OPEC members were keen to adopt a more diversified basket of currencies to replace the US dollar for oil pricing. In this context, the evolving US–Saudi relationship was paramount. On the same day that Saudi officials were meeting with a US delegation in Jeddah to finalise the agreement around the secret US Treasury purchases, the Kingdom announced that it would no longer accept sterling for its oil sales.[13] Whether this timing was mere

9 These arrangements were first documented in the pathbreaking research of David Spiro, and later corroborated in diplomatic cables released from the US National Archives in 2016. See David Spiro, *The Hidden Hand of American Hegemony Petrodollar Recycling and International Markets*, Ithaca, NY: Cornell University Press, 1999; Andrea Wong, 'The Untold Story behind Saudi Arabia's 41-Year US Debt Secret', bloomberg.com, 30 May 2016.

10 Spiro, *The Hidden Hand*, 112.

11 Ibid., 110.

12 Ibid., 122–3.

13 A lucid account of the debates and archival evidence around the US–Saudi relationship, including the 'coincidence' of this meeting and the Saudi decision to move

coincidence remains undisclosed, but, over the next few months, Saudi Arabia used its influence in OPEC to stop any move away from the US dollar, and, by 1975, dollar-only oil trading had been adopted by all OPEC members. Within OPEC as a whole, reserves held in US dollars increased from 57 per cent of the total to 93 per cent between 1973 and 1978.[14]

With the global oil trade now taking place exclusively in dollars, all countries were forced to hold large dollar reserves in order to fund their purchases of the world's most important commodity.[15] In this way, oil's centrality to global capitalism – mediated through the US alliance with Saudi Arabia and the other Gulf states – played a paramount role in cementing US dollar hegemony in a world of floating exchange rates. And because the international demand for dollars was way in excess of any domestic needs, the US could spend more abroad than it earned with less concern to the inflationary or exchange rate worries that constrained the spending policies of other countries. In essence, international holders of US dollars were funding the costs of American imperial expansion overseas. With the dollar confirmed as both the main store of value and a necessary means of purchase in world trade, it also provided a formidable source of geopolitical power to the US – the threat of sanctions or exclusion from the US banking system could cripple a country's economy without a single shot being fired. For its part, confirmation of Saudi Arabia's newfound systemic importance to global finance would come with its appointment as a permanent member of the IMF Executive Board in 1978, joining the US, West Germany, Japan, France, and Britain as the only countries in the world with individual seats on the board. This appointment depended on the support of the US, which dropped its objections once the voting rules had been

---

towards the dollar can be found in Duccio Basosi, 'Oil, Dollars, and US Power in the 1970s: Re-viewing the Connections', *Journal of Energy History/Revue d'Histoire de l'Énergie* 3, 28 May 2020, energyhistory.eu.

14 Congressional Budget Office (CBO), *The Effect of OPEC Oil Pricing on Output, Prices, and Exchange Rates in the United States and Other Industrialized Countries*, Washington, DC: CBO, 1981, 35.

15 A further important factor here was that if oil had been denominated in another currency, then the major oil exporters may have sought to shift their investments to non-US destinations or assets other than US treasuries and other equities.

changed to allow a continued American veto on all major decisions taken by the Fund.[16]

In all these ways, US Middle East policy through the 1970s was oriented towards cultivating interdependencies with the oil-producing monarchies in the region, based on the circulation of petrodollar wealth into US assets and financial markets, the provision of military protection, and an array of other political and economic ties. Initially this strategy encompassed both Iran and Saudi Arabia but following the overthrow of Iran's Pahlavi monarchy in 1979 – a revolution in which oil workers at the Abadan refinery played a critical role – the framework of US alliances in the Gulf shifted decisively towards the oil-rich Arab monarchies.[17] Without this strategic alliance between the US and the Gulf monarchies, it would have been much more difficult for the US (or the US dollar) to have become established at the core of global financial markets through the 1970s. But it is important to emphasise once again that this was not at all a one-way *external* imposition of US interests on countries in the region. The Gulf monarchies represented a thin layer of extreme wealth in a region of deprivation, and it was precisely the fragility of this class within the wider political tumult of the Middle East – vividly demonstrated in Iran in 1979 – that made the relationship with the US so essential to its survival.[18] By attaching themselves to US

16 Under IMF rules, an 85 per cent supermajority is required to pass votes on major policy issues. Because the US holds more than 15 per cent of voting power in the Fund, it has effective veto power (the only individual country to do so). Prior to 1978 the supermajority threshold was 70 per cent, and Saudi executive directorship would have meant a loss of US veto power. The figure was increased to 85 per cent as part of the negotiations around Saudi participation. David Spiro links this directly to the Saudi decision around oil pricing, although conclusive archival evidence on this is lacking. Spiro, *The Hidden Hand*, 104.

17 See Peyman Jafari, 'Fluid History: Oil Workers and the Iranian Revolution', in T. Atabaki, E. Bini, and K. Ehsani (eds), *Working for Oil: Comparative Social Histories of Labor in the Global Oil Industry*, London: Palgrave Macmillan, 2018, 69–98.

18 A major turning point in this US–Gulf relationship occurred with one of the most destructive conflicts of the twentieth century: the Iraq–Iran War, which lasted between 1980 and 1988, killing up to half a million people. Toby Jones observes that this war was a decisive step in the militarisation of the region, with the US seeing it as 'a useful conflict' and deliberately supplying 'weapons, funding, and intelligence to both sides' as a means to 'contain the belligerents and therefore ensure security elsewhere in the Gulf'. The US was also a direct participant, providing naval protection to Kuwaiti oil tankers and allowing them to fly the American flag, and repeatedly exchanging fire with Iranian warships. Toby Craig Jones, 'America, Oil, and War in the Middle East', *Journal of American History* 99, no. 1, 2012: 208–18, 215.

power, the Gulf monarchies sought to secure their own interests within an American-centred political and financial order. They gained a stake in this system, and in the process, helped to produce US power itself.

Euromarkets and the Global Debt Crisis

These Middle East investments in US goods and services, equities, and debt, formed one essential leg to the global circulation of petrodollars during the 1970s. Concurrently, however, other components of the global financial system were also emerging outside the US, and these would be no less linked to financial surpluses from the Middle East. Most essential here were the Euromarkets – de-regulated European financial markets that permitted banks and companies to deal in currencies denominated differently from their domestic markets. The largest of these Euromarkets was the 'Eurodollar' trade in the City of London, where dollar-denominated transactions (such as loans, bond issuance, and deposits) could take place outside the US itself. Launched after British financial markets were deregulated in the mid-1950s, the Eurodollar trade partly owes its origins to the rivalries of the Cold War, with the Soviet Union using the City as a site to place its international dollar liquidity without having to hold these dollars with institutions inside the US. The Euromarkets later became attractive to American companies seeking to circumvent restrictions on exporting dollars out of the US. As with today's offshore financial zones, the City of London was jurisdictionally separate from the British economy itself, and operated with few limits around currency controls, taxes, minimum deposit requirements, and interest rate regulations.[19]

The size of the Euromarkets exploded from just \$25 billion in 1968 to \$575 billion by 1980.[20] Much of this growth was driven by petrodollar wealth, with around a third of OPEC surpluses placed in Eurodollar banks through the 1970s.[21] These flows of oil wealth were routed from

19 For a history of how these markets came about, see Gary Burn, 'The State, the City and the Euromarkets', *Review of International Political Economy* 6, no. 2, Summer 1999: 225–61.

20 Youssef Cassis, *Capitals of Capital: A History of International Finance Centres, 1780–2005*, Cambridge: Cambridge University Press, 2006, 221, 236.

21 Basosi, 'Oil, Dollars, and US Power'.

the Middle East to Europe via consortium banks – joint ventures between Arab and foreign banks, mostly headquartered in London, Paris, and Geneva. Many of these banks traced their history back to Britain's earlier colonial presence in the Gulf, where they had been set up to funnel revenues from the sale of 'Sterling Oil' into British-domiciled accounts. Alongside these consortium banks, leading American and British banks also played a major role in channelling petrodollars into the Euromarkets through overseas bank branches established in Bahrain, a small island archipelago that opened an offshore banking system in 1975. Located just 60 kilometres off the coast of Saudi Arabia, Bahrain would soon displace Lebanon – then mired in a civil war – as the financial centre of the Middle East.

The link between Middle East petrodollar surpluses and the growth of the Euromarkets would be essential to the reconfiguration of global capitalism through the 1970s. Most importantly, the lightly regulated Euromarkets emerged as a key enabler of the liberalisation of cross-border finance that began from the 1970s onwards. With little government oversight, they allowed companies to borrow cheaply, eliminate exchange and transaction costs, and coordinate their global activities across a variety of markets, currencies, and interest rates. This was not simply a matter of banking and finance – it was directly linked to the internationalisation of non-financial firms, including the world's largest multinationals. Credit supplied in the Euromarkets helped fuel the cross-border activities of such firms seeking to expand their overseas operations – indeed, multinational corporations were responsible for 50 per cent of all Eurodollar trades in 1972 alone, a figure that continued to increase over the subsequent decade.[22] Much of this borrowing involved American firms that were restricted from exporting capital from their home country but could evade capital controls by borrowing in the Euromarkets. In this sense, the tremendous international extension of multinational activities that took place through this decade was directly rooted in the spectacular growth of the Euromarkets.

Alongside multinational corporations, the other major borrower on Euromarkets were poorer oil-importing countries. Faced with the two oil shocks and a prolonged global downturn, the total deficit of so-called developing (non-oil) countries rose steadily across the decade to reach

22 Ernest Mandel, *Late Capitalism*, London: Verso, 1972, 470.

$89 billion in 1980, up from just $11 billion in 1973.[23] Cash-strapped governments were left with little choice but to seek loans from commercial banks operating in the Euromarkets, which by 1979 accounted for half the total financing of Third World debt (up from around 25 per cent in 1974).[24] These loans were provided by a handful of private banks looking for profitable investment outlets for the surpluses they held on behalf of the oil-producing states. Importantly, most of these loans were made on commercial terms and at variable interest rates, a key departure from patterns of international lending prior to 1970, when loans had typically been concessional and provided by foreign governments or institutions such as the IMF.[25] Strikingly, just twenty large banks were responsible for half of all international bank loans made during this period – the majority of these banks were US or British-owned institutions.[26]

Fed by petrodollar flows and with a rising tide of credit provided in US dollars, the Euromarkets thus helped consolidate a new international financial architecture in which US financial institutions were dominant outside their own borders. This US leadership developed in close alliance with British banks and the City of London, which stood as the foremost intermediary between US financial markets and those in the rest of the world.[27] Connected to a 'spider web' of offshore zones such as the Cayman Islands, Bahrain, Bermuda, and Jersey – and other British overseas territories and crown dependencies operating under English

23 International Monetary Fund (IMF), *Annual Report*, 1983, 18.

24 H. Gibson, *The Eurocurrency Markets, Domestic Financial Policy and the International Instability*, London: Macmillan, 1989, 242. While commercial banks were the dominant lenders through the 1970s, other mechanisms also developed to complement the role of Euromarkets in recycling petrodollars – the IMF, for example, established two 'oil facilities' that channelled OPEC surpluses to countries reeling under high oil prices. The first lasted between June and December 1974, and the second between April 1975 and March 1976.

25 By 1979, 77 per cent of total Third World debt was non-concessional – a figure that had jumped from 40 per cent in 1971. David McLoughlin, 'The Third World Debt Crisis and the International Financial System', *Student Economic Review*, Trinity College Dublin, 1989: 96–101, 97.

26 Paul Mentre, 'The Fund, Commercial Banks, and Member Countries', IMF, 1984, 6. A majority of these banks were from the US and Britain, with seven and four banks respectively among the top twenty.

27 For a detailed history of this relationship, see Tony Norfield, *The City*, London: Verso, 2016.

Common Law – the City allowed the world's largest financial institutions to superintend the global lending and borrowing of multinational firms and governments.[28] This was not a simple enforcement of US financial imperatives on the City, but rather one in which US power emerged through its 'transatlantic interactivity' with Britain.[29] By siphoning off capital from around the world and redirecting it into US financial markets, institutions, and dollar-denominated assets, Britain both benefited from – and helped to shape – the nature of US financial power.

The full consequences of both this US financial predominance and the central role of the Euromarkets to international debt obligations would become apparent in 1980, when Paul Volcker, then chair of the board of governors of the US Federal Reserve, decided to raise US interest rates to more than 20 per cent. This interest rate hike – known as the Volcker Shock – was aimed at halting US inflation and strengthening the US dollar vis-à-vis other currencies.[30] But beyond these domestic effects, the Volcker Shock had a devastating impact on poorer oil-importing countries that had borrowed from the Euromarkets under variable rates. Because most of the debt owed by these countries was held in US dollars on non-concessional terms, the rise in interest rates meant a sharp increase in their debt service payments. All told, total Third World debt grew from $90 billion to $817 billion between 1971

28 For a discussion of this British 'spider-web', see Chapter 5 of Nicholas Shaxson, *Treasure Islands: Tax Havens and the Men Who Stole the World*, New York: Palgrave Macmillan, 2012.

29 Jeremy Green, 'Anglo-American Development, the Euromarkets, and the Deeper Origins of Neoliberal Deregulation', *Review of International Studies* 42, 2016: 425–49, 428.

30 For a full discussion of the Volcker Shock and its place in the making of American power, see Leo Panitch and Sam Gindin, *The Making of Global Capitalism: The Political Economy of American Empire*, London: Verso, 2012. Technically, the Federal Reserve board raised the *federal funds rate*, which is the interest rate that banks charge each other to borrow excess reserves overnight (by law, they must keep a minimum proportion of their deposits in the Federal Reserve Bank). Banks set their interest rates for other customers at a level slightly higher than the federal funds rate. The stated aim of Volcker's move was to reduce US inflation and strengthen the dollar vis-à-vis other currencies. In the US, it precipitated a deep recession (1980–82) and the highest unemployment rates since the Second World War. This was a clear goal for Volcker, who noted bluntly in 1979 that 'the standard of living of the average American has to decline'. S. Rattner, 'Volcker Asserts US Must Trim Living Standards', *New York Times*, 18 October 1979, A1.

and 1983, with debt service payments rising from $11 billion in 1971 to $131.3 billion by the end of 1982.[31] In effect, these payments on debt sucked up wealth from poorer countries and deposited it in the leading Anglo-American banks and financial institutions operating in the Euromarkets.

Pushed to the brink of insolvency – and concurrently reeling from the impact of the second oil shock – heavily indebted countries sought to renegotiate their debt schedules with these commercial lenders. But to reach an agreement on rescheduling, debtors had to consent to implementing a set of economic policies that were developed and monitored by the IMF and World Bank. These included measures such as trade liberalisation, privatisation, opening up to foreign capital flows, cutbacks to social spending, labour market deregulation, and so forth – all of which would become the staple requirements of the so-called structural adjustment programmes later imposed by the World Bank and IMF on debtor countries. Debt was thus the weapon used to compel poorer countries to open their industrial, financial, and commercial sectors to international capital. The sustained attack on global wages and social conditions launched at this time would profoundly alter the relative power of capital and labour, laying the ground for the later expansion and reorganisation of the world market through the 1990s and 2000s. Retroactively described by critics as the birth of the neoliberal 'revolution', this was a moment made possible through the deep interdependencies of oil and the global financial system that had emerged across the 1970s.

1980s Recession and the Oil Price Collapse

The economic changes that followed the Volcker Shock would also have a profound impact on the world oil industry. Most immediately, the interest rate rise triggered a global recession (1980–82) that would be the deepest economic slump since the Second World War. With the

31 McLoughlin, 'Third World Debt Crisis', 96. Eastern Bloc countries, notably Poland and Hungary, faced a similar debt crisis after also borrowing heavily from Western banks through the 1970s. See Mazen Labban, *Space, Oil and Capital*, New York: Routledge, 2008, 106.

shuttering of factories and businesses across most leading Western states, the global consumption of oil collapsed by 10 per cent between 1979 and 1983.[32] Led by an astonishing 17 per cent drop in North America and Western Europe, this remains the largest and longest fall in global oil consumption in history, even exceeding the collapse in demand that followed the COVID-19 pandemic.[33] Compounding the problems caused by this unprecedented fall in demand was a simultaneous increase in the supply of oil through the first half of the 1980s – thanks mostly to new production entering the market from non-OPEC sources.[34] Much of this non-OPEC production came from the Soviet Union, which remained the world's largest producer ahead of the US and Saudi Arabia. But two additional sources of non-OPEC supply had also appeared by the time of the 1980s downturn: Mexico and the UK (the latter from offshore fields in the North Sea). These two countries were negligible oil producers during the 1970s, but by 1984 they would displace major Middle East oil exporters to become the fourth and fifth largest producers in the world. Overall, global production from non-OPEC sources grew by 15 per cent between 1979 and 1985.[35]

This combination of increasing supply and falling demand struck at a moment of key structural change in the oil trade. By the early

32 Calculation in BP, *Statistical Review of World Energy*, 2022.

33 Over the past six decades, three major additional periods of annual decline in global consumption have been recorded: 1973–75, when oil consumption fell 2.2 per cent; 2008–09, with a fall of 1.3 per cent; and 2019–21, with a fall of 9.1 per cent. See BP, *Statistical Review of World Energy*, 2021.

34 In 1973, OPEC had held 51 per cent of world production; by 1985, this had fallen to less than 28 per cent. Bassam Fattouh, 'An Anatomy of the Crude Oil Pricing System', Oxford Institute for Energy Studies, January 2011, 18.

35 Oil production increased by 122 per cent in Mexico between 1978 and 1984, 135 per cent in the UK, 6.6 per cent in the Soviet Union. One of the effects of this non-OPEC oil was that it eroded the market share of Middle East producers, especially in Europe and North America, where short-haul oil from the new non-OPEC producers could be transported faster and more cheaply than long-haul oil from Saudi Arabia and elsewhere (it takes around six weeks for a tanker to carry oil from the Middle East Gulf to Europe). Lengthy transport duration was particularly problematic at times of heavy price volatility because the actual market price may have changed significantly by the time the oil reached the buyer. This encouraged producer governments to increase their use of spot markets (see below) in order to minimise the risks of volatility. Jonathan Stern and Adi Imsirovic, 'A Comparative History of Oil and Gas Markets and Prices: Is 2020 Just an Extreme Cyclical Event or an Acceleration of the Energy Transition?', Oxford Institute for Energy Studies, April 2020.

1980s, a growing share of oil was being bought and sold on so-called spot markets, where flexible short-term cash prices were negotiated between buyers and sellers, often for one-off transactions, rather than through long-term contracts based on OPEC's official reference price. These spot markets had become popular with new buyers – including independent oil refineries in Western Europe and other countries such as Japan, Brazil, and India – who found them cheaper and more flexible to use than procuring oil via the Western majors.[36] Producer governments were also shifting away from long-term contracts with the largest Western oil firms, towards dealing directly with governments or independent refiners (see Table 9.1).[37] In doing so, they increasingly depended on a new set of oil traders: specialised commodity-trading firms, who substituted themselves for the majors' trade networks by purchasing oil from producer governments and selling it on spot markets to buyers around the world. All of this meant that the number and diversity of oil industry actors multiplied dramatically during the 1970s, and the circulation of oil no longer took place predominantly within the integrated channels of the majors – indeed, by 1979, less than half of the world's oil circulated in this manner (Table 9.1).[38]

36 As noted in previous chapters, the growth in the number of independent refiners was partly due to the effect of Soviet oil exports and expertise.

37 The 1979 Iranian revolution hastened this shift, with the Islamic regime tearing up Iran's long-term contracts with the majors immediately after the overthrow of the shah; see Fattouh, 'An Anatomy', 17. After a doubling of the global oil price between April 1979 and April 1980 – the second oil shock – the price of oil in spot markets increased far above long-term contract prices; see Brian Levy, 'World Oil Marketing in Transition', *International Organization* 36, no. 1, 1982: 113–33, 123. This further encouraged oil-producing countries to terminate long-term contracts with the majors and instead trade directly with customers at the higher spot prices. On the buyer side, many oil consumers (governments and refiners alike) feared additional disruptions to oil supplies in the Middle East and thus sought to deal directly with producer governments rather than relying on the majors for their oil.

38 The one significant exception was the so-called Aramco Advantage, which involved Saudi Arabia and the four Aramco concession holders: Exxon, Mobil, Texaco, and Chevron. Between 1979 and 1981, Saudi Arabia continued to sell oil to these concessionaires at prices below spot market rates. The American companies then transferred this oil internally to their own foreign refineries at the lower prices, allowing the subsidiaries to make multi-billion-dollar profits when the oil was refined and sold at the high market prices then in place (Exxon's refineries made an *additional* $4.5 billion between 1979 and 1981 as a result of the Aramco Advantage). Because these profits were

In short, at the time of the 1980s downturn, OPEC and the Western majors had effectively lost control over upstream supply *and* downstream demand – and the enlarged role of spot markets had made it increasingly difficult to maintain a pricing system based on the coordinated decisions of a small number of OPEC members. The 1980s recession brought these tensions to a head, with the combination of plummeting demand and rising supply putting tremendous downward pressure on prices. Initially, OPEC's largest oil producer, Saudi Arabia, attempted to resist the erosion of prices by slashing its output from 10.2 million barrels per day in 1980 to just 3.6 million barrels per day in 1985. These efforts were largely futile, however, as other OPEC and non-OPEC producers continued to produce at increased volumes. Instead, for Saudi Arabia, the net result of the output cut was simply a loss of markets, with the Kingdom's share of world production falling from around 15 per cent in 1974 to just 6 per cent in 1985; concurrently, its share of OPEC revenues also plunged (Figure 9.1). By December 1985, Saudi Arabia's attempt to prop up prices had clearly failed. Faced with ballooning budget deficits at home, the Kingdom decided that it could no longer afford to support oil prices at the expense of falling market share. Giving up hopes of effectively moderating supply, Saudi Arabia instead increased its own production. This sudden increase in Saudi oil production drove a dramatic price collapse, with crude falling nearly 50 per cent, from $27.56 in 1985 to $14.43 in 1986.

The drop in oil prices would persist through the rest of the 1980s and most of the 1990s, with serious impact on major oil producers – including the Soviet Union, which would face years of turmoil alongside declining oil revenues, eventually culminating in the country's 1991 collapse (see next chapter). But, beyond its immediate fiscal effects, the 1985–86 price countershock marked the final denouement for the system of administered prices that had been in place since the early twentieth century (first under the Seven Sisters, and then under OPEC post-1973). After a couple of years of experimentation with alternative

made by foreign subsidiaries of the oil majors, the profits could be sheltered from the Internal Revenue Service (IRS). In 1991, the IRS took Exxon and Texaco to court to claim unpaid taxes worth more than $4 billion, but the case was won by the oil companies.

pricing mechanisms, a new market-based system of oil pricing would emerge by 1988.[39] In this system, the broad outlines of which remain with us today, the reference price of oil would be linked to the price of futures contracts – a kind of financial derivative – traded on two main financial markets, the New York Mercantile Exchange (NYMEX) and the Intercontinental Exchange (ICE). Tied in this way to the trade of so-called paper barrels, oil was transformed into a financial asset that could be bought and sold regardless of *physical* consumption. In subsequent decades, this would open up oil as a prime target for speculative capital flows – a feature of the markets that continues through to the current day.[40]

New Constellations of American Power

In a myriad of ways, the incorporation of Middle East oil surpluses into the emergent system of global finance reworked the character of US primacy following the end of the post–war boom. With the breakdown of the Bretton Woods arrangements (the dollar–gold standard), these surpluses helped institutionalise new forms of dollar supremacy across the Euromarkets and other offshore zones. The Anglo-American financial institutions that dominated global depository and lending activities took the lead in encouraging the development of these markets and pushing for further financial liberalisation. The unbridled growth of global finance enabled by these measures proceeded in lockstep with the cross-border expansion of multinational firms, itself made possible by the opening up of economies across the world following the oil-induced debt crises. In this manner, the oil shocks served to prise open the world market and simultaneously create the financial backbone for capital's global expansion – linked processes that were largely overseen by the US state.

39 The collapse in the price of oil was directly related to a Saudi decision to adopt a new pricing mechanism called netback prices. This system set the price of crude based on that of refined products (after transportation, refining, and other costs), with a guaranteed margin to refiners. It lasted until around 1988, when the current system of market pricing was consolidated. A comprehensive account of the evolution of oil pricing is provided in Fattouh, 'An Anatomy'.

40 See Adam Hanieh, 'The Commodities Fetish? Financialisation and Finance Capital in the US Oil Industry', *Historical Materialism* 29, no. 4, 2023: 70–113, for a fuller discussion of this issue.

All of this further modified the contours of alliance-making between the US and other parts of the world. While the 1974 embargo had initially seen European states propose a counterweight to US policies in the Middle East through an independent Euro-Arab dialogue, this course was stymied by the pro-Atlantic stance of the Netherlands, which at that stage was the centre of Europe's oil industry. By the mid-1970s, advocates of a stronger relationship with the US were elected in the UK, West Germany, and France, and the US took leadership in the transatlantic discussions around what to do with petrodollars and the financial system. As we have seen, an essential role in this emerging Atlantic alliance was played by the City of London, which became the main headquarters for petrodollar recycling and international lending. Crucially, however, the origins of this 'special relationship' were not simply determined by a historical affinity based on language and a shared Anglophone culture. Britain's colonial dominance of the Middle East had made it the privileged site through which oil's financial surpluses would come to buttress first sterling, and then later the dollar. The intersection of oil and dollar hegemony helped consolidate an enduring US-British relationship that continues today.

The other key dimension to US power through this period was, of course, the relationship with the oil-producing states of the Gulf. Initially, this had been mostly structured through US support for the shah of Iran – a legacy of the leading role played by the US in the 1953 coup – but this relationship was severed with the 1979 revolution. In its place, US dominance in the region came to rest on Saudi Arabia and the smaller Gulf states in the Arabian Peninsula, who went on to form a regional bloc in 1981 called the Gulf Cooperation Council (GCC). Integrated into a US security umbrella and backed by the ever-increasing sale of military hardware to the Gulf monarchies, the GCC would become central to the projection of American military power throughout the region. A network of US army and naval bases are now permanently located across various Gulf countries, and the US–Saudi relationship continues to define US strategy in the Middle East.[41]

41 As with the 1980s, a major turning point in this relationship involved Iraq, which was subject to a devastating sanctions regime through the 1990s and then a direct US- and UK-led military invasion in 2003. The 2003 invasion and subsequent occupation destroyed the fabric of Iraqi society, killing hundreds of thousands. This war was not so much about the seizure of Iraq's oil but the protection of the Gulf monarchies. As Toby

Beyond military and diplomatic dimensions, an often unacknowledged reason for the durability of this strategic alliance is the Gulf's distinctive class and social structure. Unlike Iran's Pahlavi monarchy – overthrown by labour strikes and mass protests in 1979 – there have been no major domestic political movements since the 1970s that have threatened the position of the ruling Gulf monarchs or their alliance with the US.[42] A key reason for this is that a majority of the working classes in each of the GCC states are made up of non-citizen migrants, drawn from poorer countries in South Asia, the Middle East, and elsewhere. There is no other place on the planet where such a high proportion of the workforce is comprised of temporary, rightless, migrant workers. A highly racialised citizen/migrant divide militates against political mobilisation, with strikes and protests forbidden and punished by deportation. Autocratic and heavily securitised states sustain this class structure, supported by a narrow layer of large business conglomerates that constitute the Gulf's capitalist class.[43] The internal stability of the Gulf's monarchies – despite frequent factional struggles within the ruling families – ultimately depends on this social structure. In this sense, the social relations of Gulf capitalism play a vital role in the reproduction of US power at the *global* level.

It is only by shedding light on these supremely political dimensions of the economics of petrodollar surpluses that the enduring imperial contours underlying the making of modern finance can be revealed.

Jones notes, 'Capturing oil and oil fields and establishing direct or imperial control over oil has not been part of the United States' strategic logic for war. But protecting oil, oil producers, and the flow of oil has been. This is a critical distinction.' Toby Craig Jones, 'America, Oil and War', 217.

42 The last major threat to the Gulf monarchies was the Dhofar rebellion, a powerful left-wing insurgency that sought independence from the Gulf state of Oman, and which lasted from 1963 to 1976. The rebellion was supported by a range of different communist and nationalist movements throughout the Arabian Peninsula, but was ultimately defeated with the backing of British and Iranian troops (the latter supplied with US helicopters and other weapons). See Abdel Razzaq Takriti, *Monsoon Revolution: Republicans, Sultans, and Empires in Oman, 1965–76*, Oxford: Oxford University Press, 2012.

43 For an analysis of these processes, including migration in the Gulf, see Adam Hanieh, *Capitalism and Class in the Gulf Arab States*, London: Palgrave Macmillan, 2011; and Adam Hanieh, *Money, Markets, and Monarchies: The Gulf Cooperation Council and the Political Economy of the Contemporary Middle East*, Cambridge: Cambridge University Press, 2018.

Forms of money and the rise of the Euromarkets, the dollar's position as international reserve currency, the dominance of Anglo-American financial institutions, the chains of debt and the rise of neoliberal orthodoxy – these were not the automatic outcomes of dry economic processes centred in North America and Europe, but inextricably linked to the geopolitics of oil and the US presence in the Middle East. In underlining these subterranean global roots to the emergence of a new international financial system in the 1970s, it is possible to shift the ways that we usually think about the control of oil. This is not simply reducible to territorial power and the ownership of foreign oil fields – it is also a question of the control of oil's *wealth*. And this remains no less an imperial venture than the tussles of British and American oil firms during the early years of the twentieth century.

10

Oil and Capital in Post-Soviet Russia

Earlier chapters have emphasised Russia's centrality to the story of world oil. Russian oil under early Soviet control helped paved the way for the rise of a local European oil industry, the international expansion of US firms such as SONY and Vacuum, and the push towards cartelisation expressed in the Achnacarry 'As Is' Agreement. With the West Siberia boom from the mid-1960s onwards, Soviet oil exports made it much more difficult for the established Western majors to control the world-wide production, refining, and distribution of oil. By weakening the position of the Seven Sisters, including their ability to set oil prices, the realities of Soviet oil were thus directly consequential to the rise of so-called oil nationalism, the establishment of OPEC, and the wave of national liberation movements through the 1960s and 1970s. Throughout, the key issue was never the simple fact of Russia's enormous material resources. Rather, it has been Russia's *social and political dynamics* – including the forms of property relations that govern oil – that have shaped the complex interdependencies between Russian oil production, the world market, and the structural characteristics of the international oil industry.

These interdependencies sit at the root of the major changes that ensued in the Soviet Union through the 1980s. As noted in Chapter 8, the perceived threat of a Soviet oil offensive had preoccupied US policy makers from as early as the 1960s, and it was in this context that oil emerged as a focus of US grand strategy debates in the 1970s. For Jimmy

Carter's policy makers – such as National Security Advisor Zbigniew Brzezinski, and his colleague Samuel Huntington – the oil industry could be used as a strategic lever to sap the economic and political strength of the Soviet Union. This assessment was backed up by a CIA report, issued in 1977, which predicted an imminent collapse of Soviet oil production due to declining well productivity in West Siberia, a lack of new fields, and poor technological capacity. The agency estimated that this coming energy crisis would make the Soviet Union a net importer of oil by the mid-1980s. With the hope of accelerating this collapse, Brzezinski, Huntington, and others called for export controls on US drilling and pipeline technologies as a way to stymie Soviet attempts to stave off the expected fall in oil production.[1]

In the end, the CIA's prediction of an imminent decline in Russian oil production turned out to be wholly wrong – the volume of Soviet oil exports rose by more than 70 per cent between 1980 and 1988, and the country still ranked as the world's largest producer at the time of its dissolution in 1991. US sanctions against the Soviet oil industry also proved to be ineffective, as other Western countries continued to export technology in place of American firms. Nevertheless, from the end of the 1970s onwards, it was clear that the Soviet oil industry had begun to face deep-rooted challenges requiring urgent attention. The main problem was that the first generation of West Siberian oil fields was suffering from high depletion rates (the share of new oil output required to make up for natural yearly declines) and thus demanded greater investment to find and produce new oil.[2] This did not mean that West Siberian oil was running out; rather that it was becoming more expensive to produce.

1 These calls for export restrictions were opposed by US drilling companies and other wings of the US government (such as the Department of Commerce), which disagreed with the CIA's prediction of Soviet oil decline and were sceptical of the impact of technological sanctions. Comprehensive sanctions were eventually introduced after the Soviet invasion of Afghanistan in 1979. For a detailed analysis of these debates over Soviet oil, see David Painter, 'From Linkage to Economic Warfare: Energy, Soviet–American Relations, and the End of the Cold War', in Jeronim Petrovic, *Cold War Energy: A Transnational History of Soviet Oil and Gas*, London: Palgrave Macmillan, 2017, 283–302.

2 By 1985, the depletion ratio was estimated at 85 per cent – meaning that almost all of any increase in oil output from West Siberia would be needed just to keep oil production at the same level. Thane Gustafson, *Crisis amid Plenty: The Politics of Soviet Energy under Brezhnev and Gorbachev*, Princeton, NJ: Princeton University Press, 1989, 67.

These costs were compounded by numerous inefficiencies associated with Soviet bureaucratic planning: a lack of exploration and drilling, poor oilfield management, sub-standard technology and tools, a prioritisation of output volumes over the long-term care of oil fields, and fabrication of oil data by managers in the field attempting to satisfy unrealistic central planning targets.[3]

By the early 1980s huge investments in drilling and exploration were required just to keep Soviet oil production stable – and the more that was spent on oil and gas, the less was available for other industrial sectors.[4] This had pernicious and self-reinforcing effects. Industries producing civilian machinery and tools, for example, suffered from a severe lack of investment as money went into oil exploration and drilling; but this meant that much oilfield machinery and equipment was sub-standard and obsolete, further increasing the costs of oil exploration and production. The realities of such feedback loops were felt on a daily basis by those working the oil fields; by one estimate, between a third to a half of domestically made oil equipment arriving in the field was defective.[5] Soviet leaders from Brezhnev to Gorbachev were well aware of these problems and intense inter-bureaucratic discussions took place around oil production and investment targets. Various plans were also developed to improve the country's energy conservation and substitute domestic oil use with other energy sources such as gas, coal, and nuclear power – but these efforts did little to reduce the huge expenditures required in oil production.

Nonetheless, the primary issue constraining Soviet decision-making at this time was not one of geology or planning – but, rather, the structural dependence of the Soviet bureaucracy on the income from oil exports. Oil revenues assisted the Soviet leadership in masking the contradictions and tensions within society as a whole, enabling the steady import of grain, meat, technology, and other consumer goods. Through these imports, living standards could improve despite

3 See Gustafson, *Crisis amid Plenty*, for a discussion of the problems in Soviet oil production during the Brezhnev, Andropov, and early Gorbachev years.

4 One 1980 estimate claimed that, in order to keep oil's share in the Soviet energy balance at the same level through the coming years, investment in oil would need to increase nearly fourfold – more than the increased investment planned for the entirety of Soviet industry. Ibid., 29.

5 Ibid., 182.

the lack of political freedoms and heavy-handed bureaucratic repression. Subsidised oil also helped hold together the wider Soviet bloc by making available energy at below world market prices; indeed, Eastern Europe had been largely insulated from the 1970s price shocks thanks to the Soviet Union. All of this meant that the position of the bureaucracy rested fundamentally on an uninterrupted and ever-increasing flow of oil revenues – hence the stability of oil production in West Siberia.

In this context, the 1986 collapse in oil prices had a severe impact on the Soviet Union. Through the first half of the 1980s, a reckoning with the declining world oil price had been largely postponed thanks to a frenzied campaign of oil drilling and exploration in West Siberia, and an expansion of gas production that saw the Soviet Union overtake the US as the world's largest producer of natural gas. These measures enabled a steady increase in Soviet oil exports between 1980 and 1985, which provided continued supplies of hard currency despite falling world prices.[6] But with world prices collapsing by nearly half in the space of less than a year, the 1985–86 price crash upturned this status quo. At that stage, exports of crude oil and refined products represented around 60 per cent of the Soviet Union's hard currency revenues – a figure that rose to 80 per cent with the inclusion of gas (the price of gas was linked to the price of oil).[7] The price collapse thus slashed Soviet foreign income, and cost the country an estimated $20 billion a year over the rest of the decade according to Politburo archives.[8]

Compounding this loss of foreign earnings was a sudden devaluation

6 Soviet oil exports increased by more than a third between 1980 and 1986; total oil production, however, remained essentially unchanged over this period (BP Statistics).

7 Theodore Shabad, 'Soviet Oil Revenue Rose in '82', *New York Times*, 21 June 1983.

8 Marshall I. Goldman, *Petrostate: Putin, Power, and the New Russia*, New York: Oxford University Press, 2008, 52. The link between Saudi Arabia's 1985 decision to increase oil production and its effect on the oil price has led some observers to attribute the Soviet collapse to a US plot led by then CIA director William Casey acting under orders from Ronald Reagan. According to this narrative, Casey used US influence with Saudi Arabia and the Kingdom's anger with the Soviet invasion of Afghanistan to convince the Saudis to crash the oil price. There is little archival evidence for this alleged conspiracy, which, among other problems, ignores the crucial backdrop to the fall in oil prices that was sketched in the last chapter. For recent critiques of this narrative focusing more on the diplomatic record, see Painter, 'Linkage to Economic Warfare', and Goldman, *Petrostate*.

of the US dollar that began in 1985 following an agreement between the finance ministers of France, West Germany, Japan, the UK, and the US.[9] This devaluation made much of the Soviet Union's non-dollar imports relatively more expensive, further squeezing the country's budget. Low oil prices also had an impact on the export of weapons and military hardware – the Soviet Union's other major hard currency earner – as much of the demand for these goods came from Middle East oil-exporting countries that were now facing their own loss of revenue.[10] With plummeting hard currency income and rising non-dollar prices, the Soviet Union found it increasingly difficult to cover the cost of imports, including food (the country was the world's largest importer of grain) and essential technology. As a result, the country was forced to borrow heavily from Western banks and governments – net Soviet debt ballooned from $10.2 billion in 1984 to $37.3 billion by 1989.[11]

With world oil prices fluctuating between $14 and $19 per barrel over the rest of the decade, the problems facing the Soviet political economy worsened. Mired in an unwinnable war in Afghanistan, lacking hard currency and increasingly unable to supply imports, the population experienced shortages of basic goods and high inflation, fuelling protests and labour strikes across the country (notably a massive strike by coalminers in 1989). Revenue from Soviet oil exports increasingly went to paying off interest on foreign debt rather than providing for imports – a classic debt trap that was appearing across much of the rest of the world at the time. All of this put greater pressure on the oil industry to produce more oil, but while the oilmen in West Siberia attempted to find and develop new fields as an alternative to the older sites, these were unable to offset declining production and it became increasingly expensive to extract Soviet oil.[12]

9 For a discussion of this agreement and its broader political economy backdrop, see Leo Panitch and Sam Gindin, *The Making of Global Capitalism: The Political Economy of American Empire*, London: Verso, 2012.

10 In some cases, oil-exporting countries paid for military hardware in oil, which was then sold by the Soviet Union. Painter cites a CIA estimate that around 10 per cent of Soviet oil exports were actually Middle East oil that had been exchanged for weapons. Painter, 'Linkage to Economic Warfare', 299.

11 Simon Pirani, *Change in Putin's Russia: Power, Money, and People*, London: Pluto Press, 2010, 8.

12 Gustafson observes that the costs of delivering Soviet oil grew by two-thirds between 1983 and 1987. Thane Gustafson, *Wheel of Fortune: The Battle of Oil and Power in Russia*, Cambridge, MA: Belknap Press, 2012, 36.

The peak in Soviet output would be reached in 1988, hastened by over-drilling, a lack of industrial imports due to the wider economic crisis, and destructive techniques that prioritised production but damaged the long-term health of the field.[13]

It was amid these multifaceted crises that the last Soviet president, Mikhail Gorbachev, launched a series of market mechanisms and political changes in 1987, hoping to address the country's deep economic and political malaise. These initiatives, however, did not deliver on promises of improved living standards for the wider population, but instead further deepened the weaknesses of bureaucratic state planning. In 1989, Gorbachev made the fateful decision to cut the supply of subsidised Soviet oil to Eastern European allies and to insist that oil payments be made in hard currency. This intensified the problems faced by these countries – who were themselves heavily indebted to Western banks and governments – and helped drive the restoration of market economies across Eastern Europe. At the same time, secessionist movements erupted in key Soviet republics, including Ukraine, Estonia, and Azerbaijan. These republics had been the main manufacturers of drilling tools, pipes, and other materials used in the West Siberian oil fields, and around 1990, as their independence movements won power, severe equipment shortages spiralled throughout the Russian oil sector. The supply of labour was also heavily impacted, as a large proportion of oil workers were migrants from the newly independent republics. All these factors contributed to a 20 per cent fall in oil production and a nearly 50 per cent collapse in oil exports between 1988 and 1991. Oil could no longer mask the country's many internal contradictions. The failure of a coup led by a conservative faction of the bureaucracy against Gorbachev in August 1991 confirmed the exhaustion of the old system. And, in December 1991, the Soviet Union was officially disbanded.

13 One technique pioneered and used extensively in the Soviet oil industry is called water flooding. It involves injecting water at high pressures into the field, in order to force oil out. While this raised initial recovery rates, it also damaged the long-term health of the oil field.

New Capitalists

The Soviet Union did not collapse because of low global oil prices. This was certainly a major proximate factor, but the price of oil was inseparable from the wider set of global transformations that unfolded through the early 1980s: deep-rooted problems of overaccumulation and stagnant profit rates; the changes to financial markets and economic activity induced by the Volcker Shock; the subsequent global economic downturn; and the explosion in global debt. As we have seen in the previous chapter, these economic shifts were wrapped up in complex ways with changes to the global oil industry itself: new sources of supply; new industry actors; new forms of oil trading; and the eventual breakdown of the OPEC-administered pricing system in 1985–86. Taken together, these transformations in the world market – of which low oil prices were simply one manifestation – severely exacerbated the deep internal contradictions of an undemocratic and bureaucratised polity (including across the Soviet Union's larger bloc of international allies). In turn, this situation of crisis only hastened the disintegration of the country's oil industry, and thus the ability to produce and export oil. None of this was a matter of causal primacy in either global *or* domestic factors, but the interaction of the two – with the oil circuit serving as the key mediating link in this relationship.

Following the 1991 collapse, the social dynamics of the new post-Soviet capitalism continued to be fundamentally tied to the world market through the mediation of oil. The years immediately following the break-up were disastrous for most of the Russian people. A 40 per cent decline in GDP between 1991 and 1996 left more than a third of the country's population living below the poverty line; mass joblessness reappeared, and life expectancy dropped by an astounding five years following the collapse of the public health and welfare systems.[14] But, while living standards plummeted for the majority, a sliver of the population managed to capture the opportunities for wealth and power that emerged with the dismantlement of the old Soviet state apparatus. These new private owners of economic wealth did not suddenly materialise in 1991; they had been nurtured in the final years of the Soviet Union under Gorbachev's policies of market opening, which had allowed a

14 *The World Bank Research Observer* 13, no. 1, February 1998: 37–58.

small number of state managers and bureaucrats to begin to convert their political power into stable economic wealth.[15] The oil circuit was essential to this early accumulation of capital.

Unlike the vertically integrated structures of large Western oil companies, effective control of the Soviet oil industry had been dispersed across various government ministries with different responsibilities for the production, transport, refining, and export of oil. Competing geographic interests overlapped with this bureaucratic fragmentation, and federal, regional, and local authorities vied with one another over resources and decisions about oil production. During the final chaotic years of the Gorbachev period, this fragmented structure provided wealth-making opportunities for anyone able to find ways to move streams of crude and refined products outside official channels.[16] But fragmentation also meant that it was not initially possible for an individual to take control of the oil field, transport, refining, and export within one vertically integrated company. Instead, encouraged by Gorbachev's policies of market opening, alliances formed between oilfield managers, refiners, and the traders who could reach export markets. In many cases, criminal gangs played an important role in these networks, assisting with the transportation of oil and helping launder its wealth – as well as providing physical protection against rivals.

Most notable here were the traders who could move oil across borders. In the Soviet Union, the domestic price of oil was fixed at a level much lower than international prices – around a hundred times less at the time of the Soviet collapse.[17] Tempted by this huge price differential, well-connected state managers sought to obtain export licences and establish their own private trading companies linked to oil refiners and tanker companies. One such individual was Gennady Timchenko, who worked at the Ministry of Foreign Trade in the USSR and became vice president of a large state-owned oil refinery in 1988 (see Table 10.1). Timchenko obtained an export licence in 1991, which he used to ship

15 Pirani, *Change in Putin's Russia*.

16 In the final years of the Soviet Union, a very large proportion of oil exports were being diverted to secret destinations outside of official channels. According to Yegor Gaidar, Russia's first prime minister, only 22 out of 194 foreign oil shipments reached their nominal destination in 1991; see Gustafson, *Wheel of Fortune*, 81.

17 Ibid., 512.

Russian oil products to Europe in partnership with another petroleum trading firm, Urals Trading, that had been established by a former KGB agent.[18] By the early 2000s, Timchenko would have become one of the most influential people in the global oil business – his company Gunvor ranking as the fourth largest oil trader in the world.

Table 10.1: Oil and Russia's Business Conglomerates

Business owner (conglomerate name)	Estimated net worth, Forbes 2021 (Russian billionaire rank)	Connection to industry	Personal history of owner
Vladimir Potanin (Interros)	$27 billion (first)	Sidanco (Russia's fifth largest oil company during the 1990s, merged with TNK in 2001 and became part of TNK-BP)*	Potanin worked in the Ministry of Foreign Trade prior to 1991 and set up a private bank, Oneksimbank, in 1993. He devised the loans-for-shares scheme and won control over oil, nickel, machine-building, agricultural, and pharmaceuticals companies through his Interros conglomerate. He was first deputy prime minister of Russia (1996–97). He sold his interest in Sidanco in 2001; his main business interest today is Norilsk Nickel, the world's largest producer of high-grade nickel.
Leonid Mikhelson	$24.9 billion (fourth)	Sibur (Russia's biggest petrochemical firm); Novatek (largest non-state gas producer in Russia, also produces oil)	Before 1991, Mikhelson was general director of a state-owned pipeline construction firm that was one of the first companies to be privatised after the end of the Soviet Union. He is the largest shareholder in Sibur and Novatek, and a business partner of Gennady Timchenko.
Vagit Alekperov (IFD Kapital)	$24.9 billion (fourth)	President and chair of LUKoil (second largest oil company in Russia)	Alekperov was deputy minister of oil and gas in the Soviet Union and won control over LUKoil in 1993. He is also involved in banking, pension fund management, real estate, and media through IFD Kapital.

18 Andrew Higgins, Guy Chazan, and Alan Cullison, 'Secretive Associate of Putin Emerges as Czar of Russian Oil Trading', *Wall Street Journal*, 11 June 2008.

Gennady Timchenko	$18.1 billion (fifth)	Gunvor (fourth largest crude oil trader in the world); Novatek (major shareholder); Sibur (major shareholder)	In 1988, Timchenko was deputy director of the state-owned oil company that operated Kirishi refinery, one of the largest in the Soviet Union. He is a business partner of Leonid Mikhelson.
Mikhail Fridman (Alfa Group)	$15.5 billion (ninth)	Tyumen Oil Company (TNK, later merged into TNK-BP)* Onako (later merged into TNK-BP)* Wintershall DEA (one of the largest European oil and gas companies; operates in Europe, the Middle East, and Latin America)	Fridman founded a commodity trading company, Alfa-Eko, in 1989, and launched Alfa Bank in 1991. He continues to control the latter, which is the largest private bank in Russia. Alfa-EKO and Alfa Bank took over the state-owned Tyumen Oil Company (TNK) in 1997, which formed an alliance with BP in 2003. TNK-BP was the third largest Russian oil company until 2013, when it was sold to Rosneft in a deal worth $55 billion. The Alfa Group also won control over Onako in 2000, the first oil privatisation under Putin. Fridman used his share of the TNK-BP sale to establish an international holding company, LetterOne, which controls 33 per cent of Wintershall DEA along with BASF (67 per cent). Other interests of Letter One include controlling ownership of UK health food chain Holland & Barrett; largest shareholder in Veon (thirteenth largest mobile operator in the world); and second largest shareholder (20 per cent) in TurkCell (the leading mobile phone firm in Turkey).
Suleiman Kerimov	$15.8 billion (tenth)	Nafta Moskva (former state-oil trading company)	Alongside Nafta Moskva, Kerimov has held investment interests in gold, banking, steel, and real estate, and was a major shareholder in Gazprom. He was a member of the State Duma between 1999 and 2007 and is currently a member of the Federation Council from Dagestan.

Roman Abramovich (Millhouse)	$14.5 billion (eleventh)	Sibneft* (sixth largest oil company in 1995)	Abramovich took control of Sibneft in 1996 and 1997 (with Boris Berezovsky) through the loans-for-shares scheme. Sibneft was acquired by Gazprom in 2005 for $13 billion. He later became owner of Chelsea Football Club, and has major interests in aluminium, airlines, steel, mining, coal, agriculture, media, and technology. Abramovich was governor of Chukotka autonomous region between 2000 and 2008.
Leonid Fedun	$11 billion (fourteenth)	Major shareholder in LUKoil	Fedun is a former military officer.
Viktor Vekselberg (Renova Group)	$9 billion (seventeenth)	Tyumen Oil Company (TNK, later merged in TNK-BP)* Onako (later merged into TNK-BP)*	Vekselberg founded Renova Group along with Leonard Blavatnik in 1990. Renova worked in partnership with Blavatnik's Access Industries and the Alfa Group to win control of TNK in 1997, later merged in a joint venture with BP to become TNK-BP. He received $7 billion through the sale of TNK-BP to Rosneft in 2013. Vekselberg holds 32 per cent of the world's second largest aluminium producer (United Co. Rusal), and controls Russia's largest power provider (T Plus), as well as companies involved in machinery, steel manufacturing, construction, and airport management. He continues to have interests in international oil and gas through various investment vehicles.
Petr Aven (Alfa Group)	$5.3 billion (twenty-third)	Tyumen Oil Company (TNK)* Onako (later merged into TNK-BP)*	Aven is a former minister of foreign economic relations for the Russian Federation (1991–92). He joined Alfa Bank in 1993 as president, and is currently a board member of LetterOne (see Fridman).

Mikhail Gutseriev (Safmar Holding)	$2.5 billion	Slavneft* RussNeft (ninth largest oil company in Russia) Neftisa (oil producer) Forteinvest (oil refiner) Adamas (oil refiner)	Gutseriev is former president of the state-owned Slavneft, which was privatised and sold to TNK-BP and Sibneft in 2002. He went on to found RussNeft and Netsifa. He is the largest foreign investor in Belarus and is a close ally of Belarusian President Alexander Lukashenko. He is also involved in media (radio and TV), fertiliser production, coal, construction, real estate, and hotel ownership. He served as a deputy in the State Duma in 1995 and 1999.
Vladimir Bogdanov	$1.7 billion	CEO of Surgutneftegaz	Bogdanov was director-general of Surgutneftegaz from 1984 until its privatisation in 1993. He was a member of the regional parliament of Khanty-Mansi autonomous region between 1996 and 2006.
Boris Berezovsky (Logovaz)	n/a (deceased)	Sibneft*	Berezovsky was a former Duma representative, running on Putin's ticket in the 1999 legislative election. He has been a deputy prime minister and a member of the National Security Council. In addition to oil, his interests included TV and media, automobiles, and airlines (Aeroflot). After conflict with Putin, he claimed political asylum in the UK. He was found dead by hanging in his Berkshire mansion in 2013.
Mikhail Khodorkovsky (Menatep)	n/a	Yukos	Khodorkovsky was a former official in Komsomol (the youth section of the Communist Party). He was advisor at the Ministry of Fuel and Energy (post-1991).

Source: Media reports; company websites; Forbes 2021 list; Andrew Barnes, *Owning Russia: The Struggle over Factories, Farms, and Power*, Ithaca, NY: Cornell University Press, 2006: some details have changed since the beginning of the Ukraine War, as a number of the individuals listed formally divested holdings in various companies or sold to family members in an attempt to avoid sanctions.
* indicates the relationship or company no longer exists

Alongside oil traders such as Timchenko, another important group that would play a prominent role in oil at the time of the Soviet Union's break-up were state officials who controlled upstream production and the oil fields. Dubbed the 'oil generals' by Thane Gustafson, a leading expert on Russian oil, these individuals used imaginative schemes to enrich themselves from the sale of oil in the years just prior to 1991. One such scheme was to set up a joint venture (JV) with a foreign oil services company (legalised in 1988), which would then contract with a Russian producer to refurbish idle oil wells. The foreign JV would be paid in dollars for this work through the exportation of oil from enhanced oil production. By distributing the contracts for fixing these idle wells – many of which were in reality fully functional – the oil generals could route the proceeds through these JVs into overseas bank accounts.[19] Gustafson reports that hundreds of millions of dollars were earned by oil managers through these and other means, and later used to purchase stock when the oil industry was privatised.[20]

The emergence of these kinds of private actors across the oil industry reflected the acute disintegration of the command economy that had taken place by the time of the Soviet collapse. After 1991, these same individuals were well positioned to take advantage of the full privatisation of Russian oil that unfolded between 1992 and 1998. The first phase of this privatisation began with a presidential decree issued in 1992 by Russia's first post-Soviet president, Boris Yeltsin. Yeltsin's decree designated three state-owned oil companies – LUKoil, Surgutneftegaz, and Yukos – as joint stock companies, allowing up to 55 per cent of their shares to be held by private interests. At the time, these three firms accounted for around 40 per cent of all oil produced in Russia and controlled both upstream crude oil production as well as refineries.[21] Following the part-privatisation of these firms, three Soviet-era oil generals emerged as their dominant private shareholders. The new owners then moved quickly to set up alliances with oil traders (such as Gennady Timchenko) who were able to transport oil (and refined products) to foreign export markets. Through these alliances, LUKoil, Surgutneftegaz, and Yukos began to resemble vertically integrated Western oil companies, and over time, trading activities would be mostly

19 This mechanism of wealth creation continued after the collapse of the Soviet Union. By 1995, it was reported that more than a quarter of all wells in the country were idle. James Watson, 'Foreign Investment in Russia: The Case of the Oil Industry', *Europe-Asia Studies* 48, no. 3, May 1996: 429–55, 443.

20 Gustafson, *Wheel of Fortune*, 46–7.

21 Matthew J. Sagers, 'Russian Crude Oil Production in 1996: Conditions and Prospects', *Post-Soviet Geography and Economics* 37, no. 9, 1996: 523–87, 527.

brought in house. Today, LUKoil and Surgutneftegaz remain controlled by the same individuals who dominated during this first phase of privatisation.[22] As we shall see, the fate of Yukos was to be quite different.

A further part to Yeltsin's 1992 decree was the establishment of a state-owned company, Rosneft, which was designed to hold other state-owned oil assets temporarily, as a prelude to their eventual privatisation. Although it would later become one of the most powerful oil companies in the world, Rosneft was a minor player when it was formed, responsible for less than 5 per cent of Russian oil production.[23] Through 1994 and 1995, the assets sheltered in Rosneft were spun off into smaller, privately owned companies in which the state held a minority share (see Table 10.1). By 1995, the Russian oil industry was composed of fourteen firms: seven companies that had some degree of private ownership (ranging from 14 per cent to 60 per cent), and another seven firms that were fully state-owned.[24] Of these, only LUKoil, Surgutneftegaz, and Yukos could properly be considered vertically integrated; between them, they dominated Russia's oil exports and controlled nearly half of the country's oil production.

Loans-for-Shares and the Rise of a New Business Class

The second phase of oil privatisation took place between 1995 and 1998 and would see a dramatic reduction in levels of state ownership. The starting point of this phase was a scheme known as loans-for-shares, which emerged out of a proposal devised in 1994 by Vladimir Potanin, a wealthy banker (and soon to be first deputy prime minister). Potanin proposed that private banks controlled by individuals such as himself should lend the government money in return for shares and management rights in twelve large state-owned firms, six of which were oil companies. At the time, the Yeltsin government was facing a financial crisis, and if the loans could not be repaid, then the shares would be put

22 Vagit Alekperov and Vladimir Bogdanov, both Soviet-era oil generals who are now prominent Russian billionaires.

23 Sagers, 'Russian Crude Oil Production', 527.

24 Eugene M. Khartukov, 'The Potential for a Russian State Oil Company: A Critical Analysis of the Russian Oil Business', *Energy Exploration and Exploitation* 18, no. 2/3, Energy Reserves Issue 2000: 207–24, 209.

up for sale in an auction process administered by the banks themselves, for which they would receive 30 per cent of the profits (and the government the other 70 per cent). Unbeknown to most outside parties, however, these auctions were to be rigged. The banks, in acting as auctioneers, excluded competitors – in one case, shutting down an airport so rival bids could not arrive on time – and sold the shares to themselves through secretive shell companies or affiliates that hid their true identities. The sell-off occurred at bargain-basement prices and provided enormous profits to the bank owners. Potanin, for example, won control of the oil company Sidanco with an initial loan of $130 million. Less than a year later, he had sold just 10 per cent of his stake to BP for $571 million.[25]

The loans-for-shares scheme was just the first step in a series of mergers and acquisitions and a wider sell-off of state oil assets that occurred over the next three years. By 1998, industry consolidation had produced what has been described as the Russian Seven Sisters – seven privately controlled oil companies, which together held 69 per cent of explored reserves in Russia, 76 per cent of oil wells, 67 per cent of oil production, 59 per cent of refinery output, and nearly 70 per cent of crude exports.[26] As highly integrated firms, these companies wielded considerable advantages over their rivals. One example of this – borrowing from the playbook of the Western oil giants – was the use of transfer pricing to maximise profits. Oil was produced and transferred at below-value prices to subsidiaries located in low-tax regions, who would then re-sell the oil at much higher prices. By shifting the location where profits were booked, the largest integrated oil companies saved billions of dollars in taxes.[27] In some cases, the head of the regional unit that granted the tax

25 Nat Moser, *Oil and the Economy of Russia: From the Late-Tsarist to the Post-Soviet Period*, London: Routledge, 2018, 109. Likewise, Li-Chen Sim notes that '40.12 percent of Surgutneftegaz was exchanged for US$88 million worth of credits to the state, whereas this stake was worth US$340 [million] according to its domestic market capitalization . . . the state auctioned 5 percent of its shares in LUKoil for US$35.01 million of credits. However, according to its capitalization on the Russian stock market, 5 percent of LUKoil's shares was worth at least US$180 million.' Li-Chen Sim, *The Rise and Fall of Privatization in the Russian Oil Industry*, London: Palgrave Macmillan, 2008.

26 Khartukov, 'The Potential for a Russian State Oil Company', 207.

27 Mikhail Glazunov, *Corporate Strategy in Post-Communist Russia*, London: Routledge, 2016.

benefits was the also the owner of the oil company – such as the future Chelsea Football Club owner Roman Abramovich, who was owner of Russia's sixth largest oil company, Sibneft, and simultaneously governor in the remote low-tax region of Chukotka.[28] Access to foreign markets and export routes was also critical to the power of the Russian Seven Sisters – pointedly, the largest oil majors held exclusive rights over the shipping and pricing of crude through various key ports across the country.[29]

One Moscow-based energy executive later described the privatisation wave of the 1990s as an 'unprecedented clearance sale', which served to reconfigure the dominant actors throughout the oil sector.[30] Together with the former oil generals who controlled LUKoil and Surgutneftegaz, a small coterie of business conglomerates emerged as the leading force in Russian oil. In part, these conglomerates were structured around powerful private banks that had been set up by well-connected individuals (such as Potanin) in the late 1980s and early 1990s and had benefited from the loans-for-shares scheme.[31] But as Table 10.1 indicates, the owners of these conglomerates – who were fast becoming known as oligarchs – were much more than simply bankers. Alongside oil, their interests spanned the commanding heights of the Russian economy, including the import-export trade, heavy industry, media, transport, construction, and real estate. This was the birth of Russian finance capital – large, integrated ownership structures bridging banking and industry, and closely connected to the state. Banks played a fundamental role within these diversified finance capital conglomerates, enabling billions to be ferreted away in offshore jurisdictions; indeed, between 1994 and

28 Moser, *Oil and the Economy of Russia*, 101.

29 Khartukov, 'The Potential for a Russian State Oil Company', 208. For example, LUKoil was in charge of delivery and pricing for crude oil destined for Lithuania, the Czech Republic, at the Russian port of Novorossiysk, and the Ukrainian port of Odessa.

30 Ibid., 207.

31 Simon Pirani notes that many owners of these private banks were high-ranking officials in the Soviet Union, especially from the Komsomol (the youth section of the Communist Party) who were given early privileges in establishing non-state financial and trading organisations and could thus gain 'first-mover' advantage. Pirani, *Change in Putin's Russia*, 17. They profited from currency trading and the massive inflow of financial assets that entered the private banking system following the collapse of the Soviet Union. One of these individuals was Mikhail Khodorkovsky, who was a Komsomol official and became the richest man in Russia following his takeover of Yukos Oil.

1998, the peak years of oil privatisation, capital flight from Russia averaged $17 billion a year.[32]

The new business class enriched by oil privatisation through the 1990s were also important political actors, allied to Yeltsin and holding influential and powerful positions in the post-Soviet state apparatus. Indeed, Yeltsin's unlikely victory in the 1996 presidential election depended heavily on the considerable financial support offered by these individuals to his campaign, and many observers believe that the loans-for-shares scheme was actually promised by Yeltsin as a quid pro quo for this support.[33] The seamless integration of business, banking, and politics guaranteed continued access to power and wealth, regardless of who sat in the Kremlin, and despite the extreme economic polarisation that marked Russian society. The share prices of the largest companies were also booming, with the stock market nearly doubling in value between 1996 and 1997. Surveying the state of world markets in mid-1997, the *Wall Street Journal* would brazenly describe Russia as the 'best performing [market] . . . in the world'.[34] For the oil barons who sat at the centre of Russia's new business class, the future appeared promising indeed.

The 1998 Financial Crisis

These apparent certitudes would vanish following the eruption of a new financial crisis in 1998. This economic crash quickly became the deepest and most severe to hit Russia since the end of the Soviet Union, and like all such moments, it had global origins. Through the 1990s, IMF-led structural adjustment packages had lowered barriers to foreign investment across most so-called emerging markets, encouraging large

32 Ibid., 30.

33 Goldman, *Petrostate*, 68. The loans-for-shares plan was implemented by Anatoly Chubais, the principal architect of economic reform in Russia during the early 1990s and a close ally of Yeltsin. As then *Washington Post* Moscow bureau chief David Hoffman observed: 'Loans for shares should really have been called "tycoons for Yeltsin". Chubais was willing to hand over the property without competition, without openness, and, as it turned out, for a bargain price, but in a way that would keep the businessmen at Yeltsin's side in the 1996 re-election campaign.' David E. Hoffman, *The Oligarchs – Wealth and Power in the New Russia*, New York: Public Affairs, 2002.

34 Steve Liesman, 'It's Tempting to Ignore Russia, But Its Performance Is Stellar', *Wall Street Journal*, 26 June 1997.

volumes of capital to flow into these regions in pursuit of higher returns than those available in core financial markets (where interest rates were low). These huge flows of speculative capital increased debt levels and inflated stock market bubbles across Latin America, East Asia, and Eastern Europe. By mid-1997, these bubbles reached their limit following the collapse of the Thai baht, which caused a sudden withdrawal of foreign capital from the East Asia region. Russia was soon facing similar problems, with foreign investors beginning to pull their money out of the country's stock markets from December 1997 onwards.

At this time, Russia operated a fixed exchange rate system, with the government attempting to keep the rouble's value within a narrow band through intervening in the foreign exchange market. But as capital outflows continued to accelerate during the first few months of 1998, this system came under severe pressure. Despite $22 billion worth of emergency loans provided by the IMF and World Bank, the Russian authorities could not stem the capital outflows or afford to continue supporting the rouble. By August 1998, the government was forced to allow the rouble to float freely, promptly leading the Russian currency to lose more than two-thirds of its value in the space of less than three weeks.[35] At the same time as this currency devaluation, the Russian government announced that it would default on its domestic government debt obligations, many of which were held by Russian banks.

The rouble devaluation and the government domestic debt default effectively bankrupted most financial institutions in Russia, including the leading banks. However, in a flagrant illustration of the state's support to the business class, a three-pronged set of government-led measures helped save these banks.[36] First, the banks were allowed to prevent the withdrawal of customer deposits (except under specific conditions favourable to them) and were granted a three-month moratorium on external debt repayments through new government legislation.[37] Second, the government provided the banks with substantial

35 Filippo Ippolito, 'The Banking Sector Rescue in Russia', Bank of Finland Institute for Economies in Transition (BOFIT) No.12, 2002, 4.

36 Andrew Barnes, *Owning Russia: The Struggle over Factories, Farms, and Power*, Ithaca, NY: Cornell University Press, 2006, 171.

37 One of these conditions was a 'deal' offered to bank depositors through a government-supported scheme: they could transfer their funds to a state-owned bank at significant loss, or they could keep them in the original bank without

short-term capital funding. Third, and most importantly, the bank's owners simply engaged in straightforward asset-stripping: the best-performing assets were placed in a new bridge bank (with the same owners as the old bank), while liabilities were kept in the original bank that was allowed to fail.[38] Through these measures, the net outcome of the 1998 crash was simply to move 'assets from victims of economic shocks to their beneficiaries' – and most of the large conglomerate banks managed to survive in a repackaged form.[39]

Nonetheless, despite these fortuitous outcomes for the business elite, the 1998 crisis did drive a major restructuring of finance capital in Russia. As thousands of small depositors clamoured for access to their savings, the largest finance capital groups reorganised their conglomerate structures by moving financial assets out of the banking system into holding companies linked to oil and other industrial interests.[40] As a result, the accumulation of the largest conglomerates became even more firmly centred around the production and export of oil. And as global oil prices began to turn upwards in mid-1999, these finance capital groups would be the prime beneficiaries. Not only did they earn dollar revenues from their oil exports, but their operating costs – including labour, transport, and tools – were mainly denominated in roubles.[41] As the rouble fell in value and the global dollar-oil price rose, the widening differential earned billions for the private oil companies and their parent conglomerates. Much of this wealth was directed into overseas bank accounts and offshore havens through increasingly sophisticated techniques of tax avoidance and money laundering. By 2000, the Russian government was estimating

access for a year and at very low interest rates. Juliet Johnson, *A Fistful of Rubles: The Rise and Fall of the Russian Banking System*, Ithaca, NY: Cornell University Press, 2000, 220.

38 One notorious example of this was Uneximbank, controlled by Vladimir Potanin. After the crash, Potanin set up a bridge bank, Rosbank, which took over the key clients of Uneximbank, including Potanin's Interros group. The liabilities of Uneximbank, an estimated $2 billion owed to creditors, were left behind in the insolvent bank. Rosbank would later become one of the largest banks in Russia and remains controlled by Potanin.

39 Andrew Barnes, 'Russia's New Business Groups and State Power', *Post-Soviet Affairs* 19, no. 2, 2003: 154–86, 160.

40 Johnson, *Fistful of Rubles*, 221.

41 Gustafson, *Wheel of Fortune*, 197.

capital flight stood at $3 billion a month, one of the highest levels in the world.[42]

Although it was not immediately apparent at the time, a doubling of global oil prices between 1998 and 2000 marked the beginning of a new oil boom that would eventually peak in mid-2008. This was a moment that seemed to promise unprecedented opportunities for the owners of Russia's private oil companies. Despite popular anger against the business–Kremlin alliance, state-owned oil assets continued to be handed over to the largest conglomerates. In 2000, the state-owned Onako oil company was sold to the Renova-Access-Alfa group.[43] Two years later, the conglomerate-controlled companies TNK and Sibneft joined together to buy another state-owned firm, Slavneft. By 2002, private companies accounted for 80 per cent of Russian oil production, with most of this concentrated in the hands of the Russian Seven Sisters.[44] It was the control of oil that created much of the extreme wealth that emerged in Russia at this time, transforming a handful of multimillionaires into multibillionaires. And as this new business elite gobbled up state assets, Russian names finally began to appear on lists of the world's richest people. In 1997 Forbes had recorded just five Russians in its ranking of the world's top billionaires; by 2003, there would be seventeen.[45]

42 Estimates of capital flight from Russia are notoriously unreliable, but there is a consensus that the levels at this time were very high. Mark Kramer, 'Capital Flight and Russian Economic Reform', PONARS Policy Memo 128, April 2000, available at ponarseurasia.org. For discussion and comparison of Russia with other countries, see Prakash Loungani and Paolo Mauro, 'Capital Flight from Russia', IMF, 1 June 2000.

43 This alliance involved the Alfa Group (Mikhail Fridman/Petr Aven) and Renova Group (Viktor Vekselberg) (see Table 10.1) along with Ukrainian-born British-US citizen, Leonard Blavatnik, who controlled the Access Industries Group. Blavatnik had attended university with Vekselberg, and in 2022 was the fortieth wealthiest individual in the world, controlling Warner Music Group as well as a 20 per cent stake in LyondellBasell, one of the world's largest petrochemical firms.

44 Gustafson, *Wheel of Fortune*, 195.

45 F. Joseph Dresen, 'The Piratization of Russia: Russian Reform Goes Awry', wilsoncenter.org.

The Rise of Putin and Rosneft

Through the privatisation of state-owned assets and other means of wealth transfer, the Yeltsin era had produced a new capitalist class in less than a decade. This explosion of Russian finance capital was founded in control over the oil industry, which served as the crux of accumulation within a wider conglomerate structure that spanned all major economic activities. Yet this rapid process of class formation had also been accompanied by a far-reaching crisis of political legitimacy fed by the disintegration of the basic capacities of the Russian state – much of this due to the plundering of state wealth by the largest billionaires and the venality of political decision-making led by the interests of warring business factions. With the viability of the new Russian capitalism under threat from these problems of state capacity and political legitimacy, the post-1998 period was thus primarily one that involved a restructuring in the relationship between the leading business groups and the centres of political power. Once again, control over oil stood at the base of this process of state re-composition.

Outside the narrow circle of billionaires, most Russians experienced a perilous decline in living standards at the time of the 1998 crisis, with a 5.3 per cent fall in GDP marking the worst contraction of economic activity since the end of the Soviet Union. Inflation rates also spiked, reaching more than 80 per cent; real wages collapsed, and around half of all economic transactions were taking place through barter rather than with cash.[46] This social and economic crisis ripped apart Russian society, exacerbating the deep inequalities of post-Soviet life. As a result, protest and labour strikes erupted across the country, frequently directed against the largest banks and industrial conglomerates. In the maelstrom of this political instability, Boris Yeltsin appointed Vladimir Putin as prime minister in August 1999 – the fifth person to hold the position since the crisis had begun a year earlier. With Yeltsin's resignation in December 1999, Putin then became president.[47]

On assuming power, Putin's main challenge was to restore basic state functions such as tax collection, economic management, and control

46 Johnson, *Fistful of Rubles*, 204.

47 Putin was to hold that position until 2008, when he stepped back into the role of prime minister once again, before resuming the post of president in 2012.

over policymaking in the context of the severe financial crash and widespread political crisis.[48] Above all, this meant disciplining the leading business owners, whose activities (especially tax avoidance) were undermining the wider conditions for capital accumulation and the capacities of the state. In doing so, Putin's approach was not anti-market – indeed, his economic advisors were principally free-market ideologues he had brought with him to the Kremlin from St Petersburg; rather, he aimed at securing the interests of the property-owning classes as a whole.[49] The basic deal that Putin presented was straightforward: the largest finance capital conglomerates would continue to benefit handsomely from their connections to the state – in many ways even more so than in the Yeltsin period – provided they gave support to this re-composition of the Russian state, paid (more) taxes, and refrained from any political destabilisation.

Within the business class, Putin's main opponent at the time was Mikhail Khodorkovsky, a former Komsomol official (the youth section of the Communist Party) who had established one of the first private Russian banks under Gorbachev. After the fall of the Soviet Union, Khodorkovsky's financial-industrial conglomerate Menatep, became one of the main beneficiaries of the Yeltsin period, taking extensive interests in banking, shipping, petrochemicals, and food through the 1990s. A key asset over which Khodorkovsky gained control in this period was Yukos Oil, which he won in 1995 through one of Yeltsin's privatisation auctions. Yukos soon overtook LUKoil to become the largest oil company in the country, and with the collapse of Menatep's banking arm during the 1998 crash, Khodorkovsky's empire was increasingly synonymous with Yukos. In 2003, however, Khodorkovsky and several Yukos executives were arrested by Russian authorities and accused of tax fraud, embezzlement, and other economic crimes. The ensuing trial lasted until May 2005, when Khodorkovsky and his business partner Platon Lebedev were found guilty and received a nine-year sentence.[50]

48 Pirani, *Change in Putin's Russia*, 195.

49 For one of the best accounts of this relationship between the rise of Putin, the state, and Russian capitalism, see Pirani, *Change in Putin's Russia*.

50 While in prison in December 2010, Khodorkovsky was found guilty of further crimes and his sentence was extended to 2014. Eventually pardoned by Putin in 2013, he now lives in London.

As the richest man in Russia, Khodorkovsky was the highest-profile target in Putin's campaign to discipline Russia's leading business owners.[51] Numerous authors have pointed out that his activities through the Yeltsin years differed little from any of the other large oil barons – engaging in tax-optimisation schemes, transfer pricing, the use of offshore accounts, and so forth. His corporate possessions had also been acquired by similar means, translating close connections with the state into stakes in newly privatised firms through schemes such as loans-for-shares. Nonetheless, after Putin's presidential victory in 2000, Khodorkovsky had become increasingly critical of Kremlin policy, and was aggressively lobbying against the passage of new government legislation, especially around taxation. Defying Putin's explicit directive to stay out of politics, Khodorkovsky funded opposition groups and even hinted that he might enter the Duma himself.[52] Perhaps most audaciously, he had been courting Western oil firms around a possible sale of Yukos: indeed, just months before his arrest, Khodorkovsky was in separate merger negotiations with both Chevron and ExxonMobil. In the case of Chevron, a letter of agreement had been signed, and the talks only fell apart over the percentage share that Yukos would hold in the new firm.[53]

All these factors provided strong motivation for Putin to go after Khodorkovsky. But the most decisive consideration behind Putin's actions may have been the goal of using Yukos as a means of strengthening the Russian state itself. Following Khodorkovsky's trial and sentencing in 2005, Yukos was dismantled. However, rather than selling the company's substantial assets to other private oil firms, these were instead absorbed by the hitherto small, but fully state-owned, Rosneft. By taking over Yukos's upstream reserves and refineries, Rosneft was immediately catapulted into the position of Russia's largest oil company, responsible for just under a quarter of the country's total oil production (up from less than 4 per cent in 2002).[54] This had two key implications for the

51 Another important figure in the oil industry was Boris Bervosky; see Table 10.1.

52 Sim, *Rise and Fall*, 43–4.

53 This marriage of a US and a Russian Seven Sister would have created the largest oil company in the world and would certainly have had a profound effect on the subsequent trajectory of US–Russia relations – it was 'one of the most tantalizing might-have-beens in the recent history of the oil industry'; Gustafson, *Wheel of Fortune*, 299.

54 Ibid., 195.

Russian state. First, Rosneft enabled the government to capture much of the stream of oil rents that until then had been flowing largely into private pockets. The company's exports – along with the sales of oil and gas by the state-owned Gazprom – drove a major expansion in the government's financial capacities. As the oil price continued to climb, Russia's foreign reserves reached $426 billion in 2008 – fourth highest in the world, and a sixfold increase from 2003. Second, alongside this crucial financial dimension, state ownership of energy assets – and the pipelines and ports that carried them – also provided strong leverage over those countries that relied heavily on Russian energy exports.[55] Rosneft thus became integral to the projection of Russian state power at the international level.[56]

State versus Markets?

Much of the international discussion around Rosneft portrays the company as emblematic of economic policymaking in Putin's 'KGB state' – statist, anti-market, and undermining the position of private capital in Russia.[57] There are many problems with this perspective. First, it tends to downplay the ongoing and significant participation of privately owned firms in Russian oil.[58] While some of the original

55 Russia's pipeline network was never privatised, staying under the control of the state-owned company Transneft since the fall of the Soviet Union. Pipelines provided influence over energy-rich former Soviet republics such as Kazakhstan, Turkmenistan, and Uzbekistan, which depended on Russian pipelines for their oil and gas to reach Europe.

56 The strategic significance of the company is indicated by the closeness of its management to the Putin-controlled state. Since 2004 it has been led by Igor Sechin, a Putin ally often described as the second most powerful man in Russia. At the time of the Khodorkovsky trial, Rosneft's deputy chair was Sergey Naryshkin, Putin's former chief of staff, who currently directs the country's Foreign Intelligence Service.

57 On the argument that Putin is rebuilding a 'KGB state', see, for example, Catherine Belton, *Putin's People: How the KGB Took Back Russia and Then Took On the West*, New York: Harper Collins, 2020. For a different perspective, see Pirani, *Change in Putin's Russia*.

58 As Mazen Labban observes, 'the so-called nationalization of the Russian oil industry under Putin slowed down the privatization process and altered its characteristics rather than reversing it . . . what Putin effectively managed to do is to keep the oligarchs in line rather than eliminate them altogether.' Mazen Labban, *Space, Oil and Capital*, New York: Routledge, 2008, 117.

Russian oil billionaires have exited the business, most did not share the fate of Khodorkovsky, and there are numerous examples of individuals who remain involved in downstream activities or in other international oil firms (see Table 10.1).[59] In 2020, private oil companies were producing around 45 per cent of the country's total oil (down from around 60 per cent at the time of Yukos's demise).[60] The largest of these firms are LUKoil and Surgutneftegas – ranked as second and third oil producers in the country – and they are led by the same individuals who took charge in the early 1990s. The Russian Energy Ministry reported 290 active companies in the Russian oil industry in 2019, but with just nine vertically integrated firms producing more than 80 per cent of the country's oil.[61] Five of these nine firms are privately controlled.

Moreover, Rosneft has also supported the development of private capital through its listing on domestic and international stock markets. These connections began in 2006, when 13 per cent of the company was floated on the London and Moscow stock exchanges, raising $10.4 billion in the largest IPO in Russian history. Stock ownership enabled large Russian capitalists to grab a share of the oil rents generated by Rosneft, and much of the country's billionaire class invested heavily in the company at this time.[62] This includes the top leadership of Rosneft, who are major *private* shareholders in the company, and thus should

59 In 2005, the state-owned gas firm, Gazprom, bought Sibneft from the Russian billionaire Roman Abramovich in what was then the largest corporate takeover in Russian history. Sibneft was renamed Gazpromneft and is now the fourth largest producer in the country. In 2014, about a decade after the Yukos affair, Rosneft acquired the country's third biggest producer, TNK-BP.

60 European Commission, Commission Staff Working Document, 'On Significant Distortions in the Economy of the Russian Federation for the Purposes of Trade Defence Investigations', Brussels, 22 October 2020, 208.

61 These companies are Rosneft (state-owned, with 35 per cent of the country's production), LUKoil (non-state, 25 per cent), Surgutneftegas (non-state, 11 per cent), Gazpromneft (state-owned, 7 per cent), Tatneft (non-state, 5 per cent), Bashneft (state-owned, 3 per cent), Slavneft (state-owned, 2 per cent), Novatek (non-state, 2 per cent), and Russneft (non-state, 1 per cent). European Commission, 'On Significant Distortions', 208.

62 One of these investors was Roman Abramovich, who reportedly invested $300 million in the IPO, giving him around 3 per cent of Rosneft. Richard Wachman and Conal Walsh, 'Abramovich Invests $300m in Controversial Rosneft IPO', *Guardian*, 15 July 2006.

properly be seen as both capitalist owners *and* state managers.[63] Western and other non-Russian investors have also been eager to participate in Rosneft. In 2013, BP took a 20 per cent stake in the company, receiving two representatives on Rosneft's board, including BP's then CEO, Bernard Looney.[64] BP's investment was followed a few years later by the Qatar Investment Authority, which took a 19 per cent stake in Rosneft in 2018, making it the third largest shareholder behind the Russian government and BP. While BP was to divest its holdings following Russia's war on Ukraine in 2022, around a fifth of the British company's profits came from its Rosneft stake as late as 2019.[65]

More broadly, while Putin's strategy of building Rosneft as the dominant leader of the oil sector may have been detrimental to individual billionaires such as Khodorkovsky, it has been enormously beneficial for the wider property-owning class in Russia – including those outside the oil sector. Today, a third of the Russian federal budget comes from energy exports, mainly Rosneft's oil, and these state revenues are fungible – they recirculate through the state to large, privately owned, non-oil firms in a myriad of ways (such as state contracts, subsidies, and public–private partnerships).[66] In this sense, beyond the continued presence of private capital in the oil industry itself, the accumulation of Russian capital *in general* remains heavily and directly tied to the production and export of oil. All of this illustrates why it is a mistake to counterpose the *state* and the *market* as two separate and antithetical spheres of economic activity. Oil remains the nexus that mutually binds the growth of Russia's billionaire class and the repressive, authoritarian state that Putin has built.

Such patterns are replicated outside Russia and help us make sense of the newfound power of state-owned national oil companies (NOCs) across much of the Middle East, Asia, and Latin America. As we shall see in Chapter 12, these NOCs now rival Western oil majors in their size

63 In 2015, Rosneft's CEO, Igor Sechin, was reported to own 0.127 per cent of Rosneft's shares, then worth about $83 million, and was paid about $11 million annually in dividends. Henry Foy, 'We Need to Talk about Igor', *Financial Times*, 1 March 2018, ft.com. Sechin remains in control of the company.

64 Former German chancellor Gerhard Schröder was also on the board.

65 Calculated by the author from BP *Annual Report* and Form 20-F, 2019, 178.

66 European Commission, 'On Significant Distortions', 204. Between 2007 and 2018, oil averaged around 43 per cent of all Russian energy exports, significantly more than gas (around 17 per cent).

and market power. But, like Rosneft, rather than viewing these state-owned firms as antagonistic towards private capital, we need to carefully consider how they actually serve broader processes of accumulation in places like Saudi Arabia, the United Arab Emirates, or China. In all these areas, NOCs have been centrally connected to the development of domestic capital – including firms beyond the oil sector itself. They have also been crucial to the projection of state power beyond national borders, both at the regional scale and globally. As such, the rise of NOCs has been a major factor in the global geopolitical and geoeconomic shifts of the past two decades, including an apparent relative decline in US power and a sharp realignment in patterns of trade, investment, and ownership in world oil.

11

A Sorority Reborn: The Western Supermajors, 1990–2005

> For a multinational oil company, Shell, to take over US thirty billion dollars from the small, defenceless Ogoni people and put nothing back but degradation and death is a betrayal of all humanity.
>
> Ken Saro-Wiwa, 1995[1]

> Nigeria is poor, despite being Africa's leading oil producer . . . It has many development challenges.
>
> Shell, 1998[2]

Seventies Britain was a time of power blackouts, good music, and – above all – class war. Across this decade, the country experienced near continuous strikes and labour protests, culminating in the 1978–79 Winter of Discontent, a strike wave that was the largest Britain had seen since the early 1940s. For much of this decade, political power was held by the British Labour Party, which, having won the 1974 elections, was placed in the unenviable position of having to tackle both worker militancy and the deep economic crisis associated with the first oil shock. Labour Party politics rested in part on a link with the country's official trade union movement,

1 Ken Saro-Wiwa, *A Month and a Day: A Detention Diary*, London: Penguin Books, 1995, 131.

2 Shell, *Profits and Principles – Does There Have to Be a Choice? The Shell Report 1998*, 18, shell.com.

combined with a milquetoast social democracy emphasising moderation and a prudent Keynesianism. Against this traditional Labourism, a growing number of British politicians were also beginning to embrace some of the new economic ideas circulating at the time, such as the monetarist doctrines of the American economist Milton Friedman, who identified inflation – not unemployment – as the greatest threat and advocated strict control of the money supply as the antidote. Among those fervently committed to these new intellectual trends was a rising star of British politics and recently elected leader of the Conservative Party, Margaret Thatcher.

Thatcher had won the Conservative Party leadership elections in 1975. In that same year, Labour Prime Minister James Callaghan was locked in difficult negotiations with the International Monetary Fund over a $3.9 billion economic rescue package. The British currency had just experienced a major run, and the country was reeling from high levels of inflation and stagnant growth – the classic stagflation conundrum of the 1970s. The loan sought by the British government was the largest amount ever requested from the Fund, and in return the IMF demanded $2.5 billion in spending cuts. For the Labour Party's Callaghan, an old trade union leader, these cuts were difficult and politically unpalatable – especially in the context of the ongoing strike waves. But it was in this context that the Labour Party hit upon an idea that would have far-reaching implications for decades to come. To soften the blow of spending cuts, the government would raise funds through selling 17 per cent of the state-owned British Petroleum on the London Stock Exchange. At the time, this was the largest share offering in British history, and brought the British government's ownership in British Petroleum down to 51 per cent.

The Labour Party decision to part-privatise British Petroleum typically receives little more than a minor footnote in most accounts of this period, but it was a watershed moment in the story of Western oil. Most immediately, it helped pave the way for the radical embrace of privatisation that came with Margaret Thatcher's electoral victory over Labour in 1979. After further share offerings of British Petroleum during the early 1980s, Thatcher sold the final government stake in a £7 billion share sale in 1987 that was once again the largest in UK history.[3] All told, the sale of

3 The value of this sale was all the more remarkable given the fact it coincided with Black Monday, a global stock market collapse that saw more than $1.7 trillion in losses across the world.

British Petroleum made up 37 per cent of the entire privatisation proceeds earned by the British government between 1977 and the end of Thatcher's last term in 1990 – much more than any other sector. With the inclusion of two smaller state-owned oil companies in these figures (see Table 11.1), oil's share of total UK privatisation earnings during this time reaches an astonishing 43 per cent. Writing shortly after she left office, Thatcher would claim that privatisation was 'the central means of reversing the corrosive and corrupting effects of socialism . . . the centre of any programme of reclaiming territory for freedom'.[4] What she declined to mention is that the putative success of this 'programme for freedom' rested almost fully on the structural transformation of the oil sector.

The privatisation of British Petroleum was the first salvo in what would become a global phenomenon over the next decade.[5] The centre of this push to privatise was Western Europe, where around two-thirds of all oil and gas privatisations in the world (by value) took place between 1977 and 2003.[6] As with the British case, oil privatisation sat at the leading edge of a broader, economy-wide sell-off of state-owned assets, among which oil companies were by far the largest and most valuable.[7] For Italy, where a mass sell-off of state assets occurred in the 1990s, proceeds from the sale of state-owned ENI made up 27 per cent of the total government take from privatisation in that decade.[8] In the case of France, two state-owned oil companies – Elf Aquitaine and Total – would account for 20 per cent of total French privatisation revenues. Across the Atlantic, over 40 per cent of all Canadian federal government privatisation revenues between 1985 and 2004 came from the sale of a

4 Thatcher, 1993, cited in David Parker, 'The UK's Privatisation Experiment: The Passage of Time Permits a Sober Assessment', CESifo Working Paper No. 1126, February 2004, 1, cesifo.de.

5 In the US the oil industry has always been privately controlled, but a significant proportion of oil companies in the rest of the world were either fully or partially state-owned at this time (for example, ENI).

6 Calculated by author using data provided in William Leon Megginson, *The Financial Economics of Privatization*, Oxford: Oxford University Press, 2005, 352–6.

7 The one exception to this was France, where earnings from the sale of France Telecom in 1998 exceeded those of Elf Aquitaine and Total. France's privatisation of oil, however, began more than a decade before the privatisation of the country's telecommunications sector.

8 Calculated by the author from Andrea Goldstein, 'Privatization in Italy 1993–2002: Goals, Institutions, Outcomes, and Outstanding Issues', CESifo Working Paper, No. 912, Center for Economic Studies and ifo Institute (CESifo), Munich, Table 2, 2003, 36.

single oil company, Petro-Canada. The sale of oil companies would also contribute a significant share of total privatisation earnings for governments in Spain, Norway, Austria, and Finland during this period.

By the early 2000s, almost every large Western oil firm that had been fully or partially owned by the state would have been transferred to private hands, creating companies that are now among the largest in the world.[9] This historic transformation in the nature of oil ownership was accompanied by a series of major changes to the structure, operation, and practices of these Western firms. One notable aspect to this was a flurry of mega-mergers that took place through the 1990s and early 2000s, out of which emerged a small group of integrated supermajors that now dominate the industry landscape. These industry behemoths increasingly expanded into other energy sectors, such as natural gas, rebranding themselves as 'energy firms' in the process. Alongside this industry consolidation and restructuring, Western oil firms also transformed their geographical footprint, most notably through cross-border investments into upstream sectors in West and Central Africa. As we shall see in this and our final chapters, all these trends carried important implications for understanding the shape of the contemporary industry.

From Oil Privatisation to Financialisation

One of the crucial features of the 1990s privatisation of oil firms – first pioneered by Britain's Labour Party back in 1977 – is that it almost always took place through share placements on domestic and international stock markets, rather than by direct sale to new private owners.[10] A major reason for this is that Western oil production and exploration was increasingly focused on costly and remote areas such as the Arctic Circle and the Caspian Sea. It was difficult for state-owned firms to meet

9 The one partial exception to this was Norway's Statoil, now Equinor, which – while partially listed during the 2000s – remains with a large state ownership.

10 The only exception to this for the twelve companies listed in Table 11.1, was the 1994 sale of 19.6 per cent of Austria's OMV to an Abu Dhabi firm. By contrast, about 30 per cent of banks and 12 per cent of telecoms privatised across the countries listed in the table took place through asset sales. Megginson, *Financial Economics*, 287–8, 312–13.

Table 11.1 Privatisation of Western Oil Companies, 1977–2005

Country	**Company**	**Year(s) privatised**	**Share of country's total privatisation receipts between 1990 and 1999 (for years indicated)**	**Domestic stock market ranking of oil firm by market capitalisation (2002)**	**Rank in world oil by market cap (2022)**	**Name and ownership structure today**
UK	British Petroleum	1977; 1983; 1987	37 per cent (1977–90)	1	9 (BP)	Merged with US firm Amoco in 1988, and later changed its name to BP. Largest shareholders are funds controlled by JPMorgan Chase, and the asset management firms BlackRock, Vanguard, and State Street.
	Britoil	1982; 1985	4 per cent (1977–90)	n/a	n/a	Acquired by BP in 1988.
	Enterprise Oil	1984	3 per cent (1977–90)	n/a	n/a	Acquired by Royal Dutch Shell in 2002.
Canada	Petro-Canada	1991; 1992; 1995; 2004	41 per cent (1985–2004)	12	29 (Suncor Energy)	In 2009, Petro-Canada was taken over by Suncor Energy, and is now a subsidiary of this firm.
France	Total	1992; 1996	3 per cent	1 (TotalFinaElf)	6 (TotalFinaElf)	Took over Belgium's Petrofina in 1999, merged with Elf Aquitaine in 2000, now known as TotalEnergies. Largest shareholders are Goldman Sachs, BlackRock, and Amundi (French asset management firm).
	Elf Aquitaine	1986; 1991; 1992; 1994; 1996	17 per cent	1 (TotalFinaElf)	6 (TotalFinaElf)	See Total.

Italy	ENI	1995; 1996; 1997; 1998	27 per cent	1	25	Italian government owns 30.3 per cent of ENI shares. Other major investors include BlackRock and Vanguard.
Austria	OMV	1987; 1994; 1996	16 per cent (1987–99)	1	60	The Abu Dhabi state-owned Mubadala Petroleum and Petrochemicals Holding Company took a stake in OMV in 1994 and now owns around 25 per cent of it. The largest shareholder is the Austrian government (31.5 per cent).
Spain	Repsol	1989; 1993; 1994; 1995; 1996; 1997	16 per cent	6	55	Two largest shareholders are the asset management firms BlackRock and Amundi (French).
Finland	Neste	1998	11 per cent	3	39	Merged with a Finnish power company to become Fortum Oyj; later demerged and is now known as Neste (36 per cent state-owned).
Greece	Hellenic Petroleum	1998	3 per cent	10	n.a	Greek government maintains 35.5 per cent share, Latsis Group (Greek billionaire family) holds 45 per cent.
Norway	Statoil	2001; 2004–05	32 per cent (1993–2005)*	1	8 (Equinor)	Merged with oil and gas division of Norsk Hydro in 2007, rebranded as Equinor in 2018. State ownership is 67 per cent.

Source: Austria: Ansgar Belke, Friedrich Schneider, 'Privatization in Austria: Some Theoretical Reasons and First Results About the Privatization Proceeds', CESifo Working Paper, No. 1123, Center for Economic Studies and ifo Institute (CESifo), Munich, 2004; William Leon Megginson, *The Financial Economics of Privatization*, New York: Oxford Academic, 2005, 352–6; Ladan Mahboobi, 'Recent Privatisation Trends in OECD Countries', Washington, DC: OECD, 2002, 46; David Parker, 'The UK's Privatisation Experiment: The Passage of Time Permits a Sober Assessment', CESifo Working Paper Series 1126, CESifo, 2004; Canada: Allison Padlova, *Federal Commercialization in Canada*, Parliamentary Information and Research Service, Library of Parliament, 2005; Greece, Hellenic Exchanges Group, Fact Book 2003.

* Norway's figure is as a share of privatisation proceeds from telecom, banking, electricity, and oil (calculated from Megginson).

these costs when their government owners were constrained by competing fiscal and policy demands at home.[11] Stock markets, however, enabled oil companies to issue equity or sell debt, and thus raise money for overseas expansion. The high costs of exploration were also pushing oil companies into strategic alliances and partnerships with other commercial firms – being listed on a stock market meant that these partnerships could be arranged through swapping equity or using shares as payment.[12] All of this was particularly salient to Western Europe, where oil firms were hampered by the limited size of their domestic markets and faced significant pressures to internationalise in order to achieve a better balance of upstream and downstream assets.

Governments also found that stock markets were a useful means of undercutting public hostility and potential trade union resistance to the sell-off of state assets more broadly. By offering shares to ordinary citizens, privatisation could be portrayed as a step towards 'democratic ownership' and a 'people's capitalism' – a means of widening the shareholder base of major corporations and allowing the general population to benefit from economic growth.[13] In reality, however, these claims served as a smokescreen for the highly concentrated ownership structures that emerged through privatisation: the total number of shareholders in oil and other listed companies certainly increased substantially, but a tiny group of financial capitalists came to hold a very large proportion of shares. Across Western Europe as a whole, the share of total stock market wealth held by 'households' halved between 1985 and 2003, falling to just 13 per cent, despite a fourfold increase in the size of European markets.[14]

11 In France, for example, there was a growing tension between company managements that were oriented towards overseas expansion, and government officials who were interested in using state ownership of oil as a means of controlling domestic industrial policy (for example, by keeping fuel prices low). See Llewelyn Hughes, 'Transforming French Oil Market Governance', in *Globalizing Oil: Firms and Oil Market Governance in France, Japan, and the United States (Business and Public Policy)*, Cambridge: Cambridge University Press, 2014, 68–112.

12 In the case of Norway's Statoil, this was an explicit motivation for the company's part-privatisation in 2001. See Ministry of Petroleum and Energy, Storting proposition no. 36, 2000–01, 'Ownership of Statoil and Future Management of the SDFI', regjeringen.no.

13 This language was particularly evident in the French case. See Andrea Goldstein, 'Privatisations and Corporate Governance in France', BNI Corporate Review, no. 199, December 1996.

14 European Commission and Financial Services Users Group, 'Under the Tender: Who Owns the European Economy? Evolution of the Ownership of EU-listed companies between 1970 and 2012', Brussels, 2013, 18–19.

What did change, however, was the international breadth of these owners. Remarking on the British experience, Eric Dobkin – a former director of Goldman Sachs who had arranged the UK government's 1977 sale of British Petroleum – noted that privatisation 'really set the stage for the globalisation of the equity markets'.[15] Because of their size, share offerings for oil companies were marketed internationally, with financial deregulation facilitating cross-border capital flows and encouraging expanded foreign ownership. In many cases, oil companies were simultaneously listed on foreign stock markets as well (especially New York and London). As a result, the scale of cross-border investment grew dramatically – by the early 2000s, around a third of European stock market wealth was foreign-owned, a share that had more than tripled since the mid-1980s.[16] Much of this investment came from the US, further strengthening the interdependencies between North American and European financial markets.[17] Importantly, a prominent part of these cross-border flows involved new financial actors, such as US-based asset management firms, hedge funds, and private equity companies, a trend that would have substantial repercussions for future patterns of corporate control in oil (see Chapter 12).

All this meant that the privatisation of oil helped underpin an unprecedented expansion in global stock markets through the 1990s. Indeed, the total capitalisation of non-US 'developed country' stock markets increased more than elevenfold between 1983 and 1999, rising from $1.4 trillion to $16.17 trillion.[18] By 1999, stock market capitalisation as a share of world GDP – another indicator of the newfound weight of stock markets in overall economic activity – would exceed 100 per cent for the first time in

15 Owen Wild, '1987: £7.2bn BP Privatisation: The Deal That Defied Black Monday', 23 August 2013, IFR 2000 Issue Supplement, ifre.com.

16 EC and FSU, 'Under the Tender', 85.

17 In 1995, around half of all cross-border investment in global equity markets came from North America. Linda L. Tesar et al., 'The Role of Equity Markets in International Capital Flows', in Martin Feldstein (ed.), *International Capital Flows*, Chicago: University of Chicago Press, 1999, 247.

18 Calculated from data provided in Maria K. Boutchkova and William L. Megginson, 'Privatization and the Rise of Global Capital Markets', *Financial Management* 29, no. 4, Winter 2000. The term 'developed country' is theirs. It should also be noted that the growth of non-US stock markets was much faster than the US during this period. By 1999, US stock market capitalisation as a share of the world total had fallen to 47.5 per cent, down from 56.1 per cent in 1983.

history.[19] This growth signalled the beginnings of what would come to be described as *financialisation*, a major shift in accumulation through which financial markets took on a greatly expanded role in economic and social life.[20] One indication of financialisation was a change in the way that firms typically funded themselves – coming to rely more on the issuance of equity and debt securities on stock markets rather than traditional bank borrowing. Corporate behaviour and management priorities also began to shift, with business calculus moving towards the short-term maximisation of stock price and 'shareholder value' rather than longer-term business strategies. All these dynamics impacted internal firm organisation and management goals, as well as the wider vulnerability to crisis in capitalist economies.

Digging for Oil on the Stock Market

Of course, the government sale of oil firms did not single-handedly cause these trends, but as some of the largest and most internationalised companies in the world, the privatisation of oil played a vital part in creating and sustaining the momentum behind financialisation. In turn, this shift had considerable impact on the structure and operation of Western oil companies themselves. One aspect to this is that oil company managers became subject to the financial imperatives of stock market valuations and the demands of major shareholders for higher dividend payments. The traditional corporate goals of growth, oil reserve replacement, and technological innovation were now also shaped by shareholder returns – the physical and financial markets became increasingly dependent upon one another.[21] As part of this, oil companies

19 Another revealing indicator is the volume of stocks traded, which, at a global level, increased more than 3,300 per cent between 1983 and 1999.

20 For an early discussion of this term, see Gerald Epstein, *Financialisation and the World Economy*, Cheltenham: Edward Elgar, 2005. I look at later debates around the concept in the context of US oil markets in Adam Hanieh, 'The Commodities Fetish? Financialisation and Finance Capital in the US Oil Industry', *Historical Materialism* 29, no. 4, 2023: 70–113.

21 R. M. Grant, 'Oil Company Strategies from 1970 to the Present', in ENI (ed.), *Encyclopaedia of Hydrocarbons*, vol. 4, Rome: Instituto Della Enciclopedia Italiana Treccani, 2005, 301–21. For a sharp analysis of the complex relationship between financial imperatives and physical oil production, which avoids the dualism of many

increasingly engaged in share buybacks: repurchasing their own shares, in order to drive up the price.[22] While this was a practice of all major companies regardless of sector, the leading oil firms were at the forefront of such buybacks during the 1990s: Exxon alone spent $29 billion on share repurchases between the mid-1980s and 1999 – more than any other listed company.[23] Share buybacks continue to mark the financial operations of Western oil companies through to the current day (see Chapter 12).

Share buybacks represented one way in which the earnings from oil were returned to major shareholders. In the context of low oil prices during the 1990s, the goal of maximising shareholder returns also drove other cost-cutting measures by Western oil firms, most notably a large wave of job redundancies. In the US, one government study reported that the top twenty-five oil companies slashed employment by 50 per cent between 1985 and 1995.[24] Associated with this was an internal reorganisation, with many activities that had previously been performed in-house spun off to other specialised external companies – including drilling and well maintenance, marine transportation, and information technology. This wave of outsourcing is the origin of many of the big engineering and oilfield service companies that are today prominent in the global industry, such as Halliburton, Schlumberger, and Baker Hughes. Outside the US, newly privatised oil companies also responded to cost-cutting pressures by firing workers. Petro-Canada reduced its workforce by more than 40 per cent shortly after its first share issue – BP, ENI, ELF, and Repsol similarly made double-digit percentage cuts in employment following their listing on domestic markets.[25] In Argentina,

---

discussions of financialisation, see Mazen Labban, 'Oil in Parallax: Scarcity, Markets, and the Financialization of Accumulation', *Geoforum* 41, no. 4, July 2010: 541–52.

22 This practice was pioneered in US financial markets after a rule change by the Securities and Exchange Commission in 1982. When companies buy back their own shares, they remove them from the marketplace. This increases the value of the remaining shares because there is now less stock outstanding, and earnings are thus split among fewer shares. Share buybacks are particularly lucrative to senior executives who characteristically have large stock holdings.

23 Stewart C. Myers, 'Capital Structure', *Journal of Economic Perspectives* 15, no. 2, Spring 2001: 81–102, 82.

24 Energy Information Administration (EIA), *Performance Profiles of Major Energy Producers 1995*, Washington, DC: US Department of Energy, 1995, 11.

25 Energy Information Administration (EIA), 'Profiles of Petroleum Privatizations in OECD Countries', in *Privatization and the Globalization of Energy Markets*,

where the state-owned oil firm YPF was privatised and bought by Repsol in 1999, jobs were slashed from 50,000 to 6,000 in the prelude to privatisation.[26] Globally, a staggering 60 per cent of the oil industry workforce lost their jobs between 1980 and 1997.[27]

Job cuts and outsourcing were part of a broader corporate reorganisation that transformed the internal operations of most Western oil companies. While a strong corporate headquarters remained the norm, decision-making further down the organisational chain was increasingly devolved to the level of individual segments (such as upstream production, refining, chemicals, or marketing). This was part of an attempt to increase internal competitive pressures between different parts of the firm. By giving various segments the operational autonomy to meet constantly changing profitability targets, the pressure to cut costs and improve efficiencies was magnified throughout all levels of the firm. Greater decentralisation and devolution of decision-making were reflected in the adoption of performance-based management and the use of bonuses and stock options to incentivise employees – a shift that further reinforced the prioritisation of shareholder returns in financial planning. Furthermore, a corporate structure based on relatively autonomous and self-contained segments enabled management to detach and sell any business units deemed to be underperforming or no longer in line with overall business strategy.

Again, this restructuring of the corporate form was not unique to oil companies; but it represented a substantial change in one of the most vertically integrated and geographically dispersed of any industrial sector. A chief feature of this new modular structure was that it greatly facilitated a wave of mergers and acquisitions that took place during the 1990s. This industry consolidation was in part a response to pressures to reduce costs (redundant segments could be closed down following a merger). It also helped firms to balance their upstream and downstream

---

Washington, DC: US Department of Energy, 1996, eia.gov.

26 International Labour Organization, 'Global Employment in Refining Industry Remains Stable, but Pressure on Jobs Grows', press release, 23 February 1998.

27 United States House Committee on Commerce, Subcommittee on Energy and Power, *The Exxon-Mobil Merger: Hearings before the Subcommittee on Energy and Power of the Committee on Commerce, House of Representatives*, 106th Congress, first session, 10 and 11 March, Washington, DC: US Government Printing Office, 1999, 22, available at govinfo.gov.

activities without needing to build new plant or engage in physical oil exploration; they could simply identify a company that had what they lacked, and buy or merge with it through investment on the stock market. This phenomenon – akin to 'digging for oil on the stock market' – was particularly evident among American companies. Indeed, between 1997 and 2000, more than half the increase in oil reserves of the thirty-three largest US oil companies came from corporate mergers and acquisitions, rather than real-world oil exploration 'through the drill bit'.[28] By 2000, these mergers had reduced the number of vertically integrated oil firms in the US to just nine, down from nineteen in 1990 and twenty-four in 1980. The concentration of market power grew most sharply in downstream activities; by 2003, the top four US oil firms accounted for just under 40 per cent of total domestic refinery output, up from 26 per cent in 1990.[29]

Industry concentration had a self-reinforcing momentum – as the leading firms got bigger and more powerful through mergers, it forced any erstwhile competitor to also look around for a potential partner. By the late 1990s and early 2000s, this dynamic would culminate in a series of mega-mergers that transformed the face of Western oil. Most important here was the merger of the two US oil giants, Exxon and Mobil, in 1999 – creating ExxonMobil, the biggest private company in the world.[30] At the time, this was the largest industrial merger in history, surpassing an earlier oil sector deal – British Petroleum's acquisition of the American firm, Amoco, in 1998 – which had previously held that record. Other corporate consolidation included Chevron's takeover of Texaco in 2001, and the merger of Conoco Inc. and Phillips Petroleum Company to create ConocoPhillips in 2002. Outside the US, the large French oil firm Total merged with Petrofina in 1999 and then later took over Elf Aquitaine, to create Total SA (now known as TotalEnergies). The net result of these mergers was a reconfiguration of the Western oil

28 Energy Information Administration (EIA), *Performance Profiles of Major Energy Producers 2000*, Washington, DC: US Department of Energy, 2000, xiii. These figures are calculated by the EIA based on an analysis of thirty-three leading oil companies, whose share of the Fortune 500 income was 13 per cent. In 2000, these thirty-three companies accounted for 43 per cent of total US oil production, 44 per cent of natural gas production, and 87 per cent of US refining capacity. Ibid, 4.

29 Ibid., 98.

30 United States House, *Exxon-Mobil Merger*, 4.

industry around a handful of so-called supermajors that remain the dominant Western firms today: ExxonMobil (US), BP (British), Shell (British), Chevron (US), ENI (Italy), TotalEnergies (France), and ConocoPhillips (US).[31]

Oil Rebranded

Alongside this industry consolidation of the 1990s and early 2000s, many of the supermajors began projecting themselves as energy companies rather than simply oil firms. In part, this redefinition reflected increasing involvement in natural gas, solar, wind, and renewables. Gas was particularly noteworthy here, with all the leading supermajors expanding into the exploration and transport of gas following liberalisation of the wholesale and retail gas markets in the 1990s. Gas is substantially more costly than oil to transport because it must be either moved through pipelines or liquified (known as Liquified Natural Gas, LNG) and carried on specialised tankers. These expenses further encouraged industry consolidation as well as multinational joint ventures to build and operate the necessary infrastructure. Huge investments were made into gas liquification plants and export terminals in places such as Qatar, Russia, and Indonesia, and rival pipeline projects were launched that connected gas fields to consumer markets.[32] The expansion into gas also led the leading oil firms – including Shell, ExxonMobil, Total, and BP – to become directly involved in power generation and the sale of electricity.[33]

The convergence of the oil and gas industries – as well as the involvement of oil companies in renewables – would take on increasing significance as popular awareness of climate change grew through the early 2000s. Despite the fact that natural gas production is a major

31 Royal Dutch Shell changed its name to Shell in late 2021, transferring its headquarters and tax residence from the Netherlands to the UK.

32 These included the Bluestream (ENI and Gazprom) and Greenstream (ENI and Libyan National oil company) pipelines that transport gas from Russia and Libya, and the South Caucasus Pipeline (a BP-led consortium) that connects Baku and Turkey.

33 Between 1995 and 2000, net investment in the electricity generation and power sector increased eightfold for the largest US oil and gas firms. EIA, *Performance Profiles 2000*, 11.

emitter of greenhouse gases – including methane, which has a warming effect up to eighty times that of carbon dioxide over the first twenty years it reaches the atmosphere – it was marketed as a cleaner fossil fuel by the largest supermajors and their industry lobby organisations such as the American Petroleum Institute.[34] In this manner, the rebranding of oil firms as energy companies was one part of an attempt to deflect public attention from their central position in the carbon economy. This was perhaps best illustrated by British Petroleum's name change to BP in 2000, under the tagline 'Beyond Petroleum', with a new green sunburst logo. In one advertisement foregrounding the image change, BP claimed that the new name meant 'being a global leader in producing the cleanest burning fossil fuel, natural gas . . . [it] means being the largest producer of solar energy in the world . . . [it] means starting a journey that will take a world's expectation of energy beyond what anyone can see today.'[35] These claims, however, were largely a hollow PR exercise: at the time, BP remained the second largest oil company in the world and spent more on the corporate rebrand than it did on renewable energy.

Confirmation that the supermajors remained primarily in the dirty business of oil was shown by their patterns of cross-border expansion. Backed by the enormous sums of capital made available through the wave of mega-mergers, the largest firms sought to enhance their access to upstream oil and gas through investment in offshore and onshore reserves across the world. One important target was Russia, where foreign partnerships with Western companies offered the newly privatised oil firms of the Yeltsin era international legitimacy as well as access to better technologies and more financing. It was at this time that merger negotiations began between Khodorkovsky's Yukos and the American firms Chevron and ExxonMobil. As we saw in the previous chapter, these discussions were eventually scuppered by Putin's arrest of Khodorkovsky and other Yukos executives in 2003. In the same year, however, a partnership was struck between BP and Russia's fourth largest oil firm, TNK, which brought the Western giant into an alliance

34 Around 97 per cent of natural gas consists of methane. Methane's warming effect is much faster than that of CO_2, although the latter has a longer-lasting impact.

35 'BP and Greenwashing', SourceWatch, 11 October 2017, sourcewatch.org.

with one of the key business groups (the Fridman, Blavatnik, and Vekselberg conglomerate). During the ten years of its existence, TNK-BP ranked as one of the largest oil companies in the world, with upstream and downstream assets located across Russia and Ukraine.[36] ConocoPhillips also entered Russia in September 2004, taking a 20 per cent stake in LUKoil in a deal that involved the transfer of ConocoPhillips's petrol stations in the US and Western Europe to the Russian firm. Sizeable deals were also agreed between Western oil companies and governments in the former Soviet Republics of Kazakhstan and Azerbaijan.[37] Most of these Western investments in Russia would later run into trouble with the rise of Rosneft, and Russia's subsequent war with Ukraine. They were, however, immensely profitable for the largest Western firms at the time.

Alongside Russia, the most important target of Western oil expansion was the African continent. Here, the liberalisation of economic policy through the 1990s had opened up oil-rich countries in West and Central Africa to foreign investment in both onshore and offshore exploration. This expansion typically took place through production-sharing contracts (PSCs), which gave Western companies the right (and the risk) to explore and produce oil for a fixed-term period. Once oil was discovered, a portion of its earnings went to recoup the initial costs of exploration and development, while the remainder was shared with state-owned national oil companies for the term of the contract. Under this arrangement, the ownership of oil reserves remained formally in the hands of the producing state – however, for all practical purposes, most of the production and sale of oil was controlled by the Western firms.[38]

36 Under the terms of the agreement, BP and the Russian consortium each held 50 per cent of TNK-BP. The deal fell apart in 2008, following a dispute between the shareholders and growing pressure on BP from the Russian government. In 2012, BP sold its share in TNK-BP to Rosneft. Despite the end to the arrangement, BP made a 472 per cent return on its initial investment – equivalent to about $45 billion over a ten-year period. Alexander Osipovich, 'TNK-BP Saga Raises Questions about BP's Handling of Political Risk', 19 March 2013, risk.net.

37 One important example of this was the so-called 'Contract of the Century', a 400-page agreement signed between thirteen foreign oil companies – including BP, ExxonMobil, Chevron, Statoil, LUKoil – and the Azerbaijan government.

38 PSCs were also critical to the ways in which notions of liberal equality and the sanctity of contracts underpinned authoritarian states in places such as Africa. For an

The importance of African states to Western oil firms in this period stemmed from the continent's considerable oil reserves, which – for reasons explored below – could be produced cheaper than most other places in the world (except the Middle East). But beyond these cost advantages, African oil was also critical to keeping intact the *integrated form* of the largest Western firms. Under the PSC system, Western firms effectively gained direct control over upstream African crude at the point of production; they were then able to feed this oil into their downstream segments without the need to buy crude on the marketplace. In this manner, African oil helped mitigate the lack of direct access to upstream crude that faced Western supermajors as a result of the nationalisation of oil in the Middle East and Latin America. With the price of oil beginning to rise again by the early 2000s, this guarantee of stable upstream supplies was essential to the longer-term survival and expansion of the integrated Western majors.

Table 11.2 demonstrates this decisive importance of African states to the upstream activities of the seven largest Western oil majors.[39] By 2005, around 27 per cent of the total worldwide reserves held by these firms (11 billion out of just over 40 billion barrels), were located in Africa – far more than any other region of the world, including the US. With the exception of ConocoPhillips, Africa ranked as either the first or second largest source of oil for all the companies shown in the table. The significance of Africa is particularly evident in the case of the two European firms, Total and ENI, which reported that around half their global crude reserves were located in African countries in 2005. But the biggest American firms were likewise heavily dependent on African oil: ExxonMobil, for example, held more oil in Africa than it did in the US at the time. While the oil controlled by these Western companies came from a wide range of countries in Central and West Africa, the most important locations were Nigeria and Angola – between them, these

insightful discussion, along with an analysis of the mechanics of PSCs in Equatorial Guinea, see Hannah Appel, *The Licit Life of Capitalism: US Oil in Equatorial Guinea*, Durham, NC: Duke University Press, 2019.

39 Because the intent of this discussion is to emphasise the importance of Central and West Africa to the global oil economy, North African states such as Algeria, Libya, Egypt, and Tunisia are excluded from the figures provided here. Obviously, if these states were also included, the importance of African oil would be even more pronounced.

two states accounted for over 70 per cent of the continent's oil production in 2005.[40]

Table 11.2 African Share of Global Proven Reserves Held by the Supermajors, 2005

Company	Total global oil reserves (million barrels)	Total African reserves (million barrels)	Share of company's global oil reserves in Africa	Regional ranking of Africa in company's global reserves	Major countries
ExxonMobil	11,229	2,583	23 per cent	first	Angola, Nigeria, Equatorial Guinea
BP	7,161	1,074	15 per cent	second (after US)	Angola
Chevron	5,626	1,800	32 per cent	second (after US)	Nigeria, Angola, Chad, Congo
Total	5,582	2,456	44 per cent	first	Nigeria, Angola, Congo, Gabon, Cameroon
ENI	3,773	1,924	51 per cent	first	Nigeria, Angola, Congo
Shell	3,466	867	25 per cent	second (after Middle East/ Former Soviet Union)	Nigeria, Gabon, and Cameroon
ConocoPhillips	3,336	334	10 per cent	third (after US and Europe)	Nigeria, Cameroon

Source: Company Annual Financial Report (various years), net proved developed and undeveloped reserves held by consolidated subsidiaries. ConocoPhillips African reserves include the Middle East.

This recentring of Western oil production in African countries carried real and long-lasting consequences for the peoples of the continent. Most directly, oil extraction had a ruinous impact on the

40 BP Statistics, exclusive of North African states.

environment and livelihoods of communities living near wells, pipelines, oil rigs, and pumping stations. This is epitomised by Africa's largest oil producer, Nigeria, where frequent oil spills have destroyed forests, mangrove swamps, and farmland in the country's main oil region, the Niger Delta. Indeed, it has been estimated that more oil is spilled across the Niger Delta *each year* than was lost in the much more visible 2010 BP Deepwater Horizon oil spill in the Gulf of Mexico.[41] These oil spills not only pollute the ecosystems upon which many communities depend for their livelihoods, but have also produced very high rates of cancer and other health problems due to the release of toxic chemicals into water, land, and air. Such destruction lay at the root of widespread non-violent popular mobilisations that emerged in the 1990s, but which took on an increasingly militant and armed character during the 2000s following brutal repression by the Nigerian military.[42]

Conditions in the Niger Delta were the direct outcome of an oil industry allowed to operate with little concern for the ecological or social effects of its activities. Chief among the firms active in the country was Shell, which controlled an estimated 50 per cent of Nigeria's oil production in 2005.[43] At the time, Shell's Nigerian operations contributed 16 per cent of the company's entire daily global production – the second largest share of any country in the world, and just a few thousand barrels short of its daily production in the US.[44] Alongside Shell, other large companies active in Nigeria included ExxonMobil, Chevron, Total, and ENI. For these companies, operating conditions in Nigeria and elsewhere in Africa were extremely advantageous – the absence of any effective environmental or social regulations meant much lower

41 Daniel Vallero, *Unraveling Environmental Disasters*, Amsterdam: Elsevier, 2012, 147. About 4.9 million barrels of oil were lost in the Deepwater Horizon catastrophe.

42 Michael Watts, 'Crude Politics: Life and Death on the Nigerian Oil Fields', Working Paper No. 25, 2009, University of California, Berkeley. A key moment in this repression included the murder of indigenous leader Ken Saro-Wiwa by the Nigerian military in 1995. Following this killing, Saro-Wiwa's family sued Shell for their role in summary execution, crimes against humanity, and torture. After petitioning the court not to hear the case for twelve years, Shell eventually settled out of court in 2009 for $15.5 million.

43 Shell began producing oil in Nigeria in 1956, but a sustained increase in oil production began in the early 2000s, peaking in 2010.

44 In 2005, Shell produced 324,000 barrels per day in Nigeria and 333,000 barrels per day in the US. *Shell Annual Report 2005*, 28.

production costs than in most other parts of the world. Shell, for example, reported that its 2005 production costs per barrel in Africa (mostly in Nigeria) were about a third less than in the US, Russia, the Middle East, and Europe, and half that in Canada and Latin America.[45] Such figures confirm a long-standing truism of the oil industry: the bottom-line expenses associated with oil production are not simply a matter of geological luck – they are directly shaped by the social conditions under which that oil is produced. With the real costs of production displaced onto the poorest communities in the Niger Delta and elsewhere, the super-profits associated with African oil played a substantial role in buttressing the balance sheets of the largest Western firms.

Of course, the favourable conditions under which Western oil companies operated in Africa did not arise automatically; they were secured by political and economic elites and backed by autocratic state structures across West and Central Africa. Rulers in African oil-producing states were more than willing to establish such an institutional framework – including, most importantly, the repression of their own populations – in return for a share of the profits obtained through oil production. In Nigeria, of the $40 billion or so that the country was making from oil exports each year by the early 2000s, around 85 per cent was estimated to accrue to just 1 per cent of the population, and up to 40 per cent of the country's oil revenues were estimated to have been stolen – much of this ferreted away in overseas bank accounts.[46] Similarly, in Equatorial Guinea – where ExxonMobil was producing nearly 10 per cent of its total worldwide crude through the early 2000s – production was guaranteed through direct payments to the country's president, Teodoro Obiang, his family, and closest advisors.[47] In return, Obiang offered some of the most attractive investment conditions for oil companies in the world, backed by an oppressive regime that was notorious for 'unlawful killings by security forces; government-sanctioned kidnappings; systematic torture of prisoners and detainees by security forces . . . arbitrary arrest, detention, and incommunicado detention'.[48] Western oil executives were

45 Shell, *Annual Report 2005*, 27.

46 Watts, 'Crude Politics', 4.

47 Appel, *Licit Life*; Rachel Maddow, *Blowout: Corrupted Democracy, Rogue State Russia, and the Richest, Most Destructive Industry on Earth*, New York: Crown, 2019.

48 US State Department report, cited in Maddow, *Blowout*, 151.

fully aware of the quid pro quo at play here. Indeed, a 2004 US Senate Hearing detailed hundreds of millions of dollars paid by American oil companies to Obiang and his family members through Riggs Bank, a Washington DC–based US bank holding more than $700 million in accounts connected to Equatorial Guinea. The payments included disbursements to companies owned by Obiang and his allies, grants to children of high-ranking Equatorial Guinea officials studying in the US, and even a $450,000 sum transferred to a fourteen-year-old relative of Obiang for the use of office space.[49]

As Hannah Appel points out, all of this confirms the 'mutually beneficial relationship between absolute rule and transnational oil firms . . . a relationship characterized by impunity and secrecy on both sides'.[50] In the African context, the ever-present legacies of colonialism and the long histories of slavery and racial division – alongside the more recent experience of debt-driven structural adjustment – meant that Western oil companies encountered state structures that were materially weak and led by rulers eager to secure the income that oil promised. Oil money guaranteed local power and generated new social hierarchies, while driving the hothouse growth of an African business elite whose accumulation centred on the state and its connection with the international oil industry. Simultaneously, as the aggregate national income earned from oil exploded, most residents of oil-producing states saw their living standards worsen considerably.[51]

In this manner, alongside the emergence of new economic and political strata, the expansion of the largest Western firms into Africa generated poverty, ecological destruction, and authoritarianism. We should

49 Norm Coleman and Carl Levin (eds), *Money Laundering and Foreign Corruption: Enforcement and Effectiveness of the Patriot Act*, Hearing before the Permanent Subcommittee on Investigations of the Committee on Governmental Affairs, United States Senate, 108th Congress, 2nd session, Washington, DC: US Government Printing Office, 2004, 101, hsgac.senate.gov.

50 Appel, *Licit Life*, 8.

51 These highly uneven outcomes of oil production were perhaps best illustrated in Equatorial Guinea, a nation of just 1 million people that was catapulted from one of the world's poorest countries to having the highest per capita income on the African continent between 1993 and 2007. Yet while Equatorial Guinea's annual oil revenues grew from $2.1 million to $3.9 *billion* over this period, '77 percent of the population live[d] in poverty, 35 percent die[d] before the age of 40, and 57 percent lack[ed] access to safe water'. Maddow, *Blowout*, 144. Similarly stark patterns of social and economic polarisation prevailed across all African oil-producing states.

be careful, however, not to read this as confirmation of the much vaunted resource-curse theory. Oil did not *cause* these polarising outcomes, and they cannot be explained simply from the internal vantage point of the African state.[52] The root problems were not corrupt leaders, illicit money-laundering, or a lack of democratic accountability. The social and political pathologies associated with the production of oil in African states ultimately derived from the meaning that hydrocarbons had attained within the logics of the capitalist world market, and, following from this, the immense structural power that Western oil majors held in determining how this commodity flows from the oil well to the producer. All this was imbricated with the racial and colonial histories of the African continent. There was nothing automatic or natural about this 'curse' – and, indeed, for the largest integrated Western firms, African oil was very much an extraordinary blessing.

52 For two insightful critiques of the 'resource curse' concept, see Gavin Bridge, 'Global Production Networks and the Extractive Sector: Governing Resource-Based Development', *Journal of Economic Geography* 8, no. 3, 2008: 389–419; and Michael Watts, 'Resource Curse? Governmentality, Oil and Power in the Niger Delta, Nigeria', *Geopolitics* 9, no. 1, 2004: 50–80.

12

NOCs and the New East–East Hydrocarbon Axis

On 11 December 2019, a single event headlined the world's business media. That day, the Saudi government was due to list 1.5 per cent of the world's biggest oil company, Saudi Aramco, on the Tadawul, the Saudi Stock Exchange. The sale had first been mooted by the Saudi crown prince, Mohamed bin Salman, back in January 2016. After three years of controversy over where the listing would take place and how much Aramco was worth – and delays caused by rocket attacks launched by Yemeni militants on the company's oil installations – the Initial Public Offering (IPO) was finally scheduled to go ahead. By the close of trading the sale had netted around $26 billion, valuing Aramco at just under $2 trillion – more than the combined value of every company on Germany's stock market at the time. This was the biggest IPO in history, catapulting Tadawul from the twenty-second to ninth largest stock exchange in the world, ahead of Toronto, Frankfurt, Seoul, and Sydney. With a market capitalisation greater than the US tech giant Apple, Aramco was now officially the most valuable company on the planet.

The sheer size of the Aramco listing underscores a major shift that has taken place in the global oil industry over the past two decades: the rise of national oil companies (NOCs) run by governments in Saudi Arabia, China, Russia, Brazil, and elsewhere. Some of these firms originated in the OPEC nationalisations of the 1970s or were established to work with Western oil companies in the main producing states.

Collectively, they have now developed into huge, diversified corporations that have overtaken the privately owned supermajors in levels of oil production, oil reserves, market capitalisation, and export quantities. As one *Financial Times* columnist put it in mid-2022, the overall effect of the NOCs on the Western oil firms was akin to the 'Total Perspective Vortex' imagined by sci-fi humourist Douglas Adams – a torture device that worked by showing its victims their utter insignificance against the unimaginable infinity of creation.[1] The significance of this power shift is said to go far beyond simple questions of energy supplies – for many observers, the rise of the NOCs helps explain the global spread of authoritarian governments, rising corruption, and increased geopolitical instability.[2]

Much commentary on the NOCs highlights the issue of their state ownership, assuming a fundamental antagonism between private and state-owned firms and implicitly linking Western democracies with a free market in oil. This chapter takes an alternative tack, focusing instead on how the rise of the NOCs is connected to the changing world market over recent years, especially the emergence of China and the wider Asian region as core zones of global accumulation. In keeping with earlier chapters, we emphasise here the importance of approaching the NOC/supermajor rift across the entire oil circuit, including the refining and petrochemical sectors. As we shall see, a closer examination of downstream activities reveals a much more complex world industry that is fractured into interdependent regional blocs centred around different corporate structures. This carries important political implications for the future of an American-centred world order, including the status of the US dollar. It also raises a significant challenge for climate activists today: how to confront the threat posed by fossil capitalism, in a world where non-Western firms are now primary determinants of oil market dynamics.

1 'Saudi Aramco: Vast Scale of NOCs Diminishes Supermajors to Bit Players', *Financial Times*, 15 August 2022, ft.com.

2 For one example of this argument, see Paasha Mahdavi, *Power Grab: Political Survival through Extractive Resource Nationalization*, Cambridge: Cambridge University Press, 2020.

Supermajors and the Shale Revolution

The past three decades have witnessed a deep-seated transformation in the geographies of world trade, production, and accumulation. At the heart of this shift has been the rise of China – the so-called workshop of the world – where increases in foreign investment and direct commercial relationships between Chinese and international firms began to take place from the 1990s onwards. Here, massive pools of rural labour had been released for work in urban factories following changes to social protection laws in the Chinese countryside. This rural-to-urban migration – the largest of its kind in the world – enabled a substantial reduction in global labour costs for transnational firms invested in China. The country came to sit at the heart of a wider East Asian regional production system, with a dense network of intraregional flows of commodities and finance underpinning the production of goods that were then exported further afield. This 'continent of labour', pivoted much of the world's manufacturing around an East Asian axis – shifting the historical patterns of industry and trade that had marked most of the twentieth century.[3]

These far-reaching changes to the geography of global production had major implications for oil. Workshops need more than labour and machines; they also require energy and raw materials – and here the world's hydrocarbon exports were indispensable to the rise of the East. Between 2000 and 2019, annual global oil consumption increased by around 30 per cent, due predominantly to China's booming demand for hydrocarbons. In 2000, China accounted for just 6 per cent of world oil demand; by 2019, it was consuming around 14 per cent of the world's oil, more than anywhere else except the US. With China's manufacturing zones closely connected to the broader region, the demand for oil and other raw materials increased across Asia as a whole. By 2019, Asian oil consumption neared one-third of the world's total, a staggering proportion that exceeded Europe, Russia, Central Asia, Africa, and Central and South America combined.[4] Although China itself possesses

3 Dae-Oup Chang, 'From a Global Factory to Continent of Labour: Labour and Development in Asia', *Asia Labour Review* 1, 2016: 1–48.

4 Figures in this paragraph drawn from BP, *Statistical Review of World Energy 2020*, 69th edition, bp.com. Asia here includes China, Indonesia, Japan, Malaysia, South Korea, Taiwan, Thailand, Vietnam, and the Philippines.

substantial oil reserves – ranking as the sixth largest global producer for most of the past decade – these alone have been unable to meet the country's oil needs. Instead, China's rise relied on a huge increase in oil imports that pushed the world oil trade away from the West towards the East (see below).

This large increase in oil consumption from China and wider Asia helped drive a prolonged surge in oil prices through the first two decades of the new millennium.[5] From an average monthly price of around $27 per barrel in 2000, global oil prices eventually peaked at just over $147 per barrel by mid-2008. They fell back sharply with the 2008 global economic crisis but soon resumed their upward trajectory, reaching around $114 per barrel in mid-2014. This was a financial boon for major oil exporters, especially in the Middle East, where the Gulf states experienced a petrodollar bonanza worth trillions of dollars in new financial surpluses.[6] But the extended period of rising prices also benefited marginal oil producers elsewhere in the world. Most significantly, investments in the development of so-called *non-conventional* oil and gas supplies – reserves that are difficult and more expensive to extract than conventional fossil fuels – were strongly incentivised during this fourteen-year period of high oil prices.

Central to these non-conventional oil supplies are US shale: crude oil and gas that is held in shale or sandstone of low permeability, and which is typically extracted through fracturing the rock by pressurised liquid (fracking). There are a variety of ways of calculating the break-even cost of shale production, and this figure changes depending on the particular oil field and the prevailing costs of technology, labour, and taxes – but a common estimate is that most US shale producers require a price of at

5 Increased demand from China was not the only reason for this price spike. Because of the connection that has emerged between the oil price and oil futures, increased financial flows into oil financial markets also helped drive up the price of oil and other commodities during this period. For a discussion, see Adam Hanieh, 'The Commodities Fetish? Financialisation and Finance Capital in the US Oil Industry', *Historical Materialism* 29, no. 4, 2023: 70–113; and Mazen Labban, 'Oil in Parallax: Scarcity, Markets, and the Financialization of Accumulation', *Geoforum* 41, no. 4, July 2010: 541–52.

6 Adam Hanieh, *Money, Markets, and Monarchies: The Gulf Cooperation Council and the Political Economy of the Contemporary Middle East*, Cambridge: Cambridge University Press, 2018.

least \$45 per barrel to turn a profit.[7] By contrast, conventional Saudi oil has a production cost of around US\$4 per barrel and Russian oil around US\$10 per barrel.[8] These comparisons need to be interpreted with care, as Saudi Arabia and Russia are countries, not companies, and they depend heavily on oil and gas revenues to meet their budgetary needs – in this sense, the break-even price of oil for these states is much higher and fluctuates according to levels of government spending. Nonetheless, there is no doubt that the oil price spike between 2000 and 2014 helped to attract large investments into shale-field development and drove notable improvements in extraction technologies for these non-conventional supplies.

On one side, the North American shale revolution was an unmitigated ecological and social disaster, which rested on the repeated deployment of state-backed violence against indigenous populations in the US and Canada in order to make way for pipeline routes and other infrastructure.[9] But, on the back of this destruction, North American oil production underwent a spectacular boom. Between 2007 and 2014, the production of US shale oil grew more than tenfold, propelling the US into the top rank of oil producers globally.[10] By 2014, the US had overtaken Saudi Arabia to become the world's largest oil producer – a position it has maintained until this day, and a far cry from the panicked predictions of 'energy dependence' that had marked US energy policy debates in the early years of the new millennium.[11]

7 Jennifer Hiller, 'Few U.S. Shale Firms Can Withstand Prolonged Oil Price War', Reuters, 15 March 2020, reuters.com.

8 Wood Mackenzie, 'Oil Price Rout: Which Supply Is Most at Risk or Shut-in?', 30 March 2020, oilandgasmiddleeast.com.

9 For a rich account of the movements against these pipelines, including their unstable political alliances and various ideological expressions, see Kai Bosworth, *Pipeline Populism: Grassroots Environmentalism in the Twenty-First Century*, Minneapolis: University of Minnesota Press, 2022.

10 Lutz Kilian, 'How the Shale Oil Revolution Has Affected US Oil and Gasoline Prices', *VoxEU*, 14 January 2015, voxeu.org.

11 BP, *Statistical Review of World Energy 2021*, 70th Edition, 18, bp.com. World ranking of oil production varies according to whether non-conventional and natural gas liquids (NGLs) are included (as they are in BP's statistics), and whether production is measured by volume, weight, or energy. See also National Energy Policy Development Group, *Reliable, Affordable, and Environmentally Sound Energy for America's Future*, Report of the National Energy Policy Development Group to the President of the United States, Washington, DC: US Government Printing Office, 2001, nrc.gov.

Over the same period, Canadian oil production also grew massively, increasing by 70 per cent between 2009 and 2019 as a result of tar sands extraction and fracking.[12] Indeed, Canada has ranked as the world's fourth largest oil producer for nearly a decade, and is the 'only G7 country whose emissions have increased since the 2015 Paris Accord'.[13] Canadian companies have also played a leading and highly destructive role in the exploitation of Latin American oil reserves, notably in Colombia.[14] Yet despite this centrality to fossil capitalism, Canada continues to portray itself as world leader in climate efforts.[15]

This increase in oil production has been immensely profitable for the largest Western supermajors who remain the dominant players in the North American market. For these international firms, the US and Canada sit at the core of their upstream reserves; indeed, around a third of all the oil produced globally by the supermajors comes from North America, more than from any other region of the world.[16] For some of the leading supermajors such as ExxonMobil, Chevron, and BP, the share of North American oil in their total global production is even higher (around 40 per cent).[17] The significance of North America to the crude base of the largest supermajors places these firms at the forefront

12 Tar sands are a mix of sand, clay, and water from which bitumen is extracted and processed into petroleum products. This is an extremely expensive and ecologically damaging form of oil production, with significantly higher levels of carbon emissions than from conventional oil. The largest tar sands reserves are located on indigenous lands in Alberta, Canada, and indigenous communities have faced the worst impacts of this form of oil extraction and associated pipeline development. See Nicolas Graham and William K. Carroll, 'Climate Breakdown: From Fossil Capitalism to Climate Capitalism (and Beyond?)', in Greg Albo, Alfredo Saad-Filho, and Nicole Aschoff (eds), *Socialist Register 2023: Capital and Politics*, London: Merlin Press, 2022.

13 Ibid., 26.

14 Todd Gordon and Jeffery R. Webber, *Blood of Extraction: Canadian Imperialism in Latin America*, Halifax: Fernwood Press, 2016, 164–9.

15 Graham and Carroll, 'Climate Breakdown', 26.

16 Calculated by the author from ENI, *World Energy Review 2021*, Rome: ENI, 2021. Gabe Eckhouse points out that fracking has also served the interests of the US oil industry because it offers short term investment opportunities and flexibility in contrast to the long-cycle production that typifies conventional oil. This is important in the context of extreme uncertainty around the future of oil. Gabe Eckhouse, 'United States Hydraulic Fracturing's Short-Cycle Revolution and the Global Oil Industry's Uncertain Future', *Geoforum*, 2021.

17 Calculated by the author from ExxonMobil, Chevron, and BP annual reports, various years.

of some of the most destructive types of oil extraction, notably shale, tar sands, and offshore deep-water drilling. The supermajors now spend a majority of their upstream investment on these forms of oil extraction, whereas around 90 per cent of NOC upstream investment goes to conventional onshore fields.[18]

Alongside this close link with North American oil production, the supermajors continue to be deeply connected to financial markets in the US and Europe, and in keeping with the trends towards financialisation that began in the 1990s, they place a strong emphasis on short-term shareholder returns and stock market valuation.[19] This is shown by the large sums of money spent on share buybacks and dividend pay-outs: between 2015 and 2019, around 40 per cent of supermajor cash flow was returned to investors in these ways.[20] The US oil industry now spends more on share buybacks than any other business sector, a trend that has accelerated sharply following the rapid rise in oil prices through early 2022.[21] Indeed, in 2023, Shell announced plans to repurchase at least $13.5 billion of its own shares – an amount that was around three times what it planned to spend on renewable and low-carbon energy over the next three years.

There has also been a significant change in ownership structures of the leading supermajors.[22] The three biggest US oil companies by market capitalisation – ExxonMobil, Chevron, and ConocoPhillips – have between 60 to 80 per cent of their share ownership controlled by various forms of financial capital (such as investment banks, asset management firms, and private equity funds).[23] Playing a prominent role are the world's Big Three asset management firms – Vanguard, Blackrock, and State Street – which occupy the top three shareholder positions for

18 International Energy Agency (IEA), *World Energy Investment 2020*, 42.

19 Labban, 'Oil in Parallax'.

20 Calculated by author from Rystad, *Rystad Energy Data, Upstream Report*, 22 May 2022, 7.

21 Geoffrey Morgan, 'Oil and Gas Share Buybacks Boomed before Energy Prices Hit Highs', *BloombergUK*, 15 March 2022.

22 For a mapping of these ownership patterns in the context of the financialisation of oil, see Hanieh, 'The Commodities Fetish?'.

23 IEA, *World Energy Investment*, 161. Some of the most important firms in this respect are JP Morgan, Goldman Sachs, Morgan Stanley, Vanguard, Blackrock, State Street, and the Blackstone and Carlyle private equity groups. See Hanieh, 'The Commodities Fetish?'.

around a third of the largest publicly listed oil and gas firms in the US.[24] The strong presence of these and other financial conglomerates indicates that when we consider *who* profits from the Western oil industry, it is not enough to focus simply on oil companies themselves. While the supermajors drive much of the physical extraction of crude oil in North America, the dynamics of oil production are ultimately tied to the imperatives of large financial groups that act simultaneously in both financial markets and the day-to-day real world of energy production.[25] Through their deep involvement in the ownership of supermajors and the wider North American and European oil industry, these financial investors are leading beneficiaries of the carbon economy.[26]

Inter-Regional Flows

The close connection between the leading supermajors and North American crude production needs to be situated within the wider global oil market. To this end, Tables 12.1 and 12.2 provide a snapshot of international cross-border flows for both crude and refined oil products in 2022. The data confirm the highly regionalised character of North American oil production: most oil exports (crude and refined) from the US, Canada, and Mexico tend to circulate as cross-border flows within the North American bloc itself. In the case of crude oil, Canadian exports to the US account for around half of all the North American exports shown in the table (the other half is mostly made up of Mexican exports to the US, and US exports to Europe, Other Asia, and Canada).[27] Canadian crude exports feed into the US refining industry (along with US domestic crude) and the resulting products are exported back to Canada,

24 Ibid.

25 An essential aspect involves profiting from oil price volatility and financial speculation; see Anna Zalik, 'Oil "Futures": Shell's Scenarios and the Social Constitution of the Global Oil Market', *Geoforum* 41, no. 4, 2010: 553–64.

26 Adrienne Buller shows how the investment priorities of these financial groups, especially the Big Three asset management firms, also wield significant power over global climate policy responses. See Adrienne Buller, *The Value of a Whale: On the Illusions of Green Capitalism*, 2022, Manchester: Manchester University Press, especially chs 3 and 4.

27 Canadian exports to the US made up 94 per cent of all Canada's crude exports in 2022.

Table 12.1 Crude Oil Inter-Regional Trade Flows, 2022 (million tonnes)

From \ To	North America	Central and South America	Europe	Middle East and North Africa	Africa	India	China	Other Asia	Total
North America	237.4	11.0	90.1	0.1	0.0	22.2	13.9	48.7	**423.4**
Central and South America	35.7	negligible	22.8	2.6	0.6	6.9	37.3	11.3	**117.2**
Russia and Central Asia*	2.1	1.0	179.6	3.8	0.7	37.8	92.2	15.4	**332.6**
Middle East and North Africa	45.7	5.8	148.4	13.8	9.9	138	271.7	352	**985.3**
West Africa	12	6	59.5	1.3	4.1	19.4	46.5	20.4	**169.2**
Total	**332.9**	**23.8**	**500.4**	**21.6**	**15.3**	**224.3**	**461.6**	**447.8**	**2,021.3**

Source: Adapted by the author from Energy Institute, *Statistical Review of World Energy 2023*, 72nd Edition, 28, energyinst.org/statistical-review. Totals are only given for the regions included in the table, not the entire world. 'Other Asia' includes Japan, Singapore, South Korea, and Thailand.

* Russian oil exports have changed significantly since 2022 because of sanctions placed on the country during the Ukraine war (see discussion in text).

Table 12.2 Refined Products Inter-Regional Trade Flows, 2022 (million tonnes)

From \ To	North America	Central and South America	Europe	Middle East and North Africa	Africa	India	China	Other Asia	Total
North America	114.9	82.5	32.9	2.0	9.9	5.7	16.2	38.7	**302.8**
Central and South America	7.7	n.a.	4.9	0.6	3.2	0.6	3.3	8.3	**28.6**
Europe	25.4	11.8	n.a.	9.4	47	2.5	2.0	9.5	**107.6**
Russia and Central Asia	6.7	3.8	84.4	6.8	3.6	7.3	10	9.6	**132.2**
Middle East and North Africa	14.5	6.8	46.1	46.3	43.2	31.5	25.2	96.2	**309.8**
China	0.9	4.2	6.3	1.5	5.1	0.6	--	32.8	**51.4**
Other Asia	11.3	2.4	8.3	4.5	10.3	4.7	34.5	98.3	**174.3**
Total	**181.4**	**111.5**	**182.9**	**71.1**	**122.3**	**52.9**	**91.2**	**293.4**	**1106.7**

Source: Energy Institute, *Statistical Review*, 29. Refined products are naptha, fuel oil, gasoline, ethane, diesel, and kerosene. 'Other Asia' includes Japan, Singapore, South Korea, and Thailand.

Mexico, and the wider Americas (Table 12.2). Canada also has its own significant refining sector, with almost all exports of refined products going to the US. Only a small proportion of North American refined products end up beyond the Americas. These intra-regional flows of oil and refined products within North America are mostly controlled by the largest Western supermajors who profit from both the upstream and downstream components of this trade. It has been underpinned by a range of regulatory initiatives that have helped facilitate North American trade and investment flows.[28]

Unlike the predominantly self-contained North American oil circuit, the rest of the world depends much more heavily on imports *between* regions to satisfy demand. In 2022, Europe, which consumes approximately a quarter of the world's crude exports, relied on the Russia/Central Asia region for about a third of its oil imports and over 40 per cent of its imported refined products.[29] As we saw in Chapter 10, oil exports are critical to the Russian economy, and until 2022 half of the country's oil exports flowed westward to Europe either via maritime routes or the Druzbha pipeline, the world's longest.[30] With the war in Ukraine, however, the EU placed a ban in December 2022 on seaborne Russian oil imports and also imposed additional restrictions on commercial services provided to the Russian maritime oil trade.[31] Europe's direct imports of Russian oil fell noticeably as a result, although considerable quantities of Russian oil (especially refined products) continue to be shipped to Europe and elsewhere after transiting through a third country.[32] Overall, the global volume of Russian oil exports has not shrunk

28 Anna Zalik, 'The Perpetual Rescaling of Oil and Gas Production and Flows in Continental North America', *Environment and Planning A* 54, no. 8, 2022: 1661.

29 Despite oil production in the North Sea, Europe is not a major exporter of crude oil. It does, however, refine and export substantial quantities of oil products, which mostly go to Africa and North America (see Table 12.2).

30 European Federation for Transport and Environment, 'How Russian Oil Flows to Europe', Briefing, 7 March 2022, 11, transportenvironment.org.

31 The EU embargo was introduced on Russian crude oil on 5 December 2022 and on Russian refined products on 5 February 2023. It did not apply to Russian pipeline oil exports (around a third of Russian oil exports to Europe). In addition, the G7, EU, and other participating countries banned the supply of various maritime services (shipping, financing, insurance) for Russian oil shipments unless the oil was being purchased at or below a capped price.

32 Once it reaches a third-country destination, Russian oil can be blended with other crudes or refined into products, and then exported to the EU, US, or elsewhere.

significantly since 2022, with increased shipments to China, India, and other non-embargo countries making up for any shortfall in oil exports to Europe.

Although Europe remains a major consumer of imported oil, by far the most important driver of the world oil trade today is demand from China and the wider Asia region. By 2022, more than 45 per cent of all the world's oil exports were flowing to Asia – with more than half of these destined for China alone.[33] Since 2000, the increase in China's oil imports has been equivalent to a second US entering the world market. This large growth in demand has reconfigured the long-established patterns of world oil exports, especially for the Gulf countries of the Middle East. Rather than flowing to Europe or the US, Middle East crude oil exports have turned decisively eastwards, and now meet more than half of China's oil import demand (up from around a third in 2001).[34] China's booming consumption of oil is part of a wider increase in Asian energy imports that have largely been met by the Middle East – by 2022, nearly two-thirds of all the Middle East's crude oil exports (mostly from the Gulf states) were going to Asia. As Table 12.2 indicates, the Middle East has also become the leading external source of exported refined products to both China and Asia, although the bulk of Asia's demand for refined imports is met through pan-regional trade flows (see below for further discussion).

India and Turkey are two countries that have significantly increased their imports of Russian oil since the EU embargo began, and have simultaneously seen a large increase in their oil and refined product exports. In addition, tankers registered in offshore jurisdictions (such as St Kitts and Nevis) are able to circumvent sanctions against Russian-owned companies, allowing the ongoing shipment of Russian oil around the world. For a discussion of these issues, see the investigative research of the British NGO, *Global Witness*, globalwitness.org/en/campaigns/stop-russian-oil/.

33 Energy Institute, *Statistical Review 2023*, 28. This figure does not include Indian imports. If India is included, the proportion of world crude exports going to Asia rises to 57 per cent.

34 Ibid. Between 2001 and 2022, the share of Middle East oil flowing to North America and Europe fell from 40 per cent to 20 per cent. BP, *Statistical Review of World Energy 2002*, 18.

Refining and Petrochemical Power

This vast increase in Chinese/Asian oil imports has helped drive a corresponding shift in the geographies of world oil refining. As Table 12.3 shows, in the early 1990s, nearly two-thirds of the world's refining capacity was located in North America, Russia/Central Asia, and Europe. Over the 1990s and 2000s, however, this structure changed radically. On one side, the collapse of the Soviet Union led to a sharp fall in Russian refining capacity, which essentially halved between 1992 and 2005. Although it has expanded since then, the country's overall share of global refining has remained unchanged over the past two decades.[35] During this same period, however, there was a marked increase in Asian refining activity associated with the rise of China.[36] Indeed, Asian refining capacity more than tripled between 1992 and 2022, and the absolute number of refineries grew more than two-and-a-half times. By 2022, Asia's share of world refining capacity stood at 29 per cent of the world's total. With Asia's manufacturing output heavily reliant on ever-growing quantities of plastics and other synthetic materials, much of this new refining capacity was used to produce petrochemicals – as a result, the region has also overtaken the US and Europe to become the global centre of petrochemical production and consumption.[37]

35 In 2005, Russian refinery capacity stood at 6.3 per cent of the world's total. BP, *Statistical Review of World Energy 2013*, 16. In 2022, it reached 6.7 per cent.

36 Asian refining capacity had previously been concentrated in Japan, and to a lesser degree South Korea.

37 In 2022, China accounted for more than 40 per cent of global chemical sales – up from 28 per cent in 2011, and far surpassing the US (11 per cent) and the EU (15 per cent). In 2000, China held just 5 per cent of the world's production capacity for the six basic petrochemicals; by 2022, that figure had reached a staggering 38 per cent. In comparison, Europe's share of global capacity fell from 20 per cent to 12 per cent, and North America's from 25 per cent to 14 per cent. See 'Profile', in '2023 Facts and Figures of the European Chemical Industry', European Chemical Industry Council, cefic.org; and John Richardson, 'Global Oversupply of Chemicals to Hit 218m Tonnes in 2023', *Asian Chemical Connections* (blog), 8 March 2023, icis.com. Despite these trends, Western chemical companies continue to be larger than their non-Western peers, although this dominance is weakening. In 2010, thirty-two out of the top fifty chemical companies in the world (64 per cent) were headquartered in North America or Europe; by 2022, this had dropped to twenty-seven (54 per cent). 'Global Top 50', *Chemical and Engineering News (C&EN)*, 2009, cen.acs.org.

Table 12.3: Share of World Refining Capacity (per cent)

	1992	2022
Asia	15	29
North America	25	21
Europe	23	15
Middle East	7	11
Russia and Central Asia	14	8
Central/South America	8	6
Africa	4	3

Source: Energy Institute, *Statistical Review 2023*, 26; *BP Statistical Review of World Energy 2002,* 16. Major refining countries in Asia include China, South Korea, Taiwan, Japan, Singapore, Indonesia, and Thailand.

Table 12.3 also indicates that the only other region of the world that has seen a growth in its share of world refining capacity is the Middle East, where absolute capacity has more than doubled since the early 1990s, and which now holds an 11 per cent share of the world's total. As with China, much of this growth in the Middle East's refinery capacity is directly connected to the region's booming petrochemical industry, especially the manufacture of ethylene, a vital ingredient used in the production of packaging, construction materials, and automobile parts.[38] The Gulf is now the third largest production hub for ethylene in the world – just behind the US and China – with massive integrated refinery and petrochemical complexes producing this and other basic petrochemicals that are then exported eastwards.[39] Indeed, just under half of all China's ethylene imports are now supplied from the Middle East.[40] China's emergence as so-called workshop of the world would not have been possible without these guaranteed flows of basic petrochemicals from the Gulf.

This geographical shift of the world refining and petrochemical industries towards Asia and the Middle East is driving new interdependencies between the two regions: crude oil is either extracted in

38 Approximately 75 per cent of the global demand for ethylene comes from these three manufacturing activities.

39 In an integrated petrochemical complex, oil refineries are situated adjacent to petrochemical plants, and refined products (such as ethane) enter as feedstock into the production of chemicals (such as ethylene). The Gulf holds 12 per cent of the world's ethylene capacity and about 7 per cent of global petrochemical production (a share that has doubled since 2000).

40 Gulf Petrochemicals and Chemicals Association (GPCA), 'Ethylene a Litmus Test', Dubai, GPCA, November 2019, 2.

the Middle East and exported to Asia for refining; or it is extracted and refined in the Middle East, and then exported as fuels or chemicals to Asia. In both cases, the refining process is dominated by large NOCs headquartered in the Middle East, China, and wider Asia. The refined fuels and petrochemicals made from Middle East oil enter directly into Asian manufacturing networks, where commodities are produced and then exported elsewhere. Western supermajors hold a relatively marginal position within this hydrocarbon circuit stretching between Asia and the Middle East – instead, they remain dominant in the older geographies of the world oil industry: North America and Western Europe.[41]

With so much of the world's refining capacity now located in Asia and the Middle East, these regional interdependencies are shifting the corporate control of the refining industry. Globally, just fifteen companies hold around half of all the world's refining capacity (up from a 40 per cent share in 1999).[42] These fifteen firms have remained mostly the same over the past two decades, but there has been a major reshuffle in their relative ranking. In 1999, three out of the top four refiners in the world were Western supermajors: Royal Dutch Shell, Exxon, and BP Amoco. Today, the first, second, and fourth spots are taken by Chinese and Saudi companies – Sinopec, Chinese National Petroleum Corporation (CNPC), and Saudi Aramco – and only ExxonMobil remains within the top four. More broadly, among the top fifteen refining firms, around half of all refining capacity is now held by NOCs, up from 37 per cent in 1999.

This shift in the control of refining shows how the large NOCs are increasingly following the path first paved by their Western rivals: adopting a vertically integrated structure that spans both the upstream and downstream. A clear example of this is the case of Saudi Aramco, which in 2020 took a major step towards downstream integration when

41 ExxonMobil, for example, has around 75 per cent of its refineries, 88 per cent of its retail sites, and 70 per cent of its chemical sales located in North America and Europe. See ExxonMobil, *Annual Report* 2020, 44–6. NOCs control less than 10 per cent of refining capacity in North America and Europe – in contrast to Asia, the Middle East, South America, and Russia/Central Asia, where they control the largest share.

42 For further details on these companies and the structure of global refining, see Adam Hanieh, 'World Oil: Contemporary Transformations in Ownership and Oil', in Albo, Saad-Filho, and Aschoff, *Socialist Register 2023*.

it became the controlling shareholder of the Saudi Basic Industries Corporation (SABIC), now the fourth largest chemical company in the world by sales (up from twenty-ninth in 2000).[43] As part of this move to integrate its crude production, refining, and petrochemical activities, Saudi Aramco has also established several trading arms in Asia (mostly located in Singapore) and is the second largest shareholder in Bahri, a Saudi logistics and shipping company that owns the world's biggest fleet of double-hulled very large crude-oil carriers (VLCCs). As a result, Aramco is now much more than simply the world's largest supplier of crude – the firm's vast global downstream infrastructure rivals any of the largest Western supermajors.

The fact that Sinopec, Saudi Aramco, and other large NOCs are majority state-controlled does not mean that private ownership is absent from refining and petrochemical activities in either the Middle East or China and East Asia. Since 2015, China has allowed full private control in refining and petrochemicals, and about 30 per cent of the country's refining volume is privately owned.[44] Many of China's new billionaires have made their fortunes in this sector, including Chen Jianhua (worth around $7.7 billion according to Forbes 2022 Rich List), who is the owner of Hengli Petrochemical, the eleventh largest chemical company in the world.[45] Similarly in the Gulf, large privately controlled conglomerates are active in downstream activities, typically through joint ventures and shared projects with NOCs such as Saudi Aramco.[46] In this way – and much as we observed in the case of Putin's Russia – there is no contradiction between the state control of hydrocarbons and the growth of private capital; rather, it is through their *partnership* with

43 'Global Top 50'. SABIC was established by Saudi royal decree in 1976, with the goal of using the country's crude oil and gas to manufacture basic chemicals for a range of industries, including automobiles, agriculture, construction, and packaging. In the early 2000s, the company began to grow internationally through investments in Europe and the US. A major milestone was the acquisition of the plastics division of the US firm General Electric in 2007, which enabled the company to take substantial steps into advanced petrochemical production. Since that time, SABIC has expanded its activities to more than fifty countries across the world.

44 Alex Kimani, 'China's Private Oil Refiners Are Too Powerful for Beijing', oilprice.com, 22 June 2021.

45 'Global Top 50'.

46 For an analysis of the relationship between private and state-owned capital in the case of the Gulf's petrochemical sector, see Hanieh, *Money, Markets, and Monarchies*.

state-run NOCs that domestic business conglomerates across Asia and the Middle East have been able to expand and enter sectors such as refining, petrochemicals, and plastics.

An 'East–East' Hydrocarbon Axis

These patterns confirm the strong interdependencies that are emerging between the Middle East (especially the Gulf region) and East Asia (especially China) across the oil sector. This encompasses much more than the simple export of Middle East oil and oil products to Asia – rather, it involves a considerable increase in *cross-regional* investments by both the large Gulf and Asian NOCs as well as major privately owned conglomerates. As a result of these capital flows between the two areas, there is an extensive intermeshing of ownership across refining, petrochemical production, and the onward circulation of oil products to the consumer. Gulf hydrocarbon interests are now increasingly embedded within Asian production networks, and vice versa. These linkages have been accompanied by growing political ties between the two regions, represented in a recent series of bilateral agreements and other diplomatic initiatives.

To really grasp the extent of these interdependencies and their implications, we must consider all aspects of the hydrocarbon circuit: upstream, downstream, and activities such as transportation, drilling, storage, and the laying of pipelines. Across these oil-related activities, China made more than US $76 billion in outward investments globally between 2012 and 2021.[47] The first phase of these Chinese investments (2012–16) followed the announcement of the Belt and Road Initiative (BRI), and focused mainly on North America, Western Europe, and Russia and Central Asia. After 2016, however, there was a substantial reorientation in Chinese overseas oil investment. Between 2017 and 2021, more than 30 per cent of Chinese investments in oil-related industries went to the Middle East, a greater proportion than to any other world region and a fivefold increase in the Middle East's relative share compared to the 2012–16 period.

47 The figures in this paragraph are calculated by the author from Orbis Database, available at bvdinfo.com. They include investment in both upstream production as well as refining, petrochemical production, and oil and gas services (including drilling and pipelines).

This geographical reorientation in Chinese overseas investments has given Chinese firms a prominent role in the Middle East oil sector. In the UAE, for example, Chinese firms are leading partners of the state-owned oil company, the Abu Dhabi National Oil Company (ADNOC), and hold major stakes in onshore and offshore oil fields. In Iraq, a privately owned Chinese firm now operates one of the largest oil fields in the world, the supergiant Majnoon oil field. And in Kuwait, a subsidiary of the Chinese NOC Sinopec has become the largest oil-drilling contractor, controlling 45 per cent of drilling contracts in the country. The largest deal involving China in the Middle East oil sector was finalised in 2021, with Chinese participation in a multinational joint venture (JV) that owns a 49 per cent equity stake in Aramco Oil Pipelines Co., a company that will have rights to twenty-five years of tariff payments for oil transported through Aramco's crude pipeline network in Saudi Arabia.

Alongside this influx of Chinese investment into the Middle East, the Gulf states have become the primary foreign presence in the Chinese oil sector. This has occurred through numerous projects aimed at securing markets for the Gulf's crude exports, including JVs in refineries, petrochemical plants, transport infrastructure, and fuel-marketing networks. One example is the Sino-Kuwait Integrated Refinery and Petrochemical Complex, a fifty–fifty JV between Sinopec and Kuwait Petroleum Corporation that is the biggest refinery JV in China, incorporating within it the country's largest petrochemical port (completed in May 2020). Both the refinery and port are viewed as an integral component of China's BRI, enabling China to import crude oil from the Gulf to manufacture fuels and other basic chemicals that are then exported to neighbouring Asian countries. Saudi Arabia's significant presence in China is evident through several large JVs between Saudi Aramco and Chinese firms in the refining and petrochemical sector, as well as a network of over a thousand service stations in Fujian province, the first province-level fuel retail JV in the country. These partnerships involve both Chinese NOCs, such as Sinopec, as well as leading privately owned refining companies in China.[48] Qatar has also been a prominent Gulf

48 One illustration of the latter was Saudi Aramco's 2023 purchase of a 10 per cent stake in the privately owned Chinese firm Rongsheng Petrochemical, which controls the largest integrated refining and chemicals complex in China. As part of this investment, Aramco agreed to supply 480,000 barrels of crude oil a day to Rongsheng.

investor in China's energy sector, focusing particularly on securing markets for its LNG exports.

The Gulf's expansion into China is part of a broader involvement in other Asian countries. Indeed, between 2012 and 2021, nearly half all foreign investments from outside Asia (by value) into Asian oil-related assets came from the Gulf, including the four largest deals during this period.[49] Through these investments, Gulf firms now produce refined oil products and basic chemicals within Asia itself (utilising crude feedstocks imported from the Gulf), which are then circulated across Asia by the trading arms of Gulf firms. Key regional targets for this downstream diversification are South Korea, Singapore, Malaysia, and Japan. In each of these four countries, Gulf firms have taken over leading oil-related companies, as well as embarked on other kinds of joint investments.

Unsurprisingly, the chief Gulf firm in this respect has been Saudi Aramco, which now has a major presence in numerous Asian states. In 2015, for example, Saudi Aramco acquired control over the South Korean firm S-Oil, which is the third largest refining company in the country (with about 25 per cent market share) and operates the sixth largest refinery in the world (located in Ulsan, South Korea). This acquisition enabled S-Oil to expand its petrochemical capacity in Korea, and the firm is now a top producer of various refined fuels and basic chemicals that Saudi Aramco's regional trading arm (Aramco Trading Singapore) then exports to other Asian countries. Also in South Korea, Saudi Aramco became the second largest shareholder of Hyundai Oilbank following the purchase of 17 per cent of the company's shares in 2019. Hyundai Oilbank is the fourth largest refining company in Korea, and is majority owned by the Hyundai industrial conglomerate. In Malaysia, Saudi Aramco is currently building a refinery and petrochemical plant that is projected to be the largest downstream petrochemical plant in Asia on completion; the project is a fifty–fifty JV with the Malaysian NOC Petronas. And in Japan, Saudi Aramco became the second largest shareholder in Idemitsu Kosan in 2019 – the firm is the number two refiner in Japan, where it has cornered

49 Calculated by the author from Orbis Database. Asia is defined here as China (including Hong Kong), Taiwan, Korea, Malaysia, Indonesia, Japan, Thailand, Singapore, and the Philippines.

roughly a quarter of the market through six refineries and a network of 6,200 retail service stations.

Whither the US Dollar?

Alongside this new East–East hydrocarbon axis – and against the wishes of the US government – Gulf countries have also begun to endorse various schemes supported by the Chinese state, including the Shanghai Cooperation Organisation (SCO), the Belt and Road Initiative, and the Shanghai-based BRICS New Development Bank.[50] The Gulf's increasingly independent relationships with China are one reflection of a relative erosion of American power in the Middle East. While there is no immediate prospect of China or any other country replacing the US as the final backstop to the Gulf monarchs, the prevailing regional security architecture – ultimately based on the incorporation of the Gulf's oil and financial surpluses into a US-centred world market – faces significant uncertainty. All this casts the Gulf's relationship with China and wider Asia as a major determinant of continued US power at the global scale.

A vital dimension to these East–East linkages is their potential to weaken the connection between oil and the US dollar. As we saw in Chapter 9, the price of oil is today linked to two main oil benchmarks: West Texas Intermediate (WTI) and Brent, which are crude oils produced in the US and North Sea respectively. Significantly, however, the pricing system for WTI and Brent is not based on the physical exchange of oil but rather the trade of financial derivatives. These derivatives are so-called paper barrels traded on two main financial markets, NYMEX and the Intercontinental Exchange (ICE), where futures contracts specify a price for selling (or purchasing) a set quantity of oil

50 The high profile visit of Chinese President Xi Jinping to Saudi Arabia in December 2022 saw discussion of various bilateral initiatives, including a $12.5 billion Saudi–China petrochemical JV in China's Liaoning province as part of China's BRI. Shortly after Xi's visit, Saudi Arabia announced its intention to join the SCO as a dialogue partner, with full membership planned in the coming years. Kuwait, Qatar, and the UAE have also joined the SCO as dialogue partners. Saudi Arabia and the UAE have been invited to join the BRICS group from January 2024, and the Kingdom is in negotiations to become the ninth member of the New Development Bank.

(in barrels) at some date in the future. Dollar hegemony continues to be served by this system because WTI and Brent futures contracts are denominated in US dollars, and all other kinds of oil in the world are linked at some differential to the prices of these contracts. Moreover, these financial markets are located in the US (NYMEX) and Western Europe (ICE), and most of the financial trading on these markets is carried out by large US-based investment banks.[51]

In this context, it is important to note Chinese attempts to establish a new oil pricing system. In 2012, the Shanghai International Exchange (INE) announced a plan to develop an oil futures contract intended to serve as an oil price benchmark for the Asia-Pacific region. Crucially, this contract would be denominated in Chinese renminbi (RMB), marking the first time since sterling oil that the commodity would be internationally traded in a currency other than the US dollar. At a technical level, there were several compelling reasons for this move. Despite being the decisive locus of global oil demand over the past two decades, Asia has been without a satisfactory benchmark since the rise of Brent and WTI as the dominant reference points for global oil pricing. The futures trade that takes place on ICE and NYMEX reflect market conditions in Europe and North America, and largely developed around the pricing needs of producers and customers in these regions. A major aspect to this is that Middle East oil exported to China is of a different grade to Brent and WTI; as a result, companies, traders, and governments in Asia have found it much more difficult to hedge their risks using the established international benchmarks.[52]

Beyond these technical factors, Chinese policy makers explicitly framed the launch of an RMB oil futures contract around the strategic goals of strengthening the international position of the Chinese currency.[53] By denominating a significant share of the global oil trade in RMB, companies and foreign governments would be encouraged to lower

51 Hanieh, 'Commodities Fetish', provides a detailed explanation of how these benchmarks operate.

52 Middle East oil exports to China are typically 'medium sour' versus the 'light sweet' oil traded on NYMEX and ICE. For a discussion, see Shanghai International Exchange (SIE), 'Crude Oil Futures Q&A', 2018, 50, at ine.cn.

53 For further discussion of the RMB contract and its potential impact on the US dollar, see Adam Hanieh, 'World Money and Oil: Theoretical and Historical Considerations', *Science and Society* 87, no. 1, 50–75: 2023.

their proportion of dollar holdings and build up RMB reserves. As such, the new oil contract could play a major role in increasing the use of the Chinese currency within global markets, while simultaneously reducing the world's reliance on the dollar.[54] If oil-producing states such as Saudi Arabia began to sell some of their oil in RMB, they would also begin to accumulate RMB surpluses. These could be used to purchase imports from China or encourage further investment in Chinese markets. And, perhaps most importantly, RMB-denominated oil would provide China a means to continue importing oil in the event of any US financial sanctions directed against the country.[55]

The RMB oil futures contract was eventually launched in early 2018 on the INE. Trading volumes quickly exceeded those on the Dubai Mercantile Exchange (where contracts for oil destined for Asia were usually traded), propelling INE into the position of the third biggest oil exchange in the world. In mid-2020, BP became the first major global firm to supply physical oil to INE, with the delivery of three million barrels of Iraqi oil.[56] The COVID-19 pandemic gave the market a large boost, with annual INE trading volumes increasing by 20 per cent in 2020, despite the massive collapse in oil demand seen across the rest of the world. Since that time, trade in the RMB contract has continued to grow, with Chinese President Xi Jinping noting in a December 2022 speech to Gulf leaders that RMB-denominated oil was a key priority of 'a new paradigm of all-dimensional energy cooperation' between China and the Gulf.[57]

Of course, the current impact of RMB-traded oil on dollar supremacy should not be overstated. WTI and Brent continue to be the two main oil pricing benchmarks, and the volume of oil futures traded on NYMEX and ICE far exceeds that of INE. There has been no move away from dollar-denominated oil by any major oil-producing state (although

54 Leslie Hook, 'Shanghai to Launch Crude Futures Contract', *Financial Times*, 9 February 2012, ft.com.

55 The importance of this was demonstrated in 2023, as Western sanctions cut Russia off from its foreign currency reserves following the war in Ukraine. After these sanctions, RMB became the most traded currency in Russia.

56 Chen Aizhu and Shu Zhang, 'BP, Mercuria First Global Firms Delivering Oil into Shanghai Contract: Sources', Reuters, 14 July 2020, reuters.com.

57 'President Xi Jinping Attends First China-GCC Summit', Ministry of Foreign Affairs of the People's Republic of China, 10 December 2022, fmprc.gov.cn/eng/zxxx_662805/202212/t20221210_10988406.html.

the Saudi finance minister signalled in early 2023 that the Kingdom was open to trading in currencies other than the US dollar).[58] The large dollar surpluses held by the Gulf countries militate against any actions that might weaken the position of the dollar. More broadly, the US dollar still makes up about 60 per cent of world foreign reserve holdings (compared to under 3 per cent for RMB), and about half of all world trade and cross-border loans are denominated in dollars.[59] Nonetheless, what is most salient here is not so much the absolute levels of RMB traded oil but the possible directions of travel. As we have seen throughout this book, the emergence of American power across the twentieth century has been closely bound up with both the nature of oil pricing and the place of oil in the making of the post-war international financial order. Oil is not simply a physical commodity, and any breakdown in the geopolitical dominance of the US will undoubtedly *also* involve a challenge to the American currency's privileged connection to oil.

Oil Resurgent

The COVID-19 pandemic that began to spread so rapidly across the world in early 2020 delivered a profound shock to oil markets and the broader fossil fuel industry. With demand for energy in freefall during the initial months of the pandemic, world oil markets were simultaneously hit by a March 2020 'oil price war' between Russia and Saudi Arabia, which promised to increase global supplies significantly.[60] Global oil prices fell to multi-decade lows, and producers rushed to find storage space on land and sea for their oil rather than sell it at a loss. In mid-April 2020, the price of WTI oil turned negative as traders holding contracts for physical delivery were forced to pay others to take oil off their hands due to lack of storage space. At that moment, some

58 Abeer Abu Omar and Manus Cranny, 'Saudi Arabia Open to Settling Trade in Other Currencies', bloomberg.com, 17 January 2023.

59 Bafundi Maronoti, 'Revisiting the International Role of the US Dollar', *BIS Quarterly Review*, 5 December 2022, bis.org.

60 For a discussion of this price war and the broader impact of the COVID-19 pandemic, see Adam Hanieh, 'COVID-19 and Global Oil Markets', *Canadian Journal of Development Studies/Revue canadienne d'études du développement* 42, nos 1–2, 2021: 101–8.

commentators speculated that this might be a bit of good news in the context of the COVID-19 calamity: the pandemic could 'kill the oil industry and help save the climate', as an April 2020 headline in the UK's *Guardian* newspaper exclaimed, with the demise of many smaller oil producers and the weakening of oil majors bringing the world one step closer to a transition away from fossil fuel use.

Such hopes quickly unravelled. During the first year of the pandemic, low oil prices and high debt levels led to a wave of consolidation in the US shale industry, with the largest US oil firms (and other financial investors) buying up assets on the cheap. Simultaneously, the Trump administration loosened environmental regulations and provided up to $15.2 billion in direct economic support to the fossil fuel industry.[61] These corporate subsidies were not limited to the US – the EU and individual European governments also provided billions of euros in direct support to major oil and gas companies through the worst months of the pandemic. As demand for oil resumed with the relaxing of pandemic restrictions, the price of oil increased sharply, reaching a five-year peak in October 2021. The Russian invasion of Ukraine in late February 2022 further helped push oil prices to over $100 per barrel by May 2022, and also shifted the prevailing political discourse away from a *faux* concern with climate change towards a prioritisation of energy security and the ramping up of oil and gas production. By the end of 2022, global demand for oil had surpassed pre-pandemic years, reaching the highest levels ever recorded.[62] In short, rather than 'the purported death knell of oil and gas', we have seen 'the greatest commodities boom since the 2008 financial crisis and the highest daily price rallies since the 1970s'.[63]

Amid this fossil fuel resurgence, the supermajor/NOC division remains a key part of the deep tensions in play across the world market today. On one side, the large Western oil firms that have been the focus of so much of this book continue to lead in North American and European markets, with their upstream production centred on unconventional, shale, and deep-water offshore extraction. The upstream

61 Bailout Watch, *Bailed Out and Propped Up*, Bailout Watch, Public Citizen, Friends of the Earth, 2020, report.bailoutwatch.org.

62 Organization of the Petroleum Exporting Countries, *OPEC Monthly Oil Market Report – December 2022*, 26.

63 Gabe Eckhouse and Anna Zalik, 'Introduction', *Environment and Planning A* 54, no. 8, 2022: 1642.

production of these firms feeds their downstream refining and petrochemical activities, which are also predominantly located in North America or Europe. The resultant fuels are mostly consumed in Western markets or exported to South and Central America and Africa (see Table 12.2). The spike in oil prices that followed the relaxation of pandemic restrictions and the beginning of the Ukraine war has earned these firms their largest profits in history. And, as we shall see in the following chapter, oil remains the unquestionable heart of their business activities, regardless of any rhetorical commitment to green energy and a supposed net zero future.

On the other side, the trajectories of China and East Asia depend fundamentally on the steady and ever-increasing flow of oil and oil products derived from the Middle East, and it is these East–East regional networks that have helped constitute the growing power of NOCs. In this sense, the rise of Middle East and Asian NOCs can be viewed as one expression of the profound eastward shift that has taken place in the world market over the past two decades. With Gulf NOCs and other firms increasingly located *inside* Asian production networks – and not simply as suppliers of crude – we need to rethink how we approach the geographies of the global fossil fuels industry. It is not enough to focus solely on reducing the direct consumption of fossil fuels or carbon emissions in traditional Western centres. Global commodity production – including much of what actually ends up being consumed in North America and Western Europe – is grounded in an axis of fossil capitalism running between the oil fields, refineries, and factories of the Middle East and Asia. The deep connections established across this axis are a significant component of capital accumulation in both regions and help support the power of state and private business elites. From an ecological perspective, these East–East interdependencies have re-embedded fossil fuels at the centre of global production chains. They constitute a major barrier to breaking with an oil-centred world.

13

Confronting the Climate Emergency

> Every molecule of hydrocarbon will come out.
>
> Saudi oil minister, Prince Abdulaziz bin Salman, 2021[1]

> An oil company is in the business of producing profit, not oil.
>
> Barry Commoner, 1976[2]

A few weeks into 2023, the world's largest oil and gas firms began to announce their end-of-year results. ExxonMobil led the way, recording a $55.7 billion profit for 2022 – the biggest in the company's history. Shell followed, also marking a historic milestone in its 115-year existence, with profits of nearly $44 billion, over twice the amount earned in 2021. All told, the five leading Western supermajors – ExxonMobil, Shell, Chevron, BP, and TotalEnergies – reported a total of $200 billion in profits, an eyewatering $23 million for every hour of 2022. Yet even these record-breaking revenues would soon be overshadowed by Saudi Aramco. Coming in at just over $161 billion, Aramco's 2022 financial results not only exceeded the combined announcements of Shell, BP, ExxonMobil, and Chevron, they became the largest corporate profit recorded in history.

1 Javier Blas, 'The Saudi Prince of Oil Prices Vows to Drill "Every Last Molecule" ', *Bloomberg*, 22 July 2021, bloomberg.com.

2 'Oil, Energy and Capitalism: An Unpublished Talk by Barry Commoner', *Climate and Capitalism*, 30 July 2013, climateandcapitalism.com.

Such results justifiably attracted the ire of many environmental campaigners, who rightly protested unprecedented fossil fuel profits while much of the world was facing the real costs of climate change. Indeed, according to the British charity Christian Aid, the total cost of the ten largest climate-related weather events through 2022 – floods, cyclones, and droughts – was around $170 billion, much less than the collective profits earned by the five largest supermajors and just a little bit over Aramco's bumper results.[3] In human terms, the worst of these disasters were the devastating floods that occurred across Pakistan between June and October 2022, killing over 1,700 people and displacing more than 7 million. The total costs of these floods in Pakistan – caused by heavier than usual monsoon rains and melting glaciers linked to climate change – were estimated by the World Bank at over $30 billion in flood damages and related economic losses.[4] Around half of ExxonMobil's 2022 profits could have footed the bill.

Nero was (falsely) accused of having fiddled while Rome was in flames. In today's world, we face the spectacle of a handful of large oil firms that are not only standing by as the planet burns but are being handsomely rewarded for their role in the arson. This reality highlights a crucial truth of the climate emergency: left to their own devices, there is no chance that the world's largest energy firms (including those NOCs beyond Western markets) will willingly walk away from the enormous wealth to be made from continued oil and gas production. Despite talk of 'low-carbon solutions' they have no intention of ending their core focus on fossil fuels. While scientific consensus now states unambiguously that no new oil and gas projects can be brought online, and that carbon emissions must be halved by the end of the decade, the major oil companies are embarking on precisely the opposite course of action. A 2022 investigation found that the twelve largest global oil firms, led by Saudi Aramco, were planning to spend $103 million *each day* for the rest of the decade on *new* oil and gas projects.[5] The leading firms have also made final

3 Christian Aid, *Counting the Cost 2022: A Year of Climate Breakdown*, 16 December 2022, christianaid.org.uk, 5.

4 World Bank, 'Pakistan Flood Damages and Economic Losses over $30 Billion and Reconstruction Needs over $16 Billion', press release, 28 October 2022, worldbank.org.

5 Damian Carrington and Matthew Taylor, 'Revealed: The "Carbon Bombs" Set to Trigger Catastrophic Climate Breakdown', *Guardian*, 11 May 2022.

financial commitments for new projects that will produce 116 billion barrels of oil over the next seven years – equivalent to about two decades of US oil production at 2020 levels.[6] As Chevron's CEO Mike Wirth put it in early 2023: 'The reality is, [fossil fuel] is what runs the world today . . . it's going to run the world tomorrow and five years from now, 10 years from now, 20 years from now.'[7]

With such investments and new production in the pipeline, we face an unmitigated disaster. As of early 2023, the world's largest oil companies – including the NOCs – held oil, gas, and coal reserves that will release around 3,600 gigatons of CO_2 into the atmosphere if burnt.[8] This figure is more than *fourteen times* the world's remaining 'carbon budget' of 250 gigatons – the amount of carbon that can be emitted before global temperatures are likely to rise 1.5 degrees above pre-industrial levels.[9] Two decades ago, a popular theory held that the world was fast approaching *peak oil* – the idea that global production would decline as it became harder to extract oil from older fields and replacement fields became more difficult to find. The shale boom showed that this geological determinism was wrong, its proponents ignoring the economic incentives that shape production levels.[10] There is no imminent physical limit to oil supplies. But today we undoubtedly face the spectre of *peak carbon*: the world's plentiful supplies of oil and other fossil fuels *must* stay in the ground if we are to hold any chance of averting the dystopic future forewarned in the extreme weather events of recent years.

6 Ibid.

7 'What Big Oil's Bumper Profits Mean for the Energy Transition', *Financial Times*, ft.com.

8 Mark Campanale, '$1 Trillion of Oil and Gas Assets Risk Being Stranded by Climate Change', interview, 22 January 2023, brinknews.com.

9 The figure of 250 gigatons is estimated as of January 2023. R.Lamboll et al., 'Assessing the Size and Uncertainty of Remaining Carbon Budgets', *Nature Climate Change* 13, 2023: 1360–7.

10 Labban, 'Oil in Parallax', presents an excellent critique of the peak oil theory, focusing on the relation between production, investment, and financial markets.

The Myths of Net Zero and Carbon Removal

The analogy is frequently drawn between fossil fuel companies and tobacco firms. Just as the latter knew about and hid the dangers of smoking, oil companies have been fully aware of the science of climate change for at least fifty years. As far back as 1977, a senior scientist at Exxon warned the company's management committee that warming temperatures due to fossil fuel consumption meant that 'man has a time window of five to 10 years before the need for hard decisions regarding changes in energy strategies might become critical'.[11] The research and statistical models developed by oil companies in the 1960s and 1970s predicted the effects of carbon emissions on global temperatures with uncanny accuracy. In the face of this knowledge, the oil supermajors took the path trailblazed by Big Smoke – attempting to muddy the water with the idea that the science of climate change was uncertain, a matter that reasonable people could disagree on. Exxon alone would spend more than $30 million on climate change denial thinktanks between 1998 and 2014, with the simple aim of creating confusion and sowing doubt regarding a scientific consensus that the company's own research affirmed.[12] In 1998, an internal memo of the American Petroleum Institute fully acknowledged this campaign of disinformation, noting that oil companies would achieve 'victory' when 'average citizens understand (recognize) uncertainties in climate science . . . [and] recognition of uncertainties becomes part of the conventional wisdom'. These words were written just a year after adoption of the Kyoto Protocol, the first international climate treaty in history. And in this context, according to the API, the oil industry needed to make 'those promoting the Kyoto treaty on the basis of the extant science appear to be out of touch with reality'.[13]

11 Shannon Hall, 'Exxon Knew about Climate Change Almost 40 Years Ago', *Scientific American*, 26 October 2015, scientificamerican.com.

12 Greenpeace USA, 'Exxon's Climate Denial History: A Timeline', greenpeace.org.

13 Kathy Mulvey and Seth Shulman, *The Climate Deception Dossiers: Internal Fossil Fuel Industry Memos Reveal Decades of Corporate Disinformation*, Union of Concerned Scientists, July 2015, 10. The Kyoto Protocol was an international treaty adopted in 1997 that committed industrialised countries to reduce their greenhouse gas emissions to below 1990 levels. It was the first major international effort to tackle global climate change, later superseded by the 2015 Paris Agreement. Although 191 countries have backed the Kyoto Protocol since 1997, the US senate refused to ratify it, citing potential damage to the US economy.

Nonetheless, over the past decade – and after many years and millions of dollars spent on obfuscation and denial – the world's leading oil firms have reversed their public attitude towards the science of climate change. All now fully endorse the scientific consensus around global warming and have explicitly affirmed their support of the Paris Agreement goal to keep temperature rises below 1.5 degrees.[14] All have moved into a range of alternative energy technologies, and visibly brandish their low-carbon strategies in annual reports and shareholder meetings. This shift is not merely rhetorical – and here the accusations of greenwashing, while accurate in some respects, can miss the important transformations taking place in global energy today. Oil companies *are* changing. But as we have seen throughout this book, oil companies have always been dynamic, malleable institutions. In the contemporary moment, they are absorbing and adapting to the language of climate change in significant ways – and in doing so, altering the ways in which the problem of climate change itself is defined and delimited. By appearing to transform themselves into part of the solution, they not only hide their ongoing centrality to the fossil economy, but aim to frame and determine the societal *response* to climate change.

A clear illustration of these patterns is the dubious and dangerous use of the 'net zero emissions' (NZE) slogan. The term gained widespread usage in the climate lexicon following its inclusion in the Paris Agreement adopted at the UN Climate Change Conference (COP21) held in Paris, France, on 12 December 2015.[15] Essentially, NZE refers to the objective of counterbalancing emissions resulting from burning fossil fuels by removing an equivalent amount of carbon, using techniques such as planting carbon sinks in the form of forests or cropland, developing carbon capture technologies, or directly extracting carbon from the atmosphere. With the right combination of policies and technologies, the theory goes, it should be possible to offset the amount of carbon generated, thereby achieving a state of NZE. Today, NZE is the dominant concept driving global climate policy, with the Intergovernmental

14 Public endorsement of the Paris Agreement includes Shell, BP, ExxonMobil, TotalEnergies, Chevron, Occidental, Aramco, and Equinor.

15 The Paris Agreement aims to hold the increase in global average temperature to well below 2 degrees Celsius above pre-industrial levels and to pursue efforts to limit the temperature increase to 1.5 degrees Celsius. As of early 2024, 194 countries and the EU were parties to the agreement.

Panel on Climate Change (IPCC) asserting that net zero must be achieved globally by 2050 to avert the dire consequences of exceeding the 1.5 degree Celsius warming threshold. Over 140 countries, as well as numerous cities and regions globally, have committed to NZE targets as of mid-2024.[16]

Oil companies have become enthusiastic converts to the idea of NZE. One of the foremost reasons for this is their leading role in carbon capture and storage (CCS) technologies. CCS refers to various techniques that can remove CO_2 emitted in manufacturing or other industrial processes, which can then be stored underground or used in other sectors.[17] Today, CCS is largely an untested technology that fails to capture a significant proportion of the carbon it is supposed to remove. Indeed, as of 2023, there were only forty-one operational CCS plants worldwide, capturing just 49 million tonnes of carbon annually.[18] Even more important than the limited scale of CCS, however, is a critical point in the fine print regarding this technology: for twenty-nine out of the forty-one existing CCS plants, the captured carbon is used in a process known as enhanced oil recovery (EOR), a technique developed by the oil industry in the 1970s that uses pressurised CO_2 injected into oil and gas reservoirs to increase the quantity of hydrocarbons that can be extracted. More than 80 per cent of all CO_2 captured in operational CCS projects is earmarked for EOR, and for this reason oil companies dominate the nascent carbon capture industry.[19] ExxonMobil alone claims control of more than 10 per cent of global carbon capture capacity, including ownership of the largest CCS facility in the US at Shute Creek in Wyoming.[20]

---

16 For a detailed analysis of the global endorsement of the net zero target, see zerotracker.net.

17 According to IEA projections for a NZE scenario, industry will account for 40 per cent of CO_2 captured by 2050, electricity for 20 per cent, and 30 per cent for fuels (including hydrogen and biofuels, discussed below). The remaining 10 per cent is captured through direct air capture, a speculative technology that does not yet exist at scale.

18 Calculated by author; see Global CSS Institute, *Global Status of CCS, 2023*, 11, 77–8, status23.globalccsinstitute.com. In 2023, global CO_2 emissions from burning fossil fuels totalled over 37 billion tonnes.

19 Ibid.

20 ExxonMobil, *Advancing Climate Solutions, Progress Report*, 2023, 61. ExxonMobil captures around 7 million tonnes of CO_2 per year from a gas-processing plant that it owns at the site. In addition to its use in EOR, around half of the CO_2 that

This link between CCS and EOR raises the distinct possibility that the push to net zero might actually lead to an *increase* in overall levels of oil production. The oil industry denies this, even going so far as to claim that the oil produced through EOR is lower carbon, because the carbon injected into oil wells is now trapped underground rather than being released into the atmosphere, and thus needs to be subtracted from the overall carbon footprint of the oil barrel that is produced.[21] But this faulty logic rests on the assumption that EOR oil will substantially displace conventional oil production. Much more likely – indeed this is why oil companies developed EOR in the first place – is that CCS technology will enable oil to be extracted from declining fields and unconventional shale oil and gas reservoirs that would have otherwise been unrecoverable. Industry experts are quite explicit about this likelihood, with some studies identifying over 280 billion barrels of *additional* oil that could be extracted in the US alone using CO_2-EOR – about sixty-five years' worth of US crude oil production at 2022 levels.[22]

The use of CCS today remains mostly limited to the oil industry, and there are currently no large-scale plants that capture carbon from industry for underground storage.[23] Nonetheless, the rapid roll-out of CCS is essential to meeting the targets established in various NZE models. According to the NZE scenario of the International Energy Agency (IEA), the total amount of captured CO_2 must reach 7,600 million tonnes by 2050 – more than 150 times today's figure. Without this expansion, it will be impossible to achieve NZE by the deadline. To this end, many countries are offering significant state subsidies and tax

---

ExxonMobil has extracted from the gas has simply been vented into the atmosphere. 'Shute Creek – World's Largest Carbon Capture Facility Sells CO_2 for Oil Production, but Vents Unsold', Institute for Energy Economics and Financial Analysis, 1 March 2022, ieefa.org.

21 One study claims that an EOR-produced barrel reduces carbon emissions by 37 per cent compared to conventional oil. Deepika Nagabhushan and John Thompson, 'Carbon Capture and Storage in the United States Power Sector', Clean Air Task Force, February 2019, 8.

22 V. Kuuskraaa, R. Petrusaka, and M. Wallace, 'Residual Oil Zone "Fairways" and Discovered Oil Resources: Expanding the Options for Carbon Negative Storage of CO_2', *Energy Procedia* 114, 2017: 5438–50.

23 There is also a real danger of CO_2 leakage from underground storage, as one study of two storage sites in Norway has recently shown. See Grant Hauber, 'Norway's Sleipner and Snohvit CCS: Industry Models or Cautionary Tales?', Institute for Energy Economics and Financial Analysis, 14 June 2023, ieefa.org.

benefits in support of carbon capture. Unsurprisingly given their existing connection to CCS, most of this support is flowing to oil companies. In the US, for example, the oil industry has lobbied heavily for an increase to tax credits for carbon removal. Their efforts met with success in 2022, when the Biden administration amended Section 45Q of the tax code, increasing tax credits from $50 to as much as $180 for each tonne of captured carbon. More than $1 billion in tax credits were awarded under 45Q between 2010 and 2019, almost all of which (99.86 per cent) went to just ten companies.[24] In short, the development of carbon capture appears to be replicating the patterns we have seen throughout the history of the oil industry: billion-dollar subsidies directed from the state to oil companies, albeit this time in the name of a green transition.[25] Such subsidies for captured carbon will be instrumental in its further commodification, turning an industrial waste product (CO_2) into a profitable good that oil companies can either use in their own EOR activities, sell to other oil producers or industrial sectors, or bank as tax credits.

But beyond these monetary considerations, CCS also plays an important role in the oil companies' own NZE aspirations. At first glance, claims of a net zero oil company may appear paradoxical – after all, how could a barrel of oil not produce any emissions? But the key to deciphering this contradiction lies in the sleight of hand that oil companies use in their own carbon accounting. When oil companies report their carbon emissions, they refer only to the carbon involved in the actual *production* of a barrel of oil – not the carbon released when that oil is consumed.[26] In reality, however, at least 85 per cent of the carbon

24 'Menendez Releases Inspector General Investigation Finding Fossil Fuel Companies Improperly Claimed Nearly $1B in Clean Air Tax Credits', 30 April 2020, available at menendez.senate.gov.

25 Tax subsidies for carbon capture is one reason why American oil companies continue to pay among the lowest taxes of any business sector despite their record-making profits: in 2021, ExxonMobil had an effective tax rate of just 2.8 per cent, and Chevron of only 1.8 per cent. Ryan Koronowski, Jessica Vela, and Zahir Rasheed, 'These 19 Fortune 100 Companies Paid Next to Nothing – or Nothing at All – in Taxes in 2021', *American Progress*, 26 April 2022, americanprogress.org.

26 The 1998 Greenhouse Gas Protocol (GGP) grouped emissions into three 'scopes' for carbon accounting purposes: scope 1 emissions are those that come from the direct activities of the company; scope 2 from purchased or acquired energy; and scope 3 from the product itself. The world's largest oil companies do not set scope 3 targets. Some companies (including BP, Shell, and TotalEnergies) mention scope 3 'ambitions',

emissions associated with the industry come from oil's final consumption – not its drilling, extraction, and refining. As such, oil companies can bank CCS against the emissions associated with their operations, claiming they are supporting the transition to net zero (and earning large tax benefits to boot), all the while ignoring the fact their product is the main driver of global warming. To return to the tobacco analogy, this is a bit like Philip Morris disavowing responsibility for cigarette deaths because lung cancer rates were very low among workers on the company's assembly line.[27]

All of this highlights the basic problem with the NZE framework: by claiming that the use of some (as yet mostly speculative) technologies will eventually cancel out future carbon emissions, the oil industry is able to expand production in the here and now. As with the most effective kinds of advertising, NZE works by appearing as something it is not: net zero is *not zero carbon*, and the focus on *net* emissions deflects attention away from the oil companies' *absolute* levels of hydrocarbon production. The perverse incentives that animate the calculus of carbon accounting are driving us towards even greater levels of oil production, led by newly greened oil companies. It is a dangerous wager, ultimately premised on a future technological fix, which serves to legitimise ongoing fossil fuel production and consumption. Or, as three scientists who once embraced the NZE concept now put it: 'In practice it helps

yet these are framed in terms of 'carbon intensity' (the amount of carbon emitted per unit of energy produced). This means that as long as they increase the proportion of 'cleaner' fuels in their energy products, they can claim to be reducing 'carbon intensity' – even though the absolute volume of their fossil fuel emissions continues to climb. This is not merely hypothetical. As the climate NGO Earthworks notes: 'In 2020 Chevron celebrated meeting all of their intensity-based metrics set in 2016. While meeting these goals they also increased their emissions from 607 million metric tons (Mmt) CO_2e in 2016 to 645 Mmt CO_2e by the end of 2020.' Earthworks, *Tricks of the Trade: Deceptive Practices, Climate Delay and Greenwashing in the Oil and Gas Industry*, Washington, DC: Earthworks, 2022, 8, earthworks.org.

27 Additional accounting tricks are also used by oil companies to emulate progress towards NZE, while actually doing the opposite. These include undercounting or underreporting the emissions from individual oil wells, counting divestment of assets as cuts in emissions even when these have just been transferred, excluding emissions produced by part-owned companies, providing information on emission intensity rather than total emissions, and adding caveats to emission goals with nebulous statements, such as 'in step with society'. For a detailed discussion, see Earthworks, *Tricks of the Trade*.

perpetuate a belief in technological salvation and diminishes the sense of urgency surrounding the need to curb emissions now. We have arrived at the painful realisation that the idea of net zero has licensed a recklessly cavalier "burn now, pay later" approach which has seen carbon emissions continue to soar.'[28]

Low Carbon Solutions in a Burning World

While the chimerical promise of net zero might disguise the continued expansion of fossil fuel production, this does not mean that the major oil companies stand apart from the growing markets for renewables and alternative forms of energy production. Indeed, precisely the opposite is the case: the oil industry clearly recognises that global strategies to address climate change have significant potential to open up new and profitable market opportunities. This is a continuation of the transformation that most oil companies embarked on in the 1990s – a shift towards becoming *energy* firms: grounded in oil, but with a mix of different energy portfolios and downstream activities. The popular image of Big Oil as a dinosaur being dragged reluctantly towards the inevitable end of the fossil era is false; these companies are taking a leading role in determining future energy choices. There is no silver lining – the trajectories established by the oil industry serve to prioritise dubious technologies and policies, create false narratives, and foreclose the necessary alternatives that are now urgently demanded. Rather than being antithetical to their interests, these pathways further entrench the position of Big Oil at the heart of our energy system.

These realities are illustrated through a closer examination of three key technologies: bioenergy, electric vehicles (EV), and hydrogen. Each of these technologies has been identified by the IEA and other international organisations as essential to the energy transition. In fact, models such as the IEA's NZE scenario assume their widespread adoption onto the positive side of the net zero balance sheet – a means of directly displacing fossil fuel use, and thus reducing emissions. Major oil firms are also championing these technologies as the centrepiece of their new

28 James Dyke, Robert Watson, and Wolfgang Knorr, 'Climate Scientists: Concept of Net Zero Is a Dangerous Trap', theconversation.com, 22 April 2021.

low-carbon strategies. While oil company spending on conventional fossil fuels remains many orders of magnitude higher – and is projected to do so for the coming decades – these technologies have become increasingly integral to how the oil industry projects itself within the discourse of the climate emergency. As the adoption of these technologies deepens, they are providing new supplementary sources of revenue that further bolster the social power of oil. They are also driving significant changes to how oil firms are positioned in relation to other business sectors and the emerging infrastructures of the so-called green transition.

Bioenergy

Bioenergy is energy derived from recently living organic material known as biomass. Biomass can include wood or wood waste from forests, as well as food crops like sugar cane, corn, and soybeans. These forms of biomass can be burnt to produce heat or electricity (as with wood), or converted into a liquid or gaseous fuel known as biofuel. They are classified as renewable because they can be produced from organic waste or from crops that can be regrown. In all major climate models, biomass and biofuels figure prominently as a replacement for fossil fuels. They are seen as particularly important to decarbonising the transport sector – especially heavy-duty trucks, ships, and planes – where electric battery technology is not currently feasible. Today, bioenergy is the largest source of renewable energy, making up around 6 per cent of the global energy supply. Its supply is projected to increase 10 per cent per year between 2021 and 2030 in the IEA's NZE scenario, eventually reaching 13 per cent of total global energy supply by the end of the decade.[29] Globally, the expansion of bioenergy is heavily supported by governments through policies such as fuel emission standards, and requirements in some countries for refiners to blend a certain proportion of biofuels with the production of gasoline.[30] It is often linked with carbon

29 IEA, *Net Zero by 2050, A RoadMap for the Global Energy Sector*, 2022, 195.

30 Biden's 2022 Inflation Reduction Act, which provides tax credits for biofuel producers. In the US, refiners are mandated to blend biofuels in their production of gasoline (typically ethanol produced from corn). Likewise, in Brazil, gasoline must contain a minimum 20 per cent share of ethanol, usually made from sugar cane.

capture in a hybrid approach called BECCS (bioenergy with carbon capture and storage).

Bioenergy may have potential to reduce overall carbon emissions, but current methods of production are seriously flawed. One problem is that growing crops for fuel sets up competition with other kinds of land use, such as food production. In the US, for instance, more than a third of the country's corn production and 40 per cent of soybean oil were allocated to biofuels in 2022.[31] Food prices can potentially be impacted by this increased demand for certain crops, as during 2006–08, when biofuels were widely attributed as an important factor in a global food price spike.[32] While the IEA's NZE scenario is careful to emphasise that biofuel production should be based on 'wastes, residues and dedicated crops that do not compete with food' this kind of sustainable production only made up 8 per cent of biofuel consumption in 2021.[33] More broadly, producing enough biofuels to substantially displace fossil fuels would place an enormous strain on existing land and water use. One projection suggests that if biofuels were to satisfy just one-fifth of the world's energy needs by 2050, it would require a biomass equivalent to all plants currently harvested worldwide, including the entirety of crops, crop residues, wood, and grasses consumed by livestock.[34] Even when combined with carbon capture in a BECCS scheme, the crop area required to keep global warming under 2 degrees Celsius would take up virtually all of the current cropland

31 Emiko Terazono and Camilla Hodgson, 'Food vs. Fuel: Ukraine War Sharpens Debate on Use of Crops for Energy', *Financial Times*, 12 June 2022. Similarly, the EU's 'Fit for 55 Initiative', which aims to bring EU legislation in line to reduce net greenhouse gas emissions by 55 per cent by 2030, would turn over about a fifth of Europe's cropland to the production of biofuels. Craig Hanson et al., 'The Ukraine Crisis Threatens a Sustainable Food Future', World Resources Institute, 1 April 2022, wri.org.

32 One World Bank report at the time estimated that biofuels were responsible for 70–75 per cent of the price increase. Donald Mitchell, 'A Note on Rising Food Prices', World Bank Development Prospects Group, July 2008, 17.

33 IEA, 'Biofuels', 2023, iea.org/reports/biofuels.

34 Tim Searchinger, 'Why Dedicating Land to Bioenergy Won't Curb Climate Change', World Resources Institute, 28 January 2015, wri.org. With the war in Ukraine in 2022, and fears of global food shortages due to the interruption of crop supplies from Ukraine and Russia, one research institute noted that all the lost exports of Ukrainian wheat, corn, barley, and rye could be compensated for by halving the grain used in biofuels destined for Europe and the US. Hanson et al., 'Ukraine Crisis Threatens'.

available on the planet (and about twice the amount of water currently used in agriculture).[35]

Bioenergy in the form of wood biomass can also have a severe impact on natural ecosystems. Although wood burning has traditionally been used for cooking and warmth, the projections modelled in various climate scenarios refer instead to 'modern biomass' – wood and wood waste that is industrially harvested and burnt to produce electricity or heat.[36] It is not widely recognised that wood biomass is the largest component of renewable energy supplies today: as of 2022, it accounted for an average of 40 per cent of EU member states' renewable energy, surpassing solar or wind power.[37] One of the consequences of this reliance on wood is that it incentivises deforestation, destroying natural carbon sinks and wildlife habitats. Wood also releases enormous quantities of carbon into the air when it is burnt – more so, in fact, than coal, per unit of energy that is generated.[38] Regrowing forests takes a long time, so the carbon released from burning wood will continue to raise global temperatures for decades – from 44 to 104 years after harvesting, according to one estimate, depending on the type of forest.[39] For all these reasons, reliance on woody biomass can have the pernicious outcome of *increasing* carbon emissions – especially if it is promoted at the expense of solar and wind.[40]

The global expansion of the bioenergy market is primarily being driven by Western oil firms, which are now displacing the first

35 Andreas Malm and Wim Carton, 'Seize the Means of Carbon Removal: The Political Economy of Direct Air Capture', *Historical Materialism* 29, no. 1, 2021: 3–48, 6.

36 Traditional use of biomass (such as in cooking) is still widespread, representing around 4 per cent of global energy supply in 2020. It is, however, inefficient and polluting, linked to 2.5 million premature deaths in 2020 according to the IEA. The IEA's NZE scenario sees this phased out by 2030.

37 Fern, RED Revision, 'Will EU Countries Stop Paying Energy Companies to Burn Forests?', 21 October 2022, fern.org.

38 John D. Sterman, Lori Siegel, and Juliette N. Rooney-Varga, 'Does Replacing Coal with Wood Lower CO_2 Emissions? Dynamic Lifecycle Analysis of Wood Bioenergy', *Environmental Research Letters* 13, no. 1, January 2018.

39 Ibid.

40 As more than 700 prominent scientists put it in a letter protesting the EU's decision to designate wood obtained from logging forests as a renewable energy source: 'Overall, allowing the harvest and burning of wood . . . will transform large reductions otherwise achieved through solar and wind into large increases in carbon in the atmosphere by 2050.' 'Letter from Scientists to the EU Parliament Regarding Forest Biomass', 11 January 2018, available at euractiv.com.

generation of smaller independent bioenergy producers. In the US, for example, which is the largest producer of biofuels in the world, more than half the capacity of renewable diesel and other biofuels plants is directly controlled by petroleum companies, with firms such as Chevron, ExxonMobil, Valero, and Marathon playing a dominant role in bioenergy production.[41] The largest US biodiesel producer, the Renewable Energy Group, was recently acquired by Chevron for more than $3 billion. Similarly in Brazil, the world's second biggest producer of biofuels, the two largest biofuel companies in the country are joint ventures (JVs) involving BP and Shell respectively.[42] In Canada, the ExxonMobil-controlled Imperial Oil is currently building the country's biggest renewable diesel facility. In Europe, oil companies such as BP, Shell, Neste, ENI, and TotalEnergies dominate the refining and marketing of biofuels, including the distribution infrastructure that is located throughout their service station networks.[43]

This recent and rapidly growing entry of Big Oil into bioenergy is reconfiguring the traditional scope of the petroleum industry and generating new interdependencies between oil firms and other sectors. An essential element to this is the supply of crop feedstock for bioenergy production. Much like the patterns of vertical integration that marked the past century of world oil, many of the leading oil firms are expanding into the actual production and management of biomass feedstocks through JVs and acquisitions that involve agribusiness firms. Shell, BP, Marathon, Chevron, and ExxonMobil are now all directly involved in companies that supply agricultural crops or forestry products.[44] This marks a new stage in the long-standing relationship between fossil fuels

41 'U.S. Renewable Diesel Fuel and Other Biofuels Plant Production Capacity', US Energy Information Administration, 7 August 2023, eia.gov.

42 On the Brazilian biofuel industry and its close connections to the state and wealthy landowners, see Leandro Vergara-Camus, 'Sugarcane Ethanol: The Hen of the Golden Eggs? Agribusiness and the State in Lula's Brazil,' in Jeffrey R. Webber and Susan Spronk (eds), *Crisis and Contradiction*, Leiden: Brill, 2014, 211–35.

43 The other major global market for biofuel production is Indonesia, which uses palm oil as a feedstock unlike the US (corn) and Brazil (sugar). Indonesian palm oil production is dominated by the Singapore-based agribusiness firm Wilmar International.

44 Shell is collaborating with Norway's second largest sawmill company, Bergene Holm, to produce fuels from woody biomass. In 2022, ExxonMobil bought a 49.9 per cent stake in Norway's Biojet, which aims to convert forestry and wood waste into biofuels.

and modern agriculture. Alongside oil's role as a crucial input into the production of food and other agricultural commodities, the control of agribusiness itself is converging with control of the energy circuit. This will undoubtedly have far-reaching implications for the global supply of food and the management of cropland and forests.

Electric Vehicles (EV)

The second major element of the oil industry's pivot to low carbon energy is its involvement in the burgeoning EV market. The roll-out of EVs is accelerating across many parts of the world, with global EV sales growing fivefold between 2019 and 2022. Europe has the highest rate of electric cars sold as a share of new automobile sales, somewhat ironically led by Europe's largest oil producer, Norway, where EV made up 88 per cent of new car sales in 2022. The uptake of EV is also significant in Iceland (70 per cent of new car sales), Sweden (54 per cent) and the Netherlands (35 per cent).[45] But expressed in absolute terms, China dominates the global EV market, with more EVs sold in the country in 2021 than across the entire world in 2020.[46] The US ranks as the third largest market in the world, with about 8 per cent of new car sales made up of electric vehicles in 2022. China, the EU, and the US have all offered subsidies and incentives to encourage EV use, seeing the growth in EV as central to reducing carbon emissions.[47] The pace of growth is much slower elsewhere in the world, with EV making up only 4 per cent of car sales outside these three key markets.[48]

There are significant problems with this focus on EV as a means of reducing climate emissions. For one, the current expansion of the EV market, while substantial, lags far behind the rate needed to make marked reductions in carbon emissions from vehicle transport. The IEA

45 'Global EV Data Explorer 2023', IEA, iea.org.

46 IEA, *Net Zero by 2050*, 16.

47 China introduced subsidies as early as 2009 and, until 2021, were offering consumers the RMB equivalent of more than $1,500 for a new EV purchase. In Europe, regulations are looking to phase out the sale of internal combustion engine (ICE) automobiles by 2035, and in the US, President Biden's Inflation Reduction Act aims to boost EV sales with a significant tax credit.

48 IEA, *Net Zero by 2050*, 15.

assumes that EV will need to make up 60 per cent of new car sales by 2030 in order to reach its zero emissions scenario by 2050. Today, the global EV rate of new car sales sits at around 14 per cent, and accounting for the existing and planned policies of governments around the world, is on track to reach only 20 per cent of total automobile sales by 2030.[49] Without a radical global shift in policy, it appears extremely unlikely that EV will reach a majority of new car sales any time over the coming two decades. These figures, moreover, focus on *new* car sales, and thus provide a misleading image of EV's capacity to reduce vehicle emissions. If absolute numbers of traditional internal combustion engine (ICE) vehicles continue to grow, for instance, even at a slower rate to EV, then there will be no reduction in overall emissions (in fact, these will likely increase).[50]

Another misconception associated with much of the discussion around EV is the widely held belief that they are emissions-free. EV are manufactured in complex cross-border production chains involving mining, processing, and assembly, requiring the transport of various materials over long distances. All of this activity releases considerable amounts of carbon, and it takes several years of on-road use before this carbon debt of an EV is 'repaid'.[51] The batteries that EVs run on must also be charged, and if the extra demand for electricity is generated by fossil fuels (including natural gas), then any widespread roll-out of EVs will potentially increase emissions from power generation.[52] As a result of these embodied emissions, the carbon accounting of an EV depends

49 Even accounting for the announced targets and stated ambitions of governments – regardless of whether these have been legislated for or not – the figure rises to only 33 per cent.

50 In the EU, EV as a proportion of new car sales increased from 0.5 per cent to 18 per cent between 2013 and 2021 (IEA). Over the same time period, the number of ICE vehicles increased 13 per cent. Without information about trends in the types of vehicles used (SUV vs light passenger), the scrap rate of older vehicles, and overall vehicle numbers, EV penetration rates do not tell us anything about emissions. 'Electric Vehicles', iea.org; and 'Passenger Cars, by Type of Motor Energy and Size of Engine', Eurostat, ec.europa.eu/Eurostat/en.

51 For a clear discussion of this point and several other methodological fallacies associated with climate claims around EV, see Jamie Morgan, 'Electric Vehicles: The Future We Made and the Problem of Unmaking It', *Cambridge Journal of Economics* 44, 2020: 953–77.

52 In China, for instance, where most of the world's EVs are produced and sold, coal and other fossil fuels make up more than 70 per cent of power generation.

heavily on the trajectory of absolute growth in car use and the overall societal energy mix. If policies to encourage EV use mean a greater reliance on private modes of transport and a growth in the overall number of vehicles on the road – even if these are battery-powered – then there is little likelihood that overall vehicle emissions will decline at a rate fast enough to meet the Paris goals.

Finally, and most significantly, the critical minerals necessary to produce EV and their batteries (such as cobalt and lithium) are scarce, expensive, and ecologically damaging to mine. In the case of lithium for example, the IEA estimates that global supplies would need to increase by up to a third by the end of the decade in order to meet the projected demand for EV batteries.[53] This is setting up a new global scramble for control over the extraction and trade in rare minerals, which increasingly shapes wider geopolitical fissures. For those countries that are major sources of these minerals – notably Chile (copper and lithium), Bolivia (lithium), Indonesia (nickel), and the Democratic Republic of the Congo (cobalt) – the kinds of predatory and ecologically damaging practices that are set in motion by this competition for resources evoke the practices of the oil industry discussed at many points throughout this book (as in Chapter 9, for example).[54] This new *extractivism* – which promises hugely destructive consequences for much of the Global South – is the hidden underside to global EV growth.

Despite these substantial problems with a reliance on EV as the solution to vehicle emissions, oil companies are rapidly positioning themselves to profit from the growth in EV uptake, especially in Western markets. This is not occurring in the manufacture of EVs, which continues to be controlled by traditional automobile firms or specialised EV companies, such as Tesla and the Chinese firms BYD Auto and SAIC. Rather, oil companies are pursuing two related strategies within the EV space. The first of these is an attempt to gain a foothold in the mining of lithium, a critical metal used in the manufacture of EV batteries. Leading oil companies have recently bought up lithium technology companies as well as large tracts of land containing salt brines from where lithium can

53 IEA, *Net Zero by 2050*, 7.

54 Martín Arboleda, *Planetary Mine: Territories of Extraction Under Late Capitalism*, New York: Verso Books, 2020.

be extracted.[55] Second, oil companies are playing a key role in the most profitable segment of the EV value chain: setting up and operating the charging points used to power EV batteries. In this regard, the response of Big Oil to the roll-out of EV resembles the same kind of strategy these companies pursued alongside the initial rise of a car-centred society: control of the marketing and distribution of energy at point of contact with the consumer. In the early twentieth century, this strategy focused on the growth of branded service stations, which developed over time into a range of other profit-making opportunities such as road-stops and convenience stores in service station forecourts. Today, the service station remains at the centre of oil's EV strategy, together with the roll-out of other charging points positioned alongside roads, and in car parks and retail centres.

This struggle to control EV charging points is ongoing and has set oil firms against a variety of different corporate competitors, including automobile firms, power utilities, and smaller dedicated charging companies. For the Western oil majors, the main battlegrounds of this struggle are in North America and Europe. In the US, Tesla and a range of other charging firms are dominant, although Shell has a significant presence. BP has identified the US as a major target of its EV strategy, and in February 2023 acquired TravelCenters America (TCA), the largest operator of truck stops in the US with nearly 650 restaurants under its management across North America. The acquisition was motivated by BP's goal of establishing charging points at TCA sites, as part of its global aim of controlling more than 100,000 such points by 2030.[56] In Europe, where EV uptake is much higher than the US, oil company subsidiaries play a prominent role in EV charging networks. In the UK, just under a third of all EV charging points are controlled by oil companies (as of January 2023), including the country's largest operator, Ubitricity, a Berlin-based firm bought by Shell in 2021.[57] EV charging

55 Harry Dempsey and Derek Bower, 'Oil and Gas Majors Step Up Efforts to Diversify into Lithium', *Financial Times*, 25 June 2023. On the disastrous ecological effects of this mining, especially in Chile's Atacam Desert, where most of the world's lithium is found, see Thea Riofrancos, 'The Rush to "Go Electric" Comes with a Hidden Cost: Destructive Lithium Mining', *Guardian*, 14 June 2021, theguardian.com.

56 Jenny Strasburg, 'BP Adds to EV-Charging Network with TravelCenters Deal', *Wall Street Journal*, 16 February 2023, wsj.com.

57 Zap Map, zap-map.com.

networks operated by other European oil companies are also among the largest in Germany, the Netherlands, Italy, Spain, and Portugal.[58]

The expansion of EVs reflects the wider significance of electrification within the societal energy mix. While oil companies have long been the major suppliers of the primary energy that generates much of society's electricity – oil and gas – they have traditionally been less involved in actual power generation or the direct distribution of electricity. This may well change in coming years, and several of the leading oil companies have signalled their intentions to move into the business of electricity and power generation. While this might include truly renewable energy, such as solar and wind, the predominant focus remains gas (and increasingly hydrogen). Oil companies are also active in the wholesale electricity market, buying electricity and then selling this at a premium to companies or households. It will be important to watch these trends moving forward, as they may presage growing connections between the diversified energy business of oil firms and the large utility companies.

Hydrogen

The third main focus of the climate strategies embraced by Big Oil has been the aggressive promotion of hydrogen as a supposedly clean fuel. Hydrogen has an energy density about three times greater than conventional petrol, and when used in a fuel cell it releases only water with no carbon emissions. It can be stored as a compressed gas and is seen as a potential means of decarbonising sectors such as long-distance maritime transport and aviation, where battery technology is insufficient due to the lack of charging facilities. Hydrogen also holds promise for certain industrial processes such as steelmaking, which require very high temperatures and currently rely on carbon-intensive fossil fuels (coal and gas). Nonetheless, despite these potential applications, the present-day realities of hydrogen are deeply interlaced with fossil fuels.

58 This includes BP (largest number of ultra-fast charging sites in Germany), ENI (Italy's second largest charging operator), Repsol (largest network in Spain and Portugal), and TotalEnergies (major operator in France, Belgium, and the Netherlands; aims to have 150,000 charge points across Europe by 2025).

Understanding why requires a quick tour through the different colours of hydrogen.

Currently, almost all the world's hydrogen is made from natural gas, using a method called steam methane reforming (SMR) that converts the methane in the gas into hydrogen and CO_2. The hydrogen produced in this manner is known as *grey hydrogen*, and its manufacture releases enormous amounts of CO_2 and methane into the atmosphere.[59] Indeed, according to the IEA, the global production of hydrogen released more carbon emissions in 2019 than the UK and Indonesia combined; if hydrogen were a country, it would be the sixth largest source of CO_2 emissions in the world.[60] Most of this grey hydrogen is manufactured by the oil industry, which uses it in crude oil refineries to reduce the sulphur levels in diesel fuel.[61] About 6 per cent of the world's natural gas consumption is used to produce grey hydrogen – and this intrinsic link with natural gas is one part of understanding the oil industry's enthusiastic support of hydrogen today.

Alongside the continued manufacture of grey hydrogen, the oil industry has turned over the past decade to promoting two other hydrogen colours: blue and green. Much like grey hydrogen, *blue hydrogen* is made by converting natural gas into hydrogen and CO_2 using SMR. But instead of releasing the CO_2 into the atmosphere, the goal is to remove and store it using carbon capture and storage (CCS). As discussed earlier, the basic problem with this is that CCS technology does not exist at adequate scale and is unable to capture all the CO_2 produced. One report from early 2022 pointed out that there were only four blue hydrogen projects in operation, and the highest rate of carbon capture achieved in these was just 43 per cent.[62] But even more serious is the large amount of methane released in the extraction and transport of natural gas. Methane is a potent greenhouse gas with over eighty times the warming impact of CO_2 over a twenty-year period,

59 The other main form of hydrogen today is brown hydrogen, produced using coal.

60 IEA, 'The Future of Hydrogen', 2019, iea.org.

61 Sasan Saadat and Sara Gersen, *Reclaiming Hydrogen for a Renewable Future: Distinguishing Oil and Gas Industry Spin from Zero Emission Solutions*, Earthjustice, August 2021, 10, earthjustice.org.

62 Jonas Moberg and Sam Bartlett, 'The Mirage of Blue Hydrogen Is Fading', Green Hydrogen Organisation, 28 January 2022, gh2.org.

and it is not removed by CCS. For this reason, blue hydrogen has a *worse* greenhouse gas footprint than traditional fossil fuels, estimated at '20 percent greater than burning natural gas or coal for heat and some 60 percent greater than burning diesel oil for heat'.[63] As one academic study concludes, 'there really is no role for blue hydrogen in a carbon-free future'.[64]

Alternatively, *green hydrogen* is generated from water molecules that are split using electrolysis powered by electricity. Unlike grey and blue hydrogen, it does not originate in natural gas, and thus releases no carbon dioxide or methane when produced. However, the electricity used to produce green hydrogen must be 100 per cent renewable, otherwise the substantial amount needed to electrolyse the water will increase emissions. Indeed, one study found that electrolysis powered by the average energy mix currently available on the US electricity grid would generate around double the emissions of grey hydrogen.[65] This is not merely a theoretical problem: under draft rules proposed by the EU in February 2023, green hydrogen was defined in such a way as to allow it to be produced from electricity generated by gas or even coal – a definition, as one NGO put it, that set 'a gold standard for greenwashing'.[66] Furthermore, the electrolysis required to make green hydrogen is highly energy-intensive, and would demand a sixfold increase in the world's solar and wind capacity by 2050, all of which would need to be devoted solely to the production of hydrogen.[67] For most applications, including heating buildings, it is generally much more efficient to use that electricity directly rather than convert it into hydrogen.[68]

---

63 Robert Howarth and Mark Jacobson, 'How Green Is Blue Hydrogen?', *Energy Science and Engineering* 9, 2021: 1676–87.

64 Ibid.

65 Jay Bartlett and Alan Krupnick, *Decarbonized Hydrogen in the US Power and Industrial Sectors: Identifying and Incentivizing Opportunities to Lower Emissions*, Washington, DC: Resources for the Future, 2020, 8, rff.org.

66 Global Witness, 'EU Green Hydrogen Plans "A Gold Standard for Greenwashing" Which Would Burn More Fossil Fuels', press release, 13 February 2023, globalwitness.org.

67 International Renewable Energy Agency (IRENA), *Global Hydrogen Trade to Meet the 1.5°C Climate Goal*, 2022, 10, irena.org.

68 Moreover, if green hydrogen is scaled up to levels projected by the IEA, consumption of freshwater will exceed one-quarter of today's global annual consumption. John Szabo and Gareth Dale, 'Hiding Behind Hydrogen', *Ecologist*, 13 January 2023, theecologist.org.

These drawbacks – and the essentially speculative nature of green hydrogen production – largely rule it out as a means of rapidly reducing carbon emissions by 2030. Despite this fact, the notion of green hydrogen plays a fundamental part in the rhetorical greening of the oil industry. By projecting present-day hydrogen production, especially blue, as paving a path to a climate-safe future powered by green hydrogen, the oil industry hides the dirty realities of hydrogen today. Powerful lobby groups have been set up by the fossil fuel industry to promote this narrative, led by the Hydrogen Council, whose steering group includes BP, Shell, Aramco, Equinor, Sinopec, and TotalEnergies. Under its definition of 'clean hydrogen', the Hydrogen Council includes blue hydrogen derived from natural gas – arguing that up to 40 per cent of the world's hydrogen supply will need to be blue by 2050 in order to meet net zero targets.[69] Such levels of blue hydrogen production would have the effect of massively increasing global demand for natural gas – offering, as one UN-sponsored study put it, 'a lifeline to fossil fuel incumbents who may see in hydrogen an opportunity and excuse to maintain and expand their gas and fuel-oriented infrastructure in a decarbonized future economy'.[70]

In short, hiding behind the promise of green hydrogen, support for blue hydrogen ultimately aims at securing a future for natural gas, a fossil fuel that the oil industry deceptively promoted as clean in the 1990s, but which is, in reality, highly damaging to the biosphere (especially because of methane). Indeed, according to the Hydrogen Council's own analysis, 70 per cent of planned global 'clean hydrogen' projects with committed investment between 2022 and 2030 actually involve blue hydrogen.[71] Recognition of this fact even led the chair of the UK Hydrogen & Fuel Cell Association (UK HFCA), Christopher Jackson, to resign in 2021, stating that he 'would be betraying future generations by remaining silent on the fact that blue hydrogen is at best an expensive distraction, and at worst a lock-in for continued fossil fuel use that guarantees we will fail to meet our decarbonisation goals'.[72] In all these ways,

69 Leigh Collins, ' "The World Will Need up to 280 Million Tonnes of Blue Hydrogen a Year by 2050": Hydrogen Council', 3 November 2021, rechargenews.com.

70 Andrew Lee, ' "Beware Fossil Fuel Vested Interests": UN Backs Renewable Hydrogen to Meet Climate Goals', Recharge, 21 October 2021, rechargenews.com.

71 Hydrogen Council and McKinsey & Company, *Hydrogen Insights 2022*, 8.

72 Jillian Ambrose, 'Oil Firms Made "False Claims" on Blue Hydrogen Costs, Says Ex-lobby Boss', *Guardian*, 20 August 2021, theguardian.com.

the oil industry's embrace of hydrogen ranks as one of the most dangerous developments in climate politics today – a means of entrenching present-day fossil fuel consumption under the guise of confronting climate change.

Planning for Disaster: What Do Oil Companies *Think*?

The technologies just surveyed illustrate the problematic ways that the climate crisis is both perceived and tackled. A search for saviour technologies leaves existing patterns of market-based consumption – and the social behaviour that supports this consumption – essentially untouched. This can be seen, for instance, in the all-important transport sector, which currently contributes around a quarter of the world's greenhouse emissions and is the main destination for most of the world's fossil fuels. Biofuels, EVs, and hydrogen all purport to tackle the problem of a fossil fuel–based transport system, but they do not address the underlying structural issue: a system of mobility that is centred on individualised road transport, in which both the means of transport *and* the means of energy that power these vehicles are commodified. This is an irrational system that is destructive of the biosphere, harmful to human health, and erodes the liveability of urban spaces. A faster reduction in emissions (and dramatic improvement in city living) could be achieved through provision of free, clean, and well-funded green public transit – with urban spaces designed to prioritise and enable non-commodified modes of transport. Instead, the solutions offered by so-called clean fuels leave the underlying systems intact, reproducing many of the same problems of the internal combustion engine in a different form (and with no likelihood of substantially reducing emissions in the time required).[73]

73 The maritime sector is another leading source of transport emissions, accounting for around 3 per cent of global greenhouse gas emissions in 2022, and with few alternatives to the diesel oil fuels first pioneered in the early twentieth century. As with road transport, the question of maritime emissions highlights the systemic barriers that prevent more rational and sustainable energy use. For instance, a significant reduction in emissions could be immediately achieved through a reduction in global trade and slowing down ship speeds (it is estimated that a 10 per cent reduction in shipping speeds would reduce emissions by more than 20 per cent). Such measures, however, carry implications for global value chains and the turnover time of commodities, and contradict the basic motivations of neoliberal trade patterns.

Of course, our current transport system did not appear accidentally – it emerged through concrete political and social choices that were made in lockstep with the rise of an oil-centred world. But framing the problem as one of technological salvation ignores the social and historical roots of our present predicament. And, as any lapsed believer knows, the problem with a salvation-based politics is that it defers deliverance to an unspecified date in the future, providing fervent rapture on Sunday while continuing with business as usual during the week. In the same way, the climate technologies on offer encourage a kind of political passivity, holding out the promise of far-reaching transformation delivered from above but demanding no fundamental reorganisation of society or change in social behaviour. The underlying dynamics of capitalist markets continue unimpeded – endless growth, extractive economies, and individualised modes of production and consumption. This is the status quo wrapped in techno-fetishism – a pretence of action that will not avert climate catastrophe.

Such an approach also absolves the oil majors of any kind of direct responsibility for the climate crisis. Instead, they are able to portray themselves as part of the solution through their championing of new low-carbon technologies and scientific innovations. This apparent change in direction is a dangerous deception. As we have seen, large oil companies have *always* been diversified, moving in and out of different forms of energy production (nuclear, gas, coal, electricity) depending on economic opportunities. Oil companies have also always aimed at controlling the critical infrastructures of energy: pipelines, refining, shipping, service stations, and marketing. The increased share of renewables in the coming decades may well alter the forms of this infrastructural power, but it does not represent any decisive shift in the patterns of vertical integration that have defined the largest oil companies for over a century. In all these ways, low-carbon technologies have become additional arrows in the oil industry quiver, complementary and potentially highly profitable markets that serve to support rather than erode the power of fossil capital in our current energy pathways. This is part and parcel of the new 'green capitalism' – where 'the threat of a deteriorating natural world is transformed to a new frontier for accumulation'.[74]

74 Adrienne Buller, *The Value of a Whale: On the Illusions of Green Capitalism*, 2022, Manchester: Manchester University Press, 232.

But, despite this diversification into new technologies and energy interests, the core focus of the oil industry undoubtedly remains traditional hydrocarbons. Proof of this can be found in the scenario modelling that oil companies conduct as part of their strategic planning. These scenarios project the impact of future climate change policy and different pathways of technological innovation on energy use and CO_2 emissions. They draw heavily on work by the IEA and the UN's Intergovernmental Panel on Climate Change (IPCC), but also integrate geopolitical and social factors into their consideration. While oil companies are at pains to stress these modelling exercises are not intended as solid predictions about the future, they are an essential part of developing corporate investment strategy. As ExxonMobil puts it, scenario modelling 'forms the basis for our business planning . . . underpinned by a deep understanding of long-term fundamentals . . . [and] seeks to identify potential impacts of climate-related government policies'.[75] As such, these models provide a valuable insight into what the major companies actually *think* about the future of the world and their plans for energy production.

Two of the more robust examples of these modelling exercises are those conducted by ExxonMobil and Shell, which are both accompanied by a serious discussion of methodology, data sources, and assumptions (including political and social factors). In all the scenarios imagined by these companies the future is clear: none actually foresee meeting the critical goal of halving global emissions by 2030, and all anticipate the continued centrality of fossil fuels for many decades to come. ExxonMobil, for example, considers that wind and solar will make up only 10 per cent of primary energy demand by 2050 (up from less than 2 per cent today), and that oil and gas will still account for more than half of the world's primary energy at that time.[76] In two of Shell's scenarios – the most likely pathways according to the company, euphemistically named the Waves and Islands scenarios – oil and other fossil fuels continue to make up the majority of the world's energy mix until some time between 2050 and 2070.[77] In neither of these two scenarios do emissions drop below half until after 2070, and both

75 ExxonMobil 2023, *Advancing Climate Solutions*, 23.

76 Ibid., 24.

77 Shell, *The Energy Security Scenarios*, 2023, 26, shell.com.

estimate that the global temperature rise will have exceeded 2 degrees Celsius by 2050. Even in its most unlikely scenario, Sky 1.5, which Shell describes as demanding 'extremely challenging conditions and energy system changes', fossil fuels remain the majority of the world's primary energy until past 2045, and emissions do not halve until 2050.[78] This would increase global temperatures by well over 1.5 degrees Celsius by the middle of the century.[79]

These models are not greenwashing; they clearly establish what the major oil companies believe the future to hold. On this basis, they also inform the oil industry's investment priorities over the short to medium term. And here the results are also unequivocal. Despite the scientific consensus that there can be no new development of oil, gas, and coal projects if we are to stand any chance of averting severe temperature increases, oil firms are planning to direct trillions of dollars into fossil fuel projects over the coming decade.[80] Even in the best-case climate scenarios, firms such as ExxonMobil and BP estimate up to $11 trillion of new investment will flow into upstream oil and gas through to 2050.[81] This is not an abstract or speculative exercise conducted by disinterested actors, it is the future envisioned by those currently responsible for such investment choices. The path they see before us is one of unambiguous disaster: there will be no curtailment of emissions in the time frame required to meet the Paris goals, and within the eschatology of the leading oil firms, catastrophic climatic change will almost certainly occur.

78 Ibid., 75.

79 Shell's Sky 1.5 scenario contains a range of completely unrealistic assumptions, including the reforestation of around 700 million hectares of land (an area equivalent to more than 40 per cent of the world's current cropland) and the capture and storage of more than half of the world's carbon emissions by 2055 (in 2023, CCS accounted for about one-thousandth of world emissions).

80 Fiona Harvey, 'No New Oil, Gas or Coal Development if the World Is to Reach Net Zero by 2050, Says World Energy Body', *Guardian*, 18 May 2021, theguardian.com.

81 ExxonMobil, *Advancing Climate Solutions*, 37. ExxonMobil estimates around $11 trillion in the IEA's Net Zero Emissions scenario, a path which the company states 'society is not on' (ibid., 33). Similarly, BP arrives at a figure of between $9 to $11 trillion up to 2050 – and this *excludes* operating costs and the costs of building major LNG infrastructure. BP, *Energy Outlook 2023*, 82, 95, bp.com

Plastic Elephants

A striking absence in much of the discussion around future climate scenarios is the question of petrochemicals and plastics. As we have seen throughout this book, the synthetic revolution was a major factor in how oil became woven into the very fabric of our social existence – yet the omnipresence of petrochemicals has hidden them from view. This fact was noted recently by the executive director of the International Energy Agency (IEA), Fatih Birol, who has described petrochemicals as 'one of the key "blind spots" of the energy system', poorly understood even by energy professionals.[82] Today, petrochemicals are decisive to the future trajectories of fossil fuel use. The IEA estimates that petrochemicals will make up more than a third of the growth in oil demand to 2030, and nearly half to 2050 – an amount greater than trucks, aviation, or shipping (the other components of oil demand that are difficult to replace with existing technologies).[83] It is perhaps conceivable that some of the demand for oil and gas *as energy sources* can be reduced through alternative technologies and improved efficiencies, but there is no possibility of ending our reliance on oil as long as petroleum remains the fundamental material basis for commodity production. For this reason, industry analysts and oil firm representatives alike speak openly of petrochemicals as a solid guarantee for 'the future of oil'.[84]

The consumption of petrochemicals sits elephant-like in the ecological crisis of the present. The starkest illustration of this is the exponential growth in the most pervasive of all petroleum products: plastics. The annual global production of plastics grew nearly two hundredfold between 1950 and 2015, and the pace of growth is accelerating – quite remarkably, around half of all plastics ever made were produced in the past twenty years.[85] This seemingly unstoppable demand in the consumption of plastics is driven by the systematic displacement of natural materials across all industrial and household sectors. To give but

82 International Energy Agency (IEA), *The Future of Petrochemicals: Towards More Sustainable Plastics and Fertilisers*, IEA, 2018, 14.

83 Ibid., 11.

84 Alexander Tullo, 'Why the Future of Oil Is in Chemicals, Not Fuels', *Chemical and Engineering News*, 20 February 2019, cen.acs.org.

85 R. Geyer, J. R. Jambeck, and K. L. Law, 'Production, Use, and Fate of All Plastics Ever Made', *Science Advances* 3, no. 7, 2017: 1–5, 1.

one example, the production of polyester fibre now exceeds that of all other fibres combined, including wool and cotton, and now makes up around 60 per cent of total global fibre production.[86] Writing in the late 1950s, the French philosopher Roland Barthes once foresaw a future in which 'the hierarchy of substances is abolished [and] a single one replaces them all: the whole world can be plasticized.'[87] That synthetic reality is now firmly upon us.

For good reasons, much of the discussion around the problem of plastics and petrochemicals has focused on their toxicity to both humans and the natural environment.[88] Plastics are, by their very nature, incompatible with normal biological cycles, and can only be disposed of in three basic ways: by dumping, incineration, or recycling.[89] More than 90 per cent of all plastic waste ever produced by humankind has been dumped into the ecosystem or incinerated, both routes that release toxic materials and cause long-term and cumulative damage to life itself.[90] Today, recycling rates sit at around 9 per cent of total plastic waste, and substantial quantities of this waste ends up being exported from North America and Europe to countries where its ultimate fate is usually impossible to determine.[91] Indeed, alongside China's role as a key global producer of plastics, the country also became the final graveyard of the world's plastic waste – between 1992 and 2018, just under half of all global plastic waste was exported to China.[92] China banned the import of plastic waste in 2018, and most of this trade has now been diverted to countries such as Malaysia, Indonesia, and Turkey.

86 IEA, *Future of Petrochemicals*, 20. As noted in Chapter 7, it is this shift to synthetic fibre that underpins the rise of 'fast fashion.'

87 Roland Barthes, *Mythologies*, New York: Noonday Press, 1972, 99.

88 Rebecca Altman's writing provides a rich historically grounded account of the emergence of various plastics and their toxic effects; see rebecca-altman.com.

89 'None of the mass-produced plastics biodegrade in any meaningful way; however, sunlight weakens the materials, causing fragmentation into particles known to reach millimeters or micro-meters in size . . . Research into the environmental impacts of these "microplastics" in marine and freshwater environments has accelerated in recent years, but little is known about the impacts of plastic waste in land-based ecosystems.' Geyer, Jambeck, and Law, 'Production, Use, and Fate', 3.

90 Ibid.

91 OECD, *Global Plastics Outlook: Economic Drivers, Environmental Impacts and Policy Options*, Paris: OECD Publishing, 2022, 14.

92 Duane Dickson, Aijaz Hussain, and Bob Kumpf, *The Future of Petrochemicals: Growth Surrounded by Uncertainy*, Deloitte, 2019, 7, deloitte.com.

While their environmental toxicity is well recognised, much less attention has been given to the impact of plastics on climate change. Across their entire lifecycle, plastics are associated with significant quantities of greenhouse gas emissions – indeed, if plastic were a country, it would rank as the world's fifth largest greenhouse gas emitter, after China, the US, India, and Russia.[93] Much of these plastic-related emissions arise in the initial production of petrochemicals, which consumes more energy than any other industrial sector (including iron, steel, and cement).[94] But, even after it is discarded, plastic continues to release greenhouse gases as it degrades under the impact of UV light and water erosion. This is a particularly acute problem in the world's oceans, where the most common form of plastic waste is low-density polyethylene (LDPE), a substance used in packaging, plastic bottles, and many other applications. LDPE is lightweight and tends to float on the surface of the water. With the churn of oceans and exposure to sunlight, LDPE breaks down and emits methane, ethane, and other greenhouse gases. The process of fragmentation also increases the surface area of the plastic waste exposed to environmental degradation, which means that the rate of greenhouse gas emissions tends to accelerate over time.[95] With many plastics able to last for centuries in the environment before they decompose, our perception of discarded plastic as *waste* is perhaps a misnomer: the hundreds of millions of tonnes of plastics that find their way *annually* to landfills, rivers, and oceans are an active, ever-growing accelerant to the climate crisis that have far greater permanence than any individual human life.[96] We have become the organic detritus within a synthetic world of our own creation.

There may also be alarming, mutually reinforcing links between the toxicity of plastics and their contribution to a warming planet. Current research suggests that microplastics – tiny plastic fragments below 5 mm in size – can interfere with the ability of the ocean to act as a sink

93 P. J. Landrigan et al., 'The Minderoo-Monaco Commission on Plastics and Human Health', *Annals of Global Health* 89, no. 1, 2023: 1–215, 51.

94 IEA, *Future of Petrochemicals*, 27.

95 S. J. Royer et al., 'Production of Methane and Ethylene from Plastic in the Environment', *PLoS ONE* 13, no. 8, 2018: e0200574.

96 In 2019, 353 million tonnes (Mt) of plastic waste was produced globally, with 6.1 Mt of this leaking into rivers, lakes, and the ocean. OECD, *Global Plastics Outlook*, 14.

that captures carbon from the atmosphere.[97] This is due to the toxic effect of microplastics on the microscopic plants (phytoplankton) that absorb CO_2 from the surface of the ocean. Microplastics can also disrupt the metabolism and reproductive abilities of the small animal organisms (zooplankton) that consume phytoplankton and deposit the captured carbon (in the form of faecal matter) into the deep oceans from where it cannot re-enter the atmosphere. Since the 1850s, up to 40 per cent of human-made carbon emissions have been absorbed by this zooplankton/phytoplankton food chain – the largest natural sink for anthropogenic greenhouse gases on the planet. The potential effects of plastic pollution on this critical carbon sink constitutes another of the many 'tipping points' that threaten to accelerate runaway climate change.

It is estimated that greenhouse gas emissions from plastics may reach 15 per cent of the world's carbon budget by 2050 – in that same year, about a fifth of the world's oil consumption will go towards the production of plastics.[98] As such, the question of plastics and petrochemicals must be placed front and centre in the global struggle against a warming planet. But as we have seen in earlier chapters, the problem presented by the petrochemical revolution is not a simple technical issue of substituting one material substrate for another. Our synthetic world arose due to the place of petrochemicals in the wider logics of capital accumulation, especially their role in facilitating cheap mass production and enabling a throwaway culture that is a necessary component of ever-accelerating consumption.[99] As a result, our contemporary sensibilities – especially in the key Western markets that have historically been the centres of global consumption – are built on notions of temporary use and disposability – an out of sight, out of mind approach that is a direct *consequence* of the continuous drive to expand the market. Any shift away from the use of petrochemicals requires a break with this underlying

97 For a discussion of this process, see Centre for International Environmental Law, *Plastic and Climate: The Hidden Costs of a Plastic Planet*, 2019, 74–7, ciel.org/plasticandclimate.

98 Landrigan et al., 'Minderoo-Monaco Commission', 105.

99 As part of this process, plastic and petrochemical firms have waged an unrelenting struggle against anti-plastic regulations in a manner not dissimilar to oil companies' efforts to influence climate change policies. See Jennifer Clapp, 'The Rising Tide against Plastic Waste: Unpacking Industry Attempts to Influence the Debate', in Stephanie Foote and Elizabeth Mazzolini (eds), *Histories of the Dustheap: Waste, Material Cultures, Social Justice*, Cambridge, MA: MIT Press, 2012, 199–225.

logic – in other words, a different system of production aimed at human needs, not more accumulation. To do so requires going beyond a focus on recycling and waste disposal.[100] The development of sustainable alternatives for material production demands a massive programme of scientific research that prioritises social and ecological concerns rather than private profit. It is exceedingly unlikely that a social system that has led us to this juncture is capable of taking such an alternative path.[101]

Last Man Standing?

In assessing these possible futures, we must remember that the problem of climate change is embedded in a sharply hierarchical world that oil helped to make. There is an ecological debt associated with the historical emergence of the world market, in which the extraction of energy and other resources from the Global South has fed the development of countries and classes in the Global North. The polarisation of wealth is associated with the polarisation of emissions, with the world's richest populations – largely concentrated in the Global North – bearing primary responsibility for rising temperatures. One study, for instance, notes that about half of the world's carbon emissions are produced by the wealthiest 10 per cent of the world's population, while the poorest half of the world generates only 10 per cent.[102] Another found that the private jets, superyachts, and mansions of an average billionaire emitted the same amount of carbon in *two hours* as did someone in the poorest half of the world's population over an *entire year*.[103]

100 As Max Liboiron and Josh Lepawsky point out, too much discussion of waste reduces to a question of individual behaviours, ignoring the social and economic determinants of what becomes waste in the first place. See *Discard Studies: Wasting, Systems, and Power*, MIT Press, 2022.

101 For a powerful critique of the petrochemical and plastics industry, its connection to the imperative of limitless growth, and a discussion of what can be done to move away from our dependence on these substances, see Alice Mah, *Plastic Unlimited: How Corporations Are Fuelling the Ecological Crisis and What We Can Do about It*, Cambridge: Polity Books, 2022.

102 Michael J. Lynch et al., 'Measuring the Ecological Impact of the Wealthy: Excessive Consumption, Ecological Disorganization, Green Crime, and Justice', *Social Currents*, May 2019, 3.

103 Oxfam Methodology Note, 'Carbon Billionaires', November 2022, 5, policy-practice.oxfam.org. The study examined twenty well-known billionaires to arrive at this estimate: the private jet fleet in the US emits as much CO_2 as the entire nation of Burundi.

There can be no just solution to the climate crisis that does not tackle (and provide restitution for) these enduring inequalities.

Dominant approaches to the so-called green transition are merely reproducing these relationships anew: intensifying the search for (and control over) critical materials such as lithium, cobalt, and sand; encouraging landgrabs for solar, wind, and biofuel projects; and of course continuing to expand the hydrocarbon frontier through fracking and deep-sea oil and gas projects. This is one major problem with much mainstream climate politics across North America and Europe. By leaving the current structure of the world market intact, they feed the illusion that the climate crisis can be tackled at the national scale and within capitalism. Like the original post-war Keynesian programme, they sanction the global chains of exploitation and flows of wealth (including the historic ecological debt) that underpin public policymaking in the Global North. Not only are the worst effects of the climate crisis displaced onto the world's poorest – but so too are the extreme costs of the *faux* solutions presented to tackle this crisis.[104]

Yet, while the North–South division is critical to assessing potential paths of the climate crisis, we must reject straightforwardly binary models of the world market. As earlier chapters emphasised, the advent of the post-1970s world oil order was closely linked to the emergence of new economic elites in previously colonised or dependent countries outside North America and Europe. The growing dominance of the NOCs is a more recent reflection of this trend, which complicates the dynamics of fossil fuel production and consumption today. A perspective on the climate crisis that ignores these trends – concentrating its fire on the Western oil companies while ignoring the oil-rich states of the Middle East and Latin America, or the Russian, Brazilian, and Chinese NOCs – is out of step with the realities of world oil.[105] Likewise, the emergence of states such as China and Russia as major global actors

104 David Camfield rightly notes: 'As the climate changes, social arrangements will determine how many people will die and who they will be. They will also determine what adaptation to climate change will look like and who will pay for it.' David Camfield, *Future on Fire*, New York: PM Press, 2022, 7.

105 It is also important to consider the impact of extractive models on political and social movements in resource-rich states. For a careful discussion of this, see Thea Riofrancos, *Resource Radicals: From Petro-Nationalism to Post-Extractivism in Ecuador*, Durham, NC: Duke University Press, 2020.

does not promise any alternative to fossil capitalism or a break with extractivist models of development.

Global campaigns need to theorise, map, and confront the role of these states and their NOCs in the climate crisis much more effectively. Most important here are the Gulf Arab monarchies, which can no longer be viewed simply as giant oil reserves coveted by the Western majors. As the quote that began this chapter indicates, these states see much to be gained from hanging on to an oil-centred world for as long as possible and have no intention of reducing fossil fuel production. Their actions will determine the paths of a warming climate over the next decades. Saudi Aramco, for instance, invested more in oilfield expansion in 2022 than any other company in the world. The company has also announced that it intends to increase oil-production capacity by more than 8 per cent by 2027, reaching 13 million barrels per day. As the *Financial Times* put it, Aramco 'is doubling down' on oil, aiming to be 'the last oil major standing' and 'betting that it can continue to do what it does best: pump oil for decades to come and gain even more market power as other producers cut back'.[106] All the hydrocarbon-rich states in the Gulf have signalled their intention to follow the same course – even though they also face ruinous prospects as a result of climate change.[107]

But much like the Western majors, the intended expansion of oil and gas production in the Gulf states is occurring alongside their embrace of the new green technologies and the language of low carbon. Saudi Arabia, for example, has announced a raft of climate initiatives in the past few years, including the goal of producing half the country's electricity from renewables by 2030 (faster than targets set in most other parts of the world, including the EU). This goal, however, is explicitly framed in terms of *expanding* the country's export of oil: by reducing oil consumption at home, the country will have more available for export abroad. The Saudi energy minister, Prince Abdulaziz bin Salman, describes this as a 'triple-win situation': greater oil exports, a cheaper

106 Tom Wilson, 'Saudi Aramco Bets on Being the Last Oil Major Standing', *Financial Times*, 12 January 2023.

107 Some scientists estimate that climate change will make the Gulf uninhabitable by 2070. Jim Krane, *Energy Kingdoms: Oil and Political Survival in the Persian Gulf*, New York: Columbia University Press, 2019, 94.

energy bill at home, and the prestige of meeting its emissions targets.[108] There is no necessary contradiction between the expansion of oil and the growth in renewables.

All the leading Gulf NOCs have expressed support for the Paris Agreement goals and endorsed their countries' net zero pledges.[109] In brandishing their climate achievements, however, these companies deploy the same carbon accounting tricks as the Western firms. One of these is to measure only the emissions generated in the actual production of oil – not the remaining 85–90 per cent of emissions released when the oil is used.[110] Another related popular climate objective used by Gulf NOCs is reduction in the so-called carbon intensity of upstream production – the greenhouse gas emissions generated in the production of oil as a proportion of the amount of oil sold.[111] The obvious flaw in using this ratio as any kind of measure for sustainability is that it places no limitations on growth in *absolute* levels of oil production: get your employees to walk to work rather than take the company bus and you can produce more oil at less intensity. Perhaps the only innovation in Gulf climate-speak is Saudi Aramco's notion of 'lower carbon oil' – the idea that Saudi oil is a more ecologically sound choice than oil from other countries because it is easier to extract and thus can be produced with lower emissions.[112] A bit like the fiction of a 'light' cigarette, this is a sure road to a nasty end.

Much like the Western oil industry, the Gulf's response to the climate emergency is not head-in-the-sand denialism. Rather, these states seek to incorporate themselves as leading partners in the global response to this emergency, all the while seeking to increase levels of oil production.

108 'Saudi Arabia's Green Agenda: Renewables at Home, Oil Abroad', *Financial Times*, 21 November 2022. The goal of reducing the Gulf's energy costs is directly connected to the region's extraordinarily high levels of domestic energy consumption: five Gulf states rank among the world's top ten energy consumers per capita, including Qatar and the UAE at numbers one and two respectively. This is partly due to the prioritisation of energy-intensive industries such as steel, aluminium, cement, and petrochemicals, as well as high demand for air-conditioning use and water desalination. See Krane, *Energy Kingdoms*.

109 Except for Qatar, all Gulf states now have NZE target dates.

110 For Aramco, see Saudi Aramco, *Sustainability Report 2021*. Even when addressing scope 1 and scope 2 emissions, the company does not see any substantial decline between 2021 and 2035 (ibid., 27).

111 Ibid., 89.

112 Wilson, 'Last Oil Major Standing'.

A major part of this has involved massive investments in new technologies such as hydrogen and carbon capture, on which the Gulf states publicly declare they intend to lead the world.[113] It has also involved leadership of international fora such as the 2022 COP27 meeting in Egypt, where the largest national pavilion was that of Saudi Arabia – followed by those of the UAE, Qatar, and Bahrain. Measuring 1,008 square metres, the Saudi pavilion was exactly double the area of the one housing the entire continent of Africa – one of the regions most directly under threat from the effects of climate change.

It says much that COP27 was little more than an exhibition space for the world's largest oil and gas producers, led by the Gulf states. The impact of the Gulf presence was undoubtedly felt in the COP27 final resolution, where language around phasing out fossil fuel use was defeated by an alliance led by Saudi Arabia and other large fossil fuel producers (backed by the Gulf-supported Egyptian military government who hosted the event). Indeed, quite bizarrely, the final COP27 text carried no mention at all of oil.

The Gulf's supposed leadership of global efforts to halt climate change continued at COP28, held in late 2023 in Dubai, UAE. Presided over by the CEO of the Abu Dhabi National Oil Company, Sultan Ahmed al-Jaber, a record 2,400 delegates connected to the fossil fuel industry attended the event – four times as many as at COP27, and more than the total number of representatives from the ten countries most vulnerable to climate change. In their coverage of this event, much of the world's media highlighted the apparent irony of seeing an oil company CEO at the helm of global climate change negotiations. But given that the COP summits have become little more than opportunities for the world's largest polluters to enact their planet-saving performances, Al Jaber's leadership seems entirely appropriate.

113 Saudi Arabia intends to be the world's largest producer and exporter of hydrogen; see Saudi and Middle East Green Initiatives, 'SGI Initiatives', greeninitiatives.gov.sa. This includes blue hydrogen, and in December 2022, Saudi Arabia became the first country in the world to ship blue hydrogen commercially (to South Korea). Riyadh is also currently planning one of the world's largest CCS plants. The other Gulf states are all planning large hydrogen production sites, which is closely connected to the expansion of their natural gas industries. The GCC produces around 10 per cent of the world's natural gas, ranking third in the world behind the US and Russia.

The Eco-Socialist Alternative

The problem we confront is twofold. On one hand, the means of energy production and the infrastructure of the energy system remain solidly in the hands of the largest oil conglomerates – including those outside the Western states – whose principal concern is the maximisation of profit. This is not an ethical failing on the part of oil firm executives, but a condition imposed by the nature of capitalism itself. It is not possible for these conglomerates to prioritise an objective other than the pursuit of profit – they act within 'a machine that no one controls. Every agent must conform to its imperatives. Fail to turn an adequate profit and [they] will not survive.'[114] This is precisely why the trajectories of low-carbon technologies are on their current path – commodified, market-driven technologies that complement the continued growth of fossil fuels, while affording minimal change to the existing system. It should not need to be said, but given the current state of the world it must: there can be no effective response to climate change steered by the oil industry.

The second part of the problem is that we are faced with more than the corporate power of oil. As we have seen throughout this book, behind the oil industry lies deeper structural forces that have embedded oil into every aspect of life across the twentieth and twenty-first centuries. Beyond its central roles as energy and transport fuel, oil and its derivatives underline all forms of commodity production. Our food and our financial systems rest on oil. Oil's centrality stems from what it does for the imperatives of accumulation: its ability to accelerate and expand capital's turnover, cheapen the costs of production (including labour), and knit together an international market. No other commodity plays this role. The immense power of the firms that make up Big Oil – and their close association with the rise of the US through the twentieth century – stems from this foundational place in capitalism. For this reason, while these oil firms are indeed a major obstacle to ending our dependence on fossil fuels, they are a *manifestation*, not a cause, of the underlying problem. We must confront the multiple logics of a social system that has served to centre oil throughout all aspects of our lives. And we cannot extricate ourselves from oil's pervasiveness – certainly

114 David McNally, cited in Camfield, *Future on Fire*, 21.

not at the pace necessary to halt runaway climate change – while remaining within this social system.

Systemwide transformation rooted in democratic control over energy and technology is thus urgently needed. Many activists now refer to such change as *ecosocialism*, a label that highlights the need to go beyond capitalism, while centring ecology and the repair of the biosphere at the heart of any radical shift. Ecosocialism means ending the blind pursuit of growth and endless accumulation that drives capitalism, replacing this with the prioritisation of social needs and the recuperation of the planet. This can only happen with a reconsideration of how, what, why, and where things are produced and consumed – a decommodification of our social existence.[115] This would mean an end to wasteful and destructive forms of production and consumption (including fossil fuels, advertising, inbuilt obsolescence, private jets, and superyachts). It would also expand the availability of some social goods (such as education, health, housing), and radically increase the free time individuals can devote to the cultivation of their abilities, interests, and passions.

Unlike many other perspectives on the climate crisis, ecosocialism recognises the indivisibility of climate struggles and other movements for social and economic justice. The connection of these struggles lies in the fact that capitalism is the root cause of both the climate emergency and other forms of exploitation. As the climate crisis worsens, its effects are felt most sharply by those who are most marginalised. Movements for racial justice and gender equality, the rights of indigenous peoples, and the defence of migrants and refugees must inevitably take on an ecological edge. The central place of labour in capitalism gives a particular weight to the struggles of urban and rural workers, including those in the informal sector and outside official trade union structures. The climate crisis reinforces and helps to spawn numerous other crises, including wars and conflict, mass displacement, and a permanent state of economic polarisation and austerity. All of this means that the climate crisis can only be resolved as part of broader social change. By pointing to the interconnectedness of both the problems and the necessary

115 For a clear summary of the key tenets of the ecosocialist perspective, see Michael Löwy et al., 'For an Ecosocialist Degrowth', *Monthly Review*, 1 April 2022, monthlyreview.org.

solution, ecosocialism provides hope and a source of social power – centring solidarity, collective action, and a recognition of common interests despite difference.

Given all of this, what to do? As numerous ecosocialist writers and activists have pointed out, there is a range of demands that can be fought for in the here and now and that provide a bridge to more deep-seated change. Most immediately, we could dismantle the major oil companies and polluters, taking their enormous skills and resources and using these rapidly to phase out the production of fossil fuels and support a genuine green transition. Demilitarisation would cut the world's largest source of carbon emissions – first and foremost, the US military.[116] Massive investment can be directed into developing new technologies, including some of those discussed above, which can be appropriately introduced alongside encouraging changes to social behaviour. We can expand the infrastructure for truly renewable energies and develop sustainable materials and agro-ecological forms of food production. The highly polluting conspicuous consumption of the world's ultra-rich can be ended, beginning with the confiscation and decommissioning of private jets and superyachts. Urban spaces and modes of transit could be reorganised around free, accessible, and clean public transport, bike tracks, and pedestrian walkways. We can end production models built around inbuilt obsolescence and disposability, and immediately prioritise energy efficiency and conservation.

Measures such as these need to be global in scope. The majority of the world's population that has been adversely incorporated into the world market over the past decades has an unequivocal right to energy, material growth, and an improvement in living standards. This must be supported and enabled in sustainable ways by those who live in areas that have profited from over a century of fossil capitalism. The first step in this is the cancellation of sovereign debt owed by the Global South, and a massive programme of reparations could transfer the necessary technologies and resources to lift billions of people out of fuel and material poverty in sustainable ways.

116 Part of this should involve reparations for the historic social cost of military emissions on countries in the Global South. For a discussion and estimates of this cost, see Patrick Bigger et al., *Less War, Less Warming: A Reparative Approach to US and UK Military Ecological Damages*, Common Wealth, 6 November 2023, available at common-wealth.org.

These proposals might sound utopian, but without them we stand no chance of dealing with the climate catastrophe. Capitalism's ecological crisis poses such demands as both necessary and possible, and there are no technical or material reasons why they could not be immediately implemented. The barriers to taking such steps (and many others) are purely *social*: a narrow layer of global society – extending far beyond oil companies – benefits from our current social arrangements and will resist any fundamental challenge to their position. We cannot behave as if the problem of capitalism does not exist, or can be ignored, or as if our current rulers can be convinced to take an alternative path through the sheer force of scientific evidence. This is an irrational economic system that pits the interests of a tiny few against the vast majority, and only by taking political and economic power away from the logic of the market will it be possible to build a different and better world.

Index